The International Companion to the Scottish Novel

INTERNATIONAL COMPANIONS TO SCOTTISH LITERATURE

Series Editors: Ian Brown and Thomas Owen Clancy

Titles in the series include:

International Companion to Lewis Grassic Gibbon
Edited by Scott Lyall
ISBN 978-1-908980-13-7

International Companion to Edwin Morgan
Edited by Alan Riach
ISBN 978-1-908980-14-4

International Companion to Scottish Poetry
Edited by Carla Sassi
ISBN 978-1-908980-15-1

International Companion to James Macpherson and The Poems of Ossian
Edited by Dafydd Moore
ISBN 978-1-908980-19-9

International Companion to John Galt
Edited by Gerard Carruthers and Colin Kidd
ISBN 978-1-908980-27-4

International Companion to Scottish Literature 1400–1650
Edited by Nicola Royan
ISBN 978-1-908980-23-6

International Companion to Scottish Literature of the Long Eighteenth Century
Edited by Leith Davis and Janet Sorensen
ISBN 978-1-908980-31-1

International Companion to Nineteenth-Century Scottish Literature
Edited by Sheila M. Kidd, Caroline McCracken-Flesher, and Kenneth McNeil
ISBN 978-1-908980-35-9

International Companion to Scottish Children's Literature
Edited by Maureen A. Farrell and Robert A. Davis
ISBN 978-1-908980-41-0

International Companion to the Scottish Novel
Edited by Cairns Craig
ISBN 978-1-908980-43-4

The International Companion to the Scottish Novel

Edited by Cairns Craig

Scottish Literature International

Published by
Scottish Literature International
Scottish Literature
7 University Gardens
University of Glasgow
Glasgow G12 8QH

Scottish Literature International is an imprint of
the Association for Scottish Literature

www.asls.org.uk

ASL is a registered charity no. SC006535

First published 2025

Text © ASL and the individual contributors

All rights reserved. No part of this book may be
reproduced, stored in a retrieval system, or
transmitted in any form or means, electronic,
mechanical, photocopying, recording or otherwise,
without the prior permission of the
Association for Scottish Literature.

A CIP catalogue for this title
is available from the British Library

ISBN 978-1-908980-43-4

Our authorised representative in the EU for product safety is
JGU Scotland HUB, Johannes Gutenberg Universität Mainz
Jakob-Welder-Weg 18, 55128 Mainz, Germany
scotland@uni-mainz.de

Contents

Series Editors' Preface vii
Acknowledgements ix

Introduction 1
Cairns Craig
1. Smollett and the Novel in Scotland 20
Aileen Douglas
2. The Philosophical Foundations of the Scottish Novel. 34
Cairns Craig

Document 1 – Mrs Oliphant: 'Walter Scott' 50

3. Walter Scott, the Reader, and the Times after Time 60
Caroline McCracken-Flesher

Document 2 – Georg Lukács: from *The Historical Novel* . . . 74

4. The Scottish Novel in the Wake of Walter Scott, 1815–1830 79
Charles Snodgrass
5. The Victorian Novel of Spiritual Crisis and the Disruption of
Scottish Literary History 95
Juliet Shields

**Document 3 – Robert Louis Stevenson: 'A Humble
Remonstrance'** 108

6. From the Nineteenth to the Twentieth Century 112
Andrew Nash

Document 4 – Edwin Muir: from *Scott and Scotland* 129

7. The Scottish Novel in the Interwar Years. 134
Glenda Norquay

Document 5 – Lewis Grassic Gibbon: 'Literary Lights'. . . . 153

8. From the Second World War to the 1970s. 159
Eleanor Bell

Contents (continued)

Document 6 – Muriel Spark: from 'The Desegregation of Art' 173

9. The Scottish Novel 1979–1999 178
   Carole Jones

Document 7 – James Kelman: 'Elitism and English Literature' 192

10. The First Hundred Years of the Gaelic Novel 206
    Moray Watson
11. Scottish Detective Fiction 217
    Matthew Wickman
12. Scottish Science Fiction and Fantasy 232
    Anna McFarlane
13. Scottish Children's and Young Adult Fiction 246
    Fiona McCulloch
14. Into the Twenty-First Century 264
    Cairns Craig

Endnotes 285
Further Reading 329
Notes on Contributors 339
Index 343

Series Editors' Preface

This volume complements earlier Companions in the long-running series of Edinburgh/International Companions to Scottish Literature under our overall editorship. It offers a completion of the sequence of earlier generic volumes: on Scottish Drama (2011) and Scottish Poetry (2015). It offers a comprehensive overall vision to complement the earlier volumes on specific Scottish novelists, including Walter Scott (2012), James Hogg (2012), John Galt (2017), Robert Louis Stevenson (2010), Lewis Grassic Gibbon (2015), Muriel Spark (2010), James Kelman (2010) and Irvine Welsh (2010). It complements references to the novel in such period volumes as those covering the Twentieth Century (2009), the Long Eighteenth Century (2021) and the Nineteenth Century (2022) and such themed volumes as those on Scottish Children's Literature (2024) and the forthcoming Gaelic Literature volume.

The series was conceived as having volumes which fell into four time-limited strands: generic, author, period and thematic. This volume concludes the generic series. Brilliantly edited by Cairns Craig, it draws together an international team of scholars to offer a wide-ranging exploration of key figures and insights into important themes in the development of the Scottish novel. As series editors, we are grateful to its distinguished contributors. We are grateful to the editorial team at Scottish Literature International, the academic imprint of the Association for Scottish Literature, Duncan Jones and Pip Osmond-Williams, and we are grateful, above all, to Cairns Craig.

Ian Brown
Thomas Owen Clancy

Acknowledgements

My thanks to Ian Brown and the team in the Association for Scottish Literature for their patience in the production of this volume. It was originally intended to be completed in 2020-21, but was overtaken by the Covid lockdowns, which seriously affected the ability of some contributors to deliver their chapters to our original timetable, and meant that some others had to pull out altogether (which is why I appear as the author of more chapters than I had originally planned). This pushed the completion date back to 2023, by which time I was retiring from the University of Aberdeen, moving to a new home and dealing with the consequences of the death of Scoto-French poet Kenneth White, which were considerable, given that I was in the midst of editing Volumes 3 and 4 of his *Collected Works* for Edinburgh University Press. As a result, this *Companion* volume was delivered only in 2024, and I thank all the contributors, some for their patience and others for their resilience in the face of difficult circumstances.

'Document 2', from *The Historical Novel* by Georg Lukács, translated by Hannah and Stanley Mitchell (1963), is used with permission of Beacon Press; permission conveyed through Copyright Clearance Center, Inc.; 'Document 4', from *Scott and Scotland* by Edwin Muir, appears courtesy of Birlinn Ltd and is reproduced with permission of the Licensor through PLSclear. 'Document 7', Muriel Spark's essay on 'The Desegregation of Art' appears courtesy of David Higham Associates and Penelope Jardine, who included it in her edition of Spark's writings, *The Golden Fleece: Essays*, published by Carcanet Press (Manchester) in 2014. 'Document 8' has been provided by James Kelman as an updated version of the essay 'Elitism and English Literature' which first appeared in *'And the Judges Said': Essays* (London: Secker & Warburg, 2002), pp. 57–75, and will appear in this form in a forthcoming volume of essays to be published by PM Press, Oakland, CA.

As an academic, I was a specialist in twentieth-century poetry and only began to take an interest in the Scottish novel for classes organised by the Workers Educational Association and for the Scottish Universities International Summer School in the 1970s. And I only began to consider publishing my thoughts on the Scottish novel in the 1980s at the encouragement of the Board of the magazine *Cencrastus*, and I would like to thank those who gave me that opportunity, especially its editors Glen Murray and Geoff Parker, and those who helped focus the issues we sought to tackle, particularly Craig Beveridge.

My thanks, too, to my former colleagues at the University of Edinburgh, particularly Ian Campbell, Randall Stevenson and Penny Fielding, for their support, both personal and intellectual, as well as to my more recent colleagues at the University of Aberdeen, Michael Brown, Alison Lumsden, Catherine Jones, Brad Bow and Sarah Sharp. I owe a particular debt of gratitude to Professor Tim Baker of the University of Aberdeen, who generously agreed to be the backstop for the editing of this volume if I was unable to complete it: I hope its completion is as much of a relief to him as it is to me.

Cairns Craig

Introduction

Cairns Craig

In what was, in 1903, a groundbreaking attempt at a substantial *Literary History of Scotland*, John Hepburn Millar (1864–1929) noted that 'Down to the date of the Union of the Parliaments, the author's task was a perfectly plain-sailing one', but thereafter it was often unclear 'whether a particular writer of undoubted Scottish nationality should or should not be included in what professes to be a record of Scottish literature'. Millar's decision was 'to abstain from attempting anything like adequate criticism of men like James Thomson, James Boswell, and Thomas Carlyle',[1] because Scots who made their careers in London were contributors to 'English' rather than 'Scottish' literature, despite the fact that the literary history Millar was recording was not that of the various literary languages that had been employed in Scotland, which would have included Gaelic and Latin, but 'the literature of the English-speaking Scots'.[2] For Millar, only Scots who wrote in English – or its local version, Scots – in Scotland count as contributors to the literary history of Scotland, thereby reflecting in reverse what was to become a standard procedure in literary histories of England, which would adopt the Thomsons, Boswells and Carlyles, despite their country of origin, as honorary Englishmen. What is to count as 'Scottish' in literary terms, and *how* it is to count as Scottish, cannot escape the pressure of what is, at the same time, being defined as 'English', and of the ways in which the Englishness of English literature is justified and defined.

As Robert Crawford has argued in *The Scottish Invention of English Literature* (1998), the study of English literature began in Scotland with lectures on rhetoric by Adam Smith in Glasgow and Hugh Blair in Edinburgh, which were intended to equip their Scottish students with the language and culture they would have to work with as a result of the Union of 1707. Social advancement required Scots to become sophisticated in the use of the English language, an accomplishment which could most easily be achieved through acquaintance with literary texts and the national history which had generated them. Those innovations were subsequently replicated in nineteenth-century England in the colleges which offered education to working men, for they too needed to acquire 'proper' English if they were to prosper. It was not, however, until the 1920s and 1930s that there was a sustained effort to make 'English' fundamental to modern education in England – in the title of George Sampson's influential book of 1921, *English for the English*. Thus at the very moment when English had become a world language and the vehicle for many cultures around the world, the advice to the British government from the Newbolt report of 1924 (of which Sampson was a member) was that 'English literature' was crucial to the identity and the morale of the English people and, for the good of their country, their Englishness should be reinforced by making English literature a core element of the educational system.[3]

It was a view that was to become firmly embedded in the new university discipline of English Literature as it fought off the increasing influence of the United States, both in the production of a modern literature in English and in the study of the English literary past. English literature became, in effect, the vehicle for the reassertion of England's cultural primacy in the modern world, even as the success of the empire which had justified that primacy began to evaporate. Thus the spate of books in the latter part of the twentieth century, from F. R. Leavis's *The Great Tradition* (1948) through to Raymond Williams's *The Country and the City* (1993), which did not need to distinguish between the large abstractions in their titles and those that were specific to England: the generality of the titles underlined that the history of modernity is identical with the history of England because modernity, as the technological transformation of the conditions of human life, had happened first in England. As Raymond Williams put it,

> It ought in any case to be clear that the English experience is especially significant. In that one of the decisive transformations, in the relations between country and city, occurred there very early and with a thoroughness which is still in some ways unapproached'.[4]

In the next paragraph, Williams acknowledges that he was born into 'a predominantly urban and industrial Britain'[5] but it is 'England', not Britain, that is his subject: the Empire may be British, the state may be the United Kingdom or Great Britain, but its cultural traditions are those of England.

English Literature, therefore, has to be presented as something *internal* to English culture itself and not the product of the interaction of England with other cultural traditions within the territory of the United Kingdom or the Empire.

One of the most influential examples of this mode of English literary criticism is Ian Watt's *The Rise of the Novel* (1957), which insists that the rise of the modern world's most successful genre is a specifically *English* phenomenon, made possible by the English empirical tradition, and the dissemination through institutions such as the Royal Society of a belief that language should be as plain and direct as possible – should not, in effect, make itself visible between the reader and what is being represented. The novel comes fully formed into the world in the works of Daniel Defoe (1660–1731) and Samuel Richardson (1689–1761), differentiated from earlier genres by their 'formal realism'.[6] The Englishness of this account depends on excluding both the French prose narratives of the seventeenth century, from '*La Princess de Clèves* to *Les Liaisons dangereuses*',[7] as well as Cervantes's *Don Quixote* (1605–15) as founding texts for the genre of the novel, even if the consequence is that Fielding has to be accorded a lesser place in the novel's development than Defoe or Richardson because he shows too many signs of the influence of Cervantes: 'Fielding departed too far from formal realism to initiate a viable tradition'.[8] What also disappears out of Watt's account is that the narrative of Fielding's masterpiece, *Tom Jones*, is built around the Jacobite incursion into England in 1745–46. The events of Fielding's plot are carefully calibrated to the timetable of the Jacobite advance and Jones himself is, by some of the other characters, assumed to be a Jacobite sympathiser. Watt's critical argument must suppress the Scottish context of Tom Jones's escapades in order to underline the autonomous Englishness of the 'English novel' and its national 'pre-eminence in the genre',[9] undeflected by England's eighteenth-century involvement in a multi-national state. Fielding effectively invokes and then dismisses the Jacobite threat, leaving Tom and his wife Sophia both literally and metaphorically in possession of England's estate, and Watt's criticism repeats this gesture by suggesting that the society presented in the novel is shaped by a strictly internal class hierarchy, unaffected by England's relations with the other cultures on its borders.

Symptomatically, Watt sees Jane Austen as the culmination of the traditions he is exploring – 'Jane Austen's novels are also the climax of many other aspects of the eighteenth-century novel'[10] – but includes no mention of Austen's great contemporary Walter Scott, who had often been paired with her in earlier accounts of the development of the novel. J. B. Priestley, for instance, in his journey through *The English Novel* (1935), invites his readers

> to press forward to where two peaks may be seen shining in the sky, each of them representing perfection in two very different forms of fiction. One of them is Sir Walter Scott (1771–1832) and the other is Jane Austen (1775–1817).[11]

In Watt's landscape, however, the peak that had been Scott is no longer visible. While, from a European perspective, Scott continued to be, as Georg Lukács argued in *The Historical Novel* (written in 1936–37, published in English translation 1962),[12] the originator of a form which had dominated the nineteenth-century novel from Balzac to Tolstoy, Scott's works were increasingly seen from an English-language perspective as trading 'formal realism' for the escapist pleasures of historical romance. Scott's lack of commitment to 'formal realism' and, therefore, to the art of the novel, was revealed with the publication of *Ivanhoe* in 1819, a novel in which Scott explicitly abandons his Scottish historical settings for medieval England. *Ivanhoe*'s success, both in terms of sales and in terms of providing what was effectively an origin myth for England, might justify Ian Duncan's invocation of an 1820 review which suggested that, 'like a literary version of [William the] Conqueror, Scott has achieved the most effective Scottish invasion of England since the Union, and reversed the relations between imperial centre and province.'[13] Scott's *Waverley*, set in the same year as *Tom Jones*, might have taken as its theme the defeat of the Jacobites but Scott's novels were like a Jacobitism that had not turned back at Derby and had imposed itself imaginatively on the territory of England. Ironically, Scott regarded Fielding as his great predecessor in the novel but Fielding's resistance to Scottish intrusion into England was given voice in Scott's lifetime by Sarah Green's *Scotch Novel Reading or Modern Quackery* (1824), in which a character called Alice Fennel is so obsessed with Scott's novels that her conversation

> was a mere patchwork of quotations, phrases, and ill-pronounced specimens of Scotch dialect – using thee and thou, in imitation of king James, and other characters found only in romance, in the most common conversation; always saying, I ken for I know, mickle for much, wee for little, mon for man, &c. &c.[14]

Alice Fennel's imitation of the speech of Scott's characters ironically underlines how alien is Scott to her London environment (the novel is claimed to be by a 'Cockney'), but the irony goes in both directions, for whatever 'glamour' Scott's work cast on Scotland, the narrative voice of the novels, like the narrative voice of Scott's immensely successful poems in the first decade of the nineteenth century, was 'pure English'.[15] Though some of his characters spoke Scots, the linguistic priority of English in Scott's texts was replicated in the fact that so many of his protagonists are English visitors in Scotland. *Ivanhoe* was thus less of a Scottish invasion than a homecoming for an imagination thoroughly imbued with Shakespeare, Fielding and Dryden, so that for later critics it was easy to assimilate Scott to the regional traditions of English fiction. The result, as Lewis Grassic Gibbon was to argue in *Scottish Scene* (1934, written collaboratively with Hugh MacDiarmid), that later Scottish novelists produced merely regional variants of 'the English novel': 'The chief Literary Lights which modern Scotland claims to light up the scene of her night are in reality no more than the commendable writers of the interesting English county of Scotshire'.[16] The latter designation might have been printed as 'Scottshire', given the malign influence over later Scottish writing that Edwin Muir attributed to Walter Scott only a few years later in *Scott and Scotland* (1938). In the development of Scott's own career after *Ivanhoe*, as well as in his later reception by literary historians in both Scotland and England, Scotland's greatest and most influential novelist became a symptom of the failure of the novel to sustain the national literature established by the poetic tradition that ran from Dunbar and Henryson to Robert Fergusson and Robert Burns, and to which Scott himself had contributed with his *Minstrelsy of the Scottish Border* in 1802.

A consequence of this interpretation of the Scottish literary past was that even as late as 1978, Francis Russell Hart's *The Scottish Novel: A Critical Survey* (1978) was dominated by whether it was possible to identify any such thing as 'the Scottish novel', or whether there was a profound incompatibility between Scotland and the novel: James Hogg's career, Hart suggests, might 'illustrate the uncongeniality of the novel form to the fictional materials and impulses of Scottish tradition?'[17] Even as he claimed to give an account of a Scottish tradition of the novel, Hart doubted the very premise of his argument, invoking Walter Benjamin to defend the proposition that 'the vigorous survival in Scotland of folk culture, legend and traditional narrative' was 'an obstacle and a challenge to the formal development of the novel'.[18] When Edwin Muir's *Scott and*

Scotland was republished in Edinburgh in 1982, with an introduction by contemporary Scottish novelist Allan Massie, Massie argued for its continuing relevance because Muir's dilemma 'still confronts us'.[19] The notion that there might be a 'Scottish novel' independent of the 'English novel' was to become even more problematic as 'English literature' continued to find ways of extending its boundaries to include not only the works of English-born writers but 'works that come from, or bear upon, England', including works by 'Scottish, Irish, Welsh writers, and those from countries that were once part of the British Empire'.[20] If Scottish writers from Scott himself to novelists such as Robert Louis Stevenson in the nineteenth century and Muriel Spark in the twentieth, can be co-opted to a tradition of the English novel, how is Scotland's contribution to the novel to be evaluated and what, after such co-options, remains of a distinctive Scottish tradition?

In his effort to unveil such a possibility, however, Hart had sketched an alternative approach to Scott and his contemporaries which was to have significant consequences. What was characteristic of the Scottish novel, Hart suggested, was that it was rooted not in the 'formal realism' that Watt had identified as central but in two apparently different inheritances from the eighteenth century: first, the social analyses of the Scottish Enlightenment philosophers in their attempt to create 'a science of man' and, second, the recovery of the 'Gothic' as a northern alternative to the classical culture of the Mediterranean. If the social analyses of the Enlightenment were about the possibilities of 'improvement' in everything from farming (Lord Kames's *Gentleman Farmer* of 1772) and manufacturing (Adam Smith's pin-making factory in *The Wealth of Nations*, 1776) to the fine arts (the many 'essays on taste' from Alexander Gerard, 1759, to Archibald Alison, 1790), the other strand, the 'Gothic', depended on the recovery of the styles typical of earlier, less developed cultural environments, ones in which the 'primitive' still lingered. The link between these two concerns lay in Enlightenment historiography's fascination with the earliest forms of human society as the necessary index of how far humanity had travelled in its journey from its original social conditions. James Macpherson's 'recovery' of the Ossianic *Fragments of Ancient Poetry* (1760) was both symptom and symbol of this fascination: the underlying continuity of our most basic emotions made it possible to enter sympathetically into the apparently alien culture of pre-Christian Celts to imaginatively recover and take pleasure in a set of beliefs to which we could no longer give credence. The vernacular folk poetry of the late Middle Ages and the imaginative accounts of an even earlier

Celtic heroic age provided novelists with themes and forms that could claim to be parts of a distinctive 'national' tradition, one in which, as Ian Duncan was to argue in *Modern Romance and Transformations of the Novel* (1992), 'romance' rather than 'realism' was the dominant mode. The very terms by which Scott had been found wanting by critics of the earlier part of the twentieth century – his theatrical staging of the romance of earlier phases of historical experience – were revealed as not only the foundation of their success but the basis of their claim to be considered, like Shakespeare's late comedies, as art (and artifice) of the highest order.

Such claims take their theoretical justifications from the varieties of structuralism which had helped reshape literary criticism in the 1960s and 1970s, and which displaced the Aristotelian conception of a work of literature as a *mimesis* of an action in the world with the notion that it was shaped by the conventions – literary, linguistic and cultural – which make communication possible. The most influential proponent of such structuralism in the anglophone world was Northrop Frye (1912–1991), whose 'archetypal' mode of criticism – tracing the ways in which certain 'mythic' narrative structures recur in apparently different works of literature – was in part inspired by his reading of Walter Scott, and by the recurrent patterns that Scott deployed in shaping the texture of his narratives.[21] For Frye, Scott's prose works were misdescribed as 'novels' in Watt's sense; they should be understood as 'romances', romance being the earlier form from which the novel emerged but often in a shape that continued, however secretly or unconsciously, to acknowledge its origins in works such as Spenser's *Faerie Queene* or the plays of Shakespeare. Duncan's insistence on the centrality of romance in Scott's fiction was extended in his study of Scott's contemporaries in *Scott's Shadow: The Novel in Romantic Edinburgh* (2007), which provided an alternative Scottish context for the 'rise of the novel' (the modern novel) in the first decades of the nineteenth century.

Duncan's foregrounding of romance was to be given a further contextualisation with the publication of Katie Trumpener's *Bardic Nationalism: The Romantic Novel and the British Empire* (1997), which argued that Scott's *Waverley* and much of his subsequent production were developed from Irish models of what was described as the 'National Tale', in which an English character travels to Ireland in the expectation it will be 'devoid of culture':

> Instead, under the tutelage of an aristocratic friend, he or she learns to appreciate its cultural plenitude and decides to settle there permanently.

Each national tale ends with the traveller's marriage to his or her native guide, in a wedding that allegorically unites Britain's 'national characters'.[22]

In Ireland and Scotland 'cultural plenitude' comes from the survival of earlier cultural forms, whether Celtic or feudal, that can be reappropriated and reintegrated into a new 'British' national character, as when kilts and bagpipes become emblematic of the British military in its imperial campaigns. While the national tale implies the continuing presence of an older culture within a newer, it is distinguishable from the historical novel because the latter suggests that the very structure of the newer culture requires the destruction of the older; as Georg Lukács puts it, Scott's novels are *historical* because he 'sees the endless field of ruin, wrecked existences, wrecked or wasted heroic human endeavour, broken social formations etc., which were the necessary preconditions of the end result'.[23] What is left of the earlier society are not living presences but textual fragments – Macpherson's original *Fragments of Ancient Poetry* rather than his later attempt in *Fingal* or *Temora* to reconstruct a complete epic – and the issue posed by the fragment is how has it survived, by whom has it been discovered, how has it been put into circulation? As the protagonist of Sydney Owenson's *The Wild Irish Girl* (1806) demands of a priest who is defending the virtues of ancient Irish culture, 'Where are your manuscripts, your records, your annals, stamped with the seal of antiquity to be found?'[24] The answer he is given is that 'Manuscripts, annals, and records, are not the treasures of a colonized or conquered country' because 'it is always the policy of the conqueror, (or the invader) to destroy those mementi of ancient national splendour which keep alive the spirit of the conquered or the invaded'.[25] Such questions in Scotland were posed not only in the debates over the authenticity or otherwise of Macpherson's poems – an issue of great moment to Dr Johnson and the reason for his journey with Boswell to the Western Isles – but also in relation to the folk poetry collected by those who believed in the validity of oral tradition as a medium for the transmission of ancient texts, so that 'tradition bearers' could be trusted to provide accurate renditions of ancient literary works. But could those who wrote them down be trusted? Even old manuscripts were not above suspicion, since those who copied them might have been unable to resist interpellating their own 'original' compositions. Both the romance tradition and the national tale put the authenticity not only of the events portrayed but of the text itself in question: from the tattered remains of the supposed manuscript which became the fragmentary narrative of Henry Mackenzie's *The Man of Feeling* (1771), through the various fictional editors of Walter Scott's *Tales of my Landlord* (Jedediah Cleishbotham et al.) to the recovery from his grave of the printed version of Robert Wringhim's 'autobiography' in *Private Memoirs and Confessions of a Justified Sinner* (1824), Scottish novels exploit the dubiety of their epistemological status to dramatise the states of mind of characters trapped in histories whose sources, purposes and direction have been so overwritten that no original truth can be discovered. The Whig view of English history as a continual progress towards a present that is superior to all past times was part of the inheritance of Scottish Enlightenment historiography, but it is challenged in many Scottish novels: as Adam Ferguson suggests in his *Essay on the History of Civil Society* (1767), progress involves loss as well as benefit, and even Scott's narratives, as Lukács emphasises, continually dramatise such losses. If the present represents progress from the barbarities of the past, it does so only by replacing them with new, though often unacknowledged, barbarities of its own, including the imposition of contemporary values on that past. The editor in Hogg's *Private Memoirs and Confessions of a Justified Sinner* summarises his experience of editing the surviving text:

> Were the relation at all consistent with reason, it corresponds so minutely with traditionary facts, that it could scarcely have missed to have been received as authentic; but in this day, and with the present generation, it will not go down, that a man should be daily tempted by the devil, in the semblance of a fellow-creature; and at length lured to self-destruction, in the hopes that this same fiend and tormentor was to suffer and fall along with him.[26]

The 'present generation' wipes out eighteen hundred years of Christian belief in the reality of the devil with the stroke of a pen, making itself incapable of recognising the reality of evil when it refuses to disappear from history – an experience that the generations of the 1930s and 1940s would rediscover in Hogg's work as prefiguring their own complicity with the continuing reality of evil.

The death of Scott in 1832, Galt's increasingly debilitating illness from that year till his death in 1839, James Hogg's death in 1835 and Thomas Carlyle's final departure for London in 1834 have often been presented as bringing to an end the heroic age of the Scottish novel, a period when Scottish publishers and writers together formed what Katie Trumpener describes as 'a transperipheral Irish-Scottish public sphere'[27] that dominated the English language marketplace and, especially through the French translations of Scott's works, much of the European marketplace as well. What followed has been described as a 'void',[28] and a failure to build on the achievements of the Scottish Enlightenment (as it came to be called) or Scottish Romanticism (which expired into the kitsch of Queen Victoria's tartan-clad 'Balmoralism'). Such analyses, however, generally fail to register three important considerations about the Scottish novel and the culture in which it operated.

The first is the gendering of the novel. Scott's predominance after 1814 has been presented as a masculine takeover – what Scott called his 'big bow-wow strain'[29] – of what had previously been a predominantly feminine medium. Scott himself acknowledged the influence of Maria Edgeworth, but it is clear that the historical novels of Jane Porter (1776–1850), particularly *Thaddeus of Warsaw* (1803) and *The Highland Chiefs* (1810), had already opened up the territory that *Waverley* colonised. Porter was known to Scott, as was Joanna Baillie (1762–1851), whose play *The Family Legend,* with its Highland setting, Scott helped to stage in Edinburgh in 1810. In this context, Sarah Green's *Scotch Novel Reading* might be read as a feminine riposte to such masculinisation, since the English suitor for Alice Fennel's hand has to disguise himself as a Highlander much deformed by military service in order to reveal the inappropriateness of her Scottish passions in a London environment. With a sudden drop in the publication of novels after the crash of 1826, and the rise of serial publication to offset the risk to publishers, the novel became again much more focused towards a feminine and family readership. By the second half of the nineteenth century the writer who outdid Scott in productivity, if not in sales, was Margaret Oliphant, whose designation as 'Mrs Oliphant' seemed intended to underline her status as a feminine writer – as compared, say, with her contemporary and fellow *Blackwood's* contributor, Mary Ann Evans, who of course published under the name of 'George Eliot'. The apparent failure to maintain achievements in the novel after 1830 may be (as Juliet Shields suggests in chapter 5) more to do with modern criticism's failure to take seriously the country's nineteenth-century women writers, or those novelists (often, but not exclusively, women) who used the novel to promote religious convictions shared by few modern readers.

The second issue is the apparent disjunction between Scotland's global impact in the nineteenth century and the 'provincialisation' of its domestic culture, no longer capable of competing with London's dominant role in the Empire. Scotland's migrants in this period were not just dispossessed Highlanders or displaced farm labourers, but those who had benefited from Scotland's educational system, from ministers and philosophers to doctors and botanists, and these 'intellectual migrants' established universities, religious colleges, medical schools and botanic gardens on specifically Scottish models from Ontario to Otago via Kolkata, Shanghai and Hong Kong. This vast Scottish network carried with it folk culture in Scots and Gaelic, the religion of Calvin and the traditions of freemasonry, the philosophies of Hume and Reid as well as the literature of Burns and Scott ('Ivanhoe' is one of the most common placenames in the anglophone world), but it is, the argument goes, a culture of remembrance which can produce nothing new. If, however, we return to eighteenth-century conceptions of literature as 'writing-in-general' rather than simply poetry and fiction, and if we include the sciences as part of the nation's intellectual culture, the nineteenth century in Scotland looks very far from being a 'void'. To follow just one strand from the eighteenth into the nineteenth century we might focus on the 'geological sublime' that is initiated by James Hutton's *Theory of the Earth* in 1788: it then runs from Playfair's *Illustrations of the Huttonian Theory of the Earth* (1802) through the successive editions of Charles Lyell's *Principles of Geology*, first published in the early 1830s (which Charles Darwin took with him on the voyage of the *Beagle*), to Hugh Miller's *Old Red Sandstone* (1841), which combined the practical knowledge of a stonemason with the religious implications of the new science of geology, to Alexander Geikie's *Scenery of Scotland* (1865), with its account of how the beauties of the landscape were the product of underlying geological structures. A Scotland sustaining such significant (and also popular) science was not a cultural 'void', especially when it was also home to the most ambitious attempt at consolidation of human knowledge in the eighth and ninth editions of the *Encyclopedia Britannica* (published by A. & C. Black). The ninth edition in particular included articles on the most advanced science of the era in such transformative areas as 'thermodynamics', developed in Glasgow by William Thomson (Lord Kelvin) and given theoretical shape by James Clerk Maxwell's *A Treatise on Electricity and Magnetism* (1873). One of Kelvin and Maxwell's assistants, William Robertson Smith, not only became the editor the ninth edition of *Britannica* but went on to be a significant contributor to the new discipline of anthropology, a field that would be dominated by J. G. Frazer, whose *The Golden Bough* (1890–1922) was probably the most influential Scottish contribution to twentieth-century thought in Europe and America.

These and many similar achievements in nineteenth-century Scottish culture can stand comparison with those of the eighteenth century. That they have not been given the same prominence is based on the notion, as historian William Ferguson put it, that 'the reputation won by Scotsmen in science [...] did little to enhance the culture of the country [...] for science stands independent of national contexts', and therefore 'cannot nurture the irrational bonds that make nations'.[30] Few students of the history of science would now accept such a view but the question is: to which nation did such scientific achievements belong? Thermodynamics was a very Scottish achievement, but it was represented internationally as part of Britain's competition with France and Germany for priority in developing new technologies. Its Scottish origins were, however, reflected in the writings of some of the key Scottish novelists of the late nineteenth century, their fictions stimulated by what was a 'fictional' (because untestable) thought-experiment dreamt up by James Clerk Maxwell to counter the consequences that Lord Kelvin had derived from his interpretation of the Second Law of Thermodynamics. In Kelvin's view, every action in the physical world involved both a transformation and a dissipation of energy, the latter becoming unavailable for producing further change, a process which would, in the end, reduce the universe to an undifferentiated equality in which energy is so evenly dispersed that no new interactions between its atoms are possible. The universe is running down with all the inevitability of a steam engine whose coal supply is exhausted. Maxwell's resistance to this conclusion involved an imaginary atomic-sized creature (dubbed, by Kelvin, 'Maxwell's demon') who could choose to redirect the atoms in two containers, such that the fastest (and hottest) atoms would end up in one container and the slowest (and coldest) in the other, thus preventing the anticipated common equalisation of temperatures that would end in stasis. What the thought experiment suggested was that the 'law' of physics described by Kelvin was not inevitable but a statistical probability, which could be locally reversed – the first hint of what was later to become 'chaos theory'.

It was a hint taken up in 1875 in *The Unseen Universe or Physical Speculations on a Future State* by the Professor of Natural Philosophy at the University of Edinburgh, Peter Guthrie Tait, and Balfour Stewart, a Scottish physicist with an interest 'psychical' research. Using anthropological data gathered by William Robertson Smith (who was assistant to Tait while he was also doing a degree in theology at Edinburgh), they argued that all human societies had shared a common belief in an 'unseen' world behind the visible one. Using the analogy of Maxwell's demon, they suggested that the energy used in brain activity could flow in two complementary directions, one to lay down traces in the physical brain and one 'communicated to the spiritual or invisible body', where they are stored up, forming a memory which may be made use of when the spirit is 'free to exercise its functions'.[31] The 'unseen universe' is the storehouse of our psychical energy, which will continue beyond the dissolution of our material existences, such that there is no contradiction between traditional Christian belief in an afterlife and a modern physics which interpreted the material universe as consisting entirely of transformations of energy. *The Unseen Universe* was a publishing sensation, going through six editions in its first year (1875) and seventeen by 1886. Its title, echoing the Nicene Creed's assertion that God is the 'maker of heaven and earth, / of all that is, / seen and unseen', was taken up almost immediately by Margaret Oliphant in the first of what came to be known as her 'Tales of the Seen and the Unseen', stories that explored linkages between life and the afterlife. Thus, in 'A Beleaguered City', a French town is occupied by the ghosts of those who once lived there, as though they are an invading army expelling its current inhabitants. The description of the ghostly presences echoes the energy physics of *The Unseen Universe*:

> I was in the midst of a world where all was movement. What the current was which flowed around me I know not; if it was thought which becomes sensible among spirits, if it was action, I cannot tell. But the energy, the force, the living that was in them, that no one could misunderstand [...][32]

Oliphant's presentation of the consequences of the physics of *The Unseen Universe* were to be reimagined a decade later by Robert Louis Stevenson in *The Strange Case of Dr Jekyll and Mr Hyde* (1886), in which the characters move in a cityscape very similar to that which Oliphant had described in the city invested by its ghosts:

> Mr Utterson beheld a marvellous number of degrees and hues of twilight; for here it would be dark like the back-end of evening; and there would be a glow of a rich, lurid brown, like the light of some strange conflagration; and here, for a moment, the fog would be quite broken up, and a haggard shaft of daylight would glance in between the swirling wreaths. The dismal quarter of Soho seen under these changing glimpses, with its muddy ways, and slatternly passengers, and its lamps, which had never

> been extinguished or had been kindled afresh to combat this mournful reinvasion of darkness, seemed, in the lawyer's eyes, like a district of some city in nightmare.[33]

The city is surrendering to the 'reinvasion of darkness' as though running out of energy, just as Jekyll, in his attempt to maintain the virtues of his 'higher' being, must exhaust the energy which keeps his inner darkness at bay. Each expenditure of Hyde's energy reduces Jekyll's future resources, and to prevent his permanent transformation into Hyde, Jekyll has to expend ever more energy, leaving him 'a creature eaten up and emptied by fever, languidly weak in both body and mind'.[34] The energy required for his transformation does not add to life but subtracts from it; it is an expenditure whose terminus, like entropy, is a deathly stasis.

It was the inevitability of such an entropic outcome that Maxwell's demon apparently set in doubt, and it is Maxwell's demon that J. M. Barrie adapted into the figure of Peter Pan as a defiance of ageing and death. Like the demon, Peter is the guardian of the shutter that keeps two spheres separate – in this case the sphere of Edwardian London and the sphere of the Neverland. At Peter's invitation, however, certain particles – certain children – are allowed to cross from one sphere into the other, thus renewing the energy of the Neverland at the expense of the domestic sphere from which they escape. This continual transfer of new energy safeguards Peter's experience of the Neverland from the entropy which haunts his adversary, Captain Hook, entropy symbolised by the crocodile which has already consumed his arm and which he can only evade because it has also swallowed a clock whose ticking warns of its imminent arrival. Like the entropic universe, however, the 'the clock will run down, and then he'll get you.'[35] The crocodile that has already begun to consume Hook, like the Hyde who consumes Jekyll, is indicative of the irreversibility of energy dissipation which Peter, like Maxwell's demon, is able to defy only by bringing the energy of each new generation of children to recharge the Neverland with the dynamism of a fresh imagination and a new adventure.

The consequences of Kelvin's theories had been described by David Masson, then the editor of *Macmillan's Magazine*, in his book on *Recent British Philosophy* (1865), as an example of how 'In no age so conspicuously as in our own has there been a crowding in of new scientific conceptions of all kinds to exercise a perturbing influence on Speculative Philosophy', a crowding 'almost too fast for Philosophy's powers of reception. She has visibly reeled amid their shocks.'[36] Masson was to become Professor of

Rhetoric and English Literature at Edinburgh University, and one of his students was J. M. Barrie, and from Masson Barrie learnt that the highest form of literature was not the realism aspired to by Victorian novelists but the romance revealed by Shakespeare's late plays:

> We see not why, in prose, there should not be much of that mighty licence in the fantastic, that measured riot, that right of whimsy, that unabashed dalliance with the extreme and the beautiful, which the world allows, by prescription, to verse. Why may not one in prose chase forest-nymphs, and see little green-eyed elves […]?[37]

Indeed, in the light of energy physics, romance was more true to reality than a simple mimesis of a supposedly material 'reality', which physics revealed to be, in fact, a protean insubstantiality of energy in continual transformation. It was a view that Stevenson supported against Henry James in his essay 'A Humble Remonstrance':

> A proposition of geometry does not compete with life; and a proposition of geometry is a fair and luminous parallel for a work of art. Both are reasonable, both untrue to the crude fact; both inhere in nature, neither represents it.[38]

Stevenson's refusal of the art of 'representation' and his commitment to the higher nature of artifice was at one with Clerk Maxwell's conception of science as providing 'models' rather than truths.[39] The 'reality' of the realism demanded by so many critics of nineteenth-century Scottish novels was, in effect, an illusion; the deeper, the more 'scientific' reality could only be expressed, like Maxwell's Demon, in a mode that set realism aside to make use of the techniques of fantasy and myth. This made the trajectory of the Scottish novel in the latter part of the nineteenth century (as Andrew Nash explores in chapter 6) very different from that predominantly associated with the novel in England.

Indeed, a major strand in the English novel had been initiated by Thomas Carlyle in the very period when he was completing *Sartor Resartus* and then deciding to abandon the novel as an appropriate form for his own writing. In 'Signs of the Times' (1829), Carlyle defined his times as 'the Mechanical Age', in which humanity was at 'war with rude Nature; and by our resistless engines, come off always victorious, and loaded with spoils'.[40] The Victorian age was to be the age of the machine and in his 1839 essay on 'Chartism', he insisted that mechanism had led directly to 'the Condition-of-England Question', which boiled down to a 'simple fundamental question. Can the labouring man in this England of ours, who is willing to labour, find work, and subsistence by his work?'[41] That question was to dominate the English novel from Charles Dickens's *Hard Times* and Mrs Gaskell's *North and South* (both 1854), through to Thomas Hardy's *Jude the Obscure* (1895), and on into the twentieth century in novels such as D. H. Lawrence's *The Rainbow* (1915). The 'Condition-of-England Question' was not simply whether work could produce 'subsistence' for the workman, but what kind of fulfilment work offered under the conditions of industrial mechanisation; indeed, could civilisation survive in a mechanised society? It was a question asked by a Scot who, when he wrote 'Signs of the Times', had almost no experience of industrial England, but it was a question to which, given Carlyle's tendency to refer to himself as one of 'we English',[42] there could only be English answers, stretching from Engels's *The Condition of the Working Classes in England* (1844) to E. P. Thompson's *The Making of the English Working Class* (1963). There is no nineteenth-century Scottish novel of the period which could count as a response to a 'Condition-of-Scotland Question', but it was a question which, as Glenda Norquay discusses in chapter 7, was to dominate the work of many Scottish novelists in the twentieth century. The condition under analysis, however, was very different, for if the nineteenth-century question in England was about the consequences of all-too-successful industrialisation, the question in Scotland in the twentieth was about the consequences of its decline. Loss of life in the First World War and loss of livelihood in the peace haunted Scottish politicians and novelists alike, and while it was Scotland's poets who tried in the 1920s to inspire a cultural Renaissance through the deployment of a reinvigorated Scots language, it was the novelists who attempted to capture the condition of a society, both agricultural and industrial, that was becoming redundant in a post-imperial global economy. As the last of the coal mines on which Scotland's nineteenth-century economy had been built were closing in the 1960s and 1970s, the prospects for both the Scottish and the British economies were transformed by the discovery of large reserves of oil in the North Sea, inspiring a sense of future change that an insurgent Scottish National Party tried promote as a justification for independence from the United Kingdom.

The possibility of future Scottish secession from the Union inspired a revaluation of the earlier phase of Scottish literary revivalism, marked by the publication of many forgotten novels of the 1920s and 1930s in the Canongate Classics series (edited by Roderick Watson and supported by a Scottish Arts Council, become, in effect, independent of its British predecessor, from 1968 onward no longer simply a 'Scottish Committee of the Arts Council of Great Britain'), which began in 1987 with the republication of Willa Muir's *Imagined Corners* (1931) and Nan Shepherd's *The Quarry Wood* (1928). It also saw a revitalisation of the publishing of novels by Scottish publishers, including Canongate (Alasdair Gray, *Lanark*, 1981) and Polygon (James Kelman, *Bus Conductor Hines*, 1984; Janice Galloway, *The Trick is to Keep Breathing*, 1989). The 1970s also saw the establishment of Scottish Literature as a recognised academic discipline (first at the University of Glasgow, 1972), with the Association for Scottish Literary Studies (founded in Aberdeen University in 1970, and now the Association for Scottish Literature, based in Glasgow) as its professional body. The possibility of Scottish secession also led to the establishment, by the Labour government which took office in 1997, of the devolved Scottish Parliament which began to operate in 1999. No longer a place of loss and nostalgia, Scotland's eighteenth-century history was unveiled as the leading edge of the economic and sociological understanding of the process of modernisation,[43] with David Hume, Adam Smith and Thomas Reid rediscovered by American scholars as having inspired the political and intellectual traditions of the United States.[44] Scotland's past was as profoundly transformed as its possible future: the Scottish novel had a new and changed environment to give voice to, 'voice' being, as Carole Jones describes in chapter 9, as much a defining characteristic of the Scottish novel in the last decades of the twentieth century as it had been in Walter Scott's time. This transformation of Scotland's relationship with its cultural past was given its most potent expression by Alasdair Gray's *Lanark* (1981), which combined the 'question of Scotland' issues of the first half of the twentieth century (Duncan Thaw's Glasgow is a city that cannot unfreeze its economic decline) with the romance tradition of the nineteenth-century novel (Lanark's descent into the 'Institute' that consumes human lives, and his fantasy journey to Unthank, the metropolis built by thankless exploitation, echo themes from George MacDonald's works).

These redefinitions of Scotland's cultural and institutional place within the United Kingdom and within the history of Great Britain unleashed not only a wave of Scottish creativity in the arts in general and in the novel in particular, but also led to an English backlash: if Scotland threatened to leave the United Kingdom, what did that mean for an England that had generally made no distinction between England and Britain? As A. J. P. Taylor wrote in the introduction to his contribution to the

Oxford History of England – entitled *English History 1914–1945* (1965) – he rejected the relevance of Great Britain to his topic:

> When the Oxford History of England was launched a generation ago, 'England' was still an all-embracing word. It meant indiscriminately England and Wales; Great Britain; the United Kingdom; and even the British Empire. Foreigners used it as the name of a Great Power and indeed continue to do so.[45]

A flood of reassessments of the meaning of 'England' and 'Englishness' followed devolution in 1999 and went alongside a determined effort on the part of the New Labour regime of Blair and Brown to create a new narrative of a Britishness that would be multi-ethnic and multi-cultural – promoted in relation to works such as Zadie Smith's *White Teeth* (2000) as the voice of 'Black Britain' – as a counterweight to the apparent acknowledgement of separate national identities within the United Kingdom. As Joseph H. Jackson puts it,

> The coincidence of the millennial reinvention of black Britain and the management of unruly sub-British nationalisms is to be found in what Ben Pitcher calls New Labour's 'elaborated Britishness', which combined devolutionary concessions to Scotland, Wales and Northern Ireland with an official discourse of multiculturalism.[46]

Scotland's distinctive history of novel writing is simply a portion of a renewed and more accommodating Britishness; indeed, is recognition, according to some, that the Scottish novel has always been British.[47] But as the BBC poll of the One Hundred Best British Novels in 2015 revealed, there would have been almost no difference if it had been called the One Hundred Best English Novels: the Scottish novels in the top one hundred are Ali Smith's *There but for the* at ninety-ninth (but I doubt if many readers noticed one of protagonist's admission that 'A long time ago I was Scottish'),[48] and James Hogg's *Confessions of a Justified Sinner* at ninety-fourth (the poll was of non-UK critics: I doubt if it would have come so high in a poll of English readers). In other words, there are almost no Scots in a tradition of the British novel: there is, in effect, no tradition of the British novel distinguishable from the English novel. This is hardly surprising when Scottish writers are rarely included in school or university curricula in English Literature (even in

Scotland), and when there are almost no courses in the Scottish novel even in English or American universities, or universities elsewhere that teach English literature.

Literary traditions are, of course, retrospective constructions but the lack of an identifiable British tradition in the novel distinct from the English tradition means that Scottish writers, both present and past, will rarely be recognised unless there is an identifiable tradition of the Scottish novel to which they can be seen to be significant contributors. In Andrew Greig's *Rose Nicolson*[49] (2021), a historical novel built around the figure of the Scottish poet William Fowler (1560–1612), one of Fowler's accomplices is Walter Scott of Branxholme and Buccleuch, an ancestor of Walter Scott the novelist. By its theme, its characters and form, Greig's novel invokes its own literary ancestry, thus acknowledging the continuing relevance of a Scottish tradition in the novel which Walter Scott himself was supposed to have made impossible.

CHAPTER ONE

Smollett and the Novel in Scotland

Aileen Douglas

'I was born in the northern part of this united kingdom': so the protagonist of an anonymously published novel, appearing in London in 1748, begins his first-person narration.[1] *The Adventures of Roderick Random*, by Tobias Smollett, is 'the first important novel in the English language to have a Scot as hero'.[2] As the novel progresses, terms such as 'northern part' of a 'united kingdom', and the description of the hero as 'North-Briton', are soon joined by references to 'Scots' and 'Scotland'. For Smollett, writing in the decades after the Union between Scotland and England in 1707, and immediately after the Jacobite rebellion of 1745, simply naming his native land involves dual perspectives: it is both a distinct entity, 'Scotland', and part of a larger 'united kingdom'. A significant concern for Smollett, as a novelist, is how these two perspectives relate to one another.

Born in Dalquhurn, Dunbartonshire, in 1721, Smollett trained as a surgeon in Glasgow. He left Scotland in 1739 and in the early 1740s he served as a ship's surgeon during the War of Jenkins' Ear, seeing action in the West Indies. On his return to London, he practiced medicine for some years, with no great success, and was soon working indefatigably as a writer. He gained a measure of financial stability through the success of his *Complete History of England* (1757–58), and further cultural influence through his editorship of *The Critical Review*, which he co-founded in 1756. Scottish prose fiction before Smollett had included notable representations of male heroism in versions of the romance, significant examples being the 'Admirable Scot', Crichtoun, in Sir Thomas Urquhart's *The Jewel* (1652), and the Persian Emperor, Cyrus, celebrated by Andrew Michael Ramsay in his very popular pedagogical romance, *A New Cyropaedia; or the Travels of Cyrus* (1727). *Roderick Random*, however, exemplified an emergent 'new species of writing', the novel, and its depiction of the titular hero eschewed the fantastic and the superlative in favour of the recognisable and the familiar.[3] In each of Smollett's four further novels, *The*

Adventures of Peregrine Pickle (1751, rev. 1758), *The Adventures of Ferdinand Count Fathom* (1753), *The Adventures of Sir Launcelot Greaves* (1760–61), and *The Expedition of Humphry Clinker* (1771) he exploited the form's generic instability to experiment with radically different kinds of fiction.[4] It is in his first and last novels, *Roderick Random* and *Humphry Clinker*, that Smollett is most substantially concerned with the representation of Scotland and the Scots in fiction. Written almost a quarter of a century apart, at either end of Smollett's career, the two books differ greatly in tone and even more in form. Each makes different demands on the reader, and, in turn, affords different pleasures. A first-person narrative indebted to the picaresque mode, *Roderick Random* focuses on the individual experience of its hero, a fiery, lusty, impetuous young man. In contrast, *Humphry Clinker*, a multi-voiced epistolary novel, is inflected by an enlightenment desire to represent the state of the uneasily united kingdom. These differences in fictional form have fundamental implications for Smollett's treatment of nationality. *Roderick Random* emphasises nationality as physical experience with prejudice at the heart of the hero's corporeal being. We see this in Roderick's confrontation of anti-Scots prejudice on account of his speech or appearance, but also in the way he is positively prejudiced and physically drawn towards his fellow Scots, especially young men like himself, seeking to find a place in a disordered world. Like *Roderick Random*, *Humphry Clinker* is also a novel of movement, albeit one which – unlike Smollett's first novel – has a determined itinerary. The novel consists of the letters of a family group, the squire Matthew Bramble, his termagant sister Tabitha, their Oxford-educated nephew Jery and his lovesick sister Lydia, along with Win Jenkins the maid, as the party travel from Wales, through England, and into Scotland, variously in search of health, love, and diversion. As the group progress from one Celtic periphery to another and (almost) back again, nationality and prejudice remain significant themes, but here the treatment is less immediately physical, more often elaborated through discussion and reflection as these occur between the novel's characters, and as subsequently represented in the letters these characters write.

That Smollett, over his lifetime, produced many thousands of pages of prose, makes his relative lack of direct critical comment either on the novel as genre or on his own fictions particularly remarkable. An important exception here, and one worth attending to, is the 'Preface' to *Roderick Random* in which Smollett gives a succinct account of the evolution of the novel as a literary form, notes the influences on his own first work, and explains certain features of *Roderick Random*. Elsewhere, in *Ferdinand*

Count Fathom, Smollett defined the novel as 'a large diffused picture, comprehending the characters of life, disposed in different groups, and exhibited in various attitudes, for the purposes of an uniform plan, and a general occurrence, to which every individual figure is subservient'.[5] Central to Smollett's account of the novel's development is the figure of Cervantes, whose *Don Quixote* he credits with reforming taste by ridiculing the overblown and implausible conventions of romance and making fiction 'far more useful and entertaining', by pointing out the 'follies of ordinary life' (p. xxxiv). Subsequently, Smollett would go on to publish a translation of *Don Quixote* (1755) and to author his own quixotic imitation, *The Adventures of Sir Launcelot Greaves*. *Roderick Random*, however, he declared to be 'modelled' on a work by another European writer, *Adventures of Gil Blas of Santillane* (1715–35) by the French author Alain-René Le Sage. Smollett lauded *Gil Blas* – of which he also published a translation in the same year as *Roderick Random* – for describing 'the knavery and foibles of life, with infinite humour and sagacity' (p. xxxiv). Smollett's singling out Le Sage as a precursor prompts readers to expect a version of the *pícaro*: a character always on the move, living by his wits, and not always entirely scrupulous in his confrontations with a hostile society.[6] Importantly, though, the 'Preface' also explicitly limits Smollett's allegiance to his chosen model by making it clear that he desires a rather different readerly response to that which the picaresque elicits. Whereas Le Sage exposes his protagonist to the reader's mirth, Smollett wants his reader to experience 'compassion' for his hero's misfortunes. David Daiches discusses how in Smollett's writing '[s]atire and sensibility, censoriousness and a capacity for deep yet easily released emotion, the man of wrath and the Man of Feeling, are closely allied'.[7] The deliberate hybridity of *Roderick Random* in its combination of satire of worldly corruption and appeals to the reader's sympathy is one of the work's most distinctive features.

It is towards the close of the 'Preface' that Smollett explains his varied 'reasons for making the chief personage of this work a North-Briton' (p. xxxv): the education the hero's 'birth and character required' could be obtained more cheaply in Scotland; a Scottish setting would allow representation of 'simplicity of manners', and 'the disposition of Scots, addicted to travelling' justified his 'deriving an adventurer from that country' (p. xxxv). For some critics, the fact that economic necessity compelled eighteenth-century Scots to travel means that this last claim 'should not be taken at face value'.[8] Certainly, the historical reasons for Scottish migration, and the hostile stereotype of the Scots to which that migration gave rise in England, mean that travelling cannot be simply seen as a matter of Scottish 'disposition'. At the same time, the remark underlines the compatibility of perceived Scottish attributes and Smollett's chosen fictional mode.

On beginning his narrative, Roderick gives the reader a proleptic account of his future, telling how his pregnant mother dreamed that 'she was delivered of a tennis-ball, which the devil (who to her great surprise, acted the part of a midwife) struck so forcibly with a racket, that it disappeared in an instant'. Where the ball lands on its return there springs up a 'goodly tree covered with blossoms'. A seer consulted by the anxious parents declares 'that their first-born would be a great traveller, that he would undergo many dangers and difficulties, and at last return to his native land, where he would flourish with great reputation and happiness' (p. 1). The seer's prognostication comes to pass. Owing to his grandfather's disapproval of his father's marriage, Roderick is essentially disinherited while still in the womb; he then suffers the death of his mother and disappearance of his father. After a brutal childhood he makes his way to an unnamed university town in Scotland, to commence apprentice to a surgeon, and subsequently to London, where he attempts to become a ship's surgeon only to be pressed onto a man of war and reluctantly participates in the naval battle of Cartagena (1741). Returning to England he is shipwrecked and robbed, undergoes an ignominious stint as a servant, and is kidnapped by smugglers who dump him in France. Here, he enlists in the army and fights on the French side in the Battle of Dettingen (1743). At his nadir, Roderick turns fortune-hunter in London and is imprisoned for debt, before undertaking a trading voyage to South America where the discovery of his father allows a return to the ancestral home in Scotland. The expansiveness of *Roderick Random*, as the hero bounces around a global stage, is remarkable in contemporary fiction in English, especially when compared to the works of Smollett's great rival, Henry Fielding, whose *Joseph Andrews* (1742) and *History of Tom Jones* (1749) also feature travelling heroes, but ones confined to a domestic English setting.[9]

Roderick's experience of nationality is determined by the workings of prejudice in both negative and positive aspects. On first coming to London, his unfashionable appearance and long red hair mark him out, but it is his distinctive 'dialect' (p. 63) that makes him recognisably Scottish. As critics have pointed out, Roderick is heard as Scottish by the other characters in the novel, though his speech is represented in standard English.[10] Early on, Roderick is accosted by a customer in an alehouse who, drawing on stereotypes of the Scots as impoverished religious fanatics, enquires if his knapsack contains 'oat-meal or brimstone' (p. 63). More seriously, when he presents himself at Surgeon's Hall, a hostile examiner invokes the negative stereotype of the travelling Scot: 'you Scotchmen have overspread us of late as the locusts did Egypt' (p. 86). Meanwhile, Roderick's strong attachment to home is also a source of vulnerability, easily exploited. A 'money-dropper' who hears Roderick's Scottish accent immediately appeals to the young man's prejudices, launching into a celebration of Scottish bravery, ancient families, and educated pedlars. 'This eulogium on my native country', the naïve Roderick narrates, 'gained my affection so strongly, that I believe I could have gone to death to serve the author' (p. 69). Death is not required but Roderick does lose all his money in a rigged card game. In another incident, Roderick assaults a night watchman to effect the release of a Scotsman under arrest, offering as laconic explanation, 'My prejudice in favour of my native country was so strong, that I could not bear to see any body belonging to it in distress' (p. 110).

Alongside incidents in which national prejudice – English; his own – causes Roderick to be dismissed, belittled, or exploited, occur those in which he is ineluctably drawn to his fellow Scots. Waiting at the Navy-Office in a crowd of other young men and needing advice, Roderick 'consulted the physiognomy of each, and at last made up to one whose countenance I lik'd [...]. He answered me in broad Scotch' (p. 78). Roderick's attraction to Thomson, another young Scots surgeon, is a sympathetic recognition invoking the model of social response elaborated by David Hume:

> Accordingly we find, that where, beside the general resemblance of our natures, there is any peculiar similarity in our manners, or character, or country, or language, it facilitates the sympathy. The stronger the relation is betwixt ourselves and any object, the more easily does the imagination make the transition, and convey to the related idea the vivacity of conception, with which we always form the idea of our own person.[11]

In a novel full of extraordinary meetings between compatriots, the most unlikely involves not Roderick himself but his friend Thomson, with whom Roderick is re-united when pressed onto the *Thunder*. Unable any longer to endure the grotesque cruelties of life on board Thomson jumps ship and is believed to be dead. In fact he is picked up by a schooner bound for Jamaica: 'the master's name was Robertson, by birth a North

Briton, whom I knew at first sight to be an old school-fellow of mine.—When I discovered myself to him, he was transported with surprise and joy' (p. 203). In *Roderick Random* shared nationality does not have to be explicitly or consciously acknowledged; it can make itself felt as a variety of physical experience. In this, and again in accordance with the Humean model of sympathy, it works as do more particular and familial relationships. For example, before Roderick learns that the 'Don Rodriquez' he encounters in Argentina is, in fact, his own father he feels a strong, physical response: 'the dignity of his deportment filled me with affection and awe; and in short, the emotions of my soul, in presence of this stranger, were strong and unaccountable' (p. 412).

Roderick's irresistible sympathetic responses are at odds with an alternative, performative, model of identity on which the novel also draws. Hearing the story of one of his lovers causes Roderick to contrast their gendered fates: whereas Miss Williams, a well-born young woman forced into prostitution, is destined to suffer 'eternal infamy', Roderick can veer about 'to a thousand different shifts, according to the emergencies of fate, without forfeiting the dignity of my character, beyond a power of retrieving it' (p. 136). Some of the 'shifts' to which Roderick resorts are highly unsavoury. At the lowest moral point of his adventures, he complacently lives off a friend and embarks on unscrupulous fortune-hunting, detailing for the reader his rich, extensive wardrobe (p. 256). Roderick's mutability begs the question as to whether there is any shift he would refuse, or any limit beyond which he would not go. Here, a little-discussed episode in the novel sheds some light. Roderick, and his uncle Bowling, encounter a Scottish priest in Boulogne, and the latter tries to inveigle Roderick into becoming a Catholic priest. Roderick resists, but not for religious reasons, 'for as to the difference of religion, I looked upon it as a thing of too small moment to come in competition with a man's fortune' (p. 239). Roderick's flexibility allows him to entertain changes to aspects of the self, including that of his religion, often fundamentally bound up in national identity. Through all his vicissitudes, however, his 'prejudice' in favour of his native country remains in play, even if it is less pronounced as the novel progresses.[12]

The readerly compassion Smollett seeks to elicit on Roderick's behalf parallels the novel's general representation of feeling and affection and connects to the 'simplicity of manners' cited in the 'Preface' as a factor in Smollett's making Roderick a 'North-Briton'. That Roderick leaves Scotland one quarter way through the book, not to return until its closing pages, and that the 'manners' on display in the book's early chapters have more to do with violence and brutality than 'simplicity', initially confuse this issue. It is clarified, however, by attention to two characters who disappear from view for stretches of the novel but still steadfastly care for Roderick: his uncle, Tom Bowling, whose benevolence Roderick ascribes to the 'dictates of a heart as yet undebauched by a commerce with mankind' (p. 19), and the journeyman barber Hugh Strap, Roderick's loyal friend. This latter relationship is based on Strap's subservience to Roderick's superior class position: 'though you be gentle and I simple […] I who am simple may do a good office to you who are gentle' (p. 95). The simplicity of Bowling and Strap is fully contextualised, and its ideological aspects illuminated, in the novel's closure when Roderick, his father, and his new bride return to his birthplace to be enthusiastically welcomed:

> When we came within half a league of the house, we were met by a prodigious number of poor tenants, men, women and children, who testified their joy by loud acclamations, and accompanied our coach to the gate.—As there is no part of the world, in which the peasants are more attached to their Lords, than in Scotland, we were almost devoured by their affection, in getting out of the coach: My father had always been their favourite, and now that he appeared their master, after being thought dead so long, their joy broke out into a thousand extravagancies. (pp. 433–34)

Extending and amplifying the 'simplicity of manners' personified throughout the novel by Strap, and turning it into a form of social organisation, this hyperbolic scene of feudal attachment is not just a homecoming but is also a journey backwards in time. After the harsh, corrupt, modern society through which Roderick has travelled we arrive back in an antique social world. Yet *Roderick Random* is only superficially a 'Scottish restoration narrative'.[13] The patrilineal lines of inheritance remain ruptured, and it is hard cash that enables these deliriously joyful scenes. Roderick's father has not reclaimed the family estate but purchased it with money made during his South American sojourn. Roderick's wealth comes from Atlantic trade, in gold dust, but he travels to South America on a slaving vessel and is involved in caring for the slaves on board.

Smollett denied that *Roderick Random* was an autobiographical work, insisting to a Scottish friend, Alexander Carlyle, 'the *whole* is not so much a Representation of my Life as that of many other needy Scotch Surgeons whom I have known either personaly [sic] or by Report'.[14] Decades after the book's publication he wrote to an admirer:

> The only Similitude between the Circumstances of my own Fortune and those I have attributed to Roderick Random consists in my being born of a reputable Family in Scotland, in my being bred a Surgeon, and having served as a Surgeon's mate on board a man of war during the Expedition to Carthagene. The low Situations in which I have exhibited Roderick I never experienced in my own Person.[15]

Despite Smollett's decisive denial that Roderick's less salubrious experiences were in any respect shared by his author, the 'similitude' he does admit is striking: both born into respectable Scottish families; both trained as surgeons; both experiencing the same naval battle. That author and protagonist also share a fundamental experience of exile has encouraged views of Roderick Random as one of the 'wayward or dislocated protagonists' in whose stories Smollett invested 'the same sense of alienation that he himself felt as a displaced Scot'.[16] The alienation Roderick Random experiences is occasionally extreme, but is meliorated throughout by moments of camaraderie, fellow-feeling, and national sympathy.

Soon after his arrival in Scotland and impressed by the Scotsmen with whom he has enjoyed conversation and sociability, *Humphry Clinker*'s Matthew Bramble gives a national stereotype a new spin: 'I am not at all surprised that these Scots make their way in every quarter of the globe'.[17] In *Roderick Random*, Scotland is the origin from which the hero is propelled, the 'native country' towards which he feels a strong favourable prejudice. In *Humphry Clinker* not only is the direction of travel reversed, but for the Bramble family group Scotland is unfamiliar terrain. *Humphry Clinker* is a virtuosic technical achievement in its deployment of multiple points of view and voices, from that of the crusty Matthew Bramble to the excitable, malaprop-prone servant, Win Jenkins. It is also closely linked with several of Smollett's works of the 1760s. His *Travels through France and Italy* (1766), based on his extended stay on the continent between 1763 and 1765, when he travelled in search of better health, successfully exploited the contemporary vogue for travel writings, to which *Humphry Clinker* also contributed, a fact facetiously alluded to in the fictional bookseller's letter preceding the work (pp. 2–3). Additionally, as Louis L. Martz first discussed, there are extensive correspondences between descriptions and accounts in *Humphry Clinker* and the Scottish sections of the eight-volume *The Present State of Nations*, published by Smollett in 1768–69.[18]

The 'six weeks' ramble' (p. 262) undertaken by the Bramble party in Scotland is at the heart of novel. Setting off from Wales in late March, the group have already spent time in Bath and London before they reach Tweedmouth in mid-July, sharing all the while their diverse impressions of what they have seen with their respective correspondents. Letters in which Lydia and her brother Jery record their pleasure and enjoyment of novel scenes and experiences contrast with those in which their uncle, suffering from ill-health, describes a country out of kilter. Bath he finds beset by a 'general tide of luxury, which hath overspread the nation', populated by 'Clerks and factors from the East Indies, loaded with the spoil of plundered provinces; planters, negro-drivers, and hucksters, from our American plantations' (p. 36). London, for Bramble an overgrown monster, excites a litany of vividly articulated complaints regarding gross food and promiscuous society.

A threshold period prior to the arrival in Scotland prepares the travelling party, and by extension the novel's reader, for what is to come. Bramble has already recorded his shame that as 'a British freeholder' he has never been north of the Tweed, while Jery asserts that 'South Britons' are 'woefully ignorant' as far as Scotland is concerned: 'between want of curiosity, and traditional sarcasms, the effect of ancient animosity, the people at the other end of the island know as little of Scotland as of Japan' (pp. 213–14). Jery's reflection has been excited by Tabitha's beliefs that Scotland can only be reached by sea and that there will be nothing to eat there 'but *oat-meal* and *sheep's-heads*' (p. 213). Such 'traditional sarcasms' against the Scots had recently been given fresh impetus by the unpopular ministry of the Scottish Lord Bute, effective Prime Minister 1762–63.[19] Important to the novel's preparation for the Scottish sections is the figure of Lismahago, a Scottish soldier on half-pay who makes a dramatic entry at an inn in Durham:

> A tall, meagre figure, answering, with his horse, the description of Don Quixote mounted on Rozinante, appeared in the twilight at the inn door, while my aunt and Liddy stood at a window in the dining-room.—He wore a coat, the cloath of which had once been scarlet, trimmed with Brandenburgs, now totally deprived of their metal, and he had holster-caps and housing of the same stuff and same antiquity. Perceiving ladies at the window above, he endeavoured to dismount with the most graceful air he could assume, but […] the girth unfortunately gave way, the saddle turned, down came the cavalier to the ground, and his hat and periwig falling off, displayed a head-piece of various colours, patched and plaistered in a woeful condition. (p. 188)

As the party subsequently learn, Lismahago gained his injuries when scalped and left for dead at the battle of Ticonderoga (1758) in upstate New York during the Seven Years' War. Much later in the novel, debating with Matthew Bramble the results of the Act of Union between England and Scotland, Lismahago will speak of how the Union gave England

> above a million of useful subjects, constituting a never-failing nursery of seamen, soldiers, labourers, and mechanics; a most valuable acquisition to a trading country, exposed to foreign wars, and obliged to maintain a number of settlements in all the four quarters of the globe. (p. 278)

Lismahago himself belongs to this cohort and his lurid account of torture by and captivity among the Miami emphasises the cost of colonial gains and maintaining empire.[20] Meanwhile, Lismahago's having been 'wounded, maimed, mutilated, taken, and enslaved, without ever having attained a higher rank than that of lieutenant' (p. 189) excites the indignation of the Brambles.

The three days Lismahago travels towards Scotland with the group are taken up with discussion and debate between the men of the party on recent political history, the impact of commerce, the nature of the press, the place of the Scots in the army and navy of Great Britain, and the nature of the English spoken in Scotland. On this last topic Lismahago maintains that 'the English tongue was spoke with more propriety at Edinburgh than at London' (p. 198). Eccentric, contrary, and idiosyncratic, described by Jery as a 'curiosity' (p. 202) and by his uncle as one of the 'most singular personages I ever encountered' (p. 203), Lismahago is far from being a conventional guide. Yet, he still aids the travelling party in their negotiation of national differences. So, while Jery initially finds Lismahago's views on English as spoken in Scotland ludicrous, he later accepts that this is a subject on which he has much to learn and determines to acquire in Edinburgh books Lismahago recommends: Allan Ramsay's anthology of Scots poems written before 1600, *The Ever Green* (1724), as well as Ramsay's own collected poems (1721). Similarly, Lismahago informs the group's response to the anti-Scots prejudice they see in the 'doggeral rhimes, in abuse of the Scotch nation' etched on the windows of all the inns from Doncaster onwards (p. 197). The 'composure' with which Lismahago reads one such piece of scurrility in the very parlour in which the group is sitting, and the wit with which he deflects Jery's suggestion that the Scots should break all the windows in which such abuse appears, means that the onus falls on the 'South-Briton', Matthew Bramble, both to castigate the 'scribblers of such infamous stuff' and to praise the 'philosophic forbearance of the Scots' (p. 198). Lismahago's company, accentuating the travelling party's awareness of national difference and of the intangible barriers between supposedly united peoples, readies them for their experience of Scotland. Then, however, he separates from the group and disappears from the novel for a period, leaving the entourage to cross into Scotland on their own, through a landscape Bramble represents as mysterious and slightly other-worldly:

> That part of Scotland contiguous to Berwick, nature seems to have intended as a barrier between two hostile nations. It is a brown desert of considerable extent, that produces nothing but heath and fern; and what rendered it the more dreary when we passed, there was a thick fog that hindered us from seeing above twenty yards from the carriage. (p. 215)

When the fog lifts, Bramble is pleased with the scenes of the sea on the right, the mountains at a distance and an 'agreeable plain [...] covered with as fine wheat as ever I saw in the most fertile parts of South Britain' (p. 215). The dissipating fog, and the movement from blankness to admiration, are elements in a literal account of the border crossing and a symbolic foreshadowing of a visit during which the travellers' new knowledge and positive impressions of Scotland will be recorded for the benefit of the novel's ignorant or indifferent readers.

Bramble, in his letters, declares that Scotland would be a 'perfect paradise' were it not cursed with a 'weeping climate' (p. 250). He celebrates Scottish enlightenment writing, finding Edinburgh to be 'a hot-bed of genius' (p. 233) and refers to luminaries including David Hume, William Robertson, and Adam Smith whom he is pleased to find 'as agreeable in conversation as they are instructive and entertaining in their writings' (p. 233). Glasgow proves to be one of the prettiest towns in Europe and 'one of the most flourishing in Great Britain [...] a perfect bee-hive in point of industry' whose inhabitants 'have a noble spirit of enterprise' (p. 246). The landscape around Loch Lomond Bramble finds 'romantic beyond imagination' (p. 248), while further north, near Inverary, he remarks on 'the stupendous appearance of savage nature [...]. All is sublimity, silence, and solitude' (p. 252). On the relationship between clans and their chiefs, Bramble is ambivalent, admiring a patriarchal relationship 'founded on hereditary regard and affection, cherished through a long succession of the ages' (p. 255) but opining that the most effective way to break the influence of this relationship is to give clan members 'a taste of property and independence' (p. 255) through the development of 'commercial schemes' (p. 256).

This is, however, ultimately a work of fiction in which the actions and reactions of characters provide a narratological logic and coherence. So, when Jery exclaims that a longer stay in Edinburgh will turn him into a 'downright Caledonian' (p. 221) he is registering how he has been insensibly influenced by Scottish manners and customs. It is also in Scotland that the ill-health of the valetudinarian Matthew Bramble begins to improve. In Edinburgh he begins to 'feel the good effects of exercise' (p. 219). At Loch Lomond, he is so re-invigorated that he determines to 'penetrate at least forty miles into the Highlands, which now appear like a vast fantastic vision in the clouds' (p. 249). As he prepares to leave the 'Scotch Arcadia' he announces that he has received 'so much advantage and satisfaction from this tour' that he is already projecting another, much more ambitious, expedition the following year 'to the Northern extremity of Caithness' (p. 257). *Humphry Clinker* provides an enlightenment survey of Scotland, its landscape, sociability, industry, and progress, while, at a fictional level, it places Scotland as the harbinger of returned health and vigor.

On the journey south, the Brambles are once more joined by Lismahago, who has, in the interim, visited his native place. Regarding the Scottish sections of *Humphry Clinker*, it is helpful to keep in mind that there are two itineraries in play: while the dominant narrative concerns the travels and extensive commentary of the Bramble group, the second, minor, narrative concerns Lismahago. As he separates from the Bramble group in the north of England, Lismahago explains he would be of little service to them in Scotland as 'he was utterly unacquainted with the country, which he had left in his early youth' (p. 206). Long an exile, he now feels 'an irresistible impulse' (p. 207) to revisit his paternal home. Like many of Smollett's male characters including Roderick Random, Lismahago is keen to maintain his status as a gentleman. On their first encounter, Bramble offends Lismahago by sympathising with how poorly recompensed he has been in the army to be tartly told that the Scotsman was not animated by hope of gain but 'entered the service as other gentlemen do, with such hopes and sentiments as honourable ambition inspires' (p. 190). Whereas, however, Roderick Random returns home, rich and successful to demonstrations of loyalty and a quasi-feudal tableau, Lismahago is horrified by the scenes of modern progress he encounters. Not only does he discover that his nephew has become involved in a weaving manufacture directed by his father-in-law, but on approaching the very house he hears 'the sound of treddles in the great hall' (p. 272). The transformation of his ancestral home into a place of manufacture is an element of the commerce and modernity that Lismahago cannot accept, and he determines to return to America. By the end of the novel, however, in a wryly comic parallel to his captive marriage to Squinkinacoosta, Lismahago has married Tabitha, by which means he finds a British retreat, and Bramble and his servants are free of 'a very troublesome and tyrannic gouvernante' (p. 273).

Lismahago's speech is reported in the novel but, like the eponymous servant Humphry Clinker, who turns out to be Matthew Bramble's bastard son, he writes no letters. Clinker and Lismahago are objects of scrutiny who test and challenge observers – in the title's turn of phrase they 'expedite' changed understandings – but they are also always objects of mediation. In an appreciation of *Humphry Clinker* as 'the eighteenth century's greatest novel on the theme of prejudice',[21] Robert Crawford concludes that:

> In the novel's concluding alliances the despised – Methodist Humphry, absurd Tabitha and Lismahago, persecuted 'Wilson' – find the prejudices against them dispelled and new unions made possible. Such unions parallel the treatment of the United Kingdom and, in particular, the Union of Scotland and England.[22]

Similarly, Evan Gottlieb sees the novel as a 'virtual experiment, in which the sympathetic theories of Hume and Smith are summoned, staged, and tested to determine the most effective way to promulgate more harmonious relations between the citizens of the two former states'.[23] The comedic conclusion of *Humphry Clinker* may encourage such reflections, but it also punctures them. For Janet Sorensen, Smollett turns to 'linguistic practice as a way of effacing the hierarchies of region', only to inscribe a new hierarchy of gender and class that troubles 'the inclusive posturing of nationalist rhetoric'.[24] Of the three couples married, the only cross-national alliance, and the one closest to the Union between Scotland and England, is that of two the novel's most eccentric characters, the backward-looking Lismahago and the rapacious Tabitha. Still more tellingly, the entire symbolic structure of marital union is comically undermined by the servant Win: 'We were yesterday three kiple chined, by the grease of God, in the holy bands of mattermoney' (p. 352).

Tobias Smollett's first and final novels offer different approaches to the representation of Scotland in fiction. In the first-person narration of *Roderick Random* prejudice is strongly felt and robustly expressed, with the author successfully eliciting the reader's 'compassion' for his hero. In the epistolary *Humphry Clinker*, by contrast, prejudice is variously experienced, described, and debated by characters sharing their subjective and partial responses with their individual correspondents. What this novel asks of the reader is the exercise of judgement in piecing together these diverse accounts. In the 'Prefatory Memoir' of Smollett included in *Ballantyne's Novelist's Library*, Walter Scott touched on the matter of prejudice and the reception of Smollett's final novel, noting that the 'popular odium' that then persisted against the 'Scotch nation' had caused Smollett to be charged with 'undue partiality to his own country'. Such 'fond partiality' for the scenes of his youth and early attachment, in a dying man, Scott declares to be 'not only pardonable, but praiseworthy'.[25] Although aspects of Scott's own representation of Scotland in fiction – the celebration of the Highlands as an antidote to modern commercial life, the significance of border crossing, and an emphasis on orality – were to be influenced by Smollett's example, Scott's account of the reception of *Humphry Clinker* and the issue of prejudice is one of few moments in the 'Memoir' that addresses nationality directly. Nationality is nonetheless profoundly present in the extended comparison of Henry Fielding and 'his northern contemporary' (p. xxx–xxxix), with which the 'Memoir' closes, with Scott declaring that 'In comparison with [Smollett's] sphere, that in which Fielding walked was limited' (p. xxxix). Finally, Scott compares the 'genius of Smollett' to that of Rubens: while each artist may evidence faults in conception and execution, these are redeemed by brilliant colours and 'a profusion of imagination'. Walter Scott's concluding articulation of Smollett's achievement as a novelist recognises both its scope and distinction, and is easily applied to Smollett's distinctive representation of Scotsmen abroad in the world:

> [T]here is so much of life, action, and bustle, in every group he has painted; so much force and individuality of character, that we readily grant to Smollett an equal rank with his great rival Fielding, while we place both far above any of their successors in the same line of fictitious composition. (p. xlii)

CHAPTER TWO

The Philosophical Foundations of the Scottish Novel

Cairns Craig

David Hume's *A Treatise of Human Nature* (1739) overturned the rationalism of his philosophical predecessors, Descartes, Locke and Leibniz, to emphasise that human beings are primarily driven by emotion, and are more likely to be irrational rather than rational in their beliefs and judgements: 'Reason is, and ought only to be the slave to the passions, and can never pretend to any other office than to serve and obey them.'[1] The philosophical basis for this outcome was a radical reversal of John Locke's use of what he called the 'association of ideas', the notion that when two events or states of mind are regularly experienced together they inevitably invoke each other. For Locke this explained why rational creatures, who should be able to come to the same judgements about things in the world, could, nonetheless, completely – and violently – disagree:

> Ideas that in themselves are not at all of kin come to be so united in some men's minds that it is very hard to separate them; they always keep in company, and the one no sooner at any time comes into the understanding but its associate appears with it; and if they are more than two which are thus united, the whole gang, always inseparable, show themselves together.[2]

For Locke, as the choice of the word 'gang' suggests, association is a disruptive mental mechanism, having none of the '*natural* correspondence and connexion with one another' which it is 'the office and excellency of our reason to trace'.[3] For Hume, on the other hand, association is the foundational process of the mind, and even those connections of cause and effect which science extracts as the apparently 'true' structure of the universe, are nothing but psychological connections: 'We have no other notion of cause and effect, but that of certain objects, which have been *always conjoin'd* together, and which in all past instances have been found inseparable' and 'from the constant conjunction the objects acquire an union in the imagination'.⁴ The regularities we discover or expect in the universe are the products of our own imaginings: for each of us, the world is a place so infused with imagination that it is difficult, if not impossible, to separate those events which might correspond to something 'real' in nature and those which may be no more than our imaginings.

The effort to distinguish between valid, objective conjunctions and those which are merely subjective is, Dugald Stewart argued in his *Elements of the Philosophy of the Human Mind* of 1792, at the very core of education, since it is only by 'watching over the impressions and associations which the mind receives in early life' that we can 'secure it against the influence of prevailing errors; and, as far as possible to engage its prepossessions on the side of truth'.⁵ The problem, as Adam Smith, a supporter of Hume's epistemology, discovered at the conclusion of his essay on 'Astronomy', lay in how easily apparent 'truth' could deceive us. Following on an exposition of Newton's principles of the relations of the planets, an account which has 'a degree of firmness and solidity that we should in vain look for in any other system', Smith has to remind himself that even Newton's explanations are, after all, just another product of the imagination:

> And even we, while we have been endeavouring to represent all philosophical systems as mere inventions of the imagination, to connect together the otherwise disjointed and discordant phenomena of nature, have insensibly been drawn in, to make use of language expressing the connecting principle of this one, as if they were the real chains which Nature makes use of to bind together her several operations.⁶

Newton's account of the universe is not *true* – it is simply more compelling to our imaginations than those which preceded it; the 'real chains', more powerful than gravity, are those of association.

Hume describes eloquently towards the end of Book I of the *Treatise* the psychological consequences of such an account of the world, in a passage where the style of the philosopher gives way to that of the novelist:

> The *intense* view of these manifold contradictions in human reason has so wrought upon me, and heated my brain, that I am ready to reject all belief and reasoning, and can look upon no opinion even as more probable or likely than another. Where am I, or what? From what causes do I derive my existence, and to what condition shall I return? Whose favour shall I court, and whose anger must I dread? What beings surround me? And on whom have I any influence, or who any influence on me? I am

> confounded with all these questions, and begin to fancy myself in the most deplorable condition imaginable, inviron'd with the deepest darkness, and utterly depriv'd of the use of every member and faculty.[7]

This crisis is produced by what is known as Hume's 'bundle' theory of the self, the theory that, no matter how carefully we inspect the workings of our own minds, we can never find what it is that binds together the fleeting 'impressions' and 'ideas' that flow through our consciousness: 'what we call a *mind*, is nothing but a heap or collection of different perceptions, united together by certain relations, and suppos'd, tho' falsely, to be endowed with perfect simplicity and identity'.[8] What holds experience together is not the substantiality of the self, or, indeed, the reality of the world beyond the self, but simply the processes of association – the relations of resemblance, of contiguity and of cause and effect – which determine the nature of our experience of what we call the world. In the *Treatise*, Hume's escape from his crisis, which 'reason is incapable of dispelling', is provided by the pleasures of the social world: 'I dine, I play a game of back-gammon, I converse, and am merry with my friends', such that the 'lively impressions of my senses' will 'obliterate all these chimeras'.[9] The comforts of social camaraderie set aside the solipsistic meditations of the philosopher, as he joins his *associates* in shared activities. If association might seem to lock us into the solipsism that results in the crisis of the end of Book I of the *Treatise*, association is also the means by which we escape back into the social world through our ability to share, however distantly, in others' associations: 'we find, that where, beside the general resemblance of our natures, there is any peculiar similarity in our manners, or character, or country, or language, it facilitates the sympathy'.[10] Our imaginations, which are the source of our associations, can also allow us to enter into those of others as though they were our own: this, Hume insists, is 'the nature and cause of sympathy; and 'tis after this manner we enter so deep into the opinions and affections of others, whenever we discover them'.[11] As Adam Smith suggested in his *Theory of Moral Sentiments* (1759), 'Society and conversation [...] are the most powerful remedies for restoring the mind to its tranquillity, if, at any time, it has unfortunately lost it',[12] because although our senses 'never did and never can, carry us beyond our own person', the associative imagination allows us to

> place ourselves in [another's] situation, we conceive ourselves enduring all the same torments, we enter as it were into his body, and become in

some measure the same person with him, and thence form some idea of his sensations, and even feel something which, though weaker in degree, is not altogether unlike them.[13]

Our own apparently private associations, carried along on the flow of passion or sentiment, are capable of turning into a sympathetic identification with others' experience.

Scottish novels in the century following the publication of Hume's *Treatise* are haunted by the threat that untrammelled passion and an overactive imagination will overthrow their characters' sense of self and their relationship with the social world. In Henry MacKenzie's *The Man of Feeling* (1771), for instance, we are presented with a character – Harley – whose individual identity is regularly overwhelmed by his capacity for sympathy with those whom he encounters, as though he has acquired an excess of the Humean ability to enter into others' associations. The very structures of MacKenzie's novel, which offers the reader a series of fragmentary narratives about its characters, the original manuscript having been much mutilated (we are told) for wadding in a hunting rifle, reflects the fragmentation of the 'bundle' theory of the self. In Harley, it seems, the bundle has been made powerless by the intensity of its sympathy with others' suffering: 'There were a thousand sentiments; – but they gushed so impetuously on his heart, that he could not utter a syllable.'[14] The language of 'sentiment' is conveyed not in speech but, as John Mullan has argued, through the body in 'tears, blushes and sighs'[15] – Harley's response to any story he is told is to offer 'the tribute of some tears'[16] – as well as in the body's collapse into fits and faintings. When Harley finally manages to give utterance to his love for the Miss Walton who has been the secret object of his affections, it is only as his body reaches its last gasp:

He seized her hand – a languid colour reddened his cheek – a smile brightened faintly in his eye. As he gazed on her, it grew dim, it fixed, it closed – He sighed, and fell back on his seat – Miss Walton screamed at the sight – His aunt and the servants rushed into the room – They found them lying motionless together.[17]

Emotions which cannot be expressed in language overwhelm the body.

So, in Christian Isobel Johnstone's *Clan-Albin* (1815), the protagonist, Norman Macalbin, hears unexpectedly that the woman he loves is about to marry his military commander. His comrade, Pat Leary, who has casually announced the coming nuptials, 'turned round and beheld Norman leaning against the canvas of the tent, which was dyed with blood, and blood still gushing from his mouth and nostrils'; his emotions are so intense Norman 'had burst a blood vessel'.[18] Similarly, in Mary Brunton's *Discipline* (1814), the heroine's father dies from the shock of discovering that he is bankrupt: when a servant intimates this outcome,

> A dark and shapeless dread rushed across my mind; but the cup was already full, and I could bear no more. I sunk down in strong convulsions.[19]

Having no memory of the truth which she had guessed, she enters her father's chamber: 'Upon a couch lay a form that seemed my father's. The face I saw not. A cloth frightfully stained with blood – No! – It cannot be told.'[20] The silent but bloodied body overwhelms the body of the text, which becomes similarly dumb.

Such shocks, transmitted from the mind to the body, can equally travel in the other direction, becoming so concentrated in characters' associative processes that they are entirely disconnected from external reality. Such descent into world-as-imagination according to a Humean account is most vividly represented in *The Man of Feeling* by Harley's visit to Bedlam, where the madness of a young woman who sees in her every visitor the reappearance of her dead lover leads Harley to conclude that 'the passions of men are temporary madnesses',[21] and such temporary madnesses are common in early Scottish novels. Thus, in Brunton's *Discipline*, the protagonist, Ellen, after having been turned out of her father's home and trying to survive as a governess in Edinburgh, wakes to find herself incarcerated in Edinburgh's version of Bedlam:

> I was awakened from the deepest sleep, by a cry wild and horrible. It was followed by shouts of dissonant laughter, unlike the cheering sounds of human mirth. They seemed but the body's convulsion, in which the spirit had no part.[22]

Allowed out into the exercise yard, Ellen encounters a man she believes is one of the officials of the institution:

> This belief inspired me with a very embarrassing desire to convince him of my sanity; and I endured the toil of being laboriously wise, while we moralised together on the various illusions which possessed the people

round us, and on the curious analogy of their freaks to those more sober madmen who are left at large.[23]

The world is made up of irrational beings, some in society and some in confinement, because 'it is not for the prejudiced eye to detect the almost imperceptible bound which separates soundness of mind from insanity':[24] the associations that govern each individual mind could be deemed 'insanity' by anyone who does not happen to sympathise with them.

The bi-directionality of the associative process, leading on the one hand to inner fragmentation and a world dominated by the imagination, or, on the other, leading us outwards to an identification with the experience of others, is what has made Hume's philosophy fundamental to the genre of the novel:[25] as readers we are locked within our own associative connections but through the novels we read we learn to extend the range both of our associations and our sympathies. Fictional characters become our 'associates' and the act of reading leads us from the isolated to the sociable self. It was the relation between inner and external associations that informed Hume's turn in the 1750s from the analysis of the workings of the mind to the writing of history, for his history was organised around the presentation of the 'character' of historical figures and the relationship between their inner associative processes and their external associates. Regularly in his narration, Hume pauses to summarise the characters of those involved, as, for instance, in his summation of Fairfax, a royalist leader in the English civil war:

> Fairfax was a person equally eminent for courage and for humanity; and tho' strongly infected with prejudices or principles, derived from religious and party zeal, he seems never, in the course of his public conduct, to have been seduced by private interest or ambition, from adhering strictly to these principles. Sincere in his professions; disinterested in his views; open in his conduct; he formed one of the most shining characters of that age; had not the extreme narrowness of his genius in every thing but war, and his embarrassed and confused elocution, on every occasion but when he gave orders, diminished the lustre of his merit, and rendered the part, which he acted, even when invested with the supreme command, but secondary and subordinate.[26]

Fairfax's inner associations – 'strongly infected with prejudices or principles' – are balanced against his public performance – 'sincere in his professions; disinterested in his views' – to explain how his public actions are the inevitable consequence of private associations too embedded in his nature to be resisted. What is, initially, accidental and contingent – the nature of our earliest associations – becomes, over time, the determining structure of our 'character', which is reflected in those with whom we choose to be associated.

In his delineation of character-as-association, Hume provided novelists with the means for exploring the interaction of private subjectivity with the world of public action. Appropriately, Hume's history was often bound together with Tobias Smollett's continuation of it (for Hume had refused to go beyond 1688), thus underlining how the writing of history and the writing of fiction were intimately connected when the novel was in its infancy. Indeed, the epistolary structure of Smollett's *The Expedition of Humphry Clinker* (1771) allows it to dramatise the workings of association as his letter-writers respond to the immediacy of events:

> Never did I sit down to write in such agitation as I now feel – In the course of a few days, we have met with a number of incidents so wonderful and interesting, that all my ideas are thrown into confusion and perplexity – You must not expect either method or coherence in what I am going to relate.[27]

Each of the letter writers is given a style based on their capacity to articulate their experiences in writing and the kinds of association that dominate their character – hilariously so in the case of Win. Jenkins's spelling, that reveals the anarchy of an inner life in which, for instance, 'grace' is transformed into 'grease'.[28] Nonetheless, the characters' accumulation of 'associates', from Humphry himself to the pensioned former soldier Lismahago, produces both a compact history of the preceding decades and a series of debates about the past and present condition of Scotland as part of the United Kingdom, and about the sources of the country's apparent transformation, in Edinburgh's case into 'a hot-bed of genius',[29] and in Glasgow's into 'a perfect bee-hive in point of industry'.[30] These transformations provide the travellers with new sets of associations by which both they and Smollett's readers can re-imagine Scotland. Smollett's plot plays on such transformations of association, in both of its senses. Matthew Bramble has overturned his Welsh identity, as 'Matthew Loyd of Glamorgan', in order better to reflect the superior social standing of Matthew Bramble, graduate of Oxford, and in doing so made it impossible for Humphry to track down his natural father, who was, his mother had told him, Matthew Loyd. Humphry is a lost association. He has, however, accidentally fallen into the very set of associates – the Bramble family – which ought to have been his from the beginning. The stability of one's character and the certainty of one's identity depends on achieving a comfortable fit between one's inner and external associations and in this, Smollett's novel sets a pattern of the loss and recovery of associations and associates that will underpin the plotting of novels well into the nineteenth century.

In Susan Ferrier's *Marriage* (1818), the central character, Mary, is brought up in Scotland after she has been rejected by her English mother. As she reaches maturity, she is sent to spend time in London with her mother and to meet, for the first time, her English relatives:

> The carriage drove smoothly along, and the sound of the church bell fell at intervals on the ear, 'in cadence sweet, now dying away'; and, at the holy sound, Mary's heart flew back to the peaceful vale and primitive kirk of Lochmarlie, where all her happy sabbaths had been spent. The view now opened upon the village church, beautifully situated on the slope of a green hill. Parties of struggling villagers, in their holiday suits, were descried in all directions, some already assembled in the church-yard, others traversing the neat foot-paths that led through the meadows. But, to Mary's eyes, the well dressed English rustic, trudging along the smooth path, was a far less picturesque object, than the bare-footed Highland girl, bounding over trackless heath-covered hills; and the well-preserved glossy blue coat, seemed a poor substitute for the varied drapery of the graceful plaid.[31]

Mary's valuation of her new environment is governed by her childish associations, a fact that Ferrier underlines by declaring, 'So much do early associations tincture all our future ideas'.[32] That those associations include, especially, our earliest associates, Mary discovers in the pleasure she contemplates in meeting again one of her Scottish aunts: 'Her heart warmed at the thoughts of seeing again the dear familiar face of aunt Grizzy, and of hearing the tones of that voice, which, though sharp and cracked, still sounded sweet in memory's ear'. Such emotion is explained by 'the power that early associations ever retain over the kind and unsophisticated heart'.[33] It is those early associations which will protect Mary from the culture of her new 'associates' in London, and from English wealth and dissipation to which her mother has succumbed, whose aim is that Mary should marry a Mr Down Wright, because he is 'a man of family and fortune, heir to a title, uncommonly handsome and remarkably sensible and well-informed'.[34] Mary's response echoes Hume's emphasis on character as a set of dispositions by which we can judge the likely outcomes of a person's future actions: 'I would wish to know something of his character – his principles – his habits – temper, talents – in short all those things on which my happiness would depend'.[35] Ferrier's plot allows Mary to fulfil the values of her early associations by marrying for love rather than for money or social position and thereafter returning with her husband to the scene of her early associations: 'Colonel and Mrs. Lennox agreed in making choice of Lochmarlie for their future residence'.[36] The other marriages in *Marriage* are almost all emotional failures, in each of which women find it impossible to make themselves at home with their husbands because they have no shared associations to connect past and present. Mary's sister Adelaide, for instance, 'had vainly imagined, that, in renouncing virtue itself for the man she loved, she was for ever ensuring his boundless gratitude and adoration' only to discover that she is 'an outcast from society – an object of indifference, even to him for whom she had abandoned all'.[37] For Mary, on the other hand, marriage re-establishes the associations on which her character was originally founded and so allows it to be a completion rather than a disruption of the underlying pattern of her life.

In *Thaddeus of Warsaw* (1803), Jane Porter presented a world which dramatises an alternative version of the Humean crisis. In *Thaddeus*, the protagonist, a member of the Polish royal family who has fought to prevent his country being wiped off the map of Europe, has had to flee to London, cutting him off not only from all the associations of his boyhood in his native Poland, but from all his associates in that country except for one elderly, ailing refugee:

> Whilst he sat by his bed, ministering to him with the care of a son, he dwelt with melancholy delight on his revered features, and listened to his languid voice with those tender associations which are dear to the heart, though they pierce it with regretful anguish.[38]

Since his most intimate associations are a secret he cannot share, those in England who try to get to know him find themselves 'without a hope of penetrating the thick cloud which involved him, and with which he ever baffled any attempt she had heard to discover his birth or misfortunes'.[39] The costs of nursing and then of burying his last associate results in Thaddeus being confined to a debtors' prison, ultimately stripped of all his past associations: 'He has no father, no mother, no kindred in this wide world!' cries Mary Beaufort as she tries to arouse sympathy for him. Bereft of associations, Thaddeus is reduced to a level of penury that is the outward equivalent of a psychological vacuity in which his associations no longer have any purchase on the world around him, and he is no longer identifiable as the person he once was. Like Humphry Clinker, however, it will turn out that he is, in fact, already at home since he is the son of an English aristocrat who abandoned Thaddeus's mother before the child's birth: the associations accumulated through a childhood in Poland can be replaced by English associates – an English visitor to Poland, whom Thaddeus had saved in battle, turns out to be his brother; an estate gifted to him by his guilt-stricken father brings him tenants; a lover whose admiration leads to her paying his debts and releasing him from prison will, when they marry, bring with her wealth sufficient to restore his aristocratic lifestyle. 'Can it be possible,' she asks on first getting a hint of his Polish ancestry, that the hero of Polish resistance, 'the illustrious Sobieski and my contemned Constantine are the same person?'[40] People are defined by their associations and their associates which turn out, in Thaddeus's case, in his Polish and English experiences, to be mirror images of one another.

A similar transformation takes place at the end of Brunton's *Discipline* (1814), when a Mr Maitland, whom Ellen has spurned in London, turns out to be the Henry Graham of whose virtues she has heard so much when staying with his sister, Charlotte, in Scotland. Maitland, apparently a London merchant, is in fact a Highland chief who does not use his Scottish name in London because it is associated with Jacobite rebels. Discovered by Charlotte in poverty, Ellen's life is transformed by money delivered to her from Maitland, which he claims belongs to her as part of what remains from her father's estate. Charlotte then offers to entertain Ellen at the family home in Glen Eredine, where Ellen acquires the associations with mountain scenery and Highland lochs that make her too at home in Scotland: 'in less than a week, I was as much at home as if I had been born in Glen Eredine'.[41] This transformation of her associating consciousness, impelled by her regular association with Charlotte, prepares Ellen not only to be receptive to the arrival of a Highland chief returned to the scene of his own fondest associations but at last to escape her self-imposed isolation by her sympathetic identification with 'Maitland' and his sister. *Discipline*, as in Smollett's *Humphry Clinker*, uses the travels of its central character, from London to Edinburgh and then to the Highlands, as a means of exploring the differences between the moral values of commercial London and the inherited familial values of an apparently more 'primitive' society. The novel is, in effect, tracing what came to be known as the 'stadial' view of history, the view that the modern world has developed out of earlier forms of human societies – pastoral, agricultural, commercial – each with its own distinctive social structure. The psychological associations typical in one stage of society are apparently made redundant in a later phase of social and economic development, but novelists like Brunton strove to imagine a world in which the associations of an earlier society could be incorporated into a later, as though the novelist could reoccupy the territory previously plotted by the historian.

Jane Porter's *The Scottish Chiefs* (1810), for instance, is a retelling of the story of William Wallace and the struggle for Scotland's independence in the thirteenth and early fourteenth centuries. It begins with Wallace in a condition similar to that of Thaddeus in her earlier novel, since he is trapped in a social and psychological isolation by the fact that his Scottish associates have submitted to English suzerainty: 'Withdrawn from the world, he hoped to avoid the sight of oppressions he could not redress, and the endurance of injuries beyond his power to avenge.'[42] Wallace retains the associations that gives value to the domestic environment shared with his wife – 'Nearly of the same age, and brought up from childhood together, reciprocal affection has grown with their growth; and sympathy of tastes and virtues, and mutual tenderness, made them so entirely one'[43] – but they have no public existence: 'Scotland had submitted to her enemies; he had no alternative but to bow to her oppressors, or to become an exile from man, amid the deep glens of his country.'[44] Wallace's wife's death deprives him of even those associations, but the novel then traces his accumulation of new associations and associates through whom Scotland will be freed and his wife revenged:

> He felt as a father toward Scotland. For every son and daughter of that harassed country, he was ready to lay down his life. Edwin he cherished in his heart as he would have done the dearest of his own offspring. It was a parent to whom a beloved and prodigal son had returned, that he looked on Bruce. But Helen, of all Scotland's daughters, she was the most precious in his eyes.[45]

In its attempt to trace the thought-processes of a much earlier stage of Scottish history, *The Scottish Chiefs* inaugurates a novelistic engagement with the psychology of the past which would lead to Walter Scott's 'invention' of the historical novel in *Waverley* (1814), which pitches its protagonist, Edward Waverley, both into an earlier historical period – that of the Jacobite rebellion of 1745 – and into, in Scott's depiction, a more primitive society – that of the Gaelic-speaking Highlands of Scotland – but equally into the Humean world-as-imagination, underlined by Edward's tendency to infuse his actual experiences with literary memories, as when he supplies his rather plain female neighbour 'richly, out of the stores of his own imagination, with supernatural beauty, and all the properties of intellectual wealth'.[46] The overwhelming of reality by imagination leads Waverley into the romantic world of the Jacobites, where 'all that was common-place – all that belonged to the everyday world – was melted away and obliterated',[47] and in which the figments of imagination so 'easily outweighed all prudential motives',[48] that he becomes committed to 'follow a prince who throws himself upon the affections of his people, to recover the throne of his ancestors or perish in the attempt', and whose followers are 'worthy associates in a gallant enterprise'.[49] The outcome is that Waverley has, among his new associates, lost the associations that constituted his original identity, until he hears the voice of his former commanding officer:

> It was at that instant, that, looking around him, he saw the wild dress and appearance of his Highland associates, heard their whispers in an uncouth and unknown language, looked upon his own dress, so unlike that which he had worn in infancy, and wished to awake from what seemed at that moment a dream, strange, horrible, and unnatural.[50]

His 'Highland associates' reveal how his original associations have been displaced by ones that can no longer consistently connect his present to his past: being no longer at one with his own earlier self, his identity is set radically in doubt. It is a prefiguration not only of a psychological condition which afflicts many of the characters of the Waverley novels – as, for instance, in the case of Darsie Latimer, in *Redgauntlet* (1824), who is forced to dress as a woman and discovers that he is no longer himself as he falls unrecognised into the arms of his friend Alan Fairford[51] – but will recur in novels such as Hogg's *Confessions of a Justified Sinner* (1824), when Robert Wringhim justifies his past actions by the assertion 'that I have two souls, which take possession of my bodily frame by turns, the one being all unconscious of what the other performs'.[52] Although such identity crises may be attributed to the difficulty of Scots finding their cultural place in the new British state and in the British empire, it is articulated through Hume's epistemological dissolution of the self as a foundational set of associations are displaced by a new set of associates.

Hume's epistemology provided Scottish novelists with ways of dramatising both the inner and the social lives of their characters, but like Hume's philosophical antagonist, Thomas Reid, they could not rest with Hume's scepticism. In Reid's *Inquiry into the Human Mind on the Principles of Common Sense* (1764), the world of the sceptic is indeed the world of the mad-house to which so many characters in the novels are consigned:

> I [the sceptic] resolve not to believe my senses. I break my nose against a post that comes in my way; I step into a dirty kennel: and after twenty such wise rational actions, I am taken up and clapped into a mad-house. Now, I confess I would rather make one of the credulous fools whom Nature imposes upon, than one of those wise and rational philosophers who resolve to withhold assent at all this expense. If a man pretends to be a sceptic with regard to the informations of sense, and yet prudently keeps out of harm's way as other men do, he must excuse my suspicion that he either acts the hypocrite, or imposes on himself.[53]

Hume's scepticism goes against 'common sense' and in common sense is the validation of a world created by a benign God that makes scepticism irrelevant and unsustainable: 'Such original and natural judgments are, therefore, a part of that furniture which Nature hath given to the human understanding. They are the inspiration of the Almighty [...].'[54] Philosophical reason that goes against common sense and custom ends up in the madness of 'the credulous fools whom Nature imposes upon'. It is an outcome satirised in the character of the would-be female philosopher, Bridgetina Botherim, in Elizabeth Hamilton's *Memoirs of Modern Philosophers* (1800), a character whose 'very limited understanding' is united with an 'active imagination' to deny the traditional truths of Christianity. In Hamilton's *Cottagers of Glenburnie* (1808), those truths are personified in the figure of Mrs Mason who is continually assailed by events which restrict her capacities – she is made lame for life when saving the children of her employers from a fire – and threaten her independence. Nonetheless, she attempts to educate the 'cottagers of Glenburnie' into cleanliness and Godliness, while herself providing an example of Christian stoicism:

> On taking a view of her present situation, and comparing it with the past, she carefully suppressed every feeling that could lead to discontent. Instead of murmuring at the loss of those indulgences, which long habit had almost converted into necessaries of life, she blessed God for the enjoyment of such a state of health as none of the luxuries of wealth could purchase; and for which those who possessed them so often sighed in vain.[55]

Mrs Mason accepts the 'subordinate situation in which she had been placed' because she could there learn 'the important lesson of humility'[56] while continuing her missionary efforts to improve the lives of others, even in the small terrain within which she has to work. When she watches dawn break, 'She saw the God of nature in His works, and blessed the goodness, which even in the hour of creation, ordained that they should not only contribute to use, but add to the enjoyments of the human race'.[57]

Mary Brunton, though a much more sophisticated novelist than Elizabeth Hamilton, is not less determined that her central female characters should be heroines of Christian virtue. In *Self-Control* (1811), for instance, the heroine Laura manages to escape being ravished by her lover, Hargrave (allegorically 'her grave'), and hides her embarrassment at such an encounter in her room in her father's house: 'There was in Laura's chamber one spot, which had, in her eyes, something of holy, for it was hallowed by the regular devotions of her life.' It is through the associations of this room that she able to pray and 'her anguish softened into resignation; and with the bitter tears of disappointment, those of gratitude mingled, while she thanked Him who, though he had visited her with affliction, had preserved her from guilt'.[58] The associations which accumulate around religious experiences provide an overwhelming sense of the security of the self as created and defended by God and that belief survives even being kidnapped and made prisoner by Hargrave's people and transferred to the wilderness of North America where she hopes to die before Hargrave can complete his plot to entrap her:

> The whole night preceding Hargrave's arrival, was passed by Laura in acts of devotion. In her life, blameless as it had appeared to others, she saw so much ground for condemnation, that, had her hopes rested upon her own merit, they would have vanished like the sunshine of a winter storm. Their support was more mighty; and they remained unshaken. The raptures of faith beamed on her soul. By degrees they triumphed

over every fear; and the first sound that awoke the morning, was her voice raised in a trembling hymn of praise.[59]

The American wilderness is a place, for Laura, without associations and without associates, but her prayers are answered by the discovery of an Indian canoe, which she manages to launch on to a river whose rapids and waterfalls she improbably survives until rescued by settlers. The dangers of North American rivers (as later in John Galt's *Bogle Corbet* of 1831) are symbols of a mind out of control but in search of something to hang on to that will stabilise itself and that, for Laura, is her Christianity:

> Laura was a Christian, and she could even at times rejoice that the spirit of vanity was mortified, the temptations of the world withdrawn; even where the blow was more painful, she humbly believed that it was necessary, and thankfully owned that it was kind.[60]

The strain of evangelical Christianity is equally prominent in Jane Porter's historical novels. *The Highland Chiefs*, for instance, presents Wallace as one 'who had built his heroism on the rock of Christianity',[61] and in Christian Isobel Johnstone's *Clan-Albin*, Norman's successes on the battlefields of Spain and the possibility of acquiring his father's Spanish title are rejected because 'his habits, his associations, his hopes, his prejudices were all Scottish',[62] but a portion of those associations is his assurance that 'though dust returns to dust, the spirit returns to GOD who gave it!'[63]

Scottish novelists may have been inspired by the psychological and narrative techniques of David Hume, but they remained committed to the Christian principles of Thomas Reid. How to combine the first with the second drove much of the experimentation in narrative structure and character presentation in the half century after 1770: characters were defined by their Humean psychologies but they were redeemed from its potential destructive consequences not by Hume's sociability but by divine direction. When Norman goes to inform the wife of his friend Craig-Gillian of her husband's death on the battlefield, he finds her tempted by the Catholicism of the Spanish chapel in which she has been sheltering: 'Reflection loudly suggested how inferior was this system of blended superstition and dogmatism, to the vigorous and intellectual reformed faith in which she had been so sedulously nurtured.' The widow, however, is tempted from 'that bold spirit of respectful enquiry which forms one of the best distinctions of the Protestant religion, and is indeed its very essence', but Norman 'knew that her heart alone had betrayed her understanding, and hoped that, as soon as her feelings recovered their tone, her principles would regain their original firmness'.[64]

Human experience may be played out against the secular backdrop of Hume and Smith's 'stadial history', but that history is a minor feature of a redemptive universe in which God is an active presence. In *Sartor Resartus* (1833), Thomas Carlyle proposed to reveal to us that

> This fair Universe, were it in the meanest province thereof, is in very deed the star-domed city of God; that through every star, through every grass-blade, and most through every Living Soul, the glory of a present God still beams. But Nature, which is the Time-vesture of God, and reveals Him to the wise, hides Him from the foolish.[65]

It was a revelation which remained resonant through the Disruption of the Church in 1843, and was to be reasserted in the novels of George MacDonald, such as *David Elginbrod* (1863) and *Robert Falconer* (1867). The protagonist of *David Elginbrod*, Hugh Sutherland, long after Elginbrod himself is dead, discovers that by returning to the associations and associates of his younger years when he was lodging in the peasant home of the Elginbrods, he can behold

> in the great All the expression of the thoughts and feelings of the maker of the heavens and the earth and the sea and the fountains of water. The powers of the world to come, that is the world of unseen truth and ideal reality, were upon Him in the presence of the world that now is.[66]

The Scottish tradition of the novel, like Scottish philosophy, may emerge from Hume's epistemology but it develops by refusing his Pyrrhonian scepticism in favour of a conception of humanity directly in communication with its Maker, the Author of the book of the world.

DOCUMENT 1

'A Century of Great Poets from 1750 Downwards No. II – Walter Scott'

Blackwood's Magazine, 110 (August 1871)

Mrs Oliphant

The name which we have just written [the occasion was the centenary of Scott's birth] is one which no Scotsman can pronounce or think of without a special movement of pride and pleasure – a gratification more tender, more familiar and homelike, than that even with which we bethink ourselves of Shakespeare, who is the greatest magician of all, the wizard whose magic is still more widely spreading and penetrating. Shakespeare is England's, Britain's – part of the inheritance of all who speak our language; but Scott belongs to us by a closer relationship. He has made us glad and proud in one tender, private corner of our heart, which does not open to the poet purely as a poet. There happens to be, as we write them, a special meaning in these words, but their truth is beyond times and seasons; it was as true twenty years ago as now, and will be as true as ever generations hence. A passing irritation, an affectionate anger even moves our minds that we should be supposed to feel more warmly towards him now than at any other moment. Walter Scott needs no celebrations, no feast held in his honour. Scotland herself is his monument. It is with no ephemeral enthusiasm that we regard a man whose thoughts have mixed themselves inextricably with our thoughts, whose words rise to our lips unawares, whose creations are our familiar friends, and who has thrown a glow of light and brightness over the scenes which are dearest to us. From Schiehallion to Criffel, from the soft coves and lochs of the west to the rugged eastern coast with all its rocks and storms, something of him is on every hillside and glen. We do not know any poet who has so identified himself with a country, so wrapped himself in its beauty, and enveloped it with his genius, as this greatest of our national writers has done for Scotland. His fervid patriotism (unlike as the two men are in every respect) is more like the Italianism of Dante than the milder nationality of any other poet. Dante was fierce and terrible in his narrow patriotism, Scott benign and cordial; but what Florence was to the one

Scotland was to the other. Her name was written in his heart. Had she been convulsed with the great throes of national conflict, it was in him too to have shown that wild vehemence of patriotic love and grief as truly as did Alighieri. As the days he fell upon were peaceful days, he contented himself with the sweeter task of lighting up and beautifying the country of his love. He hung wreaths and ornaments about her with lavish fondness. He adorned and decked her, sometimes with the enthusiasm a man has for a tender mother, sometimes with the passion of a lover for his bride. He is henceforward to all the world the type and model of a patriot-poet. When a critic means to bestow upon Manzoni, for instance, the highest encomium that can be given; the very grand cross of literature, he calls him the Scott of Italy [...]

The present moment [centenary of Scott's birth], of course, suggests reflections of its own; but these are apart from Scott and the real impression he has made upon the mind of his country. It suggests to us a wondering, half-smiling reflection that a hundred years ago there was no Scott known in Scotland. No Scott! no genius of the mountains, shedding colour and light upon their mighty slopes; no herald of past glory, sounding his clarion out of the heart of the ancient ages; no kindly, soft-beaming light of affectionate insight brightening the Lowland cottages! And yet more than this – there were no novels in the land. There was Richardson, no doubt [author of *Pamela*, 1744], and the beginning of the Minerva press [famous for tales of the Gothic]. But the modern novel was not, and all the amusement and instruction and consolation to be derived from it were yet in the future. The softer and lesser, but still effectual, hands which helped in the origination of this prose form of perennial poetry, Miss Edgeworth, Miss Austen, Miss Ferrier, rose with the greater magician, like secondary moons round a planet. There were no novels; and a hundred years ago the past history of Scotland was a ground for polemics only – for the contentions of a few historical fanatics, and the investigations of antiquarians – not a glowing and picturesque path in which all the world might rejoice, a region sounding with music and brilliant with colour, as living as our own, and far more captivating in the sheen and brightness of romance, than the sober-tinted present. This is but a superficial enumeration of what Sir Walter has done for us. He has made our past beautiful and dear; he has lighted up our country, and given her a charm for all the nations of the earth; but he has done even more than this. To us he has populated Scotland. He has set that enthusiasm of loyalty which belongs only to a primitive race in full and splendid relief against the darkness of the hills to which it belongs; but he has also set forth the less demonstrative faithfulness of the tamer peasant of the plains, triumphant over the complications of more artificial life and the restraints of prudence and common-sense. He has surrounded us with the beautiful, the noble, and the fair, and he has not disdained to pluck a very daisy from the soft slopes of St Leonard's [Jeanie Deans in *Heart of Midlothian*] and wear that as his crowning glory. Could we go back to that Scotland of 1771, into which a new Scott was born without much remark, of the old mosstrooping race, tamed down to all the soberness and regularity of a respectable family, how strangely different should we find it! The people we should meet would be more entertaining in themselves, more original, less like everybody else, no doubt. They would remember the '45, and still feel in their hearts some remnant of that thrill of doubt and fear and hope which must have run through the island before the ill-fated prince turned back on his way to London. But in their recollections there would have been no Vich-Ian Vohr, no Evan Dhu, no Flora [characters in *Waverley*] – high quintessence of the old Celtic race. And Arthur's Seat would have risen to the sky with no consciousness in its lion crest that David Deans's cottage lay safe below [in *Heart of Midlothian*]. And Stirling would have shone in the sun with no Fitz-James treading its lofty streets, no Douglas and no Lufra to call forth applause even from the Ladies' Rock. And Loch Katrine and her isles would have lain hidden in the darkness, with no soft courageous Ellen to bring them to human ken [from *The Lady of the Lake*]. What a strange, what an incredible difference! No Highland emigration could so depopulate those dearest hills and glens as they are depopulated by this mere imagination. A hundred years ago they were bare and naked – nay, they were not, except to here and there a wandering, hasty passenger – such a passenger, for example, as Samuel Johnson – who made what haste he could to escape from these dreary wilds. Not even Shakespeare – no poet we know of – has done so much as this for his country. And it has all been done within the century which in this month comes to an end.

*

[…] the poems of Scott were but as the preface to his work. His real and enduring glory is in his novels – the fuller and greater drama which did not naturally with him shape itself into verse, and which was quite beyond the minstrel's sphere. There is a certain confusion here in words, which we trust may not involve our meaning to the reader's apprehension. Scott was a great poet – one of the greatest – but not in verse. In verse he is ever and at all times a minstrel, and nothing more. He is the modern representative of that most perennially popular of all characters, the bard who weaves into living song the exploits and the adventures of heroes. It is no mean band, for Homer stands at the head of it, supreme in the love and admiration of all the ages; but it is essentially different from the other schools of poetry which have flourished among us, and in more recent times. It does not admit of the great impersonations of the drama proper, and at the same time it forbids, as strictly as the true drama forbids, those explanations which are permitted to reflective and philosophical poetry. The impression it makes must be conveyed rapidly, without interruption to the song; the narrative must flow swift as a stream, vivid and direct to its end. The primitive passions, the motives known to all men, the great principles of life which all can comprehend and even divine, are the materials in which alone it ever works. The fact must never be lost sight of, that the tale is told by one voice, and that this one voice sings. The story has to be done at a hearing, or at two or three hearings, but must, by its nature, never be allowed to flag or become monotonous. Neither can it be permitted to be elaborate. Directness, simplicity, comprehensibleness, are absolute necessities to it. No one must pause to ask what does this or that mean. To thrill the listeners with a rapidly succeeding variety of emotions – to hold them breathless in suspense for the *dénouement* – to carry them along with the hero through some rapid adventure – these are the minstrel's powers. If he lays his hand on the more complicated chords of existence, and tries to unravel the deeper mysteries, he forsakes his sphere. Hamlet and Lear are impossible to him, and so are the musings of Jacques, and even the delicious trifling of Rosalind [in Shakespeare's *As You Like It*]. His is a hasty muse, with staff in hand and shoes on feet. He must be doing at all hazards. He must know how to relieve the strain upon his audience by a rapid change of subject, but never by a pause. Thus he stands apart among the ranks of the poets – a great artist in his way, the most popular perhaps of all – but never attaining to that highest sphere in which the crowned singers dwell.

This is Scott's position in what is called his poetry as distinct from his prose writings, and we think it is a mistaken love which claims a higher for him. Of all poets it is perhaps the minstrel who has the largest and most sympathetic audience. When we reflect that while all the world vied in celebration of Scott, Wordsworth was known only to a handful of friends, this fact will be made very apparent. The critics who applauded the one to the echo, and fell with savage cruelty upon the other; the public who bought up edition after edition of the minstrel's lays, and left the poet unregarded among his mountains, – enforce the lesson with a clearness above all comment. And it would be wrong to say that there was no justice in the award of the world. That world was made up of – a small class of people able to appreciate the loftier flights of poetry, and to understand those researches into the depths of human nature, and those high communings with heaven and earth which are her privilege – and of myriads who were too busy, too joyous, too sick and sorrowful, too hard-working and worn with care, to have any power to enter into the depths or ascend to the heights of that divine philosophy which speaks in music and song; but these myriads at the same time were pervaded by that vague longing for beauty and sweetness, for noble deeds and thrilling tales, which is one of the broadest principles of humanity. In the midst of the flatness of their own particular lives their ears were open to the tale of passions, sufferings, and generosities – of those conflicts of love and hate which (they are always ready to believe) make the lives of some men as full of interest as their own lives are devoid of it; and for this throng, this multitude more than could be numbered, Scott took up his harp and sang. He played upon them as upon another harp. He moved them to instant excitement, to sympathy with the generous and the injured, to admiration of the lovely and good.

*

It [*Waverley*] was received with such a flash of enthusiasm as none of his works had as yet called forth. Not even the fresh delight of the 'Lay' had stirred the public mind as did the new revelation – the beginning of a new branch of literature, as it may be called – which came before it in 'Waverley'. The effect was electrical. 'Opinion!' said Lord Holland, when asked what he thought of the book: 'none of us went to bed all night, and nothing slept but my gout.' The world was once more taken by storm [...]

'It [*Waverley*] has made a very strong impression here', he writes to his friend Morritt, a few days after its publication, 'and the good people of Edinburgh are busied in tracing out the author, and in finding out originals for the portraits it contains;' he 'does not expect, however, that it will be popular in the South, as much of the humour, if there be any, is local, and some of it even professional'. In another letter he adds a piece of criticism which is true enough, and shows the impartiality with which he looked upon the children of his brain. 'The hero,' he says, 'is a sneaking piece of imbecility, and if he had married Flora she would have set him up on the chimney-piece as Count Borolaski's wife used to do with him. I am a bad hand' he continues, 'at depicting a hero properly so called, and have an unfortunate propensity for the dubious characters of Borderers, buccaneers, Highland robbers, and all others of a Robin Hood description.' This shows that Scott recognised a deficiency which is, indeed, not common to him only, but to the greatest of dramatists as well. When one recalls not only Waverley, but the Claudios, Bertrams, Bassanios, and Sebastians of Shakespeare, as well as Scott's own mild, respectable, and ineffectual band of Harry Mortons, Lovels, &c., it becomes evident that to 'depict a hero' is a very hazardous task indeed, transcending even the highest powers.

But hero apart, what a wonderful and enchanted world was there and then opened to the astonished public! Here was no astonishing Grandison ideal [hero of Samuel Richardson's novel *Sir Charles Grandison*, 1753], no work of mere imagination created out of nothing, but a revelation of a whole broad country, varied as nature is, and as true. The veil was drawn from the face of Scotland, not only to other nations, but to her own astonished delighted inhabitants, who had hitherto despised or derided the Highland caterans, but now saw suddenly with amazed eyes the courtly figure of Vich Ian Vohr descending from the mists, the stately and beautiful Flora, with all their attendants, such surrounding personages as Evan Dhu and Callum Beg, either of them enough to have made any ordinary man's fortune. We can comprehend but dimly at this distance – we who have been brought up upon the Waverley novels, and scarcely can remember when we first made acquaintance with that wonderful Highland court, any more than we can remember when it was that we first set childish foot within Prospero's enchanted isle [in Shakespeare's *The Tempest*] – it is with difficulty that we can realise the first magical effect produced by them. They had no rivals in the field. They were read everywhere, by all kinds of people; they flew from hand to hand like the news of a campaign in which everybody was personally interested; and it is easy to realise how, as book followed book, the world kept ever growing larger and larger round the astonished, entranced, breathless audience, which had enough ado to look on while the bright panorama glided before them, and sketch after sketch of new country rose brilliant out of the mists. The race whose power and place was over – the economy of the past in its last splendid, fatal outburst – became visible suddenly, as no amount of historical description could ever have made it, in the persons of Fergus MacIvor and his valiant and loyal henchman. In that wonderful flow of narrative the reader was carried along from admiration to disapproval, to blame, to enthusiasm, to regret, and finally to that scaffold and conclusion which he came to with a pang of the 'hysterica passio' in his throat, and at the same time that sense of inevitable and necessary fate which ennobles and saddens the Greek drama – all without time to breathe or pause, or escape from the spell that had seized upon him. The splendid warmth of kindly and genial humour which lighted up the absorbing tale, gave to it all the breadth of that life which goes on cheerily, feasts and laughs, and finds a sober enjoyment in the midst of the greatest convulsions.

*

The book advances, grows, lives by its own instinctive vitality. One thinks of the hand seen through the window finishing page after page without a pause [as described in Lockhart's *Life*]. Why? Because by force of genius the author had, as it were, no will in the matter. The book brought itself into being; took its own way, amusing the writer even by its waywardness, by the flow of its incidents, by the changes and slips it made in his half-conscious hands. And pouring after 'Waverley' into the world came the flood of its successors, all instinct with kindred life, proving that no adventitious help of historical interest was wanted, but that the humblest incidents of common life were enough to furnish at once drama and interest. The cottage of the Mucklebackits [in *The Antiquary*] with its simple tragedy is brought as close to us as the rude hall of the Highland chieftain, and goes even more warmly to our hearts. Scott draws them as if he had been studying fishermen and their ways all his life. His sympathy enters into everything.

The rustic dalliance on one hand, and that sorrow of the poor which has to be put aside for all the necessities of ordinary life, are all open to his sympathetic eye; and, with the touch as of a magician's wand, he conjures all coarseness out of the one, and teaches us to feel for the petulance of grief restrained – the passion of sorrow which takes the form of irritation – in the other. As the brilliant series flows on, it is as if each new study was the author's masterpiece; and so mightily does he work upon us, that even the conventional machinery of the lost child, in its different forms, gains a new interest, and becomes in his hands the most ready way of securing a picturesque arrangement of characters. More than this, however, Scott never aims at in his plot. Though we defy the most coldblooded reader to follow without excitement the story of those strange events which make Captain Brown into Henry Bertram of Ellangowan [in *Guy Mannering*], it is not upon such means of arousing and retaining the reader's interest that Scott depends. The story is but as a thread to him upon which his pearls are strung; and though each tale has its love-story, we do not suppose that any but the youngest reader is much concerned whether Waverley marries or not, or takes any great interest in the vapid loves of Lovel or Hazeldean [Lovell is the 'hero' in *The Antiquary*, but 'Hazeldean' seems to be a mistaken recollection of Scott's song 'Jock of Hazeldean']. It is the men and women whom he introduces to us who engross our interest; and besides this, which is the primary attraction, his power of simple narration is unequalled. This is almost a more rare gift than that power of creation which has peopled our earth and our country with so many new and original and noble beings. Scott not only introduces us to a crowd of men and women whom we did not know before, but he sets incidents so before us that they make as vivid an impression upon our minds as things that have happened to ourselves [...]. He takes us into a new district, and sets it before us so that we feel capable of recognising every bush and cothouse. He makes a scene so to pass before us that we feel we have been in it. In every way he pours the full tide of his own exuberant existence over the subject he has chosen; he makes it live, he makes it glow, he removes it out of the region of hypothesis, and writes certainty all over it. His novels are as vivid, as lifelike, as lavish in their vitality, as are his poems; and though the probabilities are by no means slavishly adhered to, or facts severely upheld, there are few among us who do not stand by Scott against both history and likelihood.

*

[...] there can be no question that, among so many remarkable works, the 'Heart of Midlothian' separates itself, prince or rather princess among equals. Here is the humblest, commonest tale of deception and betrayal, a story in its beginning like one of those that abound in all literature. There is the pretty, vain, foolish girl gone astray, the 'villain' who deceived her, the father and sister brokenhearted with shame, the unhappy young heroine's life spoilt, and ruined like that of a trodden-down flower; nothing, alas! can be more ordinary than the tale. Put to it but its usual moral conclusion, the only one possible to the sentimentalist, the 'only act' which the 'lovely woman' who has 'stooped to folly' can find 'her guilt to cover', and the moralist has no more well-worn subject; but the touch of Scott's hand changed all. 'Had this story been conducted by a common hand', says a judicious anonymous correspondent quoted in Lockhart's 'Life', 'Effie would have attracted all our concern and sympathy – Jeanie only cold approbation: whereas Jeanie, without youth, beauty, genius, warm passions, or any other novel-perfection, is here our object from beginning to end.' Jeanie Deans, to our thinking, is the cream and perfection of Scott's work. She is tenfold more, because in all ordinary circumstances she would be so much less interesting to us than a score of beautiful Rowenas, than even Flora [in *Waverley*] or Rebecca [in *Ivanhoe*]. She is a piece of actual fact, real as the gentle landscape in which she is first enclosed, true as her kine that browse upon the slope – and yet she is the highest ideal that Scott has ever attained. A creature absolutely pure, absolutely truthful, yet of a tenderness, a forbearance, and long-suffering beyond the power of man, willing to die rather than lie, but resolute that the truth her nature has forced her to speak shall not be used for harm if her very life can prevent it. And this flower of human nature expands and blooms out, its slow sweet blossom opening before our eyes without one moment's departure from the homely guise, the homely language, even the matter-of-fact channel in which her thoughts run by nature. She is never made anything different from what it is natural that the daughter of David Deans, cowfeeder at St Leonards, should be. In all her many adventures she is always the same simple, straightforward, untiring, one-idea-ed woman; simple, but strong not weak in her simplicity, firm in her gentleness, resisting all unnecessary explanations with a sensible decision, at which the clever, bold, unscrupulous villain of the piece stands aghast. He has not the courage to keep his secrets, he who has courage to break hearts and prisons; but Jeanie has the courage. There is not one scene in which this high valour of the heart, this absolute goodness, fails her; nor is there one in which she departs ever so little from the lowliness of her beginning. She is as little daunted by the Duke and the Queen as she is by the other difficulties which she has met and surmounted with that tremulous timidity of courage which belongs to nerves highly strung; nay, she has even a certain modest pleasure in the society of these potentates, her simple soul meeting them with awe, yet with absolute frankness; making no commonplace attempt at equality. Nothing but the beautiful unison of a soul so firm and true with the circumstances and habits appropriate to her class, could have brought out the whole of Jeanie's virtues. Nor do her dangers, or the fame and success she has won, make for a moment that effect upon her which such experiences would make upon the temperament to which a desire of 'bettering itself' – in one way as noble a desire as it is possible to entertain

– is the chief of human motives. That desire has been the parent of many fine deeds, but its introduction would have desecrated Jeanie. With a higher and nobler art, the poet has perceived that the time which has been so important to her is, after all, but a little interval in her life, and that it has no power to upset the sweet balance of her nature, or whisper into her sound and healthful brain any extravagant wishes. The accidental and temporary pass away, the perennial and natural remain. Jeanie is greater than rank or gain could make her in the noble simplicity of her nature; and the elevation which is the natural reward of virtue in every fairy tale would be puerile and unworthy of her – false to every principle of art as well as nature. The pretty Perdita [in Shakespeare's *Winter's Tale*] becomes a princess by every rule of romance, even when she is not an anonymous king's daughter to begin with; but Jeanie is above any such primitive reward. She is herself always, which is greater than any princess; and there never was a more exquisite touch than that in which, after her outburst of poetic eloquence to the Queen – eloquence to which she is stimulated by the very climax of love and anxiety – she sinks serene into herself, and contemplates Richmond Hill as 'braw rich feeding for the cows', the innocent dumb friends of her simple and unchanging soul. This is the true moderation of genius. An inferior writer would have kept Jeanie up at the poetic pitch, and lost her in an attempt to prove the elevating influence of high emotion – an elevation which in that case would have been as poor as it was artificial, and devoid of all true insight. Scott knew better; his humble maiden of the fields never ceases for a moment to be the best and highest thing he could make her – herself.

CHAPTER THREE

Walter Scott, the Reader, and the Times after Time

Caroline McCracken-Flesher

Who shall tell us a story?
Sir Walter Scott of course.

E. M. Forster, *Aspects of the Novel*

Why, half the truths I have sent you in this letter will become lies before they reach you, and some of the lies [...] may be turned into sad realities before you shall be called upon to detect them. Such are the defects of going by different chronologies. Your now is not my now; and again, your then is not my then; but my now may be your then, and vice versa. Whose head is competent to these things?

Charles Lamb, 31 August 1817

'Who shall tell us a story?' asked E. M. Forster. 'Sir Walter Scott of course' was his 1927 reply. But for Forster as a modernist novelist, this was not a compliment.[1] 'Yes – oh dear yes – the novel tells a story', he lamented: 'That is the highest factor common to all novels, and I wish that it was not so [...] not this low atavistic form.'[2]

Scott, in fact, tells many stories. Moreover, those stories multiply according to their lively inter-relation with their readers. To Forster, readers are of a lowly sort: 'We are all like Scheherazade's husband, in that we want to know what happened next.' Stories and readers together are locked in the determinations of narrative time – 'dinner coming after breakfast, Tuesday after Monday.'[3] But Scott requires and even expects a lot more of the reader. For Scott, the reader is an unpredictable creative partner, unfixed in time.

As a writer, Scott enjoyed two distinct careers: he was a successful poet, producing popular and influential works like *The Lady of the Lake* (1810) before he turned to the novel. In this second career he wrote anonymously and often under the pseudonym 'the Author of Waverley', taken from his 1814 first novel. Again, he proved successful, producing twenty-seven novels, most of them commercial and critical successes. From this height came a slump – not unusual for a writer of reputation subject to shifting trends. Scott's fall, however, is notable for the degree to which it was critically, and even nationally, imposed. This chapter considers how Scott's novels have been received and engaged in critical and popular contexts. It points to the ways in which Scott, alongside yet against his contemporary Romantic writers, created what Sophie Laniel-Musitelli and Céline Sabiron have identified as the period's 'new representations of temporal phenomena [...] generating new modes of time-consciousness'.[4] For Scott, those modes reside in that too-often despised reader.

*

Scott's reputation took its first significant decline toward Forster's mere storyteller shortly after his death in 1832. Thomas Carlyle, reviewing J. G. Lockhart's *Memoirs of the Life of Sir Walter Scott, Baronet*,[5] challenged that, although Scott's admirers 'were at one time almost all the intelligent of civilized countries', Scott had written too much.[6] He had 'spread himself into breadth and length, into superficiality and saleability'.[7] To make things worse his 'contrasts of costume'[8] and 'hasty theatrical scene-paintings' symptomised a meretricious surrender to 'novel-manufactory'.[9] Ground in the commercial mill, Scott's novels had 'no message whatever to deliver to the world'.[10] Carlyle imagined Scott's typical reader exclaiming, 'Be mine to lie on this sofa, and read everlasting Novels of Walter Scott!'[11] Scott had one story to tell, and that served only 'the every-day mind'.[12] For Carlyle, Scott appealed to low-grade readers, happy with low-grade stories. Still, the class and critical presumptions of Carlyle's opinion might give us pause. Today they encourage us to wonder how Scott engaged with the readers Carlyle neglects, and how readers engage with Scott.

Despite Carlyle, authors through the nineteenth and into the twentieth centuries have had no qualms about embracing Scott's 'story'. The Jacobite periods and plots that centre many of his novels echo into Robert Louis Stevenson's *Kidnapped* (1886), John Buchan's *The Thirty-Nine Steps* (1915), and the English D. K. Broster's Scottish trilogy (1925, 1927 and 1929). Their indirect cultural influence resounds through the American Diana Gabaldon's *Outlander* series (1991–). Yet such appropriations may superficially speak to Carlyle's critique: it is all about the costumes, the peripatetic plot, and the commercially compelling reader.

Through much of the twentieth century, criticism consolidated that possibility. In the Scotland of 1936, Edwin Muir agreed that there was a 'curious emptiness [...] behind the wealth of [Scott's] imagination'.[13] Scott's one story – which was not a story worth telling – Muir tied to a place which itself had lost the plot of cultural progress. Scott lived 'in a hiatus, in a country [...] which was neither a nation nor a province, and had, instead of a centre, a blank, an Edinburgh, in the middle of it'.[14] John Buchan's less polemical evaluation of 1932, with its focus on the historical context of Scott's writing, recognised the author's virtues, but did little to change the narrative of his limitations. Beside the reminder that the author 'knew his native land [...] as no Scotsman had ever known it before', the insight that Scott's popularity and its international extent 'has had a paralysing effect' on his critical study sounded no warning to critics determined to mark themselves separate from Scotland's supposed cultural and literary provincialism.[15]

Thus, the first important twentieth-century turn in Scott's reputation as a novelist came from abroad. Like Buchan, the Hungarian Georg Lukács valued Scott's appreciation of common people. He also saw in Scott the ability to bring 'the past to life as the prehistory of the present' and an argument – not surprising for a Marxist critic of the 1930s – 'that the most violent vicissitudes of class struggle have always finally calmed down into a glorious "middle way"'.[16] But it was through Cairns Craig's 1996 assertion that the author had assisted in pushing Scotland 'out of history', in the sense of outside conventional narratives of progress, that critical discourse started to understand how in the case of Walter Scott, it was caught in imperialist terms.[17] Although 'Enlightenment philosophers and Scott reduced Scottish history to a series of isolated narratives which could not be integrated into the fundamental dynamic of history', Craig questioned the assumption that 'the pattern of development of Scottish culture ought to be the same as English culture'.[18] In Scott's narrative space 'forces outside of history [...] are ever ready to return upon us in defiance of the apparent progress of civilization'.[19] Recognising that there are 'values which stand outside of history as we define it: not *after* history, or *before* it, but *beyond* it',[20] Craig reopened critical awareness to the strange temporalities that motivate and play through Scottish literature – and that I will suggest play creatively and freely in those undervalued stories and readers of Walter Scott.

*

While Scott has suffered the decline shared by all nineteenth-century authors of long novels, well into the twentieth century he retained almost unique popularity as an idea. In his own day, his novels immediately translated into popular plays; *Rob Roy* consolidated a tourist industry.[21] Scott enjoyed many afterlives as tours, monuments and memorabilia proliferated.[22] In Europe, his reputation and influence proved more durable – he may even have influenced European union, suggests Robert Crawford.[23] In perhaps the clearest evidence of Scott's popular resonance, his name, and the characters and places he made famous, swirl across maps far from Scotland, suggesting readers' engagement and investment beyond the norm.

Perversely, it may be the eighteenth-century affect of an author born in 1771 that makes Scott a writer for popular readers, even today. Carlyle concluded: 'No sounder piece of British manhood was put together in that eighteenth-century of time', pinning Scott to the limitations of the past.[24] Yet Scott associates with an Enlightenment more modern than the nineteenth century in which Carlyle wrote. He often quotes Sterne, who kicked loose from the determinations of time and context, not least by direct engagement with his readers. And if Muir thought Scott wrote from within a "temporal Nothing",[25] the author drew on an eighteenth-century tradition of ballad collecting that beseeched the temporal everything that included tomorrow's misreadings. Thomas the Rhymer is the second, predominant reference for a Scott who himself collected, critiqued and rewrote ballads. In 1802, Scott included the traditional verses, the Rhymer's supposed sayings, and his own conclusion to the tale in his *Minstrelsy of the Scottish Border*.[26] Carried into Elfland, Thomas of Ercildoun receives 'the tongue that can never lie',[27] lives seven years with the faeries, returns to the world, but must leave once more. To Scott, Thomas finds himself twice-over out of step with human culture. His gift, matched with the temporal disparity between worlds, produces him sporadically re-entering human time to deliver cryptic prophecy. But True Thomas's interventions, whether in the fragmentary story Scott attaches to a late edition of *Waverley* (supposedly from 1799, but elaborated in 1829), as the fictive sayings that pop up in novels such as *The Bride of Lammermoor* (1819) and *Castle Dangerous* (1831), or in the form of the Rhymer's own ghostly appearances, typically erupt out of time. They come too soon and too late – and thus pose a challenge to their recipients.[28] Which is to say that Scott's critics, undervaluing his eighteenth-century origins, often miss in his novels a polyvalence that makes mockery of progress by disrupting linearity, and that challenges temporality by beseeching a reader who will rewrite.

Viewed from the perspective of this twenty-first century, indeed, the nearest equivalent to the experience of reading a Scott novel might be open-world gaming. Far from the singular narratives Carlyle and Muir would decry, a Scott schooled in eighteenth-century experimentalism and the turns of time offered by a Thomas the Rhymer produced not one story but many, in sequence and simultaneously. We might take a clue from Scott's first novel, *Waverley* (1814). Here, an introduction which figures as 'Chapter One' brings the multiplicity of story and the impossibility of settling on any one into the body of the text.[29] The opening gambit points toward specificity: 'The title of this work has not been chosen without the grave and solid deliberation which matters of importance demand from the prudent.'[30] Imprecision, however, evolves alongside the discourse of clarification:

> what could my readers have expected from the chivalrous epithets of Howard, Mordaunt [...] or from the softer and more sentimental sounds of Belmour [...]? I have therefore, like a maiden knight with his white shield, assumed for my hero, WAVERLEY, an uncontaminated name, bearing with its sound little of good or evil, excepting what the reader shall be hereafter pleased to affix to it.

Scott then debates a series of subtitles, setting each aside because it would rouse generic expectations and limit readerly engagement: with '"Waverley, a Tale of other Days," must not every novel-reader have anticipated a castle scarce less than that of Udolpho [...] Would not the owl have shrieked and the cricket cried in my very title-page?'[31] Even in determining a time, Scott situates it negatively:

> I would have my readers understand that they will meet in the following pages neither a romance of chivalry, nor a tale of modern manners; that my hero will neither have iron on his shoulders, as of yore, nor on the heels of his boots, as is the present fashion of Bond Street.[32]

This historical novel, strangely, is both generically and temporally unfixed. It constitutes a meeting place where what we shall meet remains unclear.

Moreover, this story of Jacobite rebellion – one that becomes a template for successive authors to follow – itself resists singularity. The first five chapters in idyllic England and a childhood of unregulated reading produce young Edward Waverley as the 'dreaming boy' who will not translate well into the 'reality' that is to come.[33] Travelling into Scotland, Waverley passes quickly through his military assignment at Dundee and on into bucolic Perthshire. Subsequently in the highland fastness of Glennaquoich, he is unwittingly enlisted to the Jacobite cause. And so it goes throughout the novel, with Waverley constantly shifting space and intersecting stories that alternately figure as romance, political intrigue, travelogue and more.

In fact, Scott refused to end tidily the stories that he did appear to privilege. Responding to criticism from Lady Louisa Stuart, he admitted that in *The Black Dwarf* (1816), 'I quarrelled with my story, & bungled up a conclusion'.[34] Nonetheless, two years later Lady Louisa was complaining of *The Heart of Mid-Lothian* (1818): 'it is a lame, huddled conclusion. I know you so well in it by the by!'[35] In the intervening *Tale of Old Mortality*, the narrator deliberately opens the story's conclusion to readerly consideration. When 'Miss Martha Buskbody' quizzes him on the characters' future lives, demanding closure down to the tale of the very last goose-boy, he reports he 'took my hat and wished her a hasty good-night, ere the Demon of Criticism had supplied her with any more queries'.[36] Then he takes an equally brusque farewell of the 'gentle Reader'. If we have questions to ask, he won't be around to answer them, taking 'the liberty to withdraw myself from you for the present'. Scott set stories going that resisted completion by their number, their nature, and his own inclination.

Writ large, this is the structure of what came to be known as 'the Waverley Novels'. Scott did not figure on the title page of his first novel, and as productions of 'the Author of Waverley', over time his twenty-seven novels assembled and reassembled as a collective. The 'Author of Waverley' appears with Scott's second book, *Guy Mannering* (1815). The advertisement to *The Antiquary* (1816) declared the Author's novel writing career complete, but immediately came the 'Tales of My Landlord'.[37] These bore neither Scott's name nor 'the Author of Waverley', but fell in line with his productions to date such that the term 'Waverley Novels' was current by the 1820s.[38] A twelve-volume set of 1819 drew texts avowedly by the Author and others by 'My Landlord' together as *Novels and Tales by the Author of Waverley*. By the time of the New Edition, which ran from 1829, concluding posthumously in 1833, not only tales of the 1745 rebellion, or even of Scottish history, but also of Elizabeth's court, the crusades, imperial India, contemporary spa towns, Louis XI's France and fifteenth-century Switzerland jostled together as Waverley Novels. Jane Millgate recognises the 'extraordinary nominative power' of that term.[39] The forty-eight volumes affirm 'by their uniform bindings an inescapable kinship with one another'.[40] Still, those forty-eight, like previous assemblages of their author's works, constitute a multiplicity; within any given novel, as with *Waverley*, and within any set, Scott assembles difference. Temporally, the story of *Rob Roy* (1818) precedes its predecessor, *Waverley*; Darsie Latimer, experiencing putative rebellion in the Solway of 1765 (*Redgauntlet*, 1824) inhabits the same space and even time of *Guy Mannering*, but a very different world. Whatever E. M. Forster may have thought, in any story, and at any magnitude – collection or novel – Scott never told 'a' story, but many. The Scott reader will always meet a new circumstance.

Of course, any author's work can contain prequels and sequels and differences of place and plot. What makes it significant for Scott is, surprisingly, this supposedly 'historical' novelist's investment in a temporality that recognises simultaneity. To Cairns Craig,

> the most banal feature of our ordinary lives is one which is almost impossible to recreate in narrative, and that is simultaneity: not simply that events happen simultaneously in space around us, but are happening simultaneously in the space that is our own bodies.[41]

Behind the enforced simultaneity of Scott's forty-eight volume New Edition lies the simultaneity induced by his strategies of preface and persona – precisely those things beneath the notice of many critics yet issued as a challenge to readers.

To Angus Calder, editing *Old Mortality* for Penguin in 1974, and A. N. Wilson, presenting *Ivanhoe* ten years later, both prefaces and personae seemed extraneous to their tales. 'You should vault over the intervening pages, ignore [...] the rather tedious Cleishbotham', Calder declared, 'and begin at once with Chapter 2'.[42] Wilson actually relocated the 'Dedicatory Epistle' to the end of *Ivanhoe*.[43] If Scott had provided 'A Postscript, which should have been a Preface' to *Waverley*, his editors missed both his strategy and his goal. 'First', Scott declares,

> most novel readers, as my own conscience reminds me, are apt to be guilty of the sin of omission respecting that same matter of prefaces.

Secondly [...] it is a general custom with that class of students, to begin with the last chapter of a work; so that, after all these remarks, being introduced last in order, have still the best chance to be read in their proper place.[44]

Hence began Scott's career in extensive prefatory matter that could show up both before and after his text, as in *Old Mortality*, or accumulate into contentious layers as in *The Monastery* (1820). Here, 'Captain Clutterbuck' in his 'Introductory Epistle' begs the Author of Waverley's indulgence to adapt and co-publish a tale. In the subsequent 'Answer by "The Author of Waverley"', he is summarily denied.[45] Specifically, his diffidence about producing a novel is attacked as rich, coming from someone who is himself a utopian fiction, and ridiculous given that 'Mr Watt' of the steam engine, who has given 'the feeble arm of man the momentum of an Afrite [...] this abridger of time and space – this magician, whose cloudy machinery has produced a change on the world', likes novels. The prefaces, that is, operate as a set of tactics to disturb the apparent single 'story' of any Scott novel, with an eruption of the present to challenge both novelistic pasts and the pretensions of any reader.

Such simultaneity of pasts and presents is exacerbated through Scott's deployment of personae. Jerome McGann, channelling Henry James, has asked 'How could one possibly install an integral imaginative world with all those Jedidiah Cleishbothams and Peter Pattiesons, Drs Rochecliffe and Dryasdust, who come to tell us in no uncertain terms that "the Author of Waverley" is only making believe?'[46] As he sees, the answer is of course that one cannot. If we track just the careers of Cleishbotham (a secondary narrator behind Pattieson) and Clutterbuck, not only do they show up in numerous novels, their stories intertwine with those of one another and with additional narrative personae. Clutterbuck's first appeal to the Author in *The Monastery*, on the grounds of the Author's prior collaboration with Cleishbotham, provokes the author's annoyance that Jedidiah 'has misbehaved himself so far as to desert his original patron, and set up for himself'.[47] Scott, that is, refers not just to Jedidiah, but to an actual case of his misappropriation to launch a spurious *Tale of My Landlord* on the London market.[48] So the Author summarily kills off Jedidiah in a footnote: 'Mr Cleishbotham died some months since [...] the person assuming his name is an impostor.'[49] The dialogue between Clutterbuck and Author then skips forward through *The Abbot* (1820) to *The Fortunes of Nigel* (1822), with Clutterbuck increasingly critical of the Author's apparently commercial choices and the Author increasingly recalcitrant in face of criticism. As for Jedidiah, he suddenly reappears in the 1830s to discuss the depredations of literary pirates.[50] In the prefaces and through the personae, worlds collide; fictive tales and putative tellers strain against one another.

Having risen from the dead, perhaps it is not surprising that Jedidiah feels the world outpacing him and remarks on 'the giddiness attendant on a journey in the Manchester steam engine'.[51] But bringing the teller of the *Tales of My Landlord*, originally told by Peter Pattieson who is already dead when they are told to us, into the moment of James Watt to tell a story of fourteenth-century Scotland that has (Jedidiah complains) already been sold in the States, makes times, tellers, tales and readers productively simultaneous yet never static. In the totality that is a Waverley Novel, narrative pasts conflate with prefatory presents forcing momentum on tales that are supposedly complete. But where was that momentum headed?

Time changed for the Romantics. Whether from the rise of industrialism that made visible the accelerating edge of the Anthropocene, from the contrasting awareness of geological time, the effects of accurate timekeeping, or the collapse of time and space made possible by steam travel, their period's momentum seemed resolutely forward, while at the same time operating in 'widely varying scales, paces, and planes'.[52] That change came early for Scots, who numbered among them Watt, of the steam engine (1765), and Hutton, who published the seminal *Theory of the Earth* (1788). For Walter Scott, who belonged to the Royal Society of Edinburgh from 1810 and served as president from 1820, that society having published Hutton's theory, and who knew Watt personally, time's many turns would have been particularly evident.[53]

Recent scholarship emphasises Scott's varying scales of temporality. For Ina Ferris, the typical Waverley novel

> overlays three tracks of forward movement: the slowed down time of the printed book [...] the speeded-up global time of progress [...]; and the organic time of human and animal steps [...] Connected to both [modern and experiential] dimensions but converging with neither is the slow time of the book and reading.[54]

'Through this temporal structure', Ferris argues, 'the fictions set out to restore density and depth both to the thinned out past and to a thinning out present'. We might take one step further. In their reading of Romantic temporalities, Laniel-Musitelli and Sabiron emphasise the shift from 'the timeless and tabular representation of a Linnean nature to the more arrow-like conception of time in pre-evolutionist theories'.[55] In this dynamic, Romanticism's engagement with the future tends to be determinative: the strain in Shelley (for instance) is between 'reminiscence and prophecy'.[56] If the Romantic art includes 'subverting the course of representation', 'Romantic poetics complicates the temporality of mimesis' by 'anticipation contained within a distant memory'; 'the future is contained within the past and will blossom in the future'.[57] Scott, however, entertained more than the progressing temporalities Ferris describes, and he actively debated the solipsistic temporalities of prophetic fulfilment. This historical novelist relished a future that would engage on its own account.

Perverse temporalities are the hallmark of a Waverley novel. There are no steam trains in Waverley plots, of course, and not much geology – although the vulcanologist R. E. Raspe is spoofed in *The Antiquary*.[58] Yet characters are alternately caught in time and overtaken by a future that turns out to be disturbingly already past. Young Edward Waverley travels not only in space but also against time: heading north from England, he leaves a home at once out-of-time as idyllic, and embroiled in the political and familial present; arriving in Scotland, he enters an apparently backward space, or at least one unevenly developed – a place marked by 'stagnation of industry, and perhaps of intellect', and yet traversed by a potential for myth that comes leaping at him in 'seven-leagued boots'.[59] Then momentarily out of time, courtesy of alcohol, Edward gets his first lesson in the unpredictability of futurity: waking up after a drunken evening, he finds a duel has already been fought on his behalf for an insult he is not quite sure to have given or received. Thus begin Edward Waverley's travels in time.

Critics have noted how often Waverley finds himself missing major action – he is ill during the first muster of the clans in preparation for rebellion; under arrest as they launch their campaign. They have recognised how often this dreaming boy is raced through landscapes and summarily deposited in different pasts that may be unevenly developed presents, as he is when rescued and rushed into the Jacobite action already underway: 'The velocity, and indeed violence, with which Waverley was hurried along, nearly deprived him of sensation'.[60] Then he is ill again, and then sped between government pickets to arrive, abruptly, at Doune Castle, now 'in the service of his Royal Highness Prince Charles Edward'.[61]

Less recognised, however, is how Waverley's confusions arise from futures generated elsewhere, and unpredictable in operation. Leaving

England, his bags are stuffed with sermons he has no intention of reading, pushed upon him by his tutor; to government forces in Scotland, these confirm what they suspect, his rebellious tendencies. At Glennaquoich, Waverley catches his own name in a bardic exhortation, but having no Gaelic recognises not at all the role it has scripted for him until he is accused of already having stirred rebellion – though he does not yet fully recognise one is going on. On the field of battle,

> looking around him, he saw the wild dress and appearance of his Highland associates, heard their whispers in an uncouth and unknown language, looked upon his own dress, so unlike that which he had worn from his infancy, and wished to awake from what seemed at the moment a dream, strange, horrible, and unnatural.[62]

Still it is not until his wayward baggage catches up with him, full of letters which, had he only received them, might have produced a different reality, that he fully takes on board how fortune has taken 'delight in placing him at the disposal of others'.[63] Through Waverley's entire career, futures far other than he imagined have been instantiated by the randomised engagement of realia (those letters, tracts and songs of which he has little knowledge) with readers whom he has not yet met and who are actually reading him.

It is this future state of reading, and its impact on the present as simultaneous with times yet to be, that drives Scott's most interesting engagement with time. Multiple stories are always in operation, told of and at different times through characters and personae. And it is those who would limit stories and restrict their telling who ground the critique of temporality for a Scott novel. In *The Tale of Old Mortality*, the fanatic Burley plays the role held by the manipulative Fergus in *Waverley*. For either case, the drive is to determine another's narrative and prevent the play of a different future. If Fergus selects Waverley's experiences to incline him toward Jacobitism, Burley insists on Henry Morton as the double-determined child of father and church: 'What has your father's son to do with such profane mummeries [as a shooting contest]', he begins, before requiring Morton's service on the grounds that 'Thou canst not help it [...]; thy master has his uses for thee, and when he calls thou must obey'.[64] By contrast, both Waverley and Morton retrieve the present through supposed enemies who recognise that people are remade moment to moment according to futures they could not imagine. The minister who pleads for clemency when Waverley is arrested separates him from the documents he carries, and their import and effect, with the simple declaration: 'He says he never read them';⁶⁵ Colonel Talbot saves Waverley from the law for 'there has been no malice prepense [...] you have been trepanned [...] It is sadly foolish [...] but not nearly so bad as I was led to expect';⁶⁶ Evandale, in *Old Mortality*, recognises the determinations of circumstances Morton did not produce in his enlistment to covenanting rebellion, and does not blame him: 'considering the usage which he has received [...] what other course is open to him?'⁶⁷ Burley, in his latter-day Pandemonium, has focused so long on 'desperate schemes and sudden disappointments' that his mind has 'lost its equipoise [...], there was now in his conduct a shade of lunacy'.⁶⁸ The future, that is, cannot be grasped, either prophetically or through control of another person. It rewrites us moment to moment.

That rewriting, Scott makes clear, lies in the role of the reader. *Waverley* yields to the 'Postscript, which should have been a Preface' and its playful, deliberate engagement with those who skip prefaces and anticipate final chapters; *Old Mortality* gives way to the critiques of Miss Buskbody. And Scott repeatedly invokes those who read. Robert Mayer has noted Scott as 'eager to please the reader', yet equally finds in letters he exchanged 'recognition of the growing power of the public' and a strategy to 'actively [cultivate] a wide range of responses from his readers'.⁶⁹ Bakhtin argued that:

> In the completely real-life time-space where the work resonates [...] we find as well a real person – one who originates spoken speech as well as the inscription and the book – and real people who are hearing and reading the text. [...] these real people, the authors and the listeners or readers, may be (and often are) located in differing time-spaces, sometimes separated from each other by centuries and by great spatial distances, but nevertheless they are all located in a real, unitary and as yet incomplete historical world [...] we may call this world the world that *creates* the text.⁷⁰

For Scott, such an awareness meant that every novel could be realised in many different ways by its many different readers.

Evaluating his own work, anonymously and tongue-in-cheek in the *Quarterly Review* (1817), Scott noted the author's 'carelessness'. 'There may be something of system in it however', his review continued, remarking on the novels' dramatic form. This, Scott observed, places the reader 'in the situation of the audience at a theatre, who are compelled to decipher the meaning of the scene from what the dramatis personae say to each other'.[71] Scott, that is, invoked, involved and embraced the reader as a maker of meaning. Moreover, future readings could impact present meaning.

Scott makes this obvious in the 'Introductory Epistle' to *The Fortunes of Nigel* (1822). Here Captain Clutterbuck, who in *The Monastery* (1820) acknowledged that he had 'yawned over the last interview of MacIvor and his sister',[72] sets himself up as that most formidable of readers, the literary advisor. Meeting the veiled and mysterious Author of Waverley, the Captain starts to school him on content and style. Not surprisingly, he predicts of the next volume, 'The story is hastily huddled up, I would venture a pint of claret'.[73] Most of all, Clutterbuck deprecates the Author's hasty productivity that brings criticism. The Author, however, dismisses such concerns. He writes for the public, to whom 'I stand pretty near in the relation of the postman', with the recipient of the mail free to respond to it as they wish.[74] Scott's reader, in fact, has the latitude entirely to remake the text, for he further deflects critique by telling the tale of a cook-maid's depredations on a priceless archive. Betty Barnes, who 'singed fat fowls and wiped dirty trenchers with the lost works of Beaumont and Fletcher' has not only visited a final criticism on irreplaceable works, she has thereby made the remainder more valuable.[75]

In one of Scott's most frequent figurations of his writing in its reading context, the relation between stories and characters, personae and public, is a gamble. To Clutterbuck the Author asserts: 'I am not displeased to find the game a winning one; yet while I pleased the public, I should probably continue it merely for the pleasure of playing.'[76] 'The public favour is my only lottery', Scott wrote in his *Journal* on the verge of the financial losses that would drive him to novel-writing at industrial scale through his later years.[77] Then for *Chronicles of the Canongate*, designed to tide him through the early months of this trial, he changed format to foreground persona and preface and the challenge to writers seeking reputation and money that readers represent. Returning to Scotland, the prodigal Crystal Croftangry finds that his devaluing reputation has preceded him, so he takes to writing. But audience after audience turns critical for story after story, falling asleep, screaming at the wrong parts, or effusing without evidence. Yet through his audiences Crystal finds his place once more and is stimulated into greater productivity. As Scott would repeatedly echo *Don Quixote* through these years: 'Patience cousin and shuffle the cards.'[78] The reader constantly will reopen the written world.

Scott, that is, with an unusual degree of authorial humility, ceded the future to his readers. He recognised their impact as makers of meaning and makers, indeed, of authorial value, in conjunction with his text. Although he coaches readers then and readers yet to come through belated prefaces and upstart personae, he recognised, as Deidre Lynch and Evelyne Ender have argued, that reading is no 'punctual, self-contained act', rather it invokes 'complex, layered, and extended temporalities'.[79] This is the simultaneous reality of texts that come into being through reading.

Alert to the slow time of geology, the race of steam, the recurrences of Napoleon, and living his many lives as poet, lawyer, novelist, agriculturalist and more, Scott produced writing and reading as polyvalent experience. 'What if', William E. Connolly asks, 'time is becoming, and the future of the universe – and the multiple, interacting, and partially open temporal systems through which it is composed – is really open to an uncertain degree?'[80] With that openness in mind – of a present capable of being rewritten by the future in this moment – perhaps Scott's nearest authorial cousin might be James Hogg, too often read in opposition to the Author's supposedly 'historical' novels.[81] Perhaps his nearest heirs might be James Joyce, the Ali Smith of *Hotel World*, or even *Monty Python*.

'Who shall tell us a story'? Forster might be surprised to learn that it will not be Walter Scott. Not Scott as Author; not Scott the person. Beginning the year of his financial exigency, Scott pondered a physiological and philosophical problem of being:

> People say that the whole human frame in all its parts and divisions is gradually in the act of decaying and renewing. What a curious time-piece it would be that could indicate to us the moment this gradual and insensible change had so completely taken place that no atom was left of the original person [...] but there existed in his stead another person [...] – a new ship built on an old plank [...] Singular – to be at once another and the same.[82]

Even the Author is a different reader, and different from himself.

To paraphrase Charles Lamb, wrestling with the problems of international date lines, *my* time is not *your* time ... is not *my* time any longer. Walter Scott's telling always anticipated unexpected readers, retold tales, and rewritten times.

DOCUMENT 2

From *The Historical Novel*, translated by Hannah and Stanley Mitchell

(Merlin Press, 1962; Penguin Books, 1969)

Georg Lukács

Scott's great artistic aim, in portraying the historical crises of popular life, is to show the *human greatness* which is liberated in its important representatives by a disturbance of this all-embracing kind. There is no doubt that, consciously or unconsciously, it was the French Revolution which awoke this tendency in literature. It is already present, though very sporadically, in the period which directly prepared the Revolution, most significantly in Goethe's figure of Klärchen in *Egmont*. But this heroism, though occasioned by the Netherlands revolution, is nevertheless immediately called to life by Klärchen's love for Egmont. After the French Revolution Goethe himself finds a still more purely human expression for this tendency in his figure of Dorothea. Simple, strong, determined and heroic qualities spring to life in her as the result of the French Revolution and the fate which her immediate environment suffers through these events. Goethe's great epic art shows itself in the way he draws Dorothea's heroism. It appears in complete accord with her simple and straightforward character: a quality which has always lain dormant in her as a potentiality and which is called to life by the great events of the time. Yet this heroism is not something which entails an irrevocable change in her life and psychological constitution. When the objective necessity for her heroic behaviour is over, Dorothea returns to everyday life.

Whether Scott knew these works of Goethe at all or to any extent is immaterial. The point is that, historically, he continues and extends this tendency of Goethe. His novels abound in such stories; everywhere we find this sudden blaze of great yet simple heroism among artless, seemingly average children of the people. Scott's extension of Goethe's tendency lies primarily in the fact that he brings out, much more strongly than Goethe, the historical character of this heroism, the peculiar historical quality of the human grandeur which it expresses. Goethe draws the general outlines of popular movements, of both the Netherlands and French Revolution, with extraordinary faithfulness to life. Nevertheless, while the minor characters in Egmont exhibit very definite contemporary historical features, while Klärchen, too, in every reaction provoked by her idyllic love for Egmont remains the child of her class and people, her heroic upsurge lacks a definite and emphatic historical character. It is true-to-life and authentic, for it shows human greatness within given historical circumstances, it follows organically from Klärchen's psychology, but its peculiar quality is not characterised historically. The same applies to the characterisation of Dorothea. In neither case does the poet use specifically social-historical features when it comes to portraying the actual heroic upsurge. Such features are given prominence before in both cases (and, in the case of Dorothea, afterwards too). Yet they serve merely as a framework for the heroism itself and give it no historical colouring.

It is different in Scott. One sees this tendency at its clearest in *The Heart of Midlothian*. Here Scott has created his greatest female character in the figure of the Puritan peasant girl, Jeanie Deans. Events face the daughter of a radical soldier of Cromwell's army with a terrible dilemma. Her sister is charged with infanticide; according to the inhumane laws of the time, proof that she has kept her pregnancy secret is sufficient to condemn her to death. She was compelled to keep this secrecy, but was not responsible for the infanticide. Now Jeanie could save her sister by perjuring herself. But despite intense love for her sister, despite unending sympathy for her fate, her Puritan conscience triumphs and, accordingly, she declares the truth. Her sister is condemned to death. And so then the peasant girl, uneducated, penniless and unfamiliar with the world, walks to London in order to secure her sister's pardon from the King. The story of these inner battles and of this struggle to save her sister show the rich humanity and simple heroism of a really great human being. Yet Scott's picture of his heroine never for a moment obscures her narrow Puritan and Scottish peasant traits, indeed it is they which again and again form the specific character of the naive and grand heroism of this popular figure. Having successfully carried through her aim, Jeanie Deans returns to everyday life, and never again does she experience a similar upsurge in her life to betray the presence of such strengths. Scott draws this final stage in rather too broad and philistine a detail, while Goethe, who aims at beauty of line and classical perfection, contents himself with indicating that Dorothea's heroic life is over and that she, too, must now recede into simple everyday life. Both instances involve a formal epic requirement. But in both instances this formal requirement expresses a profound human and historical truth. The important thing for these great writers is to lay bare those vast, heroic, human potentialities which are always latently present in the people and which, on each big occasion, with every deep disturbance of the social or even the more personal life, emerge 'suddenly', with colossal force, to the surface. The greatness of the crisis periods of humanity rests to a large extent on the fact that such hidden forces are always dormant in the people, and that they require only the occasion for them to appear on the surface. The epic requirement for such figures to recede after the accomplishment of their mission underlines just how general this phenomenon is. Neither Goethe, in the case of Dorothea, nor Scott, in the case of Jeanie Deans, wished to present an exceptional human being, an outstanding talent, who rises from the people to become the leader of a popular movement (Scott draws figures of this kind in Robin Hood and Rob Roy). On the contrary, they wished to show that the possibilities for this human upsurge and heroism are widespread among the popular masses, that endless numbers of people live out their lives quietly, without this upsurge, because no opportunity has come their way to evoke such an exertion of powers. Revolutions are thus the great periods of mankind because in and through them such rapid upward movements in human capacities become widespread. Through this manner of human-historical portrayal Scott makes history live. As has been shown, he presents history as a series of great crises. His presentation of historical development, above all that of England and France, is of an uninterrupted series of such revolutionary crises. Thus if Scott's main tendency in all his novels – and which forms of them in a sense a kind of cycle – is to represent and defend progress, then this progress is for him always a process full of contradictions, the driving force and material basis of which is the living contradiction between conflicting historical forces, the antagonisms of classes and nations.

Scott affirms this progress. He is a patriot, he is proud of the development of his people. This is vital for the creation of a real historical novel, i.e. one which brings the past close to us and allows us to experience its real and true being. Without a felt relationship to the present, a portrayal of history is impossible. But this relationship, in the case of really great historical art, does not consist in alluding to contemporary events, a practice which Pushkin cruelly ridiculed in the work of Scott's incompetent imitators, but in bringing the past to life as the prehistory of the present, in giving poetic life to those historical, social and human forces which, in the course of a long evolution, have made our present-day life what it is and as we experience it. Hegel remarks:

> The historical is only then ours ... when we can regard the present in general as a consequence of those events in whose chain the characters or deeds represented constitute an essential link ... For art does not exist for a small, closed circle of the privilegedly cultured few, but for the nation as a whole. What holds good for the work of art in general, however, also has its application for the outer side of the historical reality represented. It, too, must be made clear and accessible to us without extensive learning so that we, who belong to our own time and nation, may find ourselves at home therein, and not be obliged to halt before us, as before some alien and unintelligible world.

Scott's patriotism forms the premise of this living connexion with the past. And only vulgar sociologists can see in this patriotism a glorification of the exploiting merchants. Goethe had an infinitely deeper and truer understanding of Scott's relationship to English history. In a conversation with Eckermann he speaks of Scott's *Rob Roy*, in which the central figure, interestingly enough, happens to be both a hero of the Scottish people and a peculiar compound of rebel, cattle thief and smuggler – hence a significant example of Scott's 'social equivalent'. Goethe says of this novel: 'Here, naturally everything is on the grand scale: material, content, characters, treatment ... But one sees what English history is and what it means when such a heritage falls to the lot of a capable poet.' Goethe thus clearly senses what it is that constitutes Scott's pride in English history: on the one hand, naturally, the gradual maturing of national strength and greatness, the continuity of which Scott wishes to illustrate in his 'middle way'; but on the other, and inseparable from this, the crises of this growth, the extremes whose struggle produce this 'middle way' as their end result and which could never be removed from the picture of national greatness without robbing it precisely of all its greatness, wealth and substance.

Scott sees and portrays the complex and intricate path which led to England's national greatness and to the formation of the national character. As a sober, conservative petty aristocrat, he naturally affirms the result, and the necessity of this result is the ground on which he stands. But Scott's artistic world-view by no means stops here. Scott sees the endless field of ruin, wrecked existences, wrecked or wasted heroic, human endeavour, broken social formations, etc., which were the necessary preconditions of the end-result.

Undoubtedly there is a certain contradiction here between Scott's directly political views and his artistic world picture. He, too, like so many great realists, such as Balzac or Tolstoy, became a great realist despite his own political and social views. In Scott, too, one can establish Engels's 'triumph of realism' over his personal, political and social views. Sir Walter Scott, the Scottish petty aristocrat, automatically affirms this development with a sober rationality. Scott, the writer, on the other hand, embodies the sentiment of the Roman poet, Lucan: 'Victrix causa diis placuit, sed victa Catani' (the victorious cause pleased the gods, but the vanquished pleased Cato).

CHAPTER FOUR

The Scottish Novel in the Wake of Walter Scott, 1815–1830

Charles Snodgrass

> But the truth is, that these [Scott] novels were rather the outpourings of old thoughts than new inventions.
> —Lord Henry Cockburn[1]

Casual observers of literary history might be forgiven for judging the eighteenth century as the zenith of Scotland's literary and cultural production, especially after the 'Scottish Enlightenment' came to be identified as the source of much that characterises 'modernity'.[2] The decade and a half after the publication of Walter Scott's *Waverley* in 1814 witnessed a burgeoning and sometimes frenzied literary production of the novel in Scotland. From his retrospective view of this era, Lord Henry Cockburn's (1779–1854) assessment about 'new inventions' accurately portrays formal, thematic, and ideological changes to the Scottish novel during the early nineteenth century. In terms of book production itself, many novels in Scotland from 1815 to 1830 were published as stand-alone volumes, in one-, two-, or three-volume format, depending on length; however, other novels were serialised in periodical publications, and some of those serialised novels were subsequently published as stand-alone volumes as well. In other words, in early nineteenth-century Scottish print culture, serial production and stand-alone publishing were fluid, symbiotic, and a natural consequence of the development of eighteenth-century print culture.[3] Edinburgh was at the centre of Scottish literary activity during this decade and a half but was so, in part, because it was at the core of an international network through which books and journals published in Edinburgh were then taken up and republished in London and by publishers in Dublin and North America.[4] In his influential work on the Scottish novel, Ian Duncan reminds us that

> Scotch novels and Scotch reviewers were the most brilliant constellations in a northern literary galaxy which included – besides the historical

romance and critical quarterly – a professionalized intellectual class, the entrepreneurial publisher, the nationalist ballad epic, and the monthly magazine. If not all absolutely original, here these genres and institutions acquired their definitive forms and associations, and a prestige they would bear throughout the nineteenth century.[5]

This portrait of a robust literary scene, which also encompassed Glasgow and Aberdeen, helps – together with the competition among publishers vying for authors, as well as authors furiously outwriting each other for literary celebrity – to account for the varied publishing forms of the novel during this period.

So by the time *Waverley* appeared in 1814, Scott had already captured Britain's (and increasingly Europe's) imagination by publishing eight well-received poems, including *The Lay of the Last Minstrel* (1805), *Marmion* (1808), and *The Lady of the Lake* (1810). As if long narrative poetry, letters, diary, Sheriff-Depute duties for Selkirkshire, and Court of Session clerking were not enough to keep his pen ablaze, Scott decided to get into the novel-writing business, and it was very much a 'business' because in 1814 he had entered into what would become an ultimately financially damaging partnership with Edinburgh publisher James Ballantyne.[6] After *Waverley*'s international success – so significant that in 1937 Georg Lukács would assert that Scott was the father of the 'historical novel'[7] – Scott went on to publish another twenty-seven novels between 1815 and 1832. The only other Scottish novelist who attempted a similar level of publication during this period was John Galt, who managed a mere seventeen novels. As Duncan has pointed out, '[t]he demand stimulated by the Waverley Novels made room for a proliferation of Scottish fiction by other hands'.[8] This rise in Scottish novel production during the decade and a half after Waterloo reveals two imbricated elements of print culture in Scotland in particular and in Britain at large. On the one hand, novelists like Galt, James Hogg, John Gibson Lockhart, John Wilson, and others sought to soak up lucre left by Scott's wake. On the other hand, as Clifford Siskin has argued, the wide circulation of serialised novels in periodicals and magazines stimulated an even greater demand for 'stories of greater length',[9] and novelists and their publishers were more than willing to accommodate this growing middle-class readership by committing to double- and triple-decker novels. While Galt may have rivalled Scott's pre-eminence in terms of volume of publications, others, such as James Hogg, sought to occupy adjacent territory to that which Scott, his friend, and sometime collaborator in ballad collecting, had opened up.

Though on a smaller scale of fame and literary output than Scott, James Hogg's literary reputation before *Waverley* was likewise first established through poetry, particularly with the appearance of his first substantial volume *The Mountain Bard* (1807) and the triumphantly successful narrative poem *The Queen's Wake* (1813). Unlike Scott, much of Hogg's daily life required his physical presence, shepherding in the Ettrick Forest – thus his eventual self-styled *nom de plume* 'The Ettrick Shepherd' – and as a result among the Edinburgh *literati* Hogg had to contend with elitist derision, since he had but six months of formal schooling before being required to work among livestock.[10] For instance, David Macbeth (D. M.) Moir – who appeared thinly veiled as 'Δ' in the often caustic pages of the *Noctes Ambrosianæ* in *Blackwood's Edinburgh Magazine*, 1822–1835 – derided Hogg's upbringing and mind by musing

> The intellectual history of James Hogg is certainly one of the most curious that our age has presented; and when we consider what an unlettered peasant was able to achieve by the mere enthusiasm of his genius, we are entitled to marvel certainly—not that his writing should be full of blemishes—but that his mind ever had power to burst through the Cimmerian gloom in which his earlier years seemed so hopelessly enveloped. [...]
>
> After a boyhood of poverty, half-starvation, and labour, the shepherd-poet in embryo found himself at length aged fourteen, and the possessor of five shillings—with which he bought a fiddle (! ! !) over the catgut of which he kept sawing Scottish tunes, for two or three hours every night, after retiring to his roost in the lofts of the cowhouse, where the discord could molest nobody save himself—an antitype of Orpheus—and the rats.[11]

Hogg was already dead when Moir's account appeared, but he had endured many such insults during his lifetime. Time, however, was to reverse his contemporaries' judgement, and much modern criticism has argued for the undisputable genius revealed by his novels.[12]

Rather than compete directly with Scott's novels that explored Jacobitism and Scottish national history – such as *Waverley* (1814), *Rob Roy* (1817), and later *Redgauntlet* (1824) – Hogg's initial foray into the novel settled on what was to him more familiar ground: Scottish folklore, particularly its use of the supernatural. Published by William Blackwood in 1817, *The Brownie of Bodsbeck; and Other Tales* laid the groundwork for Hogg's later psychological study in *The Private Memoirs and Confessions of a Justified Sinner* (1824). The brownie or fairie sprite that Hogg initially described in the manuscript of his novel as 'wicked and benevolent' set the stage for the later mercurial and destructive figure of Gil-Martin in *Confessions*. Early in the *Brownie*, Hogg conjures the tremulous setting his characters must endure throughout the novel:

> These mysterious and unaccountable incidents by degrees impressed the minds of the inhabitants with terror that cannot be described; no woman or boy would go out of doors after sunset, on any account whatever, and there was scarcely a man who durst venture forth alone after the fall of evening. If they could have been sure that brownies and fairies had only power to assume the human shape, they would not have been nearly in such peril and perplexity; but there was no form of any thing animate or inanimate, save that of a lamb, that they were sure of; they were of course waylaid at every turn, and kept in continual agitation.[13]

In 1818, formal and thematic features of resurrecting mysterious pasts, depicting macabre events, and exposing döppelgangers establish a formula for many Scottish novels after this period. Many historians of Scottish literature have ascribed this recurrence of curious doublings to G. Gregory Smith's account in *Scottish Literature: Character and Influence* (1919) in which, as Kirsten Stirling points out, Smith suggested 'that the very basis of Scottish literature could be found in a union of opposites, which he playfully termed "the Caledonian antisyzygy"'.[14] Smith's identification of Scottish literature as an oscillation between solid realism – 'the Dutch style […] interiors, country folk and town "bodies", farmyard and alehouse' – and an entirely antithetical pleasure 'in the fun of things thrown topsy-turvy, in the horns of elfland and the voices of the mountains'[15] – fails, however, to describe the supernatural tradition which Hogg further promotes and can be seen earlier in the curious figure of Meg Merrilies in Scott's 1815 *Guy Mannering*. Whether playful in the Derridean sense of *jouissance* or simply a jocund use of the absurd, Hogg's project in the *Brownie* – and even more certainly in *Confessions* – is more complicated than Smith's 'combination of opposites' suggests.[16] There is an uncanny aspect to these novels that requires an alternative lens. After turning Heidegger on his head by reading William McIlvanney's *Laidlaw* (1977) through Heidegger's *Being and Time* (1927), Matthew Wickman argues that 'estranging repetition, or an estrangement as a function of repetition, an uncanny double' functions not only in *Laidlaw* but in Scottish crime fiction writ large.[17] Such 'estranging repetition' can be traced back to the *Brownie*, and though that novel does not present a crime *per se* (as readers learn in the final pages), the *Confessions* can certainly be read as an early version of crime fiction. These novels reveal, however, a locus in which religious belief and morality function as a fulcrum that foregrounds the bifurcation of Self and Other and the doubling of identities. In *Confessions*, for instance, the devilish Gil-Martin entraps the antinomian Calvinist Robert Wringhim not only into belief in his own innocence in the eyes of God, but also, thereby, into murdering his family, though Wringhim has no memory of committing such acts. The tension in Hogg's 1824 *Confessions* between religious piety and the demonic is already present in the 1817 *Brownie* in which an entire village succumbs to the perceived horrors of the supposedly slighted brownie. Religious probity and Covenanting righteousness are ultimately valorised in the penultimate chapter of the *Brownie* in an almost dismissive parenthetical aside: '(for this celebrated Brownie was no other than the noted Mr John Brown, the goodman of Caldwell)'.[18] Brown (1627–1685) was a polemical leader in the Covenanting wars of the seventeenth century and martyred on the orders of Episcopalian defender, James Graham of Claverhouse (later Viscount Dundee). Given Hogg's ongoing concern with Covenanting, it seems peculiar, as Douglas Mack notes in his edition of the *Brownie*, that 'there is no clear evidence that Hogg read the proofs of the first edition', which helps explain how and why William Blackwood exercised a heavy editorial hand to bowdlerise certain religious or theological references by the Ettrick Shepherd.[19] Sharon Ragaz has argued that printer James Ballantyne's March 1818 letter to Blackwood may account for his editorial license to expurgate certain religiously inflected descriptions.[20] Yet it is precisely this kind of close-knit literary world in Edinburgh – among author, printer, publisher, critic, or friend – that emerges as a kind of coterie authorship in this period.[21] After the *Brownie* but before *Confessions*, Hogg continued to rely on this fulcrum between the diabolical and the righteous in *The Three Perils of Man* (1822), in which wizard Master Michael Scott of Aikwood – supported by his devilish pages Prig, Prim, and Pricker – is relieved from demonic possession by the mendicant monk Benjamin who had been under the devil's spell. Drawing parallels from Hogg's *Three Perils of Man* and *Three Perils of Woman* (1823) to *Confessions*, Marshall Walker views the religious fulcrum in play as 'a fugue of incongruous elements' born out of an unholy union of 'satire and the supernatural, melodrama and social iniquity, perverted theology and psychological collapse' that mirrored 'the intransigent messiness of experience, its immunity to the constraints of religious and political dogmas and its resistance to the artificialities of generic literary regulation'.[22] While an unholy union might be one way to construe Hogg's fiction, Samuel Baker has recently characterised both Hogg's and Scott's novels emerging from within the publishing House of Blackwood as creating 'a Romantic cult of the author that assumes something of the religious authority so important for literary cultures past'.[23] Arguably, the cultural resonance of a Scottish religious civil war of the previous century that reverberated in Hogg's 1817 *Brownie* can be viewed as a challenge and ideological rebuke to Scott's 1816 *Old Mortality* in terms of how post-Enlightenment Scotland should value and portray its radical Presbyterian past.

Yet in Hogg's fictive masterpiece and most famous novel *Confessions*, he confronts Calvinist assumptions embodied by the disingenuous protagonist Wringhim and his family in order to offer readers corrections to several Calvinist doctrines, such as: 1) past sins are absolved through a religious calling and 'justification' – i.e. the infusion of God's righteousness; 2) that another person is able to will certainty of election; 3) only the Chosen or Elect achieve salvation; and 4) once justified one cannot sin or fall from grace.[24] *Confessions* editor Peter Garside has suggested that Hogg juxtaposes Wringhim's wayward self-righteousness against a crucial tenet of Scottish Calvinism during the late sixteenth and early seventeenth centuries: namely, that salvation is predicated upon enacting good works which, in turn, emerge out of good faith.[25] Unfortunately, good faith was in short supply when *Blackwood's* editors – John Gibson Lockhart (Sir Walter Scott's son-in-law during the writing and publication of *Confessions*) and John Wilson (Chair of Moral Philosophy at Edinburgh since 1820) – continued to malign Hogg's literary stature and prowess, inducing Hogg to publish *Confessions* anonymously with Longman in London. In Hogg's *Memoir of the Author's Life* (1832), he retrospectively justified anonymity because 'being a story replete with horror, after I had written it I durst not venture to put my name to it';[26] however, Douglas Mack argues that Hogg 'attacks extreme and deformed Calvinism' which would have countered the novelist's devout Presbyterianism.[27] Despite *Confessions*'s lack of sales and poor reception during Hogg's own lifetime, this work survives as a touchstone in the development of the novel and in the rise of Scottish Romanticism during the early nineteenth century. This finely wrought novel's 'hideous events',[28] competing intertextual narratives, unreliable narrators, gripping antihero, serial killing, and delusional doubling of identity all lay the groundwork, to one degree or another, for ensuing Scottish novels such as Robert Louis Stevenson's *The Strange Case of Dr Jekyll and Mr Hyde* (1886), Muriel Spark's *The Ballad of Peckham Rye* (1960), Alasdair Gray's *Lanark* (1981), and Ian Rankin's *Resurrection Men* (2002). In Hogg's later career he continued to re-examine the Covenanting tradition more thoroughly in six tales collectively published as *Tales of the Wars of Montrose* (1835). Yet perhaps nowhere during this 1815–1830 period is religion, particularly Calvinism, given more sustained portrayal than in the novels of John Galt.

During this decade and a half Galt penned a prodigious amount, comprising a variety of genres and intentions, such as: stand-alone novels, serialised novels, tragedy, occasional magazine contributions, letters, bills lobbying Parliament for the Edinburgh & Glasgow Canal Union, official records for the Canada Company (first as Secretary, then as Superintendent), school textbooks, children's books, biographies of both Benjamin West and Lord Byron, and editorial work for the London evening newspaper *The Courier*. Surveying the Scottish literary landscape from an aerial view during this period, Duncan declares that in 'the early 1820s Hogg and Galt emerged as the most original authors of Scottish prose fiction next to Scott, masters of the distinctive genres developed in the Blackwood orbit, regional tale and fictional autobiography'.[29] Galt's novels remain his most successful genre, chiefly due to narrative techniques that he developed in what he later labeled as 'theoretical histories'.[30] Many of Galt's novels – whether initially serialised, then reprinted in volumes like *The Ayrshire Legatees* (1820), *The Steam-Boat* (1821), and *The Gathering of the West* (1822) – remain testaments to his social comedy, perceptive observations of human nature, and sense of place.

Rather than employ Hogg's contortions of supernaturalism to confront Calvinist rectitude, Galt drops the reader into the otherwise quotidian lives and preoccupations of rural folk, particularly presbyters in the West of Scotland. This shift from Hogg's Borders and Scott's Highlands to the rapidly commercialising and industrialising West was welcomed by both Blackwood and his growing readership. Though *The Majolo* (1815), *The Wandering Jew, The Earthquake,* and *Glenfell* (all 1820) were Galt's first forays into the novel, it was *The Ayrshire Legatees* (serialised in *Blackwood's Edinburgh Magazine*, June 1820–February 1821) that captured the imagination of *Blackwood's* magazine readership; it was so successful that Blackwood published it in book form just months later in 1821. Galt draws upon his experiences while briefly attending law school at London's Lincoln's Inn together with his childhood upbringing in Ayrshire by juxtaposing the rural sensibilities of Presbyterian minister Dr Zachariah Pringle and his family against London's bustling urban lifestyle during the period of rapid industrialisation in post-Waterloo Britain. Gone are Hogg's dubious religious figures such as John Brown in the *Brownie*, Robert Wringhim in *Confessions*, or Abbot Lawrence in *Perils of Man*. Instead, Galt portrays his clerical characters as wholesome, industrious, and inspiring figures, as he does Mrs Pringle, of whom 'there is not such another minister's wife, both for economy and management, within the jurisdiction of the Synod of Glasgow and Ayr'.[31] Galt employs two important fictive features in such descriptions: flattening out human nature to render his characters relatable to a Scottish sense of probity as well as grounding his 'theoretical histories' in a Scottish collective consciousness of place. His localities differ from Scott's imaginatively expansive scenes of Culloden Moor in *Waverley*, the Solway Firth in *Redgauntlet*, or Torquilstone Castle in *Ivanhoe*. Scots of all classes could relate to synods and parish grounds. In *The Ayrshire Legatees* Galt illustrates that his sense of place is recognisable to local people and the social worlds they inhabit by announcing in the opening pages that the 'Doctor had been for many years the incumbent of Garnock, which is pleasantly situated between Irvine and Kilwinning'.[32] Galt's Ayrshire kith and kin would have recognised immediately the specificity of this environment,[33] and the modern reader can readily see its details online by using the National Library of Scotland's map resources.

Underscoring that geography and locale were not trivial formal features for Galt, Franco Moretti examines Galt's perhaps finest novel – *The Annals of the Parish* (1821) – by mapping out the network of spatial relationships in the text onto a cultural landscape of a novel that spans the late eighteenth and early nineteenth centuries, 1760–1810. In *Graphs, Maps, Trees*, Moretti poses a seemingly innocuous question 'about literary maps: what exactly do they *do* [original emphasis]?' – only to discover that what happens when 'you make a map of the book [...] everything changes'.[34] Galt's affable narrator – with what Colin Kidd characterises as an 'avuncular warmth'[35] – is yet another Presbyterian minister, the Rev. Micah Balwhidder, who chronicles five decades of social changes in Dalmailing parish which encompasses Irville, a thinly veiled allusion to Irvine (Galt's birthplace), just south of the Garnock location in the *Legatees*. Moretti's technique of mapping spatial networks allows readers to follow two possible threads through the figure's materials. The first runs through Irville (Irvine), Glasgow, and Edinburgh, and shows the system of central places at work: school in Irville, university in Glasgow, lawyers and doctors in Edinburgh; second-hand news in Irville, and first-hand news in Glasgow; celebration dinner, honeymoon, marble headstone [...]. As services become more unusual, they move 'up' in the urban hierarchy, and further [sic] away from Dalmailing; but since Galt's world is still fundamentally one of simple everyday needs, such services are seldom required, and central places like Edinburgh or London remain barely visible.[36]

Panning into a rural community or out of a metropolis (or vice versa) in order to provide both local colour and national perspective became one of Galt's refined narrative techniques; in fact, this fictive anticipation of cinemaphotography is discernible in all of his novels. And why should not Galt's novels be mapped in such a manner, especially since Galt himself employed cartography during his tenure in the Canada Company to literally map first Upper Canada and then Lower Canada (later renamed Ontario) as well as to found the town of Guelph?[37] As if to reify Galt's colonisation efforts in Canada, it should be no surprise, then, when viewing the Irish-born artist Daniel Maclise's portrait of Galt, which appeared originally in *Fraser's Magazine* in 1830, he is standing in front of a roughly sketched yet readily identifiable map of Ontario.[38] Galt's legacy of portraying local communities *in toto* and *in situ* along with their characters' complicated network of relationships – rooted in earlier works like Oliver Goldsmith's *The Vicar of Wakefield* (1766) and (to a lesser degree) Henry Mackenzie's *The Man of Feeling* (1771) – became another hallmark of the Scottish novel that can be appreciated in works such as Margaret Oliphant's *Passages in the Life of Mrs. Margaret Maitland of Sunnyside* (1849), George Douglas Brown's *The House with the Green Shutters* (1901), Gavin Maxwell's *Ring of Bright Water* (1960, in which otters more than humans abound), and Iain Crichton Smith's *Consider the Lilies* (1968). Yet if we are to believe Galt in his 1834 *Autobiography*, Scott supposedly prevented Galt's initial literary success by publishing *Waverley* one year before Galt finished *Annals of the Parish*:

> Business, with other cares and vicissitudes, suspended the design for many years, but it was constantly remembered, though not carried into effect till the year 1813, when I perceived that the plan of a schoolmaster's register would not suit, so I altered my design into the 'Annals of the Parish.'

> When the work was nearly finished, I wrote to my old acquaintance Constable, the bookseller, what I was about, but he gave me no encouragement to proceed: Scottish novels he said, would not do, for at that time Waverley was not published, nor, if it had been, was there any resemblance between my work and that celebrated production. In consequence, however, of his letter, the unfinished manuscript was thrown into a drawer and forgotten.[39]

Granted, this account is Galt assessing his literary life retrospectively, so he might be forgiven in viewing *Annals* on a par with *Waverley* which, as Constable rightly observed, had no resemblance to the latter. However, it is inviting to consider Galt's claim of how treatment of the relatively recent rural Scottish life of 1760–1810 in *Annals* squares with the historical poignancy and pageantry of Scott's Jacobite-era tale. Katie Trumpener rose to this invitation when delineating the contours of the national tale by arguing that the Waverley Novels are challenged by Galt's "theoretical histories"' because

> where Scott's novels telescope long-term historical processes into single dramatic events, played out by small groups of major and minor actors, Galt and [Sydney] Owenson refashion the annal form to explore the temporal unevenness of development and the otherwise invisible connections between local occurrences and long-term processes, local agency and centralizing institutions[40]

– precisely the 'invisible connections between local occurrences' that Moretti mapped in *Annals*.

A Galt novel that utilises the telescopic function Trumpener elucidates, as well as one that re-engages the religious fulcrum evident in Hogg and Scott, is *Ringan Gilhaize; Or, the Covenanters* (1823). Since the appearance of Scott's *Old Mortality* in 1816, Galt and many other Presbyterian apologists felt compelled to challenge Scott's representation of Covenanters as fanatical zealots while simultaneously camouflaging the role of Royalists like James Graham of Claverhouse's in religious persecutions. Telescoping over three generations of first-person family narrative, Galt's triple-decker novel sought to rectify a misperceived fanaticism as a rebuke to Scott's caricatured antiquarian historiography. Padma Rangarajan has recently observed that 'Galt's first-person autobiographic narrative obliterates the protective distance from the violent past that Scott's nesting frames enable' so that the 'spirited backlash to [*Old Mortality*'s] representations of Covenanting history must have seemed like corpses suddenly popping up from a long interment'.[41] Galt's religious historical revisionism that portrayed Royalist and Episcopalian persecutors unfavourably did not sit well with William Blackwood who declined to publish *Ringan Gilhaize*, even though 'Galt was the first and most influential of "Blackwood novelists"',[42] with the result that Galt landed the manuscript successfully with newer Edinburgh publishers, Oliver & Boyd.

The same year that *Ringan Gilhaize* appeared, literary doyen of Edinburgh Lord Francis Jeffrey (1773–1850), who served as senior editor of the Whig *Edinburgh Review*, in 1823 categorised the editors of the Tory *Blackwood's Edinburgh Magazine*, John Wilson and John Gibson Lockhart, as 'secondary Scottish novelists'.[43] Although Jeffrey does include Galt within this secondary category, his chief criticism focuses upon Wilson's *Lights and Shadows* (1822) and *Trials of Margaret Lyndsay* (1823), as well as Lockhart's *Valerius* (1820), *Adam Blair* (1822), and *Reginald Dalton* (1823). Given that Archibald Constable was publisher of both the *Edinburgh Review* and most of Scott's novels – not to mention that Jeffrey and Scott were Court of Session colleagues – Jeffrey here pays deference to the 'Great Unknown' author of *Waverley*, which at this point was an open yet unacknowledged secret, while simultaneously depicting the Scottish novel scene as a constellation of figures who cluster around Scott's shining star:

> we cannot but regard them as much less original [than Scott], and as having performed, upon the whole, a far easier task. They have no variety of style, and but little of invention,—and are *mannerists* [original emphasis] in the strongest sense of that term. [...] and though their inferior and borrowed lights are dimmed in the broader blaze of the luminary, who now fills our Northern sky with his glory, they still hold their course distinctly within the orb of his attraction, and make a visible part of the splendour which draws to that quarter of the heavens the admiration of so many distant eyes.[44]

Jeffrey's criticism that Wilson and Lockhart are 'mannerists' is a slight at both the form and content of their novels' highly stylised features, such as romantic landscapes, spatial abstraction of plot, and characterisations of pathos. It appears decorous for Jeffrey to have excluded Susan Edmonstone Ferrier and her 1818 *Marriage*, also published by Blackwood's

– which is typically read as a novel of manners rather than mannerist fiction – because of her social and familial connections. On the one hand, her father James Ferrier (1744–1829) was Writer to the Signet in the Court of Session and, thus, a legal colleague of Scott and Jeffrey; on the other hand, since 1811 she had established a familiar and working relationship with Scott; by excluding her from his account, therefore, Jeffrey avoids any potential insult to Scott's social and family circles.

In many ways Wilson and Lockhart invited such literary scrutiny and criticism by conjuring up and participating in the literary diatribes that appeared in *Blackwood's Edinburgh Magazine*, collectively known as the *Noctes Ambrosianæ* (March 1822–February 1835), of which it was said 'no Magazine articles won more attention or favor'.[45] Set in Ambrose's Tavern,[46] these pieces were dramatised parodies of Edinburgh's *literati*, complete with acts, stage directions, and occasionally musical scores. As Trevor Royle notes, these night talks

> took the form of imaginary conversations, usually over gargantuan suppers, in Ambrose's Tavern at 15 Picardy Place, Edinburgh. Some of the participants were fictitious but most of them were real: John Wilson as 'Christopher North', James Hogg as 'The Ettrick Shepherd', Robert Sym as 'Timothy Tickler', Thomas De Quincey as 'The Opium Eater', and William Maginn as 'O'Doherty' [*sic*].[47]

Even though Hogg was both a contributor to and a character in the *Noctes*, his poetry and novels were not spared Wilson's and Lockhart's condescension. Their literary lampooning caused scandal and backlash which positioned them precariously within the constellation of the Edinburgh *literati*. When the first instalment of the *Noctes* appeared in October 1817, which included the infamous 'The Chaldee Manuscript', it laid literary ambushes on Leigh Hunt, John Keats, Percy Bysshe Shelley, Cornelius Webb, and other London-based poets and was intended to be 'a sort of fiery meteor to blaze across the Edinburgh sky' and call everyone's attention to Blackwood and the 'good cause' of Toryism.[48] The *Noctes* group deployed parody for political ends – albeit historically specific and often arcane to non-Edinburghers – which functioned as a relief-valve for potentially libellous and alarming treatments of historical personages and events. However, 'The Chaldee Manuscript' constituted 'actionable' grounds (to use Wilson's term) for libel charges. In the April 1822 instalment of the *Noctes*, Wilson and Lockhart – assuming the voice of Robert

Sym's 'Timothy Tickler' – express indignation that Scottish Whigs overreact to literary roasting:

> *Tickler.* I hate novelties. Is the prosecution mania about to subside, think you? Now-a-days, every word is said to be actionable. You cannot open your mouth, or put pen to paper, without feeing a libel-lawyer. An Edinburgh Whig, and really some of the London ones seem no better, is an animal without a skin. [...] [The Whigs] have entered into a cowardly compact to *prosecute* [original emphasis] every syllable that shall ever be written against any one of their degraded and slanderous selves.[49]

John Wilson, Chair of Moral Philosophy at Edinburgh, and John Gibson Lockhart, who married Scott's eldest daughter Sophia in 1820, had become controversial literary figures in Edinburgh, and their novels lacked the esteem of Galt, Hogg, and, certainly, Scott. To add insult to injury, the following year in 1823 Wordsworth wrote to Crabb Robinson regarding *The Trials of Margaret Lyndsay*, asserting that Wilson 'has played the plagiarist with the very tale of Margaret in *The Excursion* which he abuses'.[50] When summarising Wilson's literary efforts, Andrew Noble contends that 'Wilson was the clay-footed prophet of the British-Scots middle-class. He created a flatulent rhetoric of national feeling as an antidote to either true national consciousness or will. He exploited nationalism and religion in order to pursue class politics.'[51] Lockhart's reputation fares little better when Francis Russell Hart observes that his 'narratives are so various and versatile that he can severely satirize worldly vulgarities and yet at the same time delineate with lively dramatic sympathy passionate scenes of juvenile abandon: drinking, fighting, hunting' and suggests Lockhart 'may be seen as a distinctively presbyterian satirist of worldliness'.[52]

If critical reception encompassed an allowance for literary justice, then it seems only fair *not* to include Susan Ferrier among the Blackwoodian novelists. She is often myopically categorised so because Blackwood published the first two of her three novels: *Marriage* (1818) and *Inheritance* (1824). Yet as a female author Ferrier also had to contend with the decorum of gender during the early nineteenth century when 'women scribblers' and readers were considered morally suspect at best. Even Scott was circumspect of women's creative imagination when, in his review of *Frankenstein* in *Blackwood's* in 1818, he presumed the author was a man.[53] Fearful of censure by her father, 'who had a great contempt for female authors', family lore as recalled by her nephew claims that Ferrier read the manuscript of *Marriage* to her father surreptitiously, and

> on its conclusion she was told to get another by the same author. There was no other, his daughter told him. 'I am sorry to hear that', he said, 'for it is the best book you have ever brought me.' 'Then what will you say when I tell you that it was written by a woman?' 'Nonsense', was the rejoinder, 'no woman could ever write a book like that'.[54]

And so Ferrier ended up publishing all three of her novels anonymously, but, like the open secret of Scott as 'the Great Unknown' and 'Wizard of the North', her thinly veiled pseudonymity was evident when, for example, in 1831 she dedicated her last novel *Destiny* 'to Sir Walter Scott, Baronet, These Volumes Are Respectfully Dedicated By An Obliged Friend, Though Anonymous AUTHOR'.[55] This homage to Scott was, in the main, born out of his help in negotiating with Robert Cadell for the lucrative sum of £1700 for *Destiny*. Despite Ferrier's literary successes during this period, she and her fellow female authors were fighting a losing battle in the publishing scene compared to their male counterparts. Peter Garside and his team have revealed in painstaking research that 1800–1829 saw the flow then ebb of new novels by women writers throughout Britain – rising to a peak of over sixty per cent in 1814 but then plummeting to below thirty per cent by 1829.[56] Garside attributes this precipitous drop in novel production by women to the fact that, on the one hand, they 'attracted more sympathy as objects of pity', and, on the other, they 'were likely to have experienced greater difficulty in approaching publishers without support';[57] Scott's influence on Cadell – the former partner of Scott's publisher Constable – made practical and profitable sense for Ferrier.

Against this gendered authorship backdrop, Ferrier during her lifetime and beyond had to contend with being compared to Jane Austen – as if Austen, Ferrier, and Maria Edgeworth were the only female authors during the Romantic era. To be sure, Austen and Ferrier published anonymously, treated narrative topics involving marriage, and remained unwed in relatively closed social circles, but that is where the comparison should end. The narrative project of Ferrier's three successful novels extends much broader than Austen's, which are set provincially in southern England and only occasionally hint at locales beyond – such as Gretna Green in *Pride and Prejudice* or Antigua in *Mansfield Park*. In both

Marriage and *Inheritance* Ferrier reaffirms national identity differences between Scotland and England by deliberately bifurcating characters and settings between the two nations. Even her very titles – *Marriage, Inheritance, Destiny* – project a telescoping of the national tale whereby the 'culminating acts of union become fraught with unresolved tensions, leading to prolonged courtship complications, to marital crisis, and even [...] to national divorce'.[58] We would do well to reconsider Ferrier's relegation to a lesser novelist working in the shadow of Austen.

Any account of the Scottish novel during the post-Waterloo era would be remiss if it considered only authors within the House of Blackwood network because there were certainly many other yet lesser lights among the literary constellations during this period. It is difficult to speak of Ferrier and the national tale without also considering Christian Isobel Johnstone's *Clan-Albin* (1815), a novel that revisits the tribulations and sorrows of the Highland Clearances, a traumatic phenomenon that Scott's *Waverley* carefully avoids. Mary (*née* Balfour) Brunton's *Discipline* (1815) also takes up Highland scenes but with a counter-tourism depiction of gloomy and dubious locales. (Both *Clan-Albin* and *Discipline* are discussed in Cairns Craig's Chapter Two of this volume, 'The Philosophical Foundations of the Scottish Novel'.) Sir Thomas Dick Lauder's *The Wolf of Badenoch* (1825) and *Elizabeth de Bruce* (1827) are fourteenth-century set pieces that perform pale imitations to Scott's *Ivanhoe* (1819), and D. M. Moir's *The Life of Mansie Wauch* (1828) functions as a Kailyard prototype that focuses on the social circle centered around a Dalkeith tailor. But given that Lauder and Moir were also contributors to *Blackwood's*, a certain amount of publishing lubrication had been applied for Blackwood to publish their novels – once again underscoring the periodical press's unassailable influence in the production of novels in this period.

With the Highland regiments performing well on battlefields in Europe, North America, and India post-1815, Scotland began to reimagine and reinvent itself so that the erstwhile uncouth Jacobite figure could be rehabilitated for public and commercial consumption. Nowhere is such a reclaimed and burnished national and cultural identity more evident than in King George IV's visit to Edinburgh in August 1822, which Scott famously and meticulously orchestrated.[59] Recapturing post-Enlightenment Britain's imagination so that Scots and Scotland were viewed as sophisticated and welcoming once again drove tourism North, and the Scottish publishers and novelists played their roles in this reinvention. Although it remains to be seen whether the reputations of less well-known novelists during this era will be bolstered by future Scottish authors and academics: Ferrier's novels, for example, have been enjoying recent editing and republication.[60] Yet what is certain is Lord Cockburn's awareness that 'new inventions' in the novel during this textually and culturally rich decade and a half bespeak a nation burgeoning into the ages of industrialism and imperialism which were to shape Scotland's nineteenth-century identity.

CHAPTER FIVE

The Victorian Novel of Spiritual Crisis and the Disruption of Scottish Literary History

Juliet Shields

The years between the death of Walter Scott in 1832 and the flourishing of Robert Louis Stevenson in the 1880s have famously been described as a 'great "black hole" in Scottish creative literature and social thought', a time when Scottish literary culture suffered a dramatic 'loss of cohesion and self-confidence'.[1] However, this literary-historical narrative is slowly beginning to change. Douglas Gifford recently pointed out that 'if we take women's writing into account' (and why would we not?), Scottish literature in the latter half of the nineteenth century was in fact quite vibrant, with 'the twenty years between 1835 and 1855' forming a considerably smaller black hole.[2] Gifford, like Christopher Harvie and Paul H. Scott, blames the 'disastrous' Disruption of 1843 for the suppression of Scottish literary creativity.[3] The Disruption, when Evangelical Presbyterians broke away from Moderates to form the Free Church, did indeed have a momentous impact on Scottish literature. But it transformed rather than suppressed the development of the novel. In place of the grand romances of Walter Scott, the Disruption produced novels of spiritual crisis and social critique. For the Disruption was a social as much as a religious event, consolidating a Scottish middle class that embraced self-improvement in spiritual and worldly terms.

While some historians have construed the Disruption, in Callum J. Brown's words, 'as close to a nationalist uprising',[4] Valerie Wallace and Colin Kidd have recently argued that Scots in the nineteenth century 'perceived identity primarily in denominational terms', and that 'religion rather than nationhood was the dominant feature of Scottish literature' at this time.[5] Yet the examples that Wallace and Kidd adduce to support their otherwise persuasive argument – Walter Scott's, James Hogg's, and John Galt's depictions of the Covenanters in the 1820s, and the Nonconformity celebrated in James Barrie's, S. R. Crockett's, and Ian Maclaren's Kailyard fiction of the 1890s – leaves aside mid-nineteenth-century Scottish novels entirely. Instead, Wallace and Kidd turn to the denominational magazines that flourished in the mid-nineteenth century and that contained 'items of biblical exegesis; reviews of theological works; original poems; letters from missionaries; denominational notices; and, oftentimes, general intelligence on public affairs'.[6] Fiction is conspicuously absent from this list. Although fiction did not tend to feature in parish magazines, the mid-nineteenth-century Scottish novel was very much a creature of the periodical press. Many, if not most, Scottish novels were serialised before they were published in volume form, appearing in instalments in a range of publications from the elite *Blackwood's* and *Fraser's* to the middlebrow *Good Words* and *The People's Friend*. Accordingly, they reached a broader and more heterogeneous audience than denominational magazines, which 'were directed at male, middle-class office-bearers in the church, and male heads of households'.[7] Mid-nineteenth-century Scottish novels' explorations of questions of religious faith and denominational identity are remarkable precisely because they did not appear in sectarian publications. Victorian Scottish novelists did not preach to the choir, in other words, but assumed that these questions were of interest to a wide readership.

William Alexander's *Johnny Gibb o' Gushetneuk* (1871) and John Strathesk's *Blinkbonny, or Bell o' the Manse* (1882) are often assumed to be the first novels to represent the impact of the Disruption. But in fact, its effects were registered much earlier in Margaret Oliphant's *Passages in the Life of Mrs. Margaret Maitland of Sunnyside* (1849), which claims Free Church Presbyterianism as a middle-class movement. The eponymous narrator never names the Disruption and ostentatiously refuses to explain the doctrinal disagreements that informed the conflicts between Evangelical and Moderate Presbyterians:

> I think not that it is in any manner needful for me to write down any history of the Kirk's trials here. Truly, it is an old story in our country of Scotland; and if there should be folk of another land reading this, doubtless they may learn concerning the matter, from many books and histories [...] the reading of which, I doubt not, will be to the edification, to such as, by reason of belonging to another nation, or by reason of neglect in their upbringing, may want a sufficiency of knowledge to distinguish between the old and steadfast Kirk herself, and them that do sometimes iniquitously bear her name.[8]

Readers who are ignorant of the Church of Scotland's history, Margaret suggests, must either be poorly raised or foreign. Coming from a narrator whose father, brother, and nephew are, until the Disruption, ministers in the Church of Scotland, and who is as familiar with the Kirk's doctrines and traditions as if she herself was a minister, the literal parochialism of Margaret's judgement here is patently funny.

Yet, Oliphant invites readers to sympathise with Margaret even while they laugh at her, and there is much to love about this garrulous and good-natured spinster. *Margaret Maitland*'s focus on the parish of Pasturelands recalls John Galt's *Annals of the Parish* (1821); but as a woman, Margaret's perspective is much more bounded by the confines of the parish than is Reverend Balwhidder's. The great triumph of her youth occurred at the age of twelve, when she 'finished a sampler which had no equal in the parish'; and even after attending Miss Scrymgeour's 'genteel school for young ladies' in Edinburgh for two years, she is inclined to consider it 'a great and wicked city [...] the very distant sound of which is enough to put folk in mind of the roar of him that goeth about like a lion, seeking whom he may devour'.[9] The novel is liberally sprinkled with allusions like this one to 1 Peter 5. 8, which humorously reveal both the limitations of Margaret's parochial perspective and the extent of her Biblical knowledge.

Margaret Maitland offers readers an exegesis of everyday life, finding spiritual meaning and Providential design in her mundane experiences. The aim of her 'homely story' is to 'trace out' 'the threads of Providence [...] that folk might see how woven the web was, into which the Almighty's hand had run them'.[10] The Disruption constitutes the narrative climax of the novel, irrevocably transforming the lives of its characters. The Maitland family's decision to 'lay by the temporal providing of Kirk and Manse, and Stipend' and to follow 'the pure and free Kirk into the wilderness' happily coincides with the marriages of Margaret's niece Mary to the local laird and her nephew Claud, a clergyman, to her wealthy ward Grace.[11] These marriages allay the material inconveniences of giving up a living in the Church of Scotland by harnessing the gentry's financial support. And at the same time, the gentry is infused with the moral values of the predominantly middle-class Free Church. Grace, whom Margaret has brought up 'to the knowledge of His name' through 'daily reading of the Word', hopes to emulate her foster-mother's virtues and 'make another Sunnyside' at Oakenshaw, her estate.[12] Mary inspires Mr Allan, Laird of Elphinstone, to abandon his 'wild and gay' ways, and to look rather 'to the Word for what was right than to the world'.[13] The 'world' from which Mary weans Mr Allan is that of the fashionable elite. His moral reformation brings with it a middle-class respectability that attests to his purified spiritual state.

Margaret Maitland is an unjustly overlooked masterpiece among Oliphant's many novels. The sympathetic humour with which the twenty-one-year-old Oliphant entered the worldview of the middle-aged narrator who shares her first name suggests the importance that her family's 'warm Free Churchism' played in Oliphant's own upbringing.[14] The first-person narration that Oliphant uses to such great effect in *Margaret Maitland* distinguishes it from her better-known clerical novels *Salem Chapel* (1862) and *The Perpetual Curate* (1863), which belong to the Chronicles of Carlingford. Whereas these novels borrow from the conventions of Victorian sensation fiction, *Margaret Maitland* looks back to the pawky humour of *The Annals of the Parish* and David Moir's *Life of Mansie Wauch, Tailor* (1828). It is also a forerunner of Kailyard fiction, which similarly tends to focus on the affairs of a small rural community, and to take as their moral centre a woman who is at once pious and unworldly on one hand, and a strong domestic manager on the other.[15]

Margaret Maitland envisions a Scotland in which a middle-class identity grounded in the values of the Free Church prevails over Moderate self-interest and fashionable dissipation. Its exploration of the relationship between the spiritual and worldly in mid-nineteenth-century Scotland prepared the way for the development in the following decades of what I am calling the novel of spiritual crisis. A type of bildungsroman, the novel of spiritual crisis recounts a young man's struggles, with the help of an older mentor, to find his faith and his place in society. The genre owes an unexpected debt to Tobias Smollett's picaresque novels, although it replaces Smollett's scatological humour with an eschatological quest. Like Roderick Random or Peregrine Pickle, the protagonists in these novels must explore a wider world before they can undertake their life's work at home. The remainder of this chapter will examine three examples of the novel of spiritual crisis – Margaret Oliphant's *A Son of the Soil*, which was serialised in monthly instalments in *Macmillan's Magazine* from November 1863 until April 1865 before it was published in two volumes in 1866; George MacDonald's *Robert Falconer*, which ran in monthly instalments in *The Argosy* from December 1866 until November 1867 before it was published in three volumes in 1868; and Annie S. Swan's *Maitland of Laurieston*, which appeared monthly from January to December 1890 in *The Sunday Magazine* before it was published as a single volume in 1891. These magazines were published in London, although all three were edited by Scots: *Macmillan's* by David Masson, and the *Argosy* and *The Sunday Magazine* by Alexander Strahan. Of the three, only *The Sunday Magazine* was explicitly religious, and its orientation was broadly Evangelical. The spiritual crises portrayed in these novels may have been precipitated by uniquely Scottish Presbyterian circumstances, but they were assumed to be of interest to a broad middle-class Protestant British readership.

Novels of spiritual crises were not exclusive to Scotland. For instance, James Anthony Froude's *Nemesis of Faith* (1849) and Mary Augusta Ward's *Robert Elsmere* (1888) recount their protagonists' doubts about, respectively, Anglican doctrine and the existence of God. But the Scottish version of the genre is formally and thematically distinct. What Oliphant's, MacDonald's, and Swan's novels share in common beyond their plot structure as quest narratives or bildungsromans is their critique of a religion that judges its followers harshly and lacks the redeeming feminine qualities of compassion, beauty, and sustaining love. Women, in these novels of spiritual crisis, are associated with steadfast faith, and, in this sense, they are the descendants of Margaret Maitland. Much as these women occupy a subservient position in deeply patriarchal Victorian Scottish society, so a whole realm of traditionally feminine qualities – compassion, tenderness, and beauty, for instance – are repressed or excluded along with them. The recovery of these feminine qualities helps to resolve the protagonist's spiritual crisis and promises to regenerate the Presbyterian Church.

The cause of the protagonist's spiritual crisis in these novels originates in the unloving and unlovely severity of various forms of Presbyterianism. In *A Son of the Soil*, the Church of Scotland's harshly judgemental and emotionally sterile tendencies are displayed in parishioners' right to object to 'sitting under' a minister who does not meet their approval. During a minister's probationary period the congregation can object 'to his looks, or his manners, or his doctrines, or the colour of his hair'.[16] Colin Campbell, who hopes to become a minister in the Kirk but dreads this rite of passage, asks gloomily,

> What can there be that is splendid in my life?—a farmer's son, with perhaps the chance of a country church for my highest hope—after all kinds of signings, and confessions, and calls, and presbyteries. It would be splendid indeed [...] to be plucked by a country presbytery that didn't know six words of Greek, or objected to by a congregation of ploughmen.[17]

Colin resents the Kirk's emphasis on outward signs of conformity – the signings and confessions – over the inner spiritual state of its clergy. He also laments its rigid rejection of anything 'splendid' – that is, anything inspiring or uplifting. Colin dreams of 'working a revolution in his native Church' so that in place of 'external matters' it would take as its remit 'the wonderful bewildering life in which every soul before him had its share'.[18] An ardent lover of nature and an aspiring but inexpert poet, Colin believes that emotion, messy though it may be, is essential to religious belief.

In *Robert Falconer*, the Calvinist severity of the Anti-burgher Secession Church is embodied by Robert's grandmother, who raises him after his father absconds and his mother dies.[19] Mrs Falconer is to her grandson 'the all-seeing eye personified, – the eye of God, of the theologians of his country, always searching out the evil, and refusing to acknowledge the good'.[20] She deprives Robert's childhood of much of its beauty, burning his violin, which she regards as 'a trap set by Satan for the unwary feet of her poor Robert';[21] boarding up the passage to the Admiral's house, where the angelic Mary St John teaches him to play the piano; and confiscating his copy of *The Lady of the Lake*. Mrs Falconer's God is, in Robert's words, 'a puir, prood, bailie-like body, fu' o' his ain importance, an ready to be doon upo' onybody 'at didna ca' him by name o' 's office—aye think-thinkin' aboot's ain glory'.[22] Yet Mrs Falconer is not an entirely unsympathetic character. She is tormented by the fear that her 'prodigal son Andrew', Robert's father, must be condemned to hell for his sins, and she hopes to save Robert from the same fate.[23]

Maitland of Laurieston features a male version of MacDonald's Mrs Falconer. Maitland teaches his children to regard God as a 'harsh and terrible Being' who requires 'constant merciless abasement of self'.[24] His sons John and Michael revolt against their father's God, seeking their own systems of belief. Michael eschews the Church of Scotland in favour of the Free Church, which offers him a kind and loving God, and 'a gospel which admits that Christ died for all men'.[25] John, by contrast, goes to Edinburgh university to study philosophy, and there 'set out in solemn earnest to find the truth for himself—a tedious, struggling seeking, which found him day after day in an agony of doubt and unrest'.[26] John is driven into a state of religious scepticism because he cannot 'find strength and comfort in the religion his father had set before him in his youth'.[27]

Oliphant, MacDonald, and Swan envision an alternative to the Kirk's emotional and material austerity in the realm of the feminine. This realm encompasses not just faith, but also various sources of beauty – music, art, poetry, ornament, nature – that inspire faith. Novels of spiritual crisis suggest that just as the suppression or exclusion of this feminine realm by the Presbyterian church is the source of their protagonists' struggles, so the discovery of it might resolve their crises. These novels also flirt tentatively with the suggestion that the recovery of the feminine qualities condemned by the Kirk might re-enchant and revitalise Victorian Scotland, bringing wonder, joy, and kindness to a society characterised by industriousness, respectability, and propriety.

Maitland of Laurieston openly acknowledges its debts to *Passages in the Life of Mrs. Margaret Maitland of Sunnyside* through its exemplar of womanly faith and virtue. Margaret Maitland, John and Michael's mother, tries her best to 'hold up the sunny side' in a household darkened by her husband's harsher attributes.[28] Like her namesake, Margaret demonstrates 'that the work of women upon the earth was the ministry of love and peace to the righteous and the erring alike', and she imparts her faith to her young ward Agnes.[29] Agnes is beloved by both Michael and John, but the former, seeing that Agnes returns John's affection, does his best to hide his own. Michael shares the self-sacrificial and sustaining faith embodied by his mother and Agnes, and so does not need Agnes to anchor him as the sceptical John does.

Yet Agnes's anguish after her child's death suggests that women also have their spiritual struggles; and Michael's self-sacrificial generosity and comforting counsel suggest that men can participate in 'the ministry of love and peace' embodied by Mrs Maitland. Michael comforts Agnes when she begins to despair at the breach John's scepticism has created in their marriage, reminding her that 'The very faculties [those who doubt] exercise in their inquiries He has given them; and if they search into religious questions with a prayerful earnestness, it cannot be sinful'.[30] The breach between John and Agnes becomes a chasm when their two-year-old son drowns, and John denies 'to the little one we have lost, any right to a future life', undermining the comfort Agnes takes in the belief that their son is with God.[31] Michael suggests the fault lies with Agnes rather than John because she has failed to model for him a compassionate and enduring faith. He asks, 'In so utterly giving way to despondency, have you given testimony in favour of Him with whom all things are possible?' and urges her 'to show [John] in your own life such a bright example of Christ's service that John will be constrained to follow it'.[32] To our twenty-first-century eyes Michael's advice might seem to hold Agnes unfairly responsible for John's spiritual welfare. But to Swan's largely female readership, the idea that their own religious faith could encourage others to re-examine their beliefs might have seemed elevating and empowering. After all, John readily admits that 'you are my divinity, mother, – you and Agnes ... Surely to worship the highest womanhood is no sin. You have always been to me the embodiment of all perfection'.[33] If the sentiment is cloying, at least no one could accuse Swan of the misogyny for which MacDonald occasionally has been censured.[34]

In *A Son of the Soil*, as in *Maitland of Laurieston*, women possess a capacity for steadfast faith that seems to elude men. Colin's mother, and later his wife Alice, embody this capacity, but it is not to them that Colin turns to resolve his frustration with the Kirk's rigid rejection of anything 'splendid'. Instead, he finds solace and inspiration in the rituals of the Catholic Church. Catholicism is feminised in *A Son of the Soil* through its association with ornamental beauty and elaborate communal ceremonies, which contrast with the Kirk's material austerity and emphasis on the individual's relationship with God. When Colin travels to Italy for his health he visits 'all manner of churches [...] where there were no grand functions going on, but only every-day worship'.[35] All of these churches are decorated with 'poor daubs of saints and weak-eyed Madonnas', and in all of them, Colin is struck by the depth of devotional feeling expressed through ritual:[36]

> These worshippers had no books and did not need any. It might be words in a dead language—it might be but partially understood, or not understood at all; but at least it was known and familiar as no religious service is in England, notwithstanding all our national vaunt of the prayer-book, and as nothing could possibly be in Scotland, where we have no guide (save the 'minister') to our devotion.[37]

Oliphant's identification with England's and Scotland's national churches in this passage encapsulates the dual cultural allegiances that, according to some readers, characterise her novels.[38] To Colin, these worshippers appear untroubled by his questions regarding the worldly inequalities and injustices that seem at odds with the idea of a benevolent God. That the ornamental rituals of Catholicism are a disavowed Scottish inheritance becomes clear when Colin and his friend Lauderdale comes across the tomb of Charles Edward Stuart, Bonnie Prince Charlie, in a church in Frascati. Although 'Jacobite ideas had died out of all reality before either of them was born', the two men are moved by 'the stone with its pompous Latin lies and its sorrowful human story, as if it had been not an extinct family, but something of [their] own blood and kindred which had lain underneath'.³⁹ The tomb is a reminder of Scotland's Catholic, Jacobite past, and Colin finds in Catholicism tendencies that might 'untie the horrible bands of logic' stifling the Kirk, and 'dethrone the pragmatic and arrogant' propensities of the Presbyterianism that, since the defeat of the Jacobite cause, has become increasingly central to Scottish identity.⁴⁰ Colin feels no call to convert to Catholicism, but instead dreams of persuading 'his nation to join hands again with Christendom, to take back again the festivals and memories of Christianity, to rejoice in Christmas and sing lauds at Easter and say common prayers with a universal voice'.⁴¹ Catholic rituals reveal to him a loving and healing God by connecting him to primitive, universal Christianity.

If women in the Scottish novel of spiritual crisis tend to represent a depth of religious devotion that is not easily available to men, *Robert Falconer* illustrates in Mrs Falconer the dangers of steadfast faith – one that does not question the Church's doctrine. But the feminine, for MacDonald, is also a conduit to 'something infinitely higher and more divine' than Mrs Falconer's concept of God, leading Robert instead to 'a quaiet, michty, gran', self-forgettin', a'-creatin', a-uphaudin', eternal bein".⁴² Mary St John, who at first appears to Robert like 'an angel come down to comfort his grannie', symbolises the beauty and mystery that his grandmother takes pains to excise from life.⁴³ She is, as Robert Lee Wolff observes, both 'mother-surrogate' and 'object of sexual love' to the boy.⁴⁴ Importantly, Mary is associated with one of Robert's other great loves, music. He approaches his violin, which he refers to as 'the bonny leddy', with 'something of that awe and mystery with which a youth approaches the woman that he loves'.⁴⁵ Mary's piano playing makes her an 'enchantress' to Robert as he listens outside her window, and when he finally gains a peep 'into the paradise of Miss St John's room, [it] was a kind of salvation to the half-starved nature of the boy. All before him was elegance, richness, mystery'.⁴⁶ Mary introduces Robert to the beauties of art and music, but Robert finds his greatest source of spiritual consolation in nature, which MacDonald also associates with the feminine.

Ironically, Mrs Falconer's attempt to strip Robert's childhood of sources of aesthetic pleasure such as music and poetry sends him to a form of beauty that cannot be taken from him – 'the face and voice of Nature', which awakens in him 'a strange longing [...] the first dull and faint movement of the greatest need that the human heart possesses— the need of the God-Man', or Christ.⁴⁷ Women are flawed and fallible, as Robert learns when Mary St John and Eric Ericson, Robert's friend and mentor, fall in love. This is the more painful for Robert in that he and Ericson had their own love affair of sorts, with 'each thinking that God had forsaken him, or was not to be found by him, and each the very love of God, commissioned to tend the other's heart'.[48] Robert is excluded by Mary and Ericson's romantic love, but nature embodies God's unchanging and inclusive love for humanity. After travelling alone through Europe for several years to forget his feelings of forsakenness, Robert reawakens to the beauties of nature:

> He had thought that Nature could never more be anything to him; and she was waiting on him like a mother [...] Every wavelet of scent, every toss of a flower's head in the breeze came with a sting in its pleasure, – for there was no woman to whom they belonged. Yet he could not shut them out, for God, and not woman, is the heart of the universe.[49]

In a scene that illustrates what David S. Robb describes as MacDonald's 'debt to Romanticism', nature restores to Robert his capacity for aesthetic pleasure.[50] If women's association with both culture and nature in *Robert Falconer* seems paradoxical, it is because music, art, literature, and the natural world are all sources of the aesthetic pleasure that MacDonald likens to a 'chariot of fire in which to ascend heavenward'.[51] While nature is feminine, the God that it manifests is not. Instead, God, as a benevolent father, encompasses the feminised patience and compassion that Robert learns to emulate.[52]

Although their protagonists learn to value and take solace in the feminine realm excluded by the Presbyterian Church, the novels I have discussed here do not offer a neat resolution to the spiritual struggles they portray. This is due in part to the flawed construction that sometimes mars serialised fiction, and in part to the fact that spiritual questions rarely allow simple answers. Swan, Oliphant, and MacDonald wrote rapidly and prolifically; the latter two earned their living and supported their children through their writing. Serial publication did not allow much opportunity to revise for formal coherence, and the endings of *A Son of the Soil* and *Robert Falconer* reveal the strain of Oliphant's and MacDonald's efforts to allow their protagonists to embrace the feminised forms of religion they have discovered while adhering to the mandates of realism. Swan wrote at least two novels for serialisation most years. But *Maitland of Laurieston* is more compact than *A Son of the Soil* and *Robert Falconer*, and John's spiritual crisis is more limited in scope. He does not seek to change religious practices or the social order, but merely to resolve his doubts about God's existence. Arguably, this is challenging enough. Swan felt strongly that the 'serial public' for which she wrote deserved an ending that 'satisfies the primal need for happiness. Denied to the reader, possibly he, or more likely she, finds some assuagement in contemplating the happiness of others in an imaginary world.'[53] Yet *Maitland of Laurieston* offers a hopeful rather than a positively happy ending. While John and Agnes do reconcile, Swan cannot quickly resolve the religious doubts that have plagued John for years. She leaves him instead with a renewed intention to disavow those doubts: he is at the novel's end as 'eager in pursuit of all that would go to confirm the supremacy and power of Christianity' as he was previously keen to find 'any new and convincing argument against Christianity'.[54] John's new commitment to seeking out reasons to believe in the existence of a benevolent God signifies the waning of his father's influence. For Maitland of Laurieston comes to recognise that his own 'self-righteousness' has driven both of his sons from him, and he learns to embrace a 'spirit of charity' in its place.[55]

A Son of the Soil lacks the careful construction of *Margaret Maitland* but makes up for its uneven plotting through its heartfelt questioning of the comforts provided by religion. In January 1864, while Oliphant was in the midst of writing the novel, her oldest child Maggie died of a sudden illness in Rome, the city where Oliphant's husband had died of tuberculosis only five years earlier, and the city that Colin not coincidentally visits to recuperate from his accident. Moreover, while she was still writing *A Son of the Soil* for *Macmillan's*, Oliphant also wrote the entirety of the novel that many consider her masterpiece – *Miss Marjoribanks* – for *Blackwood's*.[56] As a number of critics have remarked, marriage, in many of Oliphant's novels is not a happy ending, but often entails a foreclosure of possibilities and the narrowing of horizons.[57] This is certainly true of both *Miss Marjoribanks* and *A Son of the Soil*, two novels that otherwise share little in common.

Colin's marriage to Alice Meredith burdens him with material cares that compromise his dreams of revolutionising the Kirk. Colin engages himself to Alice out of a mistaken sense of chivalry after her brother's death in Italy leaves the young Englishwoman alone and unprotected. Alice unquestioningly accepts that Colin is in love with her, while he dreams 'of an altogether different ideal woman', one 'who could have divined the thoughts in his mind and the movements in his heart before they came into being'.[58] Although far from this ideal, Alice makes an excellent wife to Colin, cementing his social standing in the parishes of Afton and St Rules, where 'very good society is to be found', and even 'introducing some edifying customs among the young people of the parish, which she and they were equally unaware were capable of having been interpreted to savour of papistry'.[59] But marriage inevitably tames Colin's 'revolutionary intentions' to bring beauty and ritual back to the Kirk; for, as the narrator remarks in a passing allusion to Francis Bacon's 'Of Marriage and the Single Life' (1612), 'A man who has given hostages to society, who has married a wife [...] is scarcely in a position to throw himself headlong upon the established order of things and prove its futility'.[60] Marriage leaves Colin prepared to pursue his aims in a 'milder way' and on a smaller scale than he had once intended, which is perhaps, the narrator suggests, all for the best. Small tweaks are more likely to retain 'the confidence of [...] the people and presbyters' of the Church of Scotland than grand innovations.[61]

In the third volume of *Robert Falconer*, Robert's interiority recedes from readers as that of Archibald Gordon, the hitherto anonymous narrator, emerges. Robert's spiritual reawakening brings him, like Teufelsdröckh in Thomas Carlyle's *Sartor Resartus* (1833–34), to 'the conviction that unto every man whom God had sent into the world he had given a work to do in that world'.[62] Robert's work is to find the father who abandoned him, a quest that takes him to the slums of London's East End, where Gordon observes his good work and becomes an acolyte. Readers are invited to share Gordon's worshipful admiration of Robert, who has been purified by his suffering in love and has become almost God-like in his selfless beneficence. In administering to the material and spiritual needs of London's poor, Robert displays traditionally feminine qualities, developing the patience and compassion to help his brethren while withholding judgement. It is through Robert's work as what Robb calls 'a Christ-like social worker' that we see how the feminine qualities repressed by Presbyterian severity might transform not just Scotland but the British social order, providing an antidote to the ills caused by urbanisation, industrialisation, and poverty.[63]

Paradoxically, these feminine qualities prepare Robert to become a good father to his own father, Andrew, whose addictions to opium and alcohol leave him peevish, manipulative, and in no mind to be saved by the son he abandoned years ago. When he finally finds Andrew,

> it was a poor, sad triumph that Robert had after all. How the dreams of the boy had dwindled in settling down into the reality! He had his father, it was true—but what a father! And how little he had him![64]

Robert's reunion with his father is hardly the stuff of sentimental fiction, but the version of the novel serialised in the *Argosy* did end rather mawkishly with the reconciliation of Andrew and Mrs. Falconer, just as the latter is dying.[65] Perhaps MacDonald felt responsible to Swan's 'serial public', offering them the vision of Mrs Falconer 'enter[ing] Paradise in radiant weeping' as Robert holds his father 'to his heart'.[66] The revised three-volume version of *Robert Falconer* offers no such totalising closure, instead emphasising the incompleteness of Andrew's rehabilitation and the limits of Robert's ability to assist him; for 'God must help ere a man can be saved'.[67] Robert's ongoing care for his erring parent reveals the depth of his faith, and their relationship becomes one of the novel's several embodiments of God's love for humanity.

The novel of spiritual crisis is by no means the only genre in which Scottish authors worked during the Victorian period, but it is a particularly important one because it formally and thematically registers the impact of the Disruption, raising eschatological questions that it cannot resolve. It links fiction written on one side of the black hole with that on the other, drawing on Smollett's picaresque novels and Scott's questing heroes, and planting the seeds of Kailyard fiction's Evangelical celebration of domestic womanhood. The novels I have discussed here are only a few of the hundreds written by Scots in the mid-nineteenth century. For literary production did not cease between the death of Scott and the prime of Stevenson. On the contrary, after the Disruption it developed rapidly. The flourishing of periodicals for a range of readerships required writers of serial fiction to fill their pages, and the Disruption shifted writers' attention from the grand historical events of Scotland's past to the no less important social changes of its present. The famous black hole exists only in our still incomplete narrative of Scottish literary history, and, even there, it is rapidly contracting.

DOCUMENT 3

'A Humble Remonstrance'

Longman's Magazine, 5 (December 1884)

Robert Louis Stevenson

We have recently enjoyed a quite peculiar pleasure: hearing, in some detail, the opinions, about the art they practise, of Mr Walter Besant and Mr Henry James; two men certainly of very different calibre: Mr James so precise of outline, so cunning of fence, so scrupulous of finish, and Mr Besant so genial, so friendly, with so persuasive and humorous a vein of whim: Mr James the very type of the deliberate artist, Mr Besant the impersonation of good nature. That such doctors should differ will excite no great surprise; but one point in which they seem to agree fills me, I confess, with wonder. For they are both content to talk about the 'art of fiction'; and Mr Besant, waxing exceedingly bold, goes on to oppose this so-called 'art of fiction' to the 'art of poetry'. By the art of poetry he can mean nothing but the art of verse, an art of handicraft, and only comparable with the art of prose. For that heat and height of sane emotion which we agree to call by the name of poetry, is but a libertine and vagrant quality; present, at times, in any art, more often absent from them all; too seldom present in the prose novel, too frequently absent from the ode and epic. Fiction is in the same case; it is no substantive art, but an element which enters largely into all the arts but architecture. Homer, Wordsworth, Phidias, Hogarth, and Salvini, all deal in fiction; and yet I do not suppose that either Hogarth or Salvini, to mention but these two, entered in any degree into the scope of Mr Besant's interesting lecture or Mr James's charming essay. The art of fiction, then, regarded as a definition, is both too ample and too scanty. Let me suggest another; let me suggest that what both Mr James and Mr Besant had in view was neither more nor less than the art of narrative.

But Mr Besant is anxious to speak solely of 'the modern English novel', the stay and bread-winner of Mr Mudie; and in the author of the most pleasing novel on that roll, *All Sorts and Conditions of Men,* the desire is natural enough. I can conceive then, that he would hasten to propose two additions, and read thus: the art of fictitious narrative in prose. Now the fact of the existence of the modern English novel is not to be denied; materially, with its three volumes, leaded type, and gilded lettering, it is easily distinguishable from other forms of literature; but to talk at all fruitfully of any branch of art, it is needful to build our definitions on some more fundamental ground than binding. Why, then, are we to add 'in prose'? The *Odyssey* appears to me the best of romances; *The Lady of the Lake* to stand high in the second order; and Chaucer's tales and prologues to contain more of the matter and art of the modern English novel than the whole treasury of Mr Mudie. Whether a narrative be written in blank verse or the Spenserian stanza, in the long period of Gibbon or the chipped phrase of Charles Reade, the principles of the art of narrative must be equally observed. The choice of a noble and swelling style in prose affects the problem of narration in the same way, if not to the same degree, as the choice of measured verse; for both imply a closer synthesis of events, a higher key of dialogue, and a more picked and stately strain of words. If you are to refuse *Don Juan*, it is hard to see why you should include *Zanoni* or (to bracket works of very different value) *The Scarlet Letter*; and by what discrimination are you to open your doors to *The Pilgrim's Progress* and close them on *The Faery Queen*? To bring things closer home, I will here propound to Mr Besant a conundrum. A narrative called *Paradise Lost* was written in English verse by one John Milton; what was it then? It was next translated by Chateaubriand into French prose; and what was it then? Lastly, the French translation was, by some inspired compatriot of George Gilfillan (and of mine) turned bodily into an English novel; and, in the name of clearness, what was it then?

But, once more, why should we add 'fictitious'? The reason why is obvious. The reason why not, if something more recondite, does not want for weight. The art of narrative, in fact, is the same, whether it is applied to the selection and illustration of a real series of events or of an imaginary series. Boswell's *Life of Johnson* (a work of cunning and inimitable art) owes its success to the same technical manoeuvres as (let us say) *Tom Jones*: the clear conception of certain characters of man, the choice and presentation of certain incidents out of a great number that offered, and the invention (yes, invention) and preservation of a certain key in dialogue. In which these things are done with the more art – in which with the greater air of nature – readers will differently judge. Boswell's is, indeed, a very special case, and almost a generic; but it is not only in Boswell, it is in every biography with any salt of life, it is in every history where events and men, rather than ideas, are presented – in Tacitus, in Carlyle, in Michelet, in Macaulay – that the novelist will find many of his own methods most conspicuously and adroitly handled. He will find besides that he, who is free – who has the right to invent or steal a missing incident, who has the right, more precious still, of wholesale omission – is frequently defeated, and, with all his advantages, leaves a less strong impression of reality and passion. Mr James utters his mind with a becoming fervour on the sanctity of truth to the novelist; on a more careful examination truth will seem a word of very debateable propriety, not only for the labours of the novelist, but for those of the historian. No art – to use the daring phrase of Mr James – can successfully 'compete with life'; and the art that seeks to do so is condemned to perish *montibus aviis* [by flying too high]. Life goes before us, infinite in complication; attended by the most various and surprising meteors; appealing at once to the eye, to the ear, to the mind – the seat of wonder, to the touch – so thrillingly delicate, and to the belly – so imperious when starved. It combines and employs in its manifestation the method and material, not of one art only, but of all the arts. Music is but an arbitrary trifling with a few of life's majestic chords; painting is but a shadow of its pageantry of light and colour; literature does but drily indicate that wealth of incident, of moral obligation, of virtue, vice, action, rapture and agony, with which it teems. To 'compete with life', whose sun we cannot look upon, whose passions and diseases waste and slay us – to compete with the flavour of wine, the beauty of the dawn, the scorching of fire, the bitterness of death and separation – here is, indeed, a projected escalade of heaven; here are, indeed, labours for a Hercules in a dress coat, armed with a pen and a dictionary to depict the passions, armed with a tube of superior flake-white to paint the portrait of the insufferable sun. No art is true in this sense: none can 'compete with life': not even history, built indeed of indisputable facts, but these facts robbed of their vivacity and sting; so that even when we read of the sack of a city or the fall of an empire, we are surprised, and justly commend the author's talent, if our pulse be quickened. And mark, for a last differentia, that this quickening of the pulse is, in almost every case, purely agreeable; that these phantom reproductions of experience, even at their most acute, convey decided pleasure; while experience itself, in the cockpit of life, can torture and slay.

What, then, is the object, what the method, of an art, and what the source of its power? The whole secret is that no art does 'compete with life'. Man's one method, whether he reasons or creates, is to half-shut his eyes against the dazzle and confusion of reality. The arts, like arithmetic and geometry, turn away their eyes from the gross, coloured and mobile nature at our feet, and regard instead a certain figmentary abstraction. Geometry will tell us of a circle, a thing never seen in nature; asked about a green circle or an iron circle, it lays its hand upon its mouth. So with the arts. Painting, ruefully comparing sunshine and flake-white, gives up truth of colour, as it had already given up relief and movement; and instead of vying with nature, arranges a scheme of harmonious tints. Literature, above all in its most typical mood, the mood of narrative, similarly flees the direct challenge and pursues instead an independent and creative aim. So far as it imitates at all, it imitates not life but speech: not the facts of human destiny, but the emphasis and the suppressions with which the human actor tells of them. The real art that dealt with life directly was that of the first men who told their stories round the savage camp-fire. Our art is occupied, and bound to be occupied, not so much in making stories true as in making them typical; not so much in capturing the lineaments of each fact, as in marshalling all of them towards a common end. For the welter of impressions, all forcible but all discreet, which life presents, it substitutes a certain artificial series of impressions, all indeed most feebly represented, but all aiming at the same effect, all eloquent of the same idea, all chiming together like consonant notes in music or like the graduated tints in a good picture. From all its chapters, from all its pages, from all its sentences, the well written novel echoes and re-echoes its one creative and controlling thought; to this must every incident and character contribute; the style must have been pitched in unison with this; and if there is anywhere a word that looks another way, the book would be stronger, clearer, and (I had almost said) fuller without it. Life is monstrous, infinite, illogical, abrupt and poignant; a work of art, in comparison, is neat, finite, self-contained, rational, flowing and emasculate. Life imposes by brute energy, like inarticulate thunder; art catches the ear, among the far louder noises of experience, like an air artificially made by a discreet musician. A proposition of geometry does not compete with life; and a proposition of geometry is a fair and luminous parallel for a work of art. Both are reasonable, both untrue to the crude fact; both inhere in nature, neither represents it. The novel, which is a work of art, exists, not by its resemblances to life, which are forced and material, as a shoe must still consist of leather, but by its immeasurable difference from life, which is designed and significant, and is both the method and the meaning of the work.

CHAPTER SIX

From the Nineteenth to the Twentieth Century

Andrew Nash

The study of Scottish fiction between 1880 and 1918 was long hampered by a critical framework that viewed the period either in terms of failure or as a prelude for the more serious ambitions of the interwar literary renaissance. The apparent refusal among writers to confront contemporary social problems and adopt realist modes led to an interpretation of the period as one of evasion or absence, dominated by fictional forms that viewed Scottish history and identity through a prism of escapist adventure or rural nostalgia. Recent scholarship has questioned this long-prevailing view. The socio-realist terms of earlier critical judgements have been challenged; the value of critical markers like 'Kailyard' have been questioned; and the importance of new intellectual contexts, such as science and anthropology, have been emphasised.[1] With a large body of work now existing on major writers, especially Robert Louis Stevenson, this chapter will indicate some of the wider diversity of fiction produced in this transitional era.

One way of bringing the diversity into focus is to consider developments in form and genre. Changes in the publishing industry at the end of the century generated demand for shorter fictional forms which in turn facilitated the emergence or resurgence of different genres. Scottish writers were at the heart of these developments, as both practitioners and theorists. Stevenson's critical essays and *Treasure Island* (serialised 1881–82) inspired a revival in adventure romance; Andrew Lang's writings on mythology underpinned his revitalising of the fairy story; and J. M. Barrie's early 'Thrums' sketches sparked an interest in regional 'idylls' that extended across Britain and Ireland. The heterogeneity of Stevenson's early short fiction – the playfully artificial 'Arabian' tales; the hint of the spy story in 'The Pavilion on the Links'; the folk-inspired supernatural stories 'Thrawn Janet' and 'The Merry Men'; the gothic 'Olalla'; the doppelgänger tale 'Markheim' – indicates something of the generic range.

The short story was formative to the artistic development of many new writers, but established authors also turned to shorter formats as the diversification of the market encouraged a move beyond dominant forms of domestic realism. George MacDonald returned to the 'adult' fantasy mode he had first carved out in *Phantastes* (1858) with *Lilith* (1895), while Margaret Oliphant, whose first novel had appeared in 1849 and who continued to write in the multi-volume format until its demise in the mid-1890s, produced supernatural tales for Christmas numbers of magazines.

The period's fascination with other worlds was accompanied by an increased attention to place and location. The imaginative exploration of geographically identifiable settings became less of a backdrop after 1880 and more central to writers' fictional designs. John Buchan's early stories, for example, adopt the idiom of local folklore to pit man and beast against the elemental forces of the moorlands of Galloway and the Borders. In 'The Watcher by the Threshold' (1900), a tale of demonic possession, the supernatural is built into the landscape: 'There was something uncanny in this soil and air. Framed in dank mysterious woods [...] at no great distance from the capital city, it was a sullen relic of a lost barbarism.' The narrator, jolted out of his 'clear and cheerful modern life' back into the 'old tragic stories of my Calvinist upbringing', seeks release from the 'intangible horror within', but finds only 'an inky darkness' in the outer world. It is the 'land' that keeps 'some devilish occult force, lingering through the ages'.[2] In their depiction of the hidden primitive forces of the landscape, Buchan's early stories anticipate some of the preoccupations of his later thrillers. In 'Fountainblue' (1901), a rich man who finds 'the sad elemental world of wood and mountain [...] more truly his own than this cosy and elegant civilisation' embarks on a chivalric quest framed as a rediscovery of his boyhood. In a phrase repeated almost verbatim in *The Power-House* (1916), Alec Maitland maintains that the division between civilisation and barbarism is 'a line, a thread, a sheet of glass'.[3] The assertion reveals a key intellectual undercurrent of this period: the study of myth and comparative religion. The anthropological writings of Lang and J. G. Frazer overlapped with the romance revival of the 1880s, with its lurking sub-text of what Lang referred to as 'our mixed condition, civilised at top with the old barbarian under our clothes'.[4]

The impact of these formal, thematic, and intellectual developments can be traced in changing portrayals of the Highlands. Throughout the 1880s, the dominant representation remained the novels of William Black, with their elaborate scenic descriptions and plots exploring the clash between worldly fashions and Highland simplicity. *White Heather* (1885) is typical. It begins with the journey north from London of an American millionaire, a device that allows for an outsider's impression of the scenery of Scotland and the feudal culture of the Highlands. The plot follows the love interest of a gamekeeper, Ronald Strang, who moves to Glasgow to study forestry. Ronald is a poet, and while in Glasgow his verses are set to music and performed in public; but the natural simplicity of his character does not belong in a place he likens to a 'City of the Dead', and his genius is safely returned home where he presents his verses to his beloved, saying: 'you'll understand them better in the Highlands'.[5]

Although Ronald's elevation to the position of factor allows for some closing commentary on Highland estate management, Black's novel is largely unconcerned with contemporary social issues. By contrast, Robert Buchanan's *A Child of Nature* (1881), written while the author was living in Oban, addresses the problem of absentee landlordism. An English gentleman travels incognito to the Highland estate he has inherited. His first impressions of a barbaric people living in 'habitations [...] worthy of troglodyte savages in the African wilds' are broken down as he witnesses the ruthless conduct of his factor, who believes it would be better for competition, industry, and the 'markets of the south' if the tenants were all evicted and 'transfer[red] bodily to the United States'.[6] Forced emigration is also the subject of George MacDonald's *What's Mine's Mine* (1886) where an English distiller purchases an estate in the Highlands and evicts the peasantry to build a deer forest. MacDonald's interests are more allegorical than social – the plot mainly concerns the spiritual awakening of two materialistic ladies under the tutelage of two Highlanders – and the novel condemns the faith in money and property that motivates both the distiller and the Highland Chief. As the Chief's saintly brother warns: 'God only can be ours perfectly; nothing called property can be ours at all.'[7] The novel ends with the clan preparing to set sail for Canada, the closing lines imagining a reunion between land and people only in the Chief's dreams.

The long three-volume form ensures that the matter of Highland culture is largely eclipsed in these novels by love plots or melodrama. By contrast, the fiction of Fiona Macleod (the female alter-ego of William Sharp) circulated via the more coterie publishing formats adopted by the 'Celtic Renascence' of the 1890s. The opening of Macleod's first volume, *Pharais* (1894), presents an immediately recognisable world, reminiscent of Black's fiction. A young woman awaits the arrival from Glasgow of her husband aboard the Western Isles steamer. He has learned from a professor of medicine that he possesses the 'mind-dark' of his fathers, a form of madness unique to the 'West', signifying not 'the mere insurgence of delirium' arising from human passions of 'hate', 'jealousy' or 'love', but 'that veil of darkness which [...] puts an impermeable mist or a twilight of awful gloom about the soul'.[8] Mist, twilight and gloom became the watchwords of Macleod's fiction, conveying an elegiac view of the Celt as a doomed and passing race. Characters serve as archetypes for spiritual characteristics that both transcend time and signal time's end. In *The Mountain Lovers* (1895), the tragic fate of the central characters is 'apiece with the passing of the ancient language [...] the exile of the sons [...] the coming of strangers, and strange ways [...] *It was to be: it would be*.'[9] The fatalist tone has its roots in Matthew Arnold's formation of Celticism in 'On the Study of Celtic Literature' (1867), but Macleod's intent was to remythologise the Gael so that its spirit would rise in 'glorious resurrection [...] in the heart and the brain of the Anglo-Celtic peoples'.[10] In *The Washer of the Ford* (1896), the remythologising takes the form of an exploration of the origins of Christianity in Scotland, with 'Christian rites and superstitions' depicted as a 'gloss' upon an 'antique paganism' that survives in 'the purely Celtic mind.'[11] In these 'legendary moralities', gloom and twilight are wedded to a new element of symbolic redemption.

For Neil Munro, born in Inveraray, Macleod's image of 'the purely Celtic mind' was a distorted Lowland construction. *The Lost Pibroch and other Sheiling Stories* (1896) counters Macleod's decadent tone through gruesome accounts of the 'gallant madness' of clan warfare and the destructive passions of loyalty, jealousy and vengeance.[12] The depiction of Highland history, nevertheless, remains fatalistic. The title story begins by recounting an ancient tale where, 'once on a time', a wood grew up around the children as they played 'and shut the little folks in', so that they 'grew with the firs and the alders, a quiet clan in the heart of the big wood, clear of the world out-by'.[13] The story that follows tells of an ancient pipe tune, 'the tune of the broken clans', which sets the men of the village on the road, stirred by a nameless longing for something beyond. The tune is played, and the land is emptied, leaving a derelict environment. The allegorical pattern is clear: the old Highland way of life, once integrated into the landscape, will inevitably be broken. In other stories, such as 'Castle Dark', where the phases of Highland history are told through the tale of a legendary castle, the fairy tale idiom belies Munro's stark portrayal of the effects of war, rebellion, and emigration on the land and its people.

Munro's first novel, *John Splendid* (1898), which traverses similar historical territory as Walter's Scott's *A Legend of Montrose* (1819), was one of a profusion of historical novels in the 1890s. Although Scott's legacy remained visible, the more immediate influence was Stevenson's transformation of the form a decade earlier. Although *Kidnapped* (1886), serialised in *Young Folks*, furthered the association between historical fiction and the juvenile market, Stevenson's theorisation of romance, which located the inspiration for storytelling in the childish imagination, blurred any obvious boundaries between adult and children's fiction. Much of the criticism on *Kidnapped* has read Stevenson's presentation of Scottish history and identity as 'essentially tragic and divided'.[14] Yet if the historical novel can no longer sustain Scott's 'aesthetics of reconciliation',[15] it is because in *Kidnapped* the Highlands are turned into an adventure playground where, as Stevenson puts it in 'A Gossip on Romance' (1883), the interest turns not upon what a man shall choose to do, but on 'how he manages to do it'.[16] The pivotal scene when Alan Breck challenges David Balfour's faith in 'the justice of my own country' and his claim that 'it's all Scotland',[17] leads directly onto the flight in the heather – a movement into an adventure terrain where matters of justice and national division or unity are subordinate to 'the problems of the body and of the practical intelligence'.[18] In spite of its precise historical setting and reference to actual events, *Kidnapped* depends more on the power of the story, a word written deep into the work's linguistic texture. At the height of their conflict, when David judges him 'blood-guilty in the first degree', Alan appeals to David's loyalty and understanding through 'the story of the Man and the Good People'. That stories allow for the moral complexities that political allegiances elide is further suggested when the lawyer Rankeillor hears David's 'story' with 'his spectacles thrust up and his eyes closed'. Later, when Rankeillor deliberately forgets his spectacles so that he can turn a blind eye to Alan, he refers to it as 'a farcical adventure'.[19] His actions recall Stevenson's dictum in 'A Humble Remonstrance' (1884) that 'Man's one method, whether he reasons or creates, is to half-shut his eyes against the dazzle and confusion of reality'.[20]

Storytelling is even more crucial to *The Master of Ballantrae* (1889). The 1745 uprising is the catalyst for the plot but proves incidental to the action which is filtered through the multi-layered narratives of Mackellar and Captain Burke. The increased critical focus on Mackellar and his control over the narrative has underlined Stevenson's reflexive concern with the writing of historical record. The apparently simple duality between James and Henry – Jacobite adventurer and prudent Whig;

diabolical persecutor and innocent victim – is undermined by the contradictions of Mackellar's own murderous moral discernment, which leads him to find the thought of the Master's 'deletion from this world [...] sweet in my belly'. His writing of the brothers' lives is memorialised when he chisels epitaphs on their grave, claiming underneath to have raised the stone with 'piety'.[21]

Stevenson's influence on the form of historical fiction is evident in S. R. Crockett, whose work encompassed Scottish and European settings. In *The Raiders* (1894), the adventure is one of place rather than history. Set in 'the graceless, unhallowed days after the Great Killing, when the saints of god had disappeared from the hills of Galloway and Carrick', Patrick Heron's adventure among rival groups of smugglers and gypsy outlaws is a journey through a topographical rather than historical chaos.[22] *The Grey Man* (1896) is more ambitious. Set in sixteenth-century Ayrshire, the sprawling plot follows the feuding branches of the Kennedy family and the evil machinations of the mysterious Grey Man, John Mure of Auchendrayne. Like Stevenson's Master, Mure is a diabolical figure whose evil is disguised by a veneer of respectability. In his dual guise he can pose as a man of devotion and at the same time fling a blood-stained Bible into the fire. His religion is both savage and opportunistic: 'Of the ancientest persuasion [...] for I am ready to believe in any well-disposed god whom I may chance to meet in my pilgriming.'[23] The story pits different codes of behaviour – chivalry, courtesy, diplomacy, and religion – against Mure's brutal scheming. The narrator Launcelot Kennedy has been sent to his kinsman, Sir Thomas Kennedy, to be formed as an esquire. He is more attracted by the valour and chivalry of Gilbert Bargany, who belongs to a side of the family he has been brought up to hate. Launcelot discovers, however, that neither courtesy nor chivalry can prosper in a world of deceit and dishonour. Gilbert is killed in an underhanded manner, while Sir Thomas, who embodies the hopeless causes of diplomacy and religion, is double-crossed by Mure and brutally murdered, dying with his little red Testament in his hand. There are similarities with Stevenson also in the way Launcelot's battle with Mure becomes a struggle not only for survival but for control over the story. At the King's invitation, Mure completes a history of the realm that threatens to preserve an opposing view of the conflict to that contained in Launcelot's narrative.

In its broader historical dimension, Crockett presents a nation in political vacuum. The King (James VI) is portrayed as a dandy, administering justice at whim, while Robert Bruce, minister of the Kirk in Edinburgh, who warns Launcelot about Mure's true intentions, is powerless to effect peace. But *The Grey Man* is less concerned with history than what lies beneath its surface. The plot becomes a quest to recover a stolen treasure chest that leads Launcelot to the cave of the cannibal Sawny Bean, the remnant of a primitive savagery that offers an even greater threat to his survival. Launcelot has grown up with legendary tales of men with monstrous forms and cloven feet living among the hills. The harrowing description of Sawny's cave, with human limbs hanging 'like hams and black puddings set to dry in the smoke', and the barbaric fate Mure plans for Launcelot, unlocks the savage human appetites that the veneer of history has confined to legend.[24]

John Buchan, whose first three novels were in the historical form, made no secret of his debt to Stevenson. The enmity between the two cousins in *John Burnet of Barns* (1898), set during the religious civil wars of the 1680s, recalls *The Master of Ballantrae*, but Buchan was also influenced by mid-Victorian traditions. In the early short story 'Afternoon', a young boy, imagining himself a Jacobite adventurer, re-enacts scenes from *Lorna Doone* (1869), and the battle for the hand of Marjory Veitch in *John Burnet* is patently modelled on R. D. Blackmore's novel. More important for understanding the subsequent direction of Buchan's fiction, however, is the displacement of John's sober scholarly pursuits by what he calls 'the excitement of the chase'. Just as Richard Hannay in *The Thirty-Nine Steps* (1915) relishes the prospect of adventuring with 'no plan of campaign in my head, only just to go on and on in this blessed, honest-smelling hill country',[25] so John declares: 'I cared not a straw for the loss of place and fortune if the free life of the open air and the hills was to be mine.'[26] Driven by the urgent political situation of the First World War, Buchan's thrillers take the adventure romance form of the 1890s into the modern world: 'it is all pure Rider Haggard and Conan Doyle', comments the 'literary innkeeper' when he hears Hannay's story.

The increased uncertainty about historical fiction as a clearly defined genre is suggested by Violet Jacob's disavowal that her work *Flemington* (1911) was a historical novel, 'none of the principal people in it being historic characters'.[27] Set immediately before and after the 1745 uprising, the portrayal of Archie Flemington – torn between love for the Jacobite James Logie and duty as a government spy – reflects the Stevensonian pattern of divided loyalties and realisation of personal identity through adventure. As a painter and a spy, Archie has a power of seeing that sets him apart from the extremism that blights others, including Logie, for whom 'there were only two kinds of men, those who were for the Stuarts and those who were not'. Yet Logie is driven not by political convictions but by a 'permanent need for action' which makes him 'an adventurer by nature'; for him, Culloden is a game not a cause. Similarly, it is the 'excitement' of the adventure that stirs Archie's 'blood' when he is caught up in battle. In the novel's tragic conclusion, however, shared personal affinities buckle under larger national divisions. Archie is betrayed by the amputee Skirling Wattie, who is associated with a 'brutality' of interest. As a master piper, however, Wattie is also representative of a national spirit of beauty: 'It was a strange truth that, in the voice of this coarse and humble vagabond, lay the whole distinctive spirit of the national poetry of Scotland.'[28] In a world of deceit and betrayal, the poetic goes hand-in-hand with the brutal.

Munro's *The New Road* (1914) is more closely modelled on Scott but also reflects a blurring of genres. Set in and around 1733, during the demilitarisation of the clans, the plot concerns Aeneas Macmaster's journey north from Inveraray with Ninian Macgregor, who is sent by the government to investigate vandalism and arms smuggling in the Highlands. The story has traces of the modern thriller as the characters are pursued, double-crossed, and in Aeneas's case kidnapped, before discovering the solution to the mystery of Aeneas's father's death. Beyond the adventure, however, the novel explores the workings of myth and historical change. The opening sets past against present. The ancient Highland world has been 'shaken to its mountain roots' and Inveraray has 'become a lowland town' in all except the language.[29] Aeneas's adventure dispels his dream of 'a poetic world surviving in the hills'; literally sickened by bloodshed, he concludes: 'we've aye been beasts, and cloak it up in poetry'. The beast he discovers, however, is characterised as much by the corrupt values of modern political opportunism as by barbarous customs. The development of trade, which promises to subjugate and civilise the 'savage Hielandmen', conceals the reality of extortion and fraud upon which power in the region rests. The New Road itself – designed to clear a path for soldiers and increase trade by connecting Inverness to the lowlands – is an ambiguous symbol of progress. When Aeneas looks down from the hills on the 'Old Road and the New', seeing them 'twine far down into the valley', he imagines the Old Road carrying the past, the ghosts of 'the hunters and the tribes long perished [...] It's history!' But while the New Road 'means the end of many things [...] the last stand of Scotland', Aeneas recognises that it 'will some day be the Old Road too, with ghosts on it and memories'.[30] Old and new – history and progress – will always twine together in myth and memory.

Adventure narratives were not the only way of addressing historical change. Women novelists in particular developed a tradition which might be called domestic historical fiction. In *Logie Town* (1887), Sarah Tytler (Henrietta Keddie) recreates her native Cupar in the period immediately after the Napoleonic wars, 'before the days of the penny post, railways and universal intercommunication'.[31] The central character, Lizzie Lindesey, becomes a teacher in the town school when her father, an old war captain, dies. When she loses her position, she becomes almost destitute. The main street of Logie is introduced to us as 'Lizzie's book' which she reads from her open window; but it is the characters in her book, not Logie's customs, that matter. The novel is chiefly concerned with the social stratifications that govern the lives of the town's inhabitants. Mrs Mally, the 'hereditary' owner of the Crown Inn, holds a more privileged place in the social hierarchy than the laird; the fate of several of the characters depends on the promise of her substantial legacy. In symbolic contrast, the paper-mills – the 'solitary native manufactory' in the town – are burned to the ground in an attempted insurance fraud, and the owner's nephew, in spite of his wealth, proves an unsuitable catch for Logie's young ladies. 'The wind of trade' is not far enough advanced to uproot the force of 'family gentility'.[32] Eventually, Lizzie emerges as Mrs Mally's beneficiary, but not before she is rescued from poverty by a French dancing master, who turns out to be an exiled Count.

Where marriage and inheritance are the solutions to a single woman's predicament in *Logie Town*, Margaret Oliphant's *Kirsteen* (1890) plots a different trajectory. Set during the Napoleonic wars, Kirsteen's journey into being as a successful woman of trade is elevated above the ostensibly larger forces of history which are kept in the background. The novel's subtitle, 'The Story of a Scotch Family Seventy Years Ago', has led critics to link it to Scott's *Waverley*, but there was a more immediate pre-text in Annie S. Swan's *Aldersyde: A Border Story of Seventy Years Ago* (1883), a novel Oliphant criticised in *Blackwood's Magazine* for its 'narrowness of aim'.[33] Both novels focus on the daughter of an impoverished family who refuses the path of marriage having suffered loss in love. In *Aldersyde*, Janet Nesbit's lover proves false when he realises her father's estate is entailed; Kirsteen's, by contrast, dies in a military campaign. Whereas Janet remains devoted to her family, restoring the ancestral home through self-sacrifice and domestic duty, Kirsteen finds individual fulfilment through work, rising to become partner in a profitable dressmaking business.

At the start of the novel, Kirsteen is defined wholly by the domestic sphere, her apparent destiny contrasted to that of her brother, who leaves to participate in historical events in a military campaign in India. But Kirsteen embarks on her own adventure when she travels to London to escape an enforced marriage that her father hopes will restore the family's status. Ironically, at the end of the novel, it is money earned from her trade which is used to repurchase some of the family's lost lands. That a successful businesswoman should have 'sillar at her command' is, for her father, 'just another sign that everything in this country is turned upside down'. It is one of the novel's many ambivalences, however, that Kirsteen retains pride in her noble ancestry even when she has won the benefits of the modern commercial world. She is 'as eager for the elevation of the family as he could be', purchasing the land 'on terms that would cripple her for years'.[34]

Structurally, Oliphant's novel subverts the traditional romance form in its handling of the love story and the journey motif. Kirsteen's promise to remain true to her beloved is built up as a romance narrative: 'All romance was in it, all the poetry of life [...] all the time she would be waiting for him and he would be coming to her.' When she learns of his death on the battlefield, Kirsteen rejects this narrative, referring to it as 'just an old story'. The linear teleology of the romance plot is displaced by a circularity: 'And thus life was over for Kirsteen; and life began [...] She took up her work with fresh vigour.'[35] A similar circularity is suggested by the frequent journeys Kirsteen makes back and forth between her new life and her family home after her first venture south. As Elsie B. Michie argues, the novel refuses to follow 'the fixed arc of a journey from here to there', foregrounding instead the recursive process of narrating history.[36]

Jane and Mary Findlater's *Crossriggs* (1908) translates some of the themes of *Kirsteen* into a modern idiom. The opening is reminiscent of Barrie's *A Window in Thrums* (1889), conjuring up the past through a self-consciously voiced narrative present. An imaginative world is signalled by the opening word – 'Romance' – which is likened to a rainbow, 'always a little away from the place where you stand', a metaphor for the narrator's evocation of the 'glamour of the past' world of 'old little Crossriggs'.[37] The story centres on Alex Hope, who lives with her impractical father in genteel poverty. Secretly in love with a married man, the scholarly Robert Maitland, Alex rebels against the social compulsion to marry, either for love or expediency. Like Kirsteen, she is associated throughout with work of one kind or another. Mocked by the well-to-do ladies of

Crossriggs for carrying a duster when visiting, she finds employment reading books and newspapers for an old Admiral, and later gives public recitations in Edinburgh. Unlike Kirsteen, however, for whom work means self-fulfilment, for Alex it is valuable only because it 'will pay that awful chemist's bill'.[38] Her restless mind refuses to be defined by any single form of occupation.

The novel's modernity lies in the self-reflexive way it sets Alex's interior consciousness against the surface reality of the 'tight little society of Crossriggs'. Alex contrasts her life with that of a romance heroine, and comments on the novelist's freedom to imagine both subjective and objective realities: 'It is one of the weak points of novels [...] that they prefer to pretend that the outside circumstances look like the inside'. In opposition, she asserts: 'I don't believe at all in the outward conditions of life making much difference as long as we can keep "the fires within" alive'. Her conversations with Maitland anticipate D. H. Lawrence in their ceaseless, unresolvable discoursing on consciousness, living and death. Maitland attributes his inhibition to a 'restless self-consciousness [...]. There's always something between me and my very life'. By contrast, he believes Alex has 'a genius for living' which sets her apart from the villagers who are as 'dead as stones'. Jane Findlater had explored the theme of death-in-life in an earlier novel *The Green Graves of Balgowrie* (1896) – the tragic story of two sisters trapped by their provincial surroundings living a tomblike existence. Graves and ghosts are leitmotivs in *Crossriggs*, but the novel resists the finality of the earlier story. Feeling she has reached 'the end of effort and energy', providence seems to be at hand when Alex receives an unexpected legacy. With the 'delicate encouragement' of 'a reviving of the mind', she sets out with her father to travel the world. Its realisation, however, lies beyond the pages of the novel.[39]

In its picture of a village which 'hugged itself in proud isolation' from nearby Edinburgh, *Crossriggs* could be seen as emblematic of the supposedly provincial outlook of the period.[40] In spite of the dominance of rural and small-town settings, however, depictions of urban and industrial Scotland increased from the 1880s. In Charles Gibbon's *A Princess of Jutedom* (1886), Dundee is merely a backdrop for a story of murder and sensation. Sarah Tytler's *St Mungo's City* (1885), by contrast, makes Glasgow a central figure in the drama. The story focuses on three generations of wealth: the elderly Mackinnon sisters, descended from a once prosperous tobacco lord; Tam Drysdale, who has acquired the Mackinnon property and made a fortune in calico printing; and Drysdale's son, Young Tam, born into wealth but with radical leanings. The novel explores the fluidity of class relations, but working-class experience is peripheral. Social change is viewed from the perspective of the wealthy and the treatment of poverty restricted to the elderly sisters. In one scene, Young Tam joins the working-class passengers on a steamboat excursion during the Glasgow Fair. Tytler observes that where once the people's holiday had been for all, there is now 'an entire withdrawal of the upper classes from taking any share in the gala'.[41] Shunned by the working men and women, Tam feels 'an artificial barrier' has been 'erected between him and those whom he sought to call his friends'. Later, when his family faces ruin, he feels the irony of his fate. Having once 'doubted the righteousness of the laws of labour and capital and the distribution of property', he has long since become 'reconciled to circumstances'.[42] For all its interrogation of social change, however, *St Mungo's City*, like *Logie Town*, ultimately rests on the quintessential mid-Victorian themes of marriage and inheritance. A lost document reveals that Drysdale's original purchase of his business was illegal. Ironically, it is the persistence of progeny, not the vagaries of commerce, that threatens to ruin him. The situation is resolved by the outcome of the love plots.

A novel which offers a view of mercantile Glasgow from above and below is William Sime's *King Capital* (1883), which in spite of a hackneyed plot paints a sharply ironic picture of the emptiness of commercial ambition. The egotistical Andrew Govan, a rich boiler-maker, has risen from poverty in the East End to the positions of Bailie and magistrate. Relentless in his pursuit of money and status, he starts a newspaper to help promote his image in the city, and advocates slum demolition purely to profit from the sale of land. Govan believes he has 'found favour in the eye of Heaven' and views his elevation to the bench as a divine right to 'dispense justice to all and sundry', but the success of this self-appointed member of the Elect is built on deception: he has used his more talented brother's inventions to make patents for himself.[43] His downfall comes when he arranges for a private investigator to steal his brother's latest blueprint. Alongside the comic picture of this merchant prince, a parallel storyline presents a more earnest analysis of trade unionism in Glasgow. The opening chapters juxtapose the Bailie's brand-new portico mansion with a description of his factory where, as in the nightmare world of Alasdair Gray's *Lanark*, daylight is a 'luxury [...] that the workmen did not anticipate during that month'. When a strike takes place, Govan has the union leader arrested on false charges of assault and coercion. He has no compunction announcing in court that Abel Durrand has for some time 'been under the secret surveillance of the police, known to be a man who, sooner or later would be found to commit a crime'. There is no doubt where Sime's sympathies lie. The portrayal of trade unionism is nevertheless ambivalent. Abel delivers a rousing speech at a meeting, anticipating the 'day of justice [...] when the labourer shall have his hire, not doled to him by a master anxious to increase, at all hazards, his own total, but from firm and fixed tribunals'. Later, when other trades join the boiler workers in the strike, he becomes depressed by the silence of the yards and the quietness of the river. Most of the men are content to drink away their half-pay from the Union, while others – 'thousands of dock-labourers [...] whose only unions were impossible Irish ones' – face starvation. Abel realises that the strikers will soon hate him as much as they do their masters: 'He had, he thought, been working for the future of his class [...] But here was the living present'. He resigns from the union to set up a co-operative business which will fairly exploit the patent secured from the Bailie's brother's invention. He still clings to his socialist views, but, having 'joined the great organisation of producers', he was now 'driving bargains, with as fond an eye to profits as any of them.'[44]

Industrial relations are also the subject of Annie S. Swan's *Mary Garth* (1904). Set in a Clydeside pit village, the story is ideologically conservative. The daughter of a pit owner learns that her ambitions for a more sympathetic understanding between the classes are better channelled through religious piety and familial duty than political change. A strike in a different industrial setting forms the basis of John Maclaren Cobban's *The King of Andaman* (1895). The story is set a decade after the Chartist riots of 1848, but a Prologue takes place in the immediate wake of their quelling which recounts the hope and despair for 'the Cause' among a village community of handloom weavers. In his depiction of the weaving shop, Cobban imagines the men likening the cloth they make to their own doomed existence:

> Our web has been drawn through the teeth of circumstance and spread upon the beam, and it has been woven into fabric, as this will be, piece by piece; piece by piece it has been taken from us as this will be taken by its owner – and now there is left us nothing but the thrums![45]

The allusion to Barrie must have been knowing, and the novel offers a more confrontational account of the handloom industry's decline than *Auld Licht Idylls* (1888). In this 'house of bondage', with its 'faint earthy smell, as of a tomb', the men work like 'automata'. Above, they hear a flute playing revolutionary songs and reflect on how 'their marches and meetings, their drums and their speeches' have brought only 'the bitter lesson that they will take who have the power, and they will keep who can'. The story itself follows the Quixotic dreams of the Master of Hutcheon, whose family has employed and lived among the weavers for generations. Hutcheon battles to preserve the handloom industry in the face of the steam machinery installed in a new mill by the Baillie of the nearby city of Inverdoon (Aberdeen). The Baillie tricks Hutcheon into believing he is the rightful King of Andaman Island, and the novel ends with Hutcheon departing with several of the old weavers to pursue a new life in the Indian ocean. The outlandish plot disguises the seriousness of Cobban's portrayal of a community's demise. Ilkastane, once 'so distinctly a weaving community' and 'synonymous with chartism', is now 'practically one in life and interest, as it is one in corporation, with the busy city of Inverdoon'. Hutcheon's benevolent 'feudal authority' over the weavers is contrasted to the cut-throat methods of the Baillie, who inflicts inferior terms and conditions on his employers. As Hutcheon bitterly proclaims: 'The braw mill and a' the braw things that come o't are the result o' a pretty way we've got in this country; we kick out our ain folk at the back door'.[46] The only way out for the weaving community is the fantasy of island adventure.

Minor works as they are, the novels by Tytler, Sime and Cobban demonstrate a growing interest in the spirit of materialism in Scottish society. In two landmark texts of the twentieth century, this interest is enfolded into novels that move beyond the limitations of social realism. In *The House with the Green Shutters* (1901), George Douglas Brown uses the form of Greek tragedy to present the destructive influence and eventual downfall of a man driven by 'brute force of character'. As early as the second chapter, the chorus of gossiping 'bodies' predict that the coming of the railway will bring John Gourlay down, and he is outmanoeuvred by a rival more able to transcend his own character – to 'look about me' – and so more capable of 'foreseeing "chances"' arising from industrial change.[47] John MacDougall Hay's *Gillespie* (1914), by contrast, envisions capitalist enterprise as a diabolical force. Gillespie Strang ruthlessly exploits 'the evolution of circumstance, whose wheels grind down tradition and pulverise effete laws'.[48] Though topographically more contained than Brown's novel (never venturing beyond the setting of a small fishing community based on the author's native Tarbert), *Gillespie* contrasts with the earlier work's formal containment, bursting its seams with apocalyptic imagery and prophetic patterning. A 'worshipper of things', Gillespie can manipulate everyone and everything in the material world, but he cannot prevail against the curse that hangs over his birth and his family home. His flaw is to believe himself larger than both the elemental world, which inflicts plague, storm, and shipwreck on the community, and the unseen forces that fuel the prophecies that the inhabitants of Brieston both seek out and have written into their lives. Even when his fleet of boats is destroyed, and he is visited with the wrath of God having 'committed the sin of the fallen angels', Gillespie 'order[s] his life anew for another bout with Fate'. Only the story's bloody denouement – more akin to Jacobean tragedy than novelistic realism – brings him realisation that 'things outside himself were greater than he'.[49]

Fictional depictions of urban slums at the end of the century were either instructional or gently subversive. Robina F. Hardy's *Jock Halliday: A Grassmarket Hero* (1883) exemplifies the instructional line. A rascally baker's boy learns from a wealthy New Town family how to be an influence for good in the 'dirty stairs' of the Old Town. Underneath the piety lurks a major Scottish-Victorian idea – Samuel Smiles' *Self-Help* (1859) – not only in the mantra that the poor can improve their own lives, but that knowledge and education can lead a boy like Jock to proper missionary endeavour. Crockett's *Cleg Kelly* (1896) subverts this idea. With its arresting opening line – 'It's all a dumb lie! – God's dead!'[50] – its essential theme is that Cleg possesses more natural Christian impulses than the Grassmarket missionaries who fling tracts at him. Unlike Jock, Cleg works against the forces of authority and wealth to help the lives of the slum dwellers. It was not until well into the twentieth century that anything resembling French naturalism entered Scottish fiction, in the form of Irish-born Patrick MacGill's semi-autobiographical *Children of the Dead End* (1914), which describes the down-and-out experiences of an Irish immigrant who ends up working as a navvy in the Highlands. A companion novel, *The Rat-Pit* (1915), tells the story of Norah, an Irish girl driven into prostitution in Glasgow. Although Norah's innocence is heightened for maximum sympathetic effect, and her character almost deified in death, MacGill's purpose is to portray in realistic terms Glasgow's sordid underworld. Social division in the city is neatly captured when Norah looks out from the window of the rat-pit – a lodging house for vagrant women – and sees, beyond the dirty washing hung out to dry and the rats and 'manure piled high' outside the doors of houses, the municipal buildings 'where the rich people meet and talk about the best thing to be done with houses like these'.[51]

In Frederick Niven's contemporaneous *Justice of the Peace* (1914), industrial and mercantile Glasgow, along with its central streets and rural hinterlands, are seen through an artist's eye. Based on autobiographical experiences, the story centres on the antagonism between an artist son and his puritanical mother. The title alludes to the failure of Martin Moir's father, a manufacturer and magistrate, to act as arbiter of peace in his household. Martin proves unable to apply his talent to the design department of his father's warehouse, and after attending art school achieves success in London and Paris. He returns home determined to draw 'for the credit of Glasgow'.[52] The novel presents the new art movement in the city as a vital source to artistic expression rather than an obstacle. Martin's drawing of the iron works, 'Dixon's Blazes', is printed in a Parisian magazine, and his exhibition of Clyde etchings and drawings promise to bring him critical and commercial success. In the novel's tragic conclusion, it is family relations – his mother's public enmity towards his vocation – not his cultural environment that destroys him.

In this sense, *Justice of the Peace* contrasts with earlier depictions of the artistic sensibility, such as Barrie's *Sentimental Tommy* (1896) and *Tommy and Grizel* (1900). The small-town community of Thrums cannot nurture the brilliant imagination of Tommy Sandys, who fails to win a bursary for university and is sent off to the herding, before escaping to London where he becomes a successful novelist. The more significant contrast with Niven's novel, however, is the innovative form of Barrie's fiction. The failure of Tommy's love affair with Grizel is attributed to the artist's egotistical desire to supplant reality with his own artistic creation; at one point Tommy tells Grizel: 'what a delicious book you are, and how I wish I had written you!'[53] Crucially, this portrayal of a creative artist's struggle to distinguish between art and reality is mirrored by the text's narrative form. The narrator, who adopts the guise of a biographer, repeatedly draws attention to his imaginative reconstruction of Tommy's life. Just as Tommy manipulates the emotions of others through his sentimental creative fantasies, so the narrator acknowledges his power as a writer to manipulate the reader's emotional response to the story.

Together with *The Little White Bird* (1902), a metafictional work where the invention of fiction and fantasies is folded into the narrative form itself, *Tommy and Grizel* can be seen as foundational to some of the preoccupations of later twentieth-century Scottish fiction.[54] Jane and Mary Findlater's portrayal of a woman's longing for self-realisation in *Crossriggs* can likewise be seen as pointing towards the tradition of women's writing that emerged in the interwar period. In a different way, one more tied to fixed genre conventions, Buchan's spy thrillers paved the way forward for later writers of popular fiction. Other forms and genres not covered in this chapter, such as the detective novel (largely shaped in its modern form by Arthur Conan Doyle), and the humorous strain found in J. J. Bell and Munro's 'Para Handy' tales (influential on later comic novels), suggests that the period from 1880 to 1918 was far richer and more inventive in its formal diversity than has generally been claimed.

DOCUMENT 4

From *Scott and Scotland*

(George Routledge & Sons, 1936)

Edwin Muir

The riddle which confronted me in approaching Scott himself, by far the greatest creative force in Scottish literature as well as one of the greatest in English, was to account for a very curious emptiness which I felt behind the wealth of his imagination. Many critics have acknowledged this blemish in Scott's work, but have either made no attempt to account for it, or else have put it down to a defect in Scott's mind and character. Yet men of Scott's enormous genius have rarely Scott's faults; they may have others but not these particular ones; and so I was forced to account for the hiatus in Scott's endowment by considering the environment in which he lived, by invoking the fact – if the reader will agree it is one – that he spent most of his days in a hiatus, in a country, that is to say, which was neither a nation nor a province, and had, instead of a centre, a blank, an Edinburgh, in the middle of it. But this Nothing in which Scott wrote was not merely a spatial one; it was a temporal Nothing as well, dotted with a few disconnected figures arranged at abrupt intervals: Henryson, Dunbar, Allan Ramsay, Burns, with a rude buttress of ballads and folk songs to shore them up and keep them from falling. Scott, in other words, lived in a community which was not a community, and set himself to carry on a tradition which was not a tradition; and the result was that his work was an exact reflection of his predicament. His picture of life had no centre, because the environment in which he lived had no centre. What traditional virtue his work possessed was at second hand, and derived mainly from English literature, which he knew intimately but which was a semi-foreign literature to him. Scotland did not have enough life of its own to nourish a writer of his scope; it had neither a real community to foster him nor a tradition to direct him; for the anonymous ballad tradition was not sufficient for his genius. So that my inquiry into what Scotland did for Scott came down finally to what it did not do for

Scott. What it did not do, or what it could not do. Considered historically these alternatives are difficult to separate.

Having traced Scott's greatest fault to his geographical and historical position as a writer, I began to wonder what he might have been, given his genius, if he had been born into a genuine organic society such as England, or even into a small self-subsistent state like Weimar. Could he possibly have left his picture of life in such a tentative state, half flesh and blood and half pasteboard, unreal where he dealt with highly civilized people, and real where he dealt with peasants, adventurers and beggars? Would he not have been forced to give it unity? or rather, would not a sociological unity at least have been there without his having to make a specific effort to achieve it? To ask such questions is not criticism; but the object of this book is not criticism. I wish merely to define the position of the Scottish writer, and then to inquire by what means he can come to completeness, what help Scotland can give him in doing so, and what obstacles she puts in his way. There is at present a general disposition in Scotland to blame Scottish writers who turn to the English tradition when they are faced with this problem. I shall have to consider whether they should do so, or rather whether they have any choice but to do so.

But behind this problem of the Scottish writer there is another which, if not for the individual author, for Scotland itself is of crucial importance. This is the problem of Scottish literature, and it is clearly a question for the Scottish people as a whole, not for the individual Scottish writer; for only a people can create a literature. The practical present-day problem may be put somewhat as follows: that a Scottish writer who wishes to achieve some approximation to completeness has no choice except to absorb the English tradition, and that if he thoroughly does so his work belongs not merely to Scottish literature but to English literature as well. On the other hand, if he wishes to add to an indigenous Scottish literature, and roots himself deliberately in Scotland, he will find there, no matter how long he may search, neither an organic community to round off his conceptions, nor a major literary tradition to support him, nor even a faith among the people themselves that a Scottish literature is possible or desirable, nor any opportunity, finally, of making a livelihood by his work. All these things are part of a single problem which can only be understood by considering Scottish literature historically, and the qualities in the Scottish people which have made them what they are; it cannot be solved by writing poems in Scots, or by looking forward to some hypothetical Scotland in the future. That is the problem, in the most simple terms I can find for it; and it appears to me that Scots criticism has largely ignored it.

*

Set these few scraps taken from the old poetry of Scotland against all that has been written in dialect Scots in the three and a half centuries since, and what comparison can there be? Consider also that a great deal of that old poetry has been irrecoverably lost; that in his *Lament for the Makars* Dunbar mentions twenty-two poets, most of them obviously contemporary with him, and that of these only four or five are known to us by their works. Consider the scope, the variety, the formal beauty, the high temper of the poetry which has come down to us from that time, and reflect what a loss Scotland suffered in losing its language and its civilization. The loss of civilization is bound up with the loss of language; for no civilization can exist without a speech in which it can express both its thought and its passion: without an adult tongue, for there can be no maturity except through a working relation between feeling and thought. Dialect is to a homogeneous language what the babbling of children is to the speech of grown men and women; it is blessedly ignorant of the wider spheres of thought and passion, and when it touches upon them its response is as irresponsible as that of the irremediably immature. Anyone, indeed, who chose to enter into this problem of Scottish dialect poetry from the psychological side, could make out a good case for the thesis that Scottish dialect poetry is a regression to childhood, an escape from the responsibility of the whole reason to the simplicity and irresponsibility of the infant mind. To most of us who were born and brought up in Scotland dialect Scots is associated with childhood, and English with maturity. This may be a regrettable fact, but it must be accepted; for there is no Scots language to which we can pass over from the restricted and local province of dialect: there is only English. When, therefore, having forsaken dialect speech and its associations of thought and feeling, we turn back to it again, we plunge in spite of ourselves into the simple world of childhood, with its emotions untouched by thought, its sanctioned irresponsibility and endless false hopes. I do not want to insist too much on this argument; yet if it is true it helps further to account for the simplicity of Scottish dialect poetry. In any case, compared with Scottish poetry since, that of the Makars is adult poetry. I said a little while ago that Scotland's loss of a native civilization was bound up with its loss of a native language. This does not mean that it lost its civilization because it lost its language; to find the cause of both calamities one would have to delve into Scottish history, and, as history is very largely the product of character, into the Scottish character as well. I have no space in this short book for such an extensive undertaking, and shall content myself with a few general observations. When a nation loses its language it loses an essential unifying element in its life, and as soon as that happens the things which divide it begin to take precedence over the things which unite it. Surveying English literature, one would say that the English are a people to whom the things which unite them are of more importance than the things which divide them; and surveying Scottish literature, one would come to the exactly opposite conclusion. For a little while Scottish history shows us a rich and fertile cohesion, and that short age produced a brilliant literature. But just at the moment when this literature should have flowered most splendidly it was cut off, and that dissension arose which has troubled Scotland ever since, and has not yet been composed. If this is true, then it is not fair to say of Scotland in general that the things which divide it are of more importance than the things which unite it: for that is true historically only of Protestant Scotland. The Scotland of James IV shows us a coherent civilization, and in the individual writer thought and feeling harmoniously working together. Calvinism drove a wedge between these two things, and destroyed the language in which they had been fused. Dissension can take strange forms, and Calvinism was prolific in dissensions; and I think it is plausible to assert that the splitting up of the Scottish language into a host of local dialects was merely a final result of radical internal conflicts, civil and religious, working continuously for over a century. That conflict was so bitter and remorseless that it finally tore to pieces the living fabric of language itself, and left nothing but the shreds with which Scottish poetry has had to content itself since. This is an inquiry into Scottish literature; and in writing of the loss of the Scottish language and civilization I have been concerned with its effects on Scottish literature. But it must obviously have had far more general effects as well, for such a catastrophe involves the whole of a people's existence from top to bottom.

> Things fall apart; the centre cannot hold;
> Mere anarchy is loosed upon the world,

Mr W. B. Yeats has written about our own time. We live in hope that the present state of the world will not be of century-long duration; and this makes it possible for us to bear it. But the centre has not held in Scotland for four hundred years; during all that time it has never been united, and the part has always meant more than the whole. A nation in which the mind is divorced from the feelings will act with hot savagery at times, and with chill insensibility at others; and the loss of Scottish civilization, of Scottish unity, is the only thing that can explain the peculiarly brutal form which the Industrial Revolution took in Scotland, where its chief agents are only conceivable as thoughtless or perverted children. No doubt the disunity of Scotland made it more favourable for the growth of Capitalism in the early stages of Capitalism; for then the very fact that every man was out for himself, the very fact that there was no effective community, was an actual advantage. It is since Capitalism reached what may be called its collective phase that Scotland has fallen behind as a capitalist country: there are other reasons for this as well, certainly, but this one should not be entirely lost sight of. What Scotland has suffered in the way of private and public lack of amenity, of household and official barbarity, by the loss of its civilization, it would be impossible for anyone to estimate. The destruction of a civilization and a literature is bound to draw other consequences behind it of far greater scope.

CHAPTER SEVEN

The Scottish Novel in the Interwar Years

Glenda Norquay

'Today it is the writers not the readers who are in search of Scotland', asserted J. M. Reid in 1945. 'For twenty-five years', he continues, 'Scots men [sic] of letters have felt themselves driven to write about their own country, often, to all appearances, at a considerable commercial sacrifice and usually for a limited and precarious public'.[1] This idea of compulsive quest dominates Scottish fiction of the interwar years and its critical interpretation. Literature as consciously shaped by a cause – whether the search for national or individual selfhood, for authenticity, for explanatory philosophies or politics – is a general feature of British writing in the 1920s and, especially, the 1930s. Historian Richard Overy identifies a sense of crisis in the interwar intelligentsia, partly prompted by the Great War, the decline of Empire, and the economic slump, fuelling apprehensions about a complete catastrophe of civilisation.[2] Such thoughts propelled writers towards scrutiny of the causes of war and its aftermath, drawing on science, psychoanalysis, economics, religion, myth. It led them to experiments in form, in genre, in publishing. In Scotland the aftermath of the war, including the establishment of the Irish Free State, produced a powerful, and arguably more positive, turn towards a cultural project of renewal and revival. What has come to be known as the Scottish Literary Renaissance was driven by a sense of crisis and the desire for political change. The regenerative impulses of its literary nationalism explain much of the richness of fiction produced in Scotland in the interwar years. Yet writers who remained outside or on the margins of this cultural project also contributed significantly to the novel's development.

Critical conflicts, antagonism with the past, and a search for the new that could be modernist, nationalist or socialist but was highly self-conscious shape Scottish interwar literature. Observing that 'Scots have not merely written; they have written about Scottish writing', Reid suggests this distinctive energy was fuelled by the figure of a 'single man of genius'.[3] The 'single man' to whom Reid attributes the impetus towards a new national imagining, referred to both Christopher Murray Grieve, editor of the annual anthology *Northern Numbers*, author of *Annals of the Five Senses* (1923), and his self-consciously modernist pseudonym, poet and critic, Hugh MacDiarmid. The agenda of the Scottish Literary Renaissance addressed both the revisioning of form and the mechanics of literary production. In a 1926 essay MacDiarmid complained that Scottish fiction had evolved no distinctive forms, no language or form that might develop a 'sense of Scotland'. 'No contemporary Scottish prose writer', therefore, was '"taking his country anywhere" or having the slightest real effect'.[4] But publishing, as well as writing, formed part of this nationalist contest for voice and audience. In 1934 Lewis Grassic Gibbon complained that in almost every case the new and unknown Scots writer wanting to appear in print 'must seek publication in London'. But 'he' must also 'consign his manuscript to alien publishers and the consideration of largely alien readers'.[5] A decade later Reid identified a Scottish literary resurgence as evidenced by the number of men – and, briefly mentioned, women – who returned from London to create a literary life in Scotland. William Power meanwhile asserted that new energies in Scottish fiction were liberated by engagement with European literature:

> A Scots writer can postulate the complete diapason of passion and intellect, range from heaven to hell, from hell to heaven, and reveal a European universal in a Scottish particular [...] can become a true and complete Scot only by realizing the continuity of Scots literature with world literature.[6]

The changing fortunes of Power's own publisher, the Porpoise Press, demonstrate the challenges of creating a more locally attentive culture and redressing metropolitanism while engaging with wider European contexts.[7]

In negotiating local particularity and global aspiration, questions of voice were central to (politicised) preoccupation of the interwar novel. Although eschewing MacDiarmid's version of literary nationalism, and nationalism more generally, Lewis Grassic Gibbon provocatively suggested that, 'there is not the remotest reason why the majority of modern Scots writers should be considered Scots at all'.[8] His polemic presented a harsh assessment of current writing: Naomi Mitchison commands 'respect and enthusiasm' for historical novels in modern English but 'they are in no sense Scots books though written by a Scotswoman'.[9] In Neil Gunn and George Blake, 'the reader seems to sense the haunting foreignness in an orthodox English', making Gunn 'the greatest loss to itself Scottish literature has suffered this century'.[10] Willa Muir, showing 'a depth and distinction, a sheer and splendidly un-womanly power', could become a great artist – 'But a great English artist'.[11] When John Buchan's characters talk Scots 'they do it in suitable inverted commas'.[12] Gibbon approvingly quoted James Barke – 'a remarkable Anglo-Gael' – who argued there was no imaginative literature in Gaelic culture.[13] Although the interwar years saw the publication of the third of the earliest Gaelic novels, *Cailin Sgiathanach: no Faodalach na h-Abaid* ('Skye Girl: or Foundling of the Abbey' by Seumas MacLeòid [James MacLeod]) in 1923, the appropriate balance of character, plot and voice was difficult without much precedent in the form and there was, Moray Watson observes, 'an abrupt halt in novel writing' in Gaelic until the 1950s.[14] Barke instead endorsed Fionn MacColla's (Thomas MacDonald's) fiction, remarking: 'his English is the finest Gaelic we have'.[15]

Grassic Gibbon's utopian attempts to move towards a 'language of Cosmopolis', in which a shared speech might abolish social difference, is demonstrated in *A Scots Quair* (1934), both empowered and limited by his own rootedness in place.[16] Other novelists developed their own versions of vernacular or used polyphonic techniques to express a range of Scottish voices. Some, like Barke, resisted the drive to recreate 'authentic' voices, as he explains when introducing *The Land of the Leal* (1939):

> The Scottish dialects are of great variety and beauty. But it is outwith the author's purpose to record them phonetically. And so the broad strong vowels of Galloway, the burr of the Borders, the lilt of the Fifers and the peculiar recitative of the Glaswegians has been no more than indicated.[17]

Yet Barke's own fiction produced a plurality of voice and perspective without needing phonetic rendering to endorse authenticity.[18] Some novelists integrated Scots into their narrative voice without making explicit claim to the vernacular. The highly prolific Nancy Brysson Morrison, for example, subtly underpins her narrative with Scots words while Nan Shepherd has her own flexibility in use of dialect.[19] Far from Scotland, writing before Gibbon, Lorna Moon created her own version of north-east voices.[20] As Carla Sassi notes, there is still work to be done on the diversity of voices developed by women writers.[21]

The critical passions evoked by questions of language in the 'search for Scotland' show how novelists inspired by the literary renaissance were encouraged to view their role. MacColla describes his sense of responsibility to present 'the modern Gael as he was in his actual conditions' when writing *The Albannach* (1932). Celebrating MacDiarmid's description of this novel as the 'most radical product yet' of the renaissance movement, he asserted it initiated a trend: novels of the Highlands.[22] But even novels with less explicit agendas were defined by concerns associated both with the renaissance movement and the instability of the interwar years. Novelists who did not obviously share the desire to reimagine Scotland's geographies, revive its literary self-consciousness or engage with a nationalist agenda still evinced a preoccupation with place and time, the intertwined relationship shaping selfhood, voice and community. 'Places, as men and nations, grow old', repeats Ian Macpherson in the opening chapter of his first novel, *Shepherd's Calendar* (1931).[23] From realist to experimental writing, in fiction produced across and for different classes, in novels that interrogate or endorse dominant gender structures and in a range of rural, small town, or urban settings, location is central to the negotiation with modernity. It configures the terms in which political and philosophical questions are articulated and shapes individual and community identities. In *Highland River* (1937) Neil M. Gunn's central character, Kenn, while a boy, ponders the ways in which he, and his family, inhabit social, emotional and ontological spaces and considers why they rarely display affection:

> How far did the discipline, which Kenn felt as natural because it was part of his social being, strengthen affection? In how much was affection a manifestation, a necessity, of environment – of sea and glen, of struggle and resource, of self-dependence and endurance? Had the vexed factor of race much to do with it?[24]

Cairns Craig suggests that while the historical novel was a formal breakthrough in the nineteenth century, 'it was the regional novel which became fundamental to the development of later Scottish writing'.[25] In its intense questioning of relationships between environment and self, place and community, present, past and future, Gunn's writing goes beyond 'the regional' and enacts a collision of the personal, social, historical and philosophical, produced by place, that is highly characteristic of Scottish interwar fiction. Perhaps as characteristic however is the urge, described by Jean, the central character in O. Douglas's (Anna Buchan's) *Penny*

Plain (1920), to find a way of articulating the dynamics of place on a domestic scale without being overshadowed by anti-Kailyard scorn:

> I have thought of writing and trying to give a truthful picture of Scottish life – a cross between *Drumtochty* and *The House with the Green Shutters* – but [...] it would probably be reviewed as a 'feebly written story of life in a Scots provincial town' and then I would beat my pen into a hatpin and retreat from the literary arena.[26]

This metonymic mocking of domestic literature belies an equally significant engagement with place which speaks to female experience.

Whether engaging with crofting communities or small-town Borders life, both *Highland River* and *Penny Plain* present place as indelibly shaped by the historical force of the First World War. For Kenn wartime experiences and loss of his brother, woven into a time-shifting narrative, change his relationships with land and self. For those less directly involved, the effects are still powerful. In *Penny Plain*, Jean experiences that double consciousness articulated by several women writers:[27]

> But sometimes it feels as if we comfortable people are walking on a flowery meadow that is really a great quaking morass, and underneath there is black slime full of unimagined horrors. A photograph in the newspaper makes a crack and you see down [...] The War made a tremendous crack. It seemed then as if we were all to be drawn into the slime, as if cruelty had got its fangs into the heart of the world.[28]

Writing in 1933 Angus MacDonald suggested that while, 'it would seem as if the Great War had made little difference to the types of novels written on Scotland [...] There has arisen [...] a new type – what I may call "the condition of Scotland" novel'. He goes on to qualify the Renaissance cultural project:

> The rise of the Scottish Nationalist party has possibly had a good deal to do with this new movement; but there is every chance some of these themes would have been treated, as the natural consequence of a war, which inevitably is followed by a period of unrest and dissatisfaction with the *status quo*.[29]

The underpinning horrors of the war are thus imbricated in a cultural project of renewal but extend beyond that in their effects.

Most Scottish novels in the period are death-inflected. In Eric Linklater's *White-Maa's Saga* (1929) the protagonist agrees with another student that the world is 'full of broken things': 'We're not really young, are we? We only have a kind of hard, make-believe youth that's lasting longer than the real thing would.'[30] In novels which engage less explicitly with the effects of the war, loss is still a constant presence: John Buchan's *Huntingtower* (1922) weaves a melancholic strain in references to the dying out of the Kennedy line through loss of sons; in *Penny Plain* and *White-Maa's Saga* emotional affect is located in widows who have lost several sons. In Dot Allan's *Hunger March* (1934) the war's effects underpin plot and language. Imaginings of the past shape understanding of the present. The mass social protest by the unemployed (based on the Scottish hunger march demonstrations of the early 1930s) is viewed by journalist Jimmy as new kind of battlefield: 'No screaming of shells, no thunder of guns, only this close, hard pressure of human bodies, this desperate push of starving men.'[31] Watching the March, businessman Arthur Joyce feels sharply repressed emotions at the loss of his son but also experiences a broader epiphany: 'He saw Death and Destruction like a blood-red film roll over and enfold the earth. [...] He saw Want and Hunger and Revolt' and, nearer to his heart, 'a more awful vision', 'a Legion of the Lifeless assembling on Flanders Field'.[32] The Great War also shapes social relations: in *Hunger March* and James Barke's *Major Operation* (1936) hospital doctors behave with particular tenderness towards patients who have shared their war service. In Linklater's *Magnus Merriman* (1934) and George Blake's *The Shipbuilders* (1935) communal war experiences temporarily dissolve class antagonisms.

Although Macpherson asserts that for people who worked the land an overseas war seemed insignificant – 'Mud meant little to them who spent their lives in servitude to mud' – even in novels which question the significance of the war to Scottish communities, its vocabulary is unavoidable, interwoven with the contours of the Scottish landscape.[33] In *Sunset Song* (1932) Ewan Tavendale's desertion in France is shaped by memories of 'the dung in the parks on an April morning [...] And the peewits over the rigs'.[34] For returned soldier Garry Forbes in Nan Shepherd's *The Weatherhouse* (1930), personal fury, the sounds of warfare and the blasting winds of his home landscape fuse: 'All that tormented – the whining shell, the destructive sea, lust, folly and derision, brute and insensate nature's roar – was in the cataract that crashed about his ears.'[35] In Willa Muir's *Mrs Ritchie* (1933), an ex-soldier's estrangement from his own body – 'The left leg that limped, and would for ever limp because some irrelevant pieces of shrapnel had lodged in its sinews [...] was not John Samuel's leg' – means that only in 'a blade of grass, the flutter of a bird's wing' can he recognise himself.[36]

The 'tremendous crack' of the First World War pushed writers to find new understanding of the present through contemporary politics or longer timeframes, through science, psychology or sociology. In English culture it generated quest narratives – based on the idea of a journey – which search for, yet despair of finding, a restorative balance of time and place.[37] In Scottish fiction, rather than journeying across spaces in search of an authentic individual or national identity, place becomes the original locale in which identities are produced. Whether that means being 'thirled to the land', as Macpherson describes, or feeling the pulse of the city, as Barke depicts, the contours of environment are established even while their meaning is questioned. The quest is frequently an intensely interior search, demonstrated in the range of sensitive young men negotiating their roots, desires and environments. In fiction by women quest can involve individual escape but also offer a communal exploration of being in the world. What Samantha Walton describes as an 'excavation' of the local becomes a defining feature of both.[38] Locale in turn shapes the voices of fiction, whether consciously addressing a broader cultural project or not.

In 1924, critic Agnes Stewart observed with surprise:

> In this country the novel is only becoming conscious of the town. [...] The crowding of our Highland and Lowland populations into busy commercial centres with the introduction of an Irish element, has created conditions which should lend themselves to dramatic treatment.[39]

Two years later MacDiarmid can talk about 'the new Glasgow School' including Dot Allan, Catherine Carswell, George Blake and less familiar figures, John Cockburn and John Carruthers. This growth of the urban novel is a defining feature of the period, 'prophetic of a major strand of Scottish fiction'[40] continuing throughout the twentieth century. Engaging with an urban working class and the fabric of city spaces, it is fuelled, with the exception perhaps of Carswell, by the 'condition of Scotland' question. But this issue, particularly in the 1930s, demanded recognition of the complicated relationships between urban and rural. Power vividly suggests: 'In a dying country-side the life-impulse widely and blindly asserts itself among a dying race. That is the sombre pedal-note that sounds beneath all the fuss and rattle and tintinnabulation of urbanized Scotland.'[41] As the trajectory of *A Scots Quair* demonstrates, the sweep of history pushes rural communities into new urban worlds, while the country retains a powerful imaginative and symbolic hold. In those novels most resolutely focused on Glasgow, the second city of the British empire, greenness and nature remain shadowy alternatives. In MacPherson's *Shepherd's Calendar*, Gunn's *Wild Geese Overhead* (1939), in Eric Linklater's novels, the city – whether Aberdeen or Glasgow – becomes representative of decay and desolation, while also serving as a site of political education. In considering the power of location, in both urban fiction and novels of highland life, this interdependency of place is key. Rich and highly distinctive novels from the north-east of Scotland, although less prophetic of later developments in twentieth-century fiction, further demonstrate the complexity of urban and rural intersections.

Allan's *Hunger March* and Blake's *The Shipbuilders* (1935) are paradigmatic of the Glasgow novel which emerged in this period. In both, a pall of darkness is consistently contrasted with the blood-red hue of violence or the glitter of tawdry consumption. Glasgow is frequently described in terms of foreboding:

> Hours ago, dawn had swept softly round the world, destroying the thick, tense silence, transmuting darkness into light. Yet here in the city's heart, the burden of outspread wings still lingered. A dark grey sky, indeterminate as down, sloped above a confusion of black stone.[42]

For Arthur Joyce, 'the malignancy of that sky' symbolises the demise of his business and that of the city. In contrast the glitter of office windows and luxury shops, shining out of the gloom, suggests the shallow obliviousness of those 'happily at work, pursuing mysterious occupations in a luxurious atmosphere, juggling with coins amidst a profusion of gold and silver'.[43] The palette in the magnificent *Major Operation* is even more vivid, with the setting sun of its opening pages encompassing the rich and poor, aspirational and desperate, invoking an ominous sense of destruction as 'the luridity of the blood deepened and dulled' until 'the smoke of the City reduced it to a faint and disgusting smudge'.[44] Again, in the most sensational and arguably least literary of the genre, *No Mean City* (1935), darkness at the novel's opening is metonymic of the city's decline, social decay and individual desolation: 'In the thick and stagnant darkness John Stark lay wide awake'.[45] The decline of Glasgow shipbuilding also encapsulates the loss of masculinity authenticated through labour. In *The Shipbuilders* the launch of the last ship of a failing shipyard represents the:

> high, tragic pageant of the Clyde. Yard after yard passed by, the berths empty, the grass growing about the sinking keel blocks. [...] And now only the gaunt, dumb poles and groups of men, workless, watching in silence the bitter passage of the vessel.[46]

The novel is critical of a contemporary culture in which there is no dignity in work left: a new generation is forced to find 'one of those flash, cheap, unskilled billets that lads were tumbling into nowadays: no apprenticeship, no early hours'.[47]

Structurally *The Shipbuilders*, *Hunger March* and *Major Operation* all trace the intersecting lives of men – and, to a limited extent, women – from different classes who make the city what it is. Their political and formal approaches are, however, different. *Hunger March* follows a range of characters through a single day in which the March takes place through the streets of Glasgow. Although innovative in technique, this means that characters, from worlds Allan was not entirely familiar with, are not as fully realised as some others.[48] *The Shipbuilders*, again emerging from Blake's own middle-class position, follows a more conventional unpicking of relationships in the narratives of shipyard owner Leslie Pagan and worker Danny Shields, linked by personal connection from the war where Shields served as Pagan's batman. This paternalism is emotionally explored but never fully challenged in the novel.

In contrast, *Major Operation* is an energetic, at times over-written, but also technically experimental, confrontation with the complexities of the economic decay of Glasgow in the 1930s and a call to political action by the working classes. Again, it is structured around the lives of two men – middle-class businessman, George Anderson, and dock worker, Jock MacKelvie – who find themselves in hospital at the same time, facing 'major operations', in a space where their political beliefs can be debated. Inevitably this is more of a process of education for Anderson than 'natural leader' and charismatic communist MacKelvie. While *The Shipbuilders* moves between two different interiorities, expressing the class perspective of each, Barke favours an explosive jumble of perspectives combined with a dominating, at time hectoring but often ironic, narrative voice which shapes this 'major operation' of dissecting a society. Although each of these novels appears to aim for social realism, they also develop, in different degrees, an arguably, modernist style through juxtaposition of clashing points of view and use of intersecting timelines to disrupt linearity.

In exploring postwar masculinity, all three novels locate the source of middle-class desolation in a feminine sphere. In *Major Operation* Anderson's artificial and unfaithful wife, Mabel, contributes to his ultimate destruction. In *The Shipbuilders*, Pagan's wife wants their son to 'speak decent English' and seeks to lure him towards a soft and feminine southern lifestyle. Shield's wife has an equally toxic effect, mixing with 'dubious' lower middle-class types who rejoice in social metropolitanism in an attempt to move up in the world. These female characters lead men away from authenticity, Scottish integrity and paternalistic responsibilities. Working-class women (strong, sexy Jean in *Major Operation*, or lovingly supportive Jess in *The Shipbuilders*) are little more than caricatures. *Hunger March*, with its wider range of female figures, acknowledges women who make a living in different class positions – opera star Adèle Elberstein, competent secretary Celia Ker, working-class mother Mrs Humphry, her employer middle-class Mrs Macgregor, and, most interestingly, waitress observer Fanny – but the narrative of misunderstood or betrayed men remains. If these are 'conditions of Scotland' novels, the country's future is projected in terms of masculine vitality and threatened by female characters who might weaken its cultural integrity. These representations contribute to what Alison Light has described as a reaction against the feminising of culture in the interwar years, the product of a society underpinned by divisions in gendered experience and aspiration.[49]

These urban novels also share that 'sombre pedal note' of the rural noted by Power. Although 'escaping' down south, Pagan considers emotional attachments on his final trip north:

> Queer [...] how definitely the fact of nationality asserts itself even in the matters of landscape and domestic architecture. It was Scotland that streamed past before his eyes; no other country could present that particular aspect. [...] The sense of a return to a natural element grew upon him.[50]

Land, race, and urban modernity are deeply imbricated, although here the tone is predominantly elegiac. *Major Operation*, too, unexpectedly revisits the meaning of the countryside around the city: the figure of the hiker, scorned in the opening scenes, becomes an intrinsic part of the revolution which might create a new Scotland.[51] *Wild Geese Overhead* likewise embodies tensions between rural and urban in its tale of a journalist who naively seeks escape from the 'fetid atmosphere' of Glasgow to 'stride through the country, wind and rain in my face, exhilarating like a song' although his political, philosophical and physical journey is less simple than anticipated.[52]

Novels that focus on the land are also in (sometimes unspoken) engagement with the urban. Yet their exploration of the 'condition of Scotland' and search for authentic modes of being take different formal directions from the broad social coverage of the Glasgow novel. In *The Albannach* MacColla sought to impose unity by working 'inside the hero's perceptions throughout'.[53] Its tale of Murdo Anderson, a man whose 'mind had been travelling highways and hill paths of its own that never led him within sight of the road his parents were on', demonstrates another dominant feature of interwar writing: the isolated individual, estranged from community and self.[54] For Murdo, whose 'mind swung in circles on a different plane', neither local and repressive community, university, nor city life can fully accommodate his psyche.[55] When he eventually returns to the land and the highlands, he experiences a degree of resolution: 'That was he. The work of his hands was like the green points pushing out from the brown earth, or like the sap rising in the stems of trees.'[56] But it is only after further tribulations that he arrives at a place of home in which he can contemplate a community and a future.

Similar trajectories of individual struggle (although without the overt misogyny of MacColla) are enacted in Ian Macpherson's first novel and the early fiction of Neil Gunn. They too depict a harsh and intensely affective way of life that, while apparently depressing, can be regenerative. In *Shepherd's Calendar* much of the year described bears the characteristics of winter, in a world of unyielding land, violence even in domestic beasts, and the pervading dampness of decline: 'Night brought no comfort. Fire itself seemed clammy. There were mists in the minds of men. All the ponderous machinery of decay had been set in motion, and the world listened apathetically to its slow dissolution.'[57] The novel follows, yet mocks, escape narratives underpinning both Kailyard and anti-Kailyard fiction. Staying on the land and leaving seem equally impossible. The countryside thus serves as effective metonym for both a personal and national malaise that is equally contradictory: John 'felt this was a land akin to his life. His life was desolate like this place. He was part of the weary moor. He was its high priest, high priest of Desolation.'[58]

Neil Gunn, for many years critically situated as the dominant novelist of the Scottish Literary Renaissance, also helped establish this mode. MacDiarmid identified *The Grey Coast* (1926) as a significant contribution to Scottish literature, predicting that, although Gunn's work 'remains unequal' and at times 'tinged with Celtic twilight', if he matures, 'he will rapidly take rank as the foremost of living Scottish novelists'.[59] Author of over twenty novels, Gunn's literary mastery and significant oeuvre is consistently acknowledged, as is his personal role within the renaissance movement. Kurt Wittig named him as Scotland's greatest twentieth-century novelist.[60] Success in commercial terms is evidenced by his importance to the Porpoise Press. Yet although his work has been praised for its simultaneous universality and local specificity, his positioning and politics were controversial when he began writing and have become so again. Gunn's engagement with Highland life fulfilled some of MacDiarmid's demands for a cultural project, but Barke questioned the identity politics: focusing on the exceptionalism of the Highlander led him 'clean away from the times of the present'.[61] Gunn certainly reinforces some rural/urban stereotypes. In *Wild Geese Overhead*, a doctor with neutral speech patterns can nevertheless be identified as 'a country lad' because of physical characteristics: 'Will could feel the country wind blowing about the head and shoulders, smoothing and shaping them, knotting the overbrows over the sea-coloured eyes.'[62] Criticising his superior race-theory of the Gael, Barke related Gunn to a nationalism which had dark resonances in the 1930s. He also suggested that Gunn, as a nationalist concentrating on a small field of vision, produced art of a high level but the internationalist Gibbon, 'because of the breadth of his vision' was 'a much more important artist'.[63] The gender politics of Gunn's fiction have also received critique.[64] By 2010 Ken Keir noted that Gunn's reputation in academia was at 'something of a nadir'.[65] Recent ecological interest in relationships between natural and human, landscape and self suggest, nevertheless, potential for a revival of interest.[66]

Many of Gunn's novels develop familiar narratives of constraint and escape, focusing on central characters in deep relationships with their environments, whether crofting or fishing, but also searching longer historical trajectories for significance. His interwar fiction moves from narratives of decline in Highland communities (*The Lost Glen* (1932); *Morning Tide* (1930)) to a more nuanced and regenerative perspective, driven by his interests in eastern philosophy and a political activism aimed at revitalising the Highland environment. Although Gunn's work consistently draws on the northern areas of Scotland he inhabited, he experimented with different forms – historical and speculative novels, as well as realist and semi-autobiographical fiction. *Sun Circle* (1933), focusing on an early mediaeval Scotland in which paganism and Christianity negotiate towards the future, engages with interwar interest in primitivism and early history. *Butcher's Broom* (1934) is one of the finest contributions to a genre of Clearance fiction which has shaped understanding of Scottish relationships with home and land as constructed through exile.[67]

Both 'the Glasgow novel' and 'the novel of Highland life' contribute to the Scottish Renaissance project. Yet, just as the Literary Renaissance movement for a brief period found its social centre in the north-east town of Montrose, so the area of north-east Scotland produced some of the most experimental and linguistically varied fiction of the interwar years, and the most complex examination of being in the world. This is evident in the vitality of novels by women writers from the region as well as, more obviously, the central role played by James Leslie Mitchell/Lewis Grassic Gibbon.

The north-east of Scotland offers a geographic mixture of land and sea, city and small town, less subject perhaps to linear narratives of flux and decline. Novels set here, fascinated by its topographical potential for borders and intersections, are some of the richest and least monological explorations of the 'condition of Scotland', combining individual lives and the local articulation of experience situated within broader historical contours. Although they speak to a disappearing way of life and assault on community identities, these novels sustain a vibrancy of voice and connection to the environment that works against narratives of fracture and decline. They also offer alternatives to the gendered divisions and focus on questing masculinity that inform both the Glasgow novel and 'Highland life' fiction.

This alternative is evident in the 1920s in the fiction of Lorna Moon (Nora Wilson Low) and her novel *Dark Star* (1929). Although written in Hollywood, with an appropriately dramatic plot of doomed love, *Dark Star* explores the domestic details of women's working lives in a complex and dynamic community. The narrative of Nancy Pringle's creative aspirations and thwarted romance may follow the conventions of female *bildungsroman*, yet the world evoked sets an environment of domestic duty and community surveillance against the more subversive and itinerant culture of beggars and marginal figures, folk voices and cultures, which is also vividly represented in the short stories of Violet Jacob and the fiction of Jessie Kesson.

Nan Shepherd's fiction focuses on the same north-eastern environment, a world she inhabited all her life. At least two of her novels construct fictions of female self-development, powerfully exploring the constraints of selfhood and a search for independence. But Shepherd's fiction is remarkable for the integration of such struggles with a particular attentiveness to the social and natural elements of place. They also challenge easy narratives of escape as self-realisation. The representation of a highly sensitive central figure, Martha Ironside, moving between rural agrarian setting to university and back in her first novel *The Quarry Wood* (1928), may seem familiar but is contextualised by a broader range of characters and sensibilities, including Aunt Josephine Leggatt, a woman who could 'tramp ten miles still' at the age of sixty-four and who 'made haste for no man, no, nor woman neither'.[68] In her life – and death, with which Martha is intimately involved – an alternative mode of being is suggested. Shepherd's third novel, *A Pass in the Grampians* (1933), also explores the dynamic of leaving and staying, with Jenny Kilgour, its central character, being seduced by a world beyond the Grampians. But the novel's dissection of these tensions engages with both her inner life and philosophies of being and situates these in the history of her family and a broader social context. Martha's final positioning in *The Quarry Wood* – 'she had acquiesced in her destiny and so delivered herself from the insecurity of the adventurer' – challenges the narratives of escape familiar from novels of Highland life or female *bildungsroman*.[69] 'Adventuring' might appear attractive but the term also acknowledges the power of fiction (the kind Martha's feckless mother admires) to create unrealistic expectations and deny other forms of fulfilment. Shepherd's own relationship to the genre was complicated: 'As a matter of fact, I read few novels. They bore me. I never wanted or intended to write one myself, and I can't tell you why I did it.'[70] This detachment perhaps accounts for her publishing only three novels but also informs the radical experiment that is her second novel. In the complexity of its structure, its kaleidoscope of perspectives, its confrontation with the effects of the First World War, its attentiveness to experience at all life stages and its embrace of linguistic, formal and philosophical 'difficulty', *The Weatherhouse* is arguably the great Scottish modernist and feminist novel of the period.

Willa Muir too was negotiating the limits of the novel form to examine gendered experience from a north-east setting. Although connected to the Scottish Literary Renaissance through intimate and social networks, Muir resisted 'condition of Scotland' imperatives to explore instead the boundaries of place and gender, challenging both novelistic conventions and interwar Scottish society through narratives of small-town life. In its shifting perspectives of female identity, *Imagined Corners* (1931) creates a narrative of 'escape' for its central female character, Elizabeth Shand, and combines dissection of social mores with an investigation of female consciousness that is modernist in its embrace of a complex interiority. Her second novel *Mrs Ritchie* (1933) challenges novelistic conventions further by creating an almost entirely unsympathetic central character, in a narrative full of energy and fury which presents an implicit confrontation with patriarchal endorsements of war. Again, Muir's relationship with the novel was ambivalent: her work within a range of other genres – polemic, essays, autobiography – and her unpublished novel *Mrs Muttoe and the Top Storey* suggest a writer in difficult material conditions seeking appropriate forms in which to articulate her understanding of locale and interwar life.[71]

In the writing of Moon, Shepherd and Muir the 'condition of Scotland' is examined but does not become the central – and arguably narrowing – project of their work. Nor does their fiction follow that alignment of masculinity with authenticity, and femininity with a weakening of that integrity. Nor do their female figures function as crude symbols of nation.

Lewis Grassic Gibbon's trilogy, *A Scots Quair*, dominating the period in terms of subsequent critical recognition, likewise focuses on a female consciousness and the contours of a north-eastern landscape. *Sunset Song* (1932) has become one of Scotland's most popular books, repeatedly filmed and televised. With *Cloud Howe* (1933) and *Grey Granite* (1934), this trilogy of novels focusing on the life of Chris Guthrie finds, through its central character and in the range of voices of 'the folk' it invokes, a means of capturing the intersections of time and place, of encapsulating but moving beyond 'the condition of Scotland' question. It has received international recognition as a fiction of working-class life, a bold modernist experiment in its use of language, a feminist text, a fine example of twentieth-century nostalgia for rural life and its breakdown, and a classic engagement with the effects of the First World War in its dissection of communities. The novels create a historical spectrum that gives the present moment meaning but also a life story that sharpens focus on the crushing effects of conventional moralities and conflicting roles in shaping the lives of both men and women. In this respect the trilogy is part of a longer-term experimentation in Mitchell's previous novels which, written in a standard English, demonstrate his willingness to challenge form and genre. It develops his ongoing engagement with feminist and Marxist politics, expressed in an understanding that gender, national and social politics intersect. In *Stained Radiance* (1930) he worked within a relatively realist frame to explore dynamics between personal relationships and broader politics. From the early epistolary and semi-autobiographical *The Thirteenth Disciple* (1931) to the tale of time-travelling nomads in *Three Go* Back (1932) and *Gay Hunter* (1934), 'science fiction' novels which explore the idea of civilisation, he was constantly seeking new forms and plots in which to address the larger issues he investigates in local settings in the *Quair*.[72] As Morag Shiach recognises, Mitchell is a significant figure 'in a broader Modernist project': the ways in which he 'negotiated [...] intellectual, stylistic and commercial choices' as a Scottish modernist enhances 'our understanding of European Modernism'.[73] In all his novels and under both names he is, Sassi argues, engaging in a dialectical quest 'between and across conventionally defined identities'.[74] In the *Quair* he found a frame, a form and a new kind of voice in which to synthesise these concerns. The fact that the trilogy is often understood as representative of women's experience, directed to women readers – was indeed initially perceived as being written by a woman – is not unproblematic but suggests too the powerful alignment of his work with other women writers from the same locale and time.

Energising fiction from and about the north-east fractures the rural/urban divide and adds complexity to the development of the Scottish novel. Other writers also challenge dominant paradigms: defying categorisation, Catherine Carswell, Eric Linklater and Ian Macpherson add further nuance to the picture. Carswell's two novels may be described as 'Glasgow fiction', but do not explicitly engage with the city as embodying the 'condition of Scotland'. Linklater writes of Aberdeen and Orkney but is ambivalent in response to the call of the Scottish Renaissance movement. Macpherson's novels are set in the north-east and in the Highlands but, moving through a range of forms, develop an exciting relationship with the natural world that has only recently received the recognition it deserves.[75] All three developed distinctive techniques in their fiction and push the novel in new ways. Carswell's novels, *Open the Door!* (1920) and *The Camomile* (1922) sit both in and outside the school of urban fiction. While the spaces of Glasgow thrum in their pages and are – as is frequent in other urban fiction – characterised by their contrast with alternative locales, interest in the city is also aesthetic. Glasgow here is a city of artistic sensibilities and aspirations, of the avant-garde. Carswell's evocative writing operates at levels of emotional intensity which make it modernist. Her novels anticipate the fictions of self-development in Muir and

Shepherd but more insistently combine sexual and national freedom while still remaining attentive to the contours of the local and everyday.[76]

Ian Macpherson and Eric Linklater both contribute to experimentation with genre fiction characteristic of the period. By the mid-1930s Ian Macpherson had produced a range of novels in different forms, moving from the grim *Shepherd's Calendar* to historical novels, *Land of Our Fathers* (1933) and *Pride in the Valley* (1936). In 1936 he articulated 'morbid expectations about the next war' in the extraordinary *Wild Harbour*, a novel that begins in 1944 and tells the story of a young couple who attempt to escape a second world war by retreating to mountains in Speyside and living off the land.[77] In its use of 'science fiction', this novel is unlike any other from the period in form and perspective. It views 'the social and cultural transitions of the early twentieth century as both necessary and lamentable', yet in its attentiveness to specifics of the landscape it shares the environmentalist interests anticipated by the works of Shepherd.[78]

Although he inhabited the edges of the Scottish Renaissance movement, Linklater's marginality enabled him to engage with the cultural cause while mocking it. *White-Maa's Saga* (1929), *Juan in America* (1931) and *Magnus Merriman* (1934) give their own particular twists to urban/rural dichotomies and the idea of homecoming.[79] Chris Baldick defines comic writing as a key feature of 1920s fiction; it is less evident in the Scottish canon (though Compton Mackenzie, writing fiction from 1912 to 1966 is another exception). *Magnus Merriman* (1934) is nevertheless a fine example of the genre which both deflates the pretensions of nationalist cultural politics and reinstates the desire for the return to a homeland in Orkney. *The Men of Ness* (1932) had already visited this terrain in the form of historical fiction. Indeed, historical fiction was an attractive genre for a number of novelists. Naomi Mitchison, suggests Elizabeth Maslen, is a prime example of a writer with a strong political commitment who wrote in such a way as to make her fiction accessible, 'with a keen awareness of an audience beyond her own class, a keen awareness of idiom, and a refusal to "write down"'.[80] With John Buchan, Mitchison produced the great historical novels of this period, including *The Corn King and the Spring Queen* (1931) set in 250 BC; *We Have Been Warned* (1935) which addressed contemporary politics; and *The Blood of Martyrs* (1939) set in Nero's Rome.

Moving from the adventure genre, with a greater postwar ambivalence towards its embodiment of the values of empire and masculinity, Buchan himself turned to different genres. *John Macnab* (1925), *Huntingtower* (1922) and *Castle Gay* (1930) all rewrite adventure escapades in comic form. Their questioning of dominant masculinity and gentle interrogation of identity which situate Buchan within a modernist moment also inflect his historical fiction.[81] *Midwinter* (1923) tells a Jacobite tale, but outside Scotland, in a romance highly expressive of the anxieties and desires of the period. Adventures of Jacobite protagonist, Alastair Maclean, follow a familiar pattern of secret identities, double dealing and espionage, love and betrayal, but the novel centres itself differently through the comic presence of an early Samuel Johnson and in its vision of the spaces of 'Old England', inhabited by the mysterious Midwinter. Offering a world of affinity with nature, natural justice and the folk, the novel allows Buchan to act, David Goldie argues, as 'a Conservative and Unionist who can argue powerfully for Scottish national self-determination'.[82] *Witch Wood* (1927) follows a Scottish tradition of combining the supernatural, religious fanaticism and oral culture but develops a particularly modern interest in the dynamics between the primal and the civilised, between individual repression and the collective unconscious to produce one of the great historical novels of the period and Buchan's own favourite.[83]

The sophistication of such writers in their use of genre fiction and the crossing of boundaries – both political and aesthetic– contributes to a wider interrogation of literary categories that has been fuelled by critical attention to women's writing. For example, a recognition of the 'flexibility of genre fiction' to express different ideological commitments, as in the case of Mitchison, enables Walton to argue that Josephine Tey (born Elizabeth Mackintosh and also writing prose and drama as Gordon Daviot and drama as F. Craigie Howe), used the crime genre to express a particular brand of conservative modernity.[84] By uniting Anna Buchan (O. Douglas) and Catherine Carswell in the category of 'Scottish Modernism and Middlebrow Aesthetics', Juliet Shields suggests there is more of a continuum between middlebrow and modernist fiction than has been acknowledged. Her emphasis on an innovative attention to the everyday in both writers resituates the influence of Carswell and gives overdue attention to the considerable oeuvre of Buchan who, Shields argues, contributed to an 'aesthetics of the ordinary' in the period. While this engagement may have precluded Buchan from being aligned with writers of the Scottish Renaissance, 'O. Douglas' plays her part in the constitution of a 'feminine middlebrow' which explores domestic space, courtship and marriage, class and manners.[85] The highly prolific Nancy Brysson Morrison also sits at the intersections between modernism and middlebrow. Like other women writers of the period, she was publicly active in cultural politics and literary circles but produced fiction that is harder to define. *The Gowk Storm* (1933), however, won her considerable critical acclaim.[86] Rebecca West's most explicitly Scottish novel, *The Judge* (1922), based on her early years of campaigning for the suffrage cause in Edinburgh and combining multiple perspectives with a psychological quest narrative, again offers a new model of how personal and political selves are framed. Fiction by diasporic modernist Claire Spencer is also beginning to receive attention.[87] Recovery work and refreshing new readings thus helps reconfigure the Scottish critical canon.

Scottish interwar fiction is characterised by political commitment, aesthetic energy and generic variety. It continues to inform our understanding of cultural and creative agendas in and beyond Scotland. Authors engage with national and international debate or the politics of person, place and environment. Their writing demonstrates a willingness to innovate and experiment, or to challenge, adapt, and subvert convention. What they share is a confidence in dissecting the aftermath of crisis and pursuing potential renewal on their own terms. For these reasons fiction of this period is still generating exciting critical debate that expands and reshapes our perception of Scotland's literary and geographical contours.

DOCUMENT 5

'Literary Lights'

From *Scottish Scene: The Intelligent Man's Guide to Albyn*, ed. Lewis Grassic Gibbon and Hugh MacDiarmid (Hutchinson, 1934)

Lewis Grassic Gibbon

The new and unknown Scots writer facing the publishing, printing world has the usual chances and mischances to face in a greater measure than his English compeer. Firstly, in almost every case, he must seek publication in London. Scots publishers are surely amongst the sorriest things that enter hell: their publicity methods are as antique as their format, their houses are generally staffed by those who in Bengali circles would write after their names, and as their chief qualification, 'failed B.A.' (or slightly worse, 'M.A. (St. Andrews)'). He must consign his manuscript to alien publishers and the consideration of largely alien readers.

For, however the average Scots writer believes himself Anglicized, his reaction upon the minds of the intelligent English reader (especially of the professional reader) is curiously similar to that produced by the English poems of Dr. Rabindranath Tagore. The prose – or verse – is impeccably correct, the vocabulary is rich and adequate, the English is severe, serene ... But unfortunately it is not English. The English reader is haunted by a sense of something foreign stumbling and hesitating behind this smooth facade of adequate technique: it is as though the writer did not write himself, but translated himself.

Often the Scots writer is quite unaware of this essential foreignness in his work; more often, seeking an adequate word or phrase he hears an echo in an alien tongue that would adorn his meaning with a richness, a clarity and a conciseness impossible in orthodox English. That echo is from Braid Scots, from that variation of the Anglo-Saxon speech which was the tongue of the great Scots civilization, the tongue adopted by the basic Pictish strain in Scotland as its chief literary tool.

Further, it is still in most Scots communities (in one or other Anglicized modification), the speech of bed and board and street and plough, the speech of emotional ecstasy and emotional stress. But it is not genteel. It is to the bourgeois of Scotland coarse and low and common and loutish, a matter for laughter, well enough for hinds and the like, but for the genteel to be quoted in vocal inverted commas. It is a thing rigorously elided from their serious intercourse – not only with the English, but among themselves. It is seriously believed by such stratum of the Scots populace to be an inadequate and pitiful and blunted implement, so that Mr. Eric Linklater delivers *ex cathedra* judgment upon it as 'inadequate to deal with the finer shades of emotion'.

But for the truly Scots writer it remains a real and a haunting thing, even while he tries his best to forget its existence and to write as a good Englishman. In this lies his tragedy. He has to learn to write in English: he is like a Chinese scholar spending the best years of his life in the mystic mazes of the pictographs, and emerging so exhausted from the travail that originality of research or experiment with his new tool is denied him. Consequently, the free and anarchistic experimentations of the progressive members of a free and homogeneous literary cultus are denied him. Nearly every Scots writer of the past writing in orthodox English has been not only incurably second-rate, but incurably behind the times. The Scots discovery of photographic realism in novel-writing, for example – I refer to *Hatter's Castle*, not the very different *House with the Green Shutters* – post-dated the great French and English realists some thirty or forty years. But to the Scot Dr. Cronin's work appeared a very new and terrifying and fascinating thing indeed; to the English public, astounded that anything faintly savouring of accuracy, photographic or otherwise, should come out of Scotland, it was equally amazing. At such rate of progress among the Anglo-Scots one may guess that in another fifty years or so a Scots Virginia Woolf will astound the Scottish scene, a Scots James Joyce electrify it. To expect contemporary experimentation from the Anglo-Scots themselves appears equivalent to expecting a Central African savage in possession of a Birmingham kite to prove capable of inventing a helicopter.

Consciousness of this inferiority of cultural position within the English tradition is a very definite thing among the younger generation of Anglo-Scots writers of to-day. Their most characteristic organ, *The Modern Scot*, is a constant reiteration of protest. Owned and edited by one of those genial Englishmen in search of a revolution who have added to the gaiety of nations from Ireland to Uganda, *The Modern Scot* has set itself, strictly within the English tradition, to out-English the English. As one who on a lonely road doth walk with fear and dread, very conscious of the frightful fiend who close behind doth tread, it marches always a full yard ahead of extremist English Opinion – casting the while an anxious backward glance. It decries the children of 'naturalism' with a praiseworthy but unnatural passion, championing in their place, with a commendable care for pathology, the idiot offspring begat on the modern literary scene in such numbers from the incestuous unions of Strindberg and Dr. Freud. It is eclectic to quite an obscure degree, is incapable of an article that does not quote either Proust or Paul Einzig, and raises an approving voice in praise of the joyous, if infantile tauromachie obsessions of Mr. Roy Campbell. Its motif-note, indeed, is literary Fascism – to the unimpassioned, if astounded, eye it would seem as if all the Fascist undergraduates of Scotland these days were hastening, in pimples and a passion for sophistication, to relieve themselves of a diarrhoetic Johnsonese in the appropriate privy of *The Modern Scot*. The entire being of the periodical, however, is rather an exhibitory, or sanitary, exercise, than a contributing factor towards authentic experimentation.

With a few exceptions presently to be noted, there is not the remotest reason why the majority of modern Scots writers should be considered Scots at all. The protagonists of the Scots literary Renaissance deny this. They hold, for example, that Norman Douglas or Compton Mackenzie, though they write in English and deal with un-Scottish themes, have nevertheless an essential Scottishness which differentiates them from the native English writer. In exactly the same manner, so had Joseph Conrad an essential Polishness. But few (except for the purpose of exchanging diplomatic courtesies) pretend that Conrad was a Polish writer, to be judged as a Pole. He wrote brilliantly and strangely and beautifully in English; so does Mr. Norman Douglas, so does Mr. Cunninghame Graham. Mention of the latter is peculiarly to the point. Mr. Graham has, I believe, a large modicum of Spanish blood in his veins, he writes much of Spanish or Spanish-American subjects, and his word-manipulation is most certainly not of the English orthodox. But we have still to hear of Spain acclaiming him one of her great essayists.

The admirable plays of Dr. James Bridie – such as *Tobias and the Angel* or the unforgettable *Jonah and the Whale* – have been hailed in Scotland as examples of modern Scots drama. They are excellent examples – but not of Scots drama. They are examples of how an Englishman, hailing from Scotshire, can write excellent plays. Mr. Edwin Muir writes poems of great loveliness; so does Mr. Roy Campbell; both are of Scots origin: ergo, great Scots poetry. Dumas père had negro blood in his veins and wrote excellent romances in French: ergo, great negro romance.

That such a position is untenable is obvious. Modern Scotland, the Gaels included, is a nation almost entirely lacking a Scottish literary output. There are innumerable versifiers, ranging from Dr. Charles Murray downwards to Mr. W. H. Hamilton (he of the eldritch glamour); there are hardly more than two poets; and there is no novelist at all. To be oneself a provincial or an alien and to write a book in which the characters infect one's literary medium with a tincture of dialect is not to assist in the creation or continuation of a separate national literature – else Eden Philpotts proves the great, un-English soul of Dartmoor and Tennyson in 'The Northern Farmer' was advocating Home Rule for Yorkshire. The chief Literary Lights which modern Scotland claims to light up the scene of her night are in reality no more than the commendable writers of the interesting English county of Scotshire.

Let us consider Mrs. Naomi Mitchison. She is the one writer of the 'historical' novel in modern English who commands respect and enthusiasm. Her pages are aglow with a fine essence of apprehended light. *The Conquered* and *Black Sparta* light up the human spirit very vividly and truly. And they are in no sense Scots books though written by a Scotswoman. Their author once wrote that had she had the command of Scots speech possessed by Lewis Grassic Gibbon she would have written her Spartan books (at least) in Scots. Had she done so they would undoubtedly have been worse novels – but they would have been Scots books by a Scots writer, just as the worst of Finnish peasant studies are Finnish peasant studies, infinitesimal by the side of Dostoieffski or Tolstoi, but un-Russian in language and content.

Another writer hailed as a great Scots novelist is Mr. Neil Gunn. The acclamation is mistaken. Mr. Gunn is a brilliant novelist from Scotshire who chooses his home county as the scene of his tales. His technique is almost unique among the writers of Scotshire in its effortless efficiency: he moulds beauty in unforgettable phrases – there are things in *The Lost Glen* and *Sun Circle* comparable to the best in the imaginative literature of any school or country. He has probably scarcely yet set out on his scaling of the heights. [...] But they are not the heights of Scots literature; they are not even the pedestrian levels. More in Gunn than in any other contemporary Anglo-Scot (with the exception, perhaps, of George Blake, in a very different category from Gunn, and the finest of the Anglo-Scots realists) the reader seems to sense the haunting foreignness in an orthodox English; he is the greatest loss to itself Scottish literature has suffered in this century. Had his language been Gaelic or Scots there is no doubt of the space or place he would have occupied in even such short study as this. Writing in orthodox English, he is merely a brilliantly unorthodox Englishman.

Once again, a writer who has been hailed as distinctively Scots, Mrs. Willa Muir. So far she has written only two novels – *Imagined Corners* and *Mrs. Ritchie* – and both show a depth and distinction, a sheer and splendidly unwomanly power which stir even the most jaded of enthusiasms. They suffer, perhaps, from the author's learnings and erudition-gatherings in the dull hag-forests of the German psychoanalysts, just as Neil Gunn's *Sun Circle* suffers from a crude and out-dated concept of history and the historical processes. But that psychoanalyst obsession is the common leprosy over all contemporary European imaginative literature, and Mrs. Muir's strength of spirit and true integrity of vision may yet transcend it. She has promise of becoming a great artist. But a great English artist. The fact that she is Scots herself and deals with Scots scenes and Scots characters is (to drive home the point *ad nauseam*) entirely irrelevant from the point of view of Scots literature: if she were a modern Mexican writing in Spanish and her scene was Mexico and her peasants spoke bastardized Nahuatl, would we call it a triumph of Aztec letters?

Mr. John Buchan has been called the Dean of Scots letters. Mr. Buchan writes mildly exhilarating romances in the vein of the late Rider Haggard (though without either Haggard's magnificent poetic flair or his imaginative grasp), commendable essays on a variety of topics, uninspired if competent biographies of Sir Walter Scott, the Marquis of Montrose, and the like distinguished cadaver-litter on the ancient Scottish scene. He writes it all in a competent, skilful and depressing English: when his characters talk Scots they do it in suitable inverted commas; and such characters as do talk Scots are always the simple, the proletarian, the slightly ludicrous characters.

Mr. Buchan represents no more than the great, sound, bourgeois heart of Scotshire. He has written nothing which has the least connection with Scots literature except a few pieces of verse – if verse has any connection with literature. In compiling *The Northern Muse*, however, a representative anthology of Scots 'Vernacular' poetry, he turned aside from other pursuits to render a real service to what might have been his native literary language. Yet even in that service he could envisage Braid Scots as being only a 'vernacular,' the tongue of a home-reared slave.

Mrs. Catherine Carswell is among the most interesting of the Anglo-Scots. Her *Life of Robert Burns* was one of the most unique and innocently mendacious studies of the subject ever attempted; her *Savage Pilgrimage* (which met such a sad fate in the teeth of the enraged Mr. Middleton Murry) contributed as little to our knowledge of D. H. Lawrence as it contributed greatly to our knowledge of its author. With such a personality and philosophy much more may be heard of Catherine Carswell: that the philosophy of her school appears a strange and repulsive one, as strange an aberration of the human spirit as history has ever known, merely adds a pathological to a genuine literary interest in her development. Scots letters represses its death-rattle to wave her on with a regretful relief.

Prior to writing *Hatter's Castle, Three Loves*, and *Grand Canary* Dr. A. J. Cronin descended five hundred collieries on tours of inspection. As a consequence he is notable for a kind of inky immensity, and an interestingly Latinized barbarization of the English language. While *Hatter's Castle* had a Scots scene its characters were gnomes from the sooty depths of the less salubrious regions of myth: though acclaimed as great and realistic portraits. In *Three Loves* Dr. Cronin showed a disposition to prove uneasy on the Scottish scene; in *Grand Canary* he escaped it entirely, taking his place (probably a permanent place) among the English writers of an order comparable to Miss Mannin or Mr. Gilbert Frankau. He is also the author of a history of aneurism.

Sir James George Frazer, a Scotsman by birth, is the author of the immense *Golden Bough*, a collection of anthropological studies. The author's methods of correlation have been as crude and unregulated as his industry and the cultivation of his erudition have been immense. The confusion of savage and primitive states of culture commenced by Tylor and his school has been carried to excess in the works of Sir J. G. Frazer. From the point of view of the social historian attempting to disentangle the story of man's coming and growth upon this planet he is one of the most calamitous phenomena in modern research: he has smashed in the ruin of pre-history with a coal-hammer, collected every brick disclosed when the dust settled on the debris, and then labelled the exhibits with the assiduous industry of a literary ant. His pleasing literary style in that labelling is in orthodox English.

Mr. Eric Linklater is a lost Norseman with a disposition to go Berserk amidst the unfamiliar trappings of literary civilization. This disposition came to a head in *The Men of Ness*, a story of the vikings and their raids into the regions of stern guffawdom and unpronunciability. It is a pity that this disposition should be let loose by the author of *Juan in America*, – in the genre of Mark Twain's *Tramp Abroad*, and one of the most acute and amusing picaresque studies ever perpetrated by the literary farceur. It would be even more regrettable if Mr. Linklater hampered his genius by an uneasy adherence to a so-called Scots literary Renaissance.

CHAPTER EIGHT

From the Second World War to the 1970s

Eleanor Bell

While the immediate postwar period has often been considered a relatively quiet time in the development of the Scottish novel, it was in fact a productive period even if, undeservedly, many texts have since fallen out of print and therefore out of public awareness.[1] Perhaps unsurprisingly, much postwar Scottish fiction was characterised by a strong focus on individualism and introspection, rather than on 'state of the nation' concerns. As Douglas Gifford has pointed out, 'Post-war Scottish novelists found it even more difficult than their "Renaissance" predecessors to present a positive picture of Scotland in terms of their central characters and situations. There are no Chris Guthries, no heroic figures [...]'.[2] A shift began to take place in the Scottish novel, one which often involved a testing of moral boundaries, whether in terms of formal experimentalism, unsettling engagements with class, sexuality or gender expectations; in some cases a mixture of all of these. A commonality found among many Scottish novels of the postwar period, therefore, is a satiric upturning of accepted convention; one which in turn pushes the reader to self-reflexively examine their own engagement with the text. In its consideration of such concerns, this chapter will suggest that the work of many writers from the postwar to the 1970s, while diverse in their range of literary styles and approaches, nonetheless collectively contributed to generating a disruptive spirit; one which subsequently opened out the possibilities of literary representation in significant ways, engaging with philosophical ideas of the self and, at times, testing the very limits of the novel itself.

A common structure, particularly in urban fiction, was the *Bildungsroman*, including novels such as Edward Gaiten's *Dance of the Apprentices* (1948), J. F. Hendry's *Fernie Brae: A Scottish Childhood* (1947), and Gordon Williams's *From Scenes Like These* (1968). As Liam McIlvanney has pointed out, 'the story of a sensitive youth negotiating the path to maturity in a brutal and intractable environment is a venerable stable of urban fiction, and Glasgow writers have used it widely'.³ Recurrent throughout J. F. Hendry's *Fernie Brae*, for example, is a tension between the 'colossal plunder of Nature'⁴ and the mechanistic, brutal reality of industrialism. There are clear, Joycean connections with Glasgow as a place of paralysis – 'something symbolic clung to the figure of the stone-mason at the corner, who broke up all forms of the stone that was paralysing and the throttling the life of the city'⁵ – and exile – 'Why had he spoken as he did, or run away from her and himself, making himself a permanent exile even in his own country?'⁶ The central character, David Macrae, enrols as a student at Glasgow University, but even there finds his intellectual horizons limited. Alluding to the motifs of Glasgow's Coat of Arms ('the bell that never rang, the fish that never swam, the bird that never flew, the tree that never grew'), David similarly finds that the university is a place of stasis – 'like the great bell in the tower, its clapper silenced, the University hung suspended over the city, a shell'.⁷ Towards the end of the novel Macrae and his friend Maclean debate whether, philosophically, the future lies at the national or the individual level:

> 'We must recover a sense of nationhood,' said Maclean, 'like Ireland.'
> 'I think we must first recover a sense of identity,' said David. 'Until we know who we are, there's little use in finding out what we are.'⁸

In the end, for David, leaving Glasgow is the only option: 'only the world is wide enough.'⁹

George Friel's fiction also explores this postwar disillusionment through poetic, yet often bleak depictions of Glasgow in novels including *The Bank of Time* (1959), *The Boy Who Wanted Peace* (1964), *Grace and Miss Partridge* (1969) and *Mr Alfred M.A.* (1972). Friel's fiction describes the stark desolation of industrial wastelands, reflecting the corresponding lived experience of the city's inhabitants. As he commented in interview in 1972, 'if you play Mr Glasgow and that it's a fine warm-hearted city then you are kidding yourself, kidding the public, and pledging the future to no reform'.¹⁰ Alongside this concern with exposing the underside of the city, Friel also interweaves his own experiences of being a schoolteacher. As with Hendry's *Fernie Brae*, there are Joycean references to paralysis within the educational system, as well as echoes of the work of Beckett. It is worth noting that four of Friel's novels were published outside of Scotland by Calder & Boyars, whose list also included Beckett, Eugène Ionesco, and Henry Miller.

Similar investigative, symbiotic journeys into the heart of the self and the city can be found in Archie Hind's *The Dear Green Place* (1966). Its protagonist, Mat Craig, is a writer who becomes obsessed with trying to place meaning on his existence, yet often this plight takes him to extremes of thought which leave him in a state of intellectual paralysis. There is a recurring tension in the novel between Glasgow as a 'dear, green' place as depicted in the City's Coat of Arms (a recurring motif throughout the novel), versus as a place of stasis and dereliction:

> Belongs! Belongs! [...] A dirty, filthy city. But with a kind of ample vitality which has created fame for her slums and her industry and given her moral and spiritual existence a tight ingrown wealth, like a human character, limited, but with a direct brutish strength, almost warm.[11]

Towards the end of the novel, overcome with existential anxiety, Mat destroys his manuscript in a fit of despair. Despite his 'lust for creation',[12] his domestic and environmental circumstances have coalesced against him, restricting his agency.

William McIlvanney's first novel, *Remedy is None*, also published in 1966, shared some similarities with *The Dear Green Place* in terms of its intense focus on interiority, small moments of lived experience explored in intense detail, as well of the oddities of everyday existence. After receiving a telegram, telling him about his father's impending death, the central character, Charlie Grant, returns home from university, though with a newly developed intellectual awareness of the stifling nature of his family life. The novel contains a series of philosophical, abstract reflections on the strangeness of everyday life, moments of quiet revelation, whilst also tracing Grant's downward spiral into estrangement from the world around him, to the extent that he ends up in prison for killing his mother's second husband ('Nobody can help me now. Ah've made my own hell. An it's private').[13] Such signs of self-revulsion are also found in the central character of *A Gift from Nessus* (1968). In this novel, however, the ending is more optimistic, with Eddie Cameron acknowledging that he must find a way of reconciling himself with the trappings of his conventional life:

> Somewhere in all the bright assurances he was lost in a private darkness, led on by a recurrent dream of more than he was. What means did he have to fulfil it? A family, a job, a house, a patch of garden. Suburban man's estate. With that he had somehow to contain and satisfy a hunger

that seemed grotesquely out of keeping with its habitat – a brontosaurus in suburbia. He would try.[14]

These themes with what McIlvanney describes as the 'tug o' war between self and community' are also found throughout his later fiction.[15] That 'tug o' war' is central to McIlvanney's works of the 1970s, including *Docherty* (1975), which won the Whitbread Award for the best fiction of 1975, and the first of his series of crime novels, *Laidlaw* (1977). As McIlvanney points out, the rationale for *Docherty* was 'to write a book that would create a kind of literary genealogy for the people I came from, the people whose memorials were parish registers. Since their history was largely silence, I would be constructing a communal fabric of myth'.[16] Set in the fictional mining town of Graithnock, it explores the shifting civic values of the community over several generations through the lens of Tam Docherty and his sons. As Keith Dixon has pointed out, the novel 'is a sort of urban *Sunset Song*, an elegy to the communal spirit and humour of the pre-First World War working-class, and like Grassic Gibbon's novel, a salute to a dying ethic'.[17] In its representation of working-class dispossession, often through the use of Scots, McIlvanney can be seen as an important influence on later writers, such as James Kelman and Irvine Welsh: 'Us an' folk like us hiv goat the nearest thing tae nothin' in this world. A' that filters doon tae us is shite [...]. The only thing we've goat is wan another.'[18] It is, however, McIlvanney's crime fiction for which he is now most well known, often commonly cited as the 'godfather of tartan noir' for his contributions to the genre. In *Laidlaw*, the first in the trilogy following Detective Inspector Jack Laidlaw, we see that, like Mat Craig, he is, in part, a self-selected outsider figure: 'a violent man who hated violence, a believer in fidelity who was unfaithful'; a contemplative, existential thinker who, in his desk drawer keeps 'Kierkegaard, Camus and Unamuno, like caches of alcohol [...]. He knew nothing to do but inhabit the paradoxes'.[19]

Another interesting crime writer of the period and early exponent of 'tartan noir' is Hugh C. Rae. While Rae also published romantic historical novels and thrillers under other names, his crime novels were published under his own name. (Romance novels were published under the name Jessica Stirling; he also wrote as Robert Crawford, R. B. Houston and James Albany.) His first novel, *Skinner* (1960), was based on the multiple murderer Peter Manuel, followed by *Night Pillow* (1967), *A Few Small Bones* (1968), *The Saturday Epic* (1970), *The Marksman*

(1971) and *The Shooting Gallery* (1972). The shocking violence explored in these novels is also an exposé of the darker side of industrial Glasgow, such as the examination of the motivations behind gang violence in *The Saturday Epic*.

Some of the most rebellious writers of the period are also those who consciously chose to separate themselves from Scotland. Such writers include James Kennaway, Alan Sharp and Alexander Trocchi. James Kennaway spent most of his short life (dying at the age of forty) living away from Scotland, publishing six novels during his lifetime, *Tunes of Glory* (1956), *Household Ghosts* (1961), *The Bells of Shoreditch* (1963), *The Mindbenders* (1963), *Some Gorgeous Accident* (1967) and *The Cost of Living Like This* (1969). Focusing on the central character, Jock Sinclair, *Tunes of Glory* explores power struggles within the peacetime barracks of a Highland Battalion. The closed environment of the barracks creates the space for investigation of psychological interiority, tracing the behaviour of the men as they attempt to adjust back to conventional life. The novel, however, explores the difficulties of this, the disconnect of the soldiers from themselves, as well as those around them. The irony of the novel's title further emphasises this dissociation. In his later novels, Kennaway's prose became increasingly pared down. As Glenda Norquay points out, 'the increasing brevity of style represents in itself an anarchic refusal to be controlled, in many ways more successful than the rebellious characters within his work'.[20]

Sharp's *A Green Tree in Gedde* (1965) explores the deep connection to place: generational connections to Greenock are set against the need to explore the wider, radical world of 1960s Britain opening up at the time. In doing so, the novel juxtaposes the traditional with the subversive, challenging and unsettling the reader by depicting characters whose actions and motivations are often unpredictable, at times highly controversial: the recurring theme of incest throughout the novel, for example, is never discussed in problematic terms, or viewed as scandalous. The rebellious characters in the novel often act with emotional detachment, resisting the norms of their age, with characters such as Cuffee more than ready to embrace the beginnings of 'swinging' London. While Moseby stays at home in Greenock, he also feels trapped by his circumstances in doing so: 'And quite simply he did not care about Edna and the child, looking out of the little cell at the metamorphic rock felt utterly weary of the whole pomp of pregnancy and removed beyond all reaching from its melodrama.'[21] Moseby then goes on to reflect on the 'West Coast joke': 'did you hear about the lonely prisoner; he was in his 'sel'.' For Moseby this prompts further reflection:

> And it was about now that he began to understand what being West Coast Scottish meant, with its preoccupations with guilt and sex and sin and its image of man as a monster, hiding his monsterdom from his fellow monsters.[22]

Alexander Trocchi's work was also deeply connected with themes of rebellion, controversy, and 'monstrosity'.[23] Reflecting the years he spent in Paris after leaving Glasgow, *Cain's Book* (1960) brought together existentialist ideas with the French anti-novel, or *nouveau roman*.[24] *Cain's Book* is a *roman à clef* in which the protagonist, Joe Necchi, is writing a novel also called *Cain's Book*. The novel therefore explores the various challenges faced while writing the novel 'itself', in quite metafictional ways. In *Cain's Book*, Necchi is obsessed with producing a text of literary value, yet is also full of self-doubt, with an openness of vision that fundamentally hinders him from recording his thoughts and ideas in a structured way. We are also reminded on several occasions that there is no clear story to tell, that the narrative in part emerges out of chance and arbitrarily selected memories:

> Even now I'm the victim of my own behaviour: each remembered fact of the congeries of facts out of which in my more or less continuous way I construct this document is an *act of remembrance*, a selected fiction, and I am the agent also of what is unremembered, rejected.[25]

Cain's Book therefore refuses a clear direction, or any attempt at closure, in preference to being 'true' to the strangeness of existence. While the novel contains an existentialist quest for authenticity, of writing a text (which is also, self-consciously, *Cain's Book*, the novel we are reading) that will be true to its age, at the heart of the novel is also a radical rejection of conventional society and a connection with the Situationist ideas that Trocchi was involved with at this time: 'My friends will know what I mean when I say that I deplore our contemporary industrial writers. Let them dedicate a year to pinball and think again.'[26] Commenting on the value and legacy of Trocchi's contribution to Scottish literature, Edwin Morgan has written that he was 'a Glaswegian risk-taker', one who helped to change the boundaries of what was possible within the novel at the time: 'he ripped the tent-flap apart – I don't want to see it – oh yes you do – look – look.'[27]

While a great deal of Scottish postwar fiction focused on the changing circumstances of the individual in the urban landscape, and the wider industrial West of Scotland, there are a number of important exceptions. Jessie Kesson's novels include *The White Bird Passes* (1958), *Glitter of Mica* (1963) and *Another Time, Another Place* (1983) and *Where the Apple Ripens* (1985). While Kesson moved to London in the early 1950s, much of her work is autobiographical, reflecting her early, difficult upbringing in Elgin. As Alan Bold has noted:

> The exploration of childhood is a common enough theme in Scottish literature but Jessie Kesson brought some new variations to it. For one thing she invested a difficult life with dignity; for another, she resisted the temptation to over-sugar the narrative pill and made the general reader swallow some unpalatable facts of life.[28]

Iain Crichton Smith's *Consider the Lilies* (1968) engages with tensions between religion, morality and the Highland Clearances from an individualistic perspective; a testing of religious conviction when the Church fails to intervene to help an elderly woman, Mrs Scott, being evicted from her home by Patrick Sellar, the Duke of Sutherland's factor (a historical figure who also reappears in John McGrath's 1973 play *The Cheviot, the Stag and the Black, Black Oil*). 'As far as he was concerned, she was a disposable object. As far as she was concerned, he was a stranger and to be treated with hospitality even though she was old.'[29] Ironically, it is the character of Donald Macleod, the atheist, who intervenes to protect Mrs Scott. As Isobel Murray has pointed out, 'just as the Highland Clearances can be seen as one example of man's inhumanity to man, so Scottish Calvinism for Crichton Smith is only one example of all the ideologies which people can and do use to shelter behind'.[30] Smith also published short novels in Gaelic at this period (as Iain Mac a' Ghobhainn). In particular, *An t-Aonaran* (1976), comprising seventeen untitled chapters, is a first-person exploration of a widowed, retired teacher Charles, whose welcome of a hermit to his village, distrusted by the villagers, starts well, but falters while his friend Dougie, initially distrusting, comes to be more welcoming. When Charles drives the hermit away, the rest of the community reject him. Another key Gaelic novel of this period is Tormod Caimbeul's *Deireadh an Fhoghair* (1979) following three elderly friends over two days, reminiscing about people who have gone and wondering what is to come of them.

Orcadian George Mackay Brown was primarily known as a poet (*Loaves and Fishes* (1959) and *The Year of the Whale* (1965)); then, as a writer of short stories (*A Calendar of Love* (1967) and *A Time to Keep* (1969)); before gaining recognition for his novels, including *Greenvoe* (1972) and *Magnus* (1973). Brown's work concentrates on the deep history of Orkney; as Douglas Gifford has pointed out, 'the entire symbolism of his work is consistent, moving in a slow circle as it does round the Cathedral of St Magnus in Kirkwall – and not just moving in space, but in time also'.[31]

Eric Linklater was another who had strong connections with Orkney. While many of his major novels were published in the first half of the twentieth century, including *Poet's Pub* (1929) and *Magnus Merriman* (1934), key postwar texts include *The Merry Muse* (1959), *A Man over Forty* (1964) and *A Terrible Freedom* (1966); the latter two explore subconscious dreamscapes with a new seriousness, on 'that metaphysical enquiry about man's final spiritual self, underlying the comic behaviour which had so occupied his satiric view hitherto'.[32]

Among the most prolific writers of the postwar period was Robin Jenkins, who published his first novel, *So Gaily Sings the Lark* in 1950, following it with more than thirty novels in the following five decades. His works throughout the fifties appeared in quick succession, including *Happy for the Child* (1953), *The Thistle and the Grail* (1954), *The Cone Gatherers* (1955), *Guests of War* (1956), *The Missionaries* (1957), *The Changeling* (1958) and *Love Is a Fervent Fire* (1959). Although well known for *The Cone Gatherers* (1955), as Gavin Wallace and Douglas Gifford have pointed out, 'Little is known about the man behind the writer':

> He kept himself at a distance from publishers, journalists, or other writers, and admirers. He was never anxious to appear at 'meet the author' sessions, although he would give interviews – on fiction, rarely on himself. Nor did he review other people's novels, on the ground that it was hard enough to write his own.[33]

Like many of his fictional outsider figures, Jenkins also preferred to have a sense of unreachability. Many of Jenkins's novels contain a deep moral seriousness, asking challenging questions about the nature of love, human connection, the purpose of existence: themes which shape the surface banality of many of his plots. *The Thistle and the Grail*, for example, is a seemingly light-hearted novel about football in small town West of Scotland; the 'grail' refers not only to the importance of winning the football cup, but also the search for a deeper human connection, and a self-consciousness about the complexities that such connections entail. *A Very Scotch Affair* (1968) also fluctuates between the comic and the serious, exploring themes of conscience and betrayal. In *The Changeling*, Glasgow schoolteacher Charlie Forbes attempts to 'rescue' one of pupils, Tom Curdie, from his life of poverty and squalor, though the consequences of this are shocking and catastrophic (similar to the tragic ending of *The Cone Gatherers*). As Alistair Thomson has pointed out, Jenkins consistently 'makes his novels end with a beginning from which the character goes forward with a humbler but stronger purpose [...]. Awareness of, responsiveness to, the condition of humanity is not a gentle, effete tolerance, but an active, difficult discipline.'[34]

While many of Jenkins's novels have Scottish settings and concerns, one of the most interesting periods of his career reflects his years spent abroad, teaching in Afghanistan (1957–1959), Barcelona (1959–1961) and North Borneo (1963–1968). *Dust on the Paw* (1961), for example, reflects Jenkins's time in Afghanistan. The novel examines the hypocrisies and contradictions of western attitudes within the expatriate community, largely through a white, male lens. In doing so the novel takes an ironic swipe at masculinity through the character of Howard Moffat, an entitled 'tubby and fat-bottomed' professor of English at the local university.[35] The most forceful aspect of the novel is its exposé of deep-rooted fears surrounding cultural 'respectability', especially surrounding Moffat's continual mistreatment of Abdul Wahab, a local Afghan teacher. Over the space of almost four hundred pages, Moffat becomes increasingly recognisant of his unconscious bias, gradually confronted with his previously buried layers of prejudice. The novel thus presents a piercing critique of the lingering imperialist mindset within the local white British culture. Throughout the novel Wahab grows increasingly aware of and intolerant towards this subjugation. A recurring motif throughout the novel is therefore that of being 'dust on the lion's paw', something that Wahab becomes assertively vocal about:

> I am a simple Afghan. Therefore I represent many millions of my countrymen. To treat me as if I did not matter, as if I were of as little consequence as a donkey, as if I was dust on the lion's paw, is therefore to treat most of my nation as such. This I must never tolerate.[36]

Despite its humorous nature, verging on slapstick at times, the critique of racial and cultural hierarchies in the novel were clearly provocative for its cultural moment.

Writing in 1970, Muriel Spark suggested that 'the only effective art of our particular time is the satirical, the harsh and witty, the ironic and derisive':[37] discussing the role of literature in her lecture on 'The Desegregation of Art', she commented that

> To bring about a mental environment of honesty and self-knowledge, a sense of the absurd and a general looking-lively to defend ourselves from the ridiculous oppressions of our time, and above all to entertain us in the process, has become the special calling of arts and letters.[38]

Spark's intense focus on the interconnections between the comical and the absurd, her detailed focus on the art of ridicule, can be seen from the publication of her first novel, *The Comforters* (1957), quickly followed by *Robinson* (1958), *Memento Mori* (1959), *The Ballad of Peckham Rye* (1960) and *The Bachelors* (1960). From these earliest novels onwards, Spark claimed her own terrain for the novel form, making a clean break with realist literary conventions of the time. Her characters are uniquely 'Sparkian': quirky outsider figures who continually push against the expectations of the unsuspecting reader. Consequently, the novels are often playful, yet layered with cerebral puzzles and complications. In *The Comforters*, for example, the central character, Caroline Rose, is working on a book on 'Form in the Modern Novel', but she becomes haunted by 'The Typing Ghost'. Caroline hears typewriter keys tapping in her head, which, we soon realise, is her own narrative being created and controlled simultaneously within her mind, yet also outwith her control. It seems that the 'ghost' is in fact the ultimate controller of what appears on the page, also therefore responsible for bringing together the other unlikely elements of the story, including a grandmother involved in a diamond smuggling ring (where the jewels are surreptitiously concealed in loaves of bread). It is often easy for the reader to become lost within Spark's texts, with their many layers of bizarre characters and plot twists. In this way, her novels often self-consciously question the extent to which art can mirror life and, perhaps most important of all in Spark's work, who is in ultimate control of the narrative.

Spark is perhaps best known for *The Prime of Miss Jean Brodie* (1961). In this novel, an Edinburgh school teacher carefully selects her 'set', that is, the chosen group of pupils whom she can most easily mould to her own views and whims (and whose parents will be the most unsuspecting of these). Throughout the novel there is a strong concern with power and control: not only Miss Brodie's dominance of her girls and their education, but also, as we see with Sandy Stranger's eventual betrayal of Miss Brodie, with larger questions of narrative control. The novel ends with the image of Sandy Stranger, now a nun known as Sister Helena of the Transfiguration, clutching 'the bars of her grille', a final image of her own resulting entrapment and estrangement, just as Brodie has ultimately been punished for aspiring to a God-like status. In much of her work Spark demonstrated clear allegiances with writers of the *nouveau roman* in France at the time.[39] For Alain Robbe-Grillet, for example,

> The meaning of the world around us can no longer be considered as other than fragmentary, temporary, and even contradictory, and is always in dispute. How can a work of art set out to illustrate any sort of meaning which is known in advance? The modern novel is an enquiry, but an enquiry which creates its own meaning as it goes along.[40]

In an interview by Martin McQuillan Spark has stated that:

> I was thinking the same thoughts that they were thinking, people like Robbe-Grillet. We were influenced by the same, breathing the same informed air. So I naturally would have a bent towards the *nouveau roman* but in fact I was very influenced by Robbe-Grillet.[41]

This concern with disruption and transgression of literary boundaries continued through her work, with twenty-two novels in total published from 1957 to 2004. As many critics have attested, her metafictional, experimental approach to writing fiction helped to reset the boundaries of what was possible in postwar Scottish, and wider British, fiction. In *The Driver's Seat* (1970), for example, the novel follows the central character, Lise, in her journey to Italy where, we are told on the first page, she will die. We know very little about this character, very few clues are provided as to her background or identity. The reader, however, follows Lise on the quest towards death, though in doing so the novel often raises more questions than it answers. While we seek a form of closure at the end of the novel, an explanation for the absurdity of her actions and behaviour, this is finally denied to us. The question prompted self-consciously by the novel's title is, therefore, who is really in control of this narrative? In the end, despite the minutiae of her planning, Lise does not have final control over her death. Closure is also denied to the reader: the clues do not cohere, there is no rationality as to what occurs. *The Driver's Seat* has therefore been read by some critics as a form of detective fiction, though the mystery at the heart of the story is more cryptic and metaphysical than might be expected in the genre.[42] In the end we are left pondering why does Lise want to die? It is a whydunnit, rather than a whodunnit, with the journey towards Lise's murder also being complicated by a variety of absurd characters, some of whom are clearly dropped in as figurative red herrings along the way to fox the reader and further complicate the narrative.

In his obituary of Elspeth Davie (1918–1995), Christopher Sinclair-Stevenson wrote that

> One's first impression of Elspeth Davie was of her smallness; the second of her extreme shyness. One of her friends described her as looking like a mouse, neat, nervous, undeniably small. She could also have been mistaken for one of Miss Jean Brodie's young girls, a Morningside lady mingling the intellectual with the tearoom. This would have been an error.[43]

Often compared to Muriel Spark, Davie's writing is similarly minimalist, rich in possible interpretation. Her work is more concerned with the metaphysical, the philosophical and the avant-garde than with a colourfully developed, realist plot. Despite publishing four novels and five collections of short stories from 1965 to 1992, her work has received little critical attention. Part of the reason for Davie's neglect is that her experimentalism resists clear categorisation, which has made it difficult to incorporate into a wider Scottish or British literary picture. As with Spark, in order to understand the complexities of her work in more detail, it is perhaps more helpful to establish connections with French writing and the *nouveau roman* in particular.

Creating a Scene (1971) focuses on an art teacher, Foley, and a group of his final-year pupils who are on the brink of sensing new forms of freedom. Often dialogue is omitted, presentation pared down to the bare minimum in order to push forward ideas, albeit in quite abstract ways. The relationships between characters are often blurred and strange, with a strong sense of disconnection between them. Dialogue is disjointed, where characters often seem more focused on their own trains of thought or subconscious perceptions. As other critics have observed, Davie's fiction is often concerned with such 'gaps' that represent the lack of communication between people at more philosophical levels.[44] In its concerns with abstraction and detachment, the novel continually resists readers' expectations and could be defined as metafictional, in that it is conscious of the gaps within storytelling at the same time as the story is unfolding: it forces the reader to become increasingly self-conscious of the text as artifice. As John Sturrock writes, this is a key aspect of the *nouveau roman*, that it plays with the very notion of textual expectations, reminding readers not to become too comfortable or complacent in their comprehension of the text:

> Hostile critics have been furious at being deprived of 'plot' and 'characters'. Sometimes it has seemed that the novels they are complaining of contain nothing at all, no events and no human beings. Of course they contain both, all that has changed is their presentation.[45]

It is in interesting to note that Davie (as with Friel, as noted earlier) was published by John Calder, also a key publisher of many of the *nouveau roman* writers, including Alain Robbe-Grillet, Marguerite Duras and Nathalie Sarraute. Commenting on Davie's work in particular, Calder noted that she was an example of 'still waters going deep'.[46]

While Naomi Mitchison is best known for her fictional engagements with classical mythology and history from the 1920s through to the 1940s (including *The Conquered* (1923), *The Corn King and the Spring Queen* (1931) and *The Bull Calves* (1947)), as Gill Benton has noted, Mitchison's 'retreat into the Scottish Highlands gradually ended in the 1950s' when she became increasingly politically active:

> She was particularly concerned about hydrogen bombs as NATO installations proliferated in Scotland. In 1959 [Mitchison] was a major speaker at a mass Nuclear Disarmament rally, and in 1961 in Glasgow she helped lead a march of 10000 people against the Polaris missile base planned for the Holy Loch.[47]

Mitchison's growing interest in scientific and technological development at this point are also evident in her series of science fiction novels, including *Memoirs of a Spacewoman* (1962), *Solution Three* (1975) and *Not by Bread Alone* (1983). *Memoirs of Spacewoman* was particularly experimental for its cultural moment, testing the boundaries of gender and sexuality through the representation of human reproduction with alien life forms. As Jenni Calder has pointed out, 'In her historical fiction she had transplanted human emotions and connections back in time. Now she was placing them in the future, which fascinatingly expanded the possibilities for unusual liaisons.'[48] In the same year, Mitchison also edited a large, four-hundred-page collection of articles on politics, science, psychology and contemporary forms of communication entitled *What the Human Race is Up To* (1962), a collection also noted for tapping into key scientific developments and their impact on human consciousness at that time.

Reflecting on the need for a cultural shift within Scottish culture, the need for Scottish literature to open up to new modes of expression taking place further afield in the early 1960s, Edwin Morgan commented:

> Anyone who thinks I am asking for Robin Jenkins to write like Robbe-Grillet or Iain Crichton Smith to write like Ginsberg misunderstands an essential point. What matters is that the achievements and purposes of contemporary European and American writing should be known in Scotland – known and discussed, not necessarily imitated [...] the main thing is to get our country to break out from its prickly isolation and have the self-confidence to do this and at the same time remain in Scotland, with all the demands living in Scotland makes on one's becoming a 'Scottish writer'.[49]

The sense of intellectual turn can clearly be found at the heart of many of the novels discussed in this chapter. While it has been possible only to touch on some of the key writers and themes of postwar Scottish fiction, and this chapter should be read in conjunction with Moray Watson's chapter in this volume on the Gaelic novel, it is nonetheless possible to see interconnecting strands throughout many of these works; easy to discern a dissenting spirit permeating these novels either in terms of their form or content. Through their engagements with themes such as exile, desolation (spiritual and literal), belonging, existentialism and experimentalism, many of the writers discussed self-consciously explore the need to test the boundaries of their cultural and historical moments, often making specific connections with wider literary developments in the process. While often the key periods of twentieth-century Scottish fiction are assumed to lie in the interwar Scottish Literary Renaissance, and the later 'new' renaissance at the end of the century, with a kind of hiatus in the middle, sustained focus on the intervening period reveals that much of the experiment of recent Scottish fiction is indebted to this earlier mid-century period.

DOCUMENT 6

From 'The Desegregation of Art'

From *The Golden Fleece: Essays by Muriel Spark*, ed. Penelope Jardine (Carcanet Press, 2014)

Muriel Spark

Literature, of all the arts, is the most penetrable into the human life of the world, for the simple reason that words are our common currency. We don't instinctively, from morning to night, paint pictures to each other, or play music to each other, in order to communicate; we talk, we write to each other.

And so, when I speak of the desegregation of art I begin with the art of letters. But I mean also the other arts, drama, music, painting – to-day, more than ever in process of abstracting themselves from the confines of separate faculties, already tending to become part and parcel of society, where they belong. We are living in times when there are fewer great artists, fewer great writers, but more and better art, better and more lively and a greater volume of writing. It is easy to say that poetry and the novel are on the decline compared with the great masterpieces of the past. But it seems to me that the art of speech itself has improved, standards of journalism and reportage have improved, speech has become sharper and more ready on everyone's tongue. We express ourselves more freely and with less clutter than ever before. It's true that in some parts of the world people are not permitted to say what they think; but even so, no-one can deny that they are very eloquent and very occupied to say what perhaps they don't exactly think. In Italy, where I live, when the millions of Americans flood in to enliven the summer months, we find them ready and able and eager to discuss everything and anything. And we ask ourselves where this great silent majority is that we hear about. Those quiet Americans certainly don't come to visit us.

Now leaving aside the other arts for the moment, I concentrate on the art of literature for the very reason that a distinction has to be made between the verbal communications going on every day, every moment of the day, and what we call literature.

I think that the art of literature is a personal expression of ideas which come to influence the minds of people even at second, third and fourth hand. Literature infiltrates and should fertilise our minds. It is not a special department set aside for the entertainment and delight of the sophisticated minority. And if this is true, then ineffective literature must go.

We all know that there is a lot of inferior literature about as there are inferior and boring examples of any other art. It is easy to say bad things must go. The critics, in every field of art, are never done denouncing what they feel to be bad art. They rightly prune and cultivate, they attempt to practise good husbandry. And as we become more articulate, itinerant, knowledgeable, we are more and more agreed on what is bad. And everyone knows we have to give up what is bad – it is a banal moral precept. What is wrong, what is bad, must go.

But I suggest now that we have to give up some of the good manifestations of art. Good things, when they begin no longer to apply, also must go. They must go before they turn bad on us. There is no more beautiful action than the sacrifice of good things at the intelligent season and by intelligent methods.

I'm sure you would like me to be more specific. And so I will be.

We have in this century a marvellous tradition of socially conscious art. And especially now in the arts of drama and the novel we see and hear everywhere the representation of the victim against the oppressor, we have a literature and an artistic culture, one might almost say a civilisation, of depicted suffering, whether in social life or in family life. We have representations of the victim-oppressor complex, for instance, in the dramatic portrayal of the gross racial injustices of our world, or in the exposure of the tyrannies of family life on the individual. As art this can be badly done, it can be brilliantly done. But I am going to suggest that it isn't achieving its end or illuminating our lives any more, and that a more effective technique can and should be cultivated. And then I shall offer my own idea of precisely what that method might be.

For what happens when, for example, the sympathies and the indignation of a modern audience are aroused by a play or a novel of the kind to which I have referred? I don't know for certain, but I suspect that a great number of the audience or of the readers feel that their moral responsibilities are sufficiently fulfilled by the emotions they have been induced to feel. A man may go to bed feeling less guilty after seeing such a play. He has undergone the experience of pity for the underdog. Salt tears have gone bowling down his cheeks. He has had a good dinner. He is absolved, he sleeps well. He rises refreshed, more determined than ever to be the overdog. And there is always, too, the man who finds the heroic role of the victim so appealing that he'll never depart from it. I suggest that wherever there is a cult of the victim, such being human nature, there will be an obliging cult of twenty equivalent victimisers.

I'm sure you all remember the silly old saying 'The pen is mightier than the sword'. Perhaps when swords were the weapons in current use, there was some point in the proverb. Anyway, in our time, the least of our problems is swords.

But the power and influence of the creative arts is not to be belittled. I only say that the art and literature of sentiment and emotion, however beautiful in itself, however stirring in its depiction of actuality, has to go. It cheats us into a sense of involvement with life and society, but in reality it is a segregated activity. In its place I advocate the arts of satire and of ridicule. And I see no other living art form for the future.

Ridicule is the only honourable weapon we have left.

We have all seen on the television those documentaries of the 'thirties and of the second World War, where Hitler and his goose-stepping troops advance in their course of liberating, as they called it, some city, some country or other; we have seen the strutting and posturing of Mussolini. It looks like something out of comic opera to us. If the massed populations of those times and in those countries had been moved to break up into helpless laughter at the sight, those tyrants wouldn't have had a chance. And I say we should all be conditioned and educated to regard violence in any form as something to be ruthlessly mocked.

If someone derides me, I don't like it. But at least I can begin to understand the mentality of the mocker. And I can mock back in such a way that he might understand mine. And so there may be room for a mutual understanding. But if he slides a knife between my ribs I'm unlikely to understand anything at all any more.

I would like to see in all forms of art and letters, ranging from the most sophisticated and high achievements to the placards that the students carry about the street, a less impulsive generosity, a less indignant representation of social injustice, and a more deliberate cunning, a more derisive undermining of what is wrong. I would like to see less emotion and more intelligence in these efforts to impress our minds and hearts.

Crude invective can rouse us for a time, and perhaps only end in physical violence. Solemn appeals to our sentiments of indignation and pity are likely to succeed only for the duration of the show, of the demonstration, or the prayer meeting, or the hours of reading. Then the mood passes, it goes to the four winds and love's labour's lost. But the art of ridicule, if it is on the mark – and if it is not true on the mark it is not art at all – can penetrate to the marrow. It can leave a salutary scar. It is unnerving. It can paralyse its object.

Does this sound as if I thought of the purpose of art as propaganda? Perhaps it does sound so, and perhaps I partly do. In a sense all art is propaganda since it propagates a point of view and provokes a response. But that isn't entirely my meaning.

I have often been asked to give an opinion as to what is the purpose of art. And I've thought of it a great deal. I've thought of this question for most of my life. And, so far, I've reached a generalised conclusion that the purpose of art is to give pleasure. Whether the form of art is tragic, comic, dramatic, lyrical, ironic, aggressive, it contains that element of pleasure which restores the proportions of the human spirit, opens windows in the mind. By means of art and literature our wits are sharpened, our intellect is refined, we can learn to know ourselves, how to appraise life with that pleasure which is the opposite and the enemy of boredom and of pain. This is what I mean by canvassing as I do the idea that the only effective art of our particular time is the satirical, the harsh and witty, the ironic and derisive. Because we have come to a moment in history when we are surrounded on all sides and oppressed by the absurd. And I think that even the simplest, the least sophisticated and uneducated mind is aware of this fact. I should think there is hardly an illiterate peasant in the world who doesn't know it. The art of ridicule is an art that everyone can share in some degree, given the world that we have.

The cult of the victim is the cult of pathos, not tragedy. The art of pathos is pathetic, simply; and it has reached a point of exhaustion, a point where not the subject-matter but the art-form itself is crying to heaven for vengeance. The art of protest, the art which condemns violence and suffering by pathetic depiction is becoming a cult separated from the actions of our life. Our noble aspirations, our sympathies, our elevated feelings should not be inspired merely by visits to an art gallery, a theatre, or by reading a book, but rather the rhetoric of our times should persuade us to contemplate the ridiculous nature of the reality before us, and teach us to mock it. We should know ourselves better by now than to be under the illusion that we are all essentially aspiring, affectionate and loving creatures. We do have these qualities, but we are aggressive, too.

And so when I speak of the desegregation of art I mean by this the liberation of our minds from the comfortable cells of lofty sentiment in which they are confined and never really satisfied.

To bring about a mental environment of honesty and self-knowledge, a sense of the absurd and a general looking-lively to defend ourselves from the ridiculous oppressions of our time, and above all to entertain us in the process, has become the special calling of arts and of letters.

CHAPTER NINE

The Scottish Novel 1979–1999

Carole Jones

The period 1979–1999 was one of seismic political and cultural change in Scotland. It spans the 'devolutionary' era, the period in which a case was built for the devolving of power from Westminster – between the unsuccessful campaign for a Scottish Assembly that culminated in the referendum of 1979 and the 'yes' vote of the 1997 referendum which led to the establishment of the Scottish Parliament in 1999. In the context of the onset of Thatcherism and the influence of fast-developing neoliberal global discourses, Scottish literature, and the Scottish novel in particular, entered a climate of explosive productivity in relation to which 'no period in Scottish culture has, perhaps, been as rich'.[1]

Critics pinpoint the 1979 referendum on Scottish devolution as the significant watershed moment, which at the time was seen as an instance of abject failure for Scottish self-determination. Controversially, it could be said the referendum was both won and lost; a late amendment to the Scotland Bill 1978 stipulated that more than forty per cent of the registered electorate would have to approve the bill as well as achieve a simple majority in the vote itself. In the event, though 51.6% voted yes, a very slim but winning majority, this represented well below the forty per cent turnout threshold, meaning the vote for a Scottish Assembly was legally defeated. This ultimately 'inconclusive, ambivalent and confusing' result,[2] which harboured deep divisions within Scotland between the rural north and south and the urban cities of the Lowlands, led the Scottish National Party to instigate a vote of no confidence in the Westminster government which in turn led to a general election that was won by Margaret Thatcher, installing nearly twenty years of Conservative rule. This 'disastrous double whammy'[3] signalled a steep decline in Tory support in Scotland until the referendum of 1997, which took place under the newly elected Labour government, produced a solid majority in favour of a Scottish parliament with tax-varying powers. However, the period's 'unprecedented explosion of creativity [is] often seen as a direct response'[4] to the political events of 1979.

The ignominious outcome of the 1979 referendum left the pro-devolution constituency despondent, and writers, commentators and cartoonists declared in a common image that the Scottish lion was 'feart'; William McIlvanney's poem 'The Cowardly Lion' bemoaned that 'the lion had turned to its cage and slunk away / And lives among stinking straw today'.[5] More prosaically, Neal Ascherson referred to the 'blankness' that was now the Scottish future.[6] It is not difficult to find, as Eleanor Bell observes, that 'pessimism is a significant feature of literary works in the period after the 1979 Referendum'.[7] However, in contrast, Douglas Gifford espies a 'more positive vision', arguing that 'it is tempting to see this change in confidence as somehow related to the 1979 Devolution referendum and the growing assertion of Scottish identity and its varieties that emerged almost in defiance of that quasi-democratic debacle'.[8] This signals a growing consensus that emerged in the years following that 'debacle' that Scottish literature, especially the novel, went through a profound regeneration in reaction to the referendum, becoming, according to some quarters, *the* medium of political expression for Scotland.

A consensus emerged which became a dominant and uplifting discourse. Robert Crawford expresses a common thesis that 'literature has operated in advance of political structures'[9] in Scotland, echoed by Murray Pittock's assertion that Scotland realised 'a form of cultural autonomy in the absence of its political equivalent'[10] and Liam McIlvanney's view of the Scottish novel as 'a kind of substitute or virtual polity'.[11] This refers to the political context which saw successive Conservative governments in Westminster while, by 1997, not one Tory MP was returned in Scotland, creating the widespread feeling of a 'democratic deficit', a lack of political representation for the people of Scotland. In definitive statements Randall Stevenson avows, 'what history and politics refuse, literature and culture provide'[12] and Craig asserts that 'Scotland had [...] effectively declared cultural independence'.[13] This 'second renaissance'[14] becomes a turning point in Scottish literary history, a 'devolutionary writing' proffered as having significant implications and consequences as 'always, of necessity, politically informed, or at least it was received and critiqued that way [...] inducing the Scottish people to pull more closely together and develop a more clearly defined and morally superior sense of national identity'.[15] In this narrative literary representation leads directly to the devolution success of 1997.

More recently, counter-arguments have emerged to challenge this narrative; its positive interpretation of the influence of literature is, in Matthew Wickman's words, a 'less chronological than performative'[16] history. Scott Hames, prominent in such debates, argues that 'to read some cultural histories of the past few decades, you would think Holyrood was dreamed into being by artists. It wasn't'.[17] For him the relationship is far more 'ambivalent, charged and complex', and to belittle this complexity is to support the 'conservative political process we call "devolution" [which is] no more or less than an effort to re-legitimise the UK state',[18] which ultimately 'limits the potential autonomy and counter-hegemonic force'[19] of Scottish literary texts.

This may be a valid argument. However, those more buoyant literary critics of this period have done a great deal to convince us that there is much to be gained by reading and writing outside of the dominant cultural paradigms. These saw the national stereotype of Scotland as an aberration because, as a nation, it had failed to become a state in the nineteenth-century onrush of nationalist assertion and had, therefore, only a fractured and fragmented history and culture, a culture of instability and self-division in comparison to those deemed successful in the holistic model; in the late twentieth century this Scotland became 'normal'. As Craig argued as early as 1988,

> The fragmentation and division which make Scotland seem abnormal to an earlier part of the twentieth century came to be the norm for much of the world's population [...] Scotland ceased to have to measure itself against the false 'norm', psychological as well as cultural, of the unified national tradition.[20]

This embrace of the inherent instability and negotiation involved in cultural processes enabled a significant critical movement that turned division into a 'galvanising diversity'.[21] And this has served to conceptualise the significance of writing from Scotland far beyond the borders of the nation.

A dominant literary canon has emerged of this period foregrounding the radically experimental literary fiction of prominent authors such as Alasdair Gray, James Kelman and Janice Galloway. However, this is not the only story of the cultural fertility of the time, which is one of astonishing diversity and creativity regarding the novel in Scotland, an openness of the form in this context which creates room for the literary and the popular and their fertile crossovers.

There is no question that 1979 instigated a literary self-examination in the novel characterised by feelings of uncertainty and attempts to embrace the 'courage of our doubts'.[22] In the striving for self-definition, there was a 'general shifting inward of narrative focalisation, and the development of a range of interior monologues, streams of consciousness and other registers for inner thought'.[23] In embodying William McIlvanney's assertion that 'hope begins in confronting the reality of ourselves',[24] the novel in this period turns to the individual person rather than the nation. As Ian A. Bell argues,

> Refusing to collaborate with a transcendental, totalising and finally determining sense of national identity, Scottish novelists since the 1980s have concentrated instead on individual moments of crisis, alienation and fragmentation, moments dramatising the loss and discovery of self, as they are articulated through the lives of some of those conventionally excluded from the story of Scotland.[25]

This focus on the individual suggests that writers are dealing with the period's most prevalent postmodern question, subjectivity, in relation to which the Scottish novel is part of a 'post-Enlightenment project [...] a movement within Scottish thought to disassemble the universalist ideas of Enlightenment'.[26] If this sounds hopeful for some, for others the often despairing and anxious inward excavation of the narratives of the 1980s produced 'a grey and morose beast prone to lengthy fits of self-pity'.[27] Conversely this 'thematically often bleak and pessimistic' writing can also be seen as 'a vibrant and characteristically unruly vehicle for Scottish self-representation [...] responsive to processes of apparent cultural disintegration as conducive to democratic diversification'.[28] The 'resourceful flexibility'[29] of the novel empowered a more energetic unmooring of identity in the fiction of the 1990s, when a turn outward – to Europe, postmodernism and its favoured tricks of anti-realist metafiction – transported the reader from Gavin Wallace's 'tradition of despair'[30] to Irvine Welsh's exuberant linguistic and formal shock and awe, part of a 'Scottish literature boom'[31] that challenged the boundaries of genre and opened up new horizons of possibility for fiction generally.

The first salvo in this cultural regeneration is often conceived to be Alasdair Gray's *Lanark: A Life in Four Books* published in 1981, now mythically located as the primary influence setting the route and the goal for future generations of Scottish novelists, the diverse lines of inspiration for a proliferating typology of the Scottish novel. Famously, this truly epic text explores all the possibilities of the novel form alluded to: it considers the state of the nation and the state of an individual mind; it deploys realism and postmodern metafictional fantasy; it explodes the notion of genre in what seems like an innovative creation but also echoes tradition in the way, for example, it 'develops a fluency of interchange between fantasy and reality often considered definitive of the Scottish imagination'.[32] As Craig puts it, *Lanark* 'will almost inevitably be seen as both an end and a beginning to phases of Scottish writings'.[33] Its magic is in the *madness* of its form, combining the realist and the fantastic, the autobiographical and the sci-fi, in a challenging anti-linear depiction of a bifurcated life and world. The novel tells the story of Thaw/Lanark who experiences births, deaths and rebirths between the worlds of a semi-autobiographical Glasgow (Duncan Thaw is a mural artist like Gray) and its dystopian double of Unthank where Lanark escapes the monstrous Institute but fails to prevent the destruction of the city. The novel is structured in four books placed in the order three, one, two, four across which the narratives of Thaw and Lanark waywardly echo each other. Before the end of book four there is an Epilogue in which Lanark meets the author who explains the text to him: 'The Thaw narrative shows a man dying because he is bad at loving. It is enclosed by your narrative which shows civilisation collapsing for the same reason.'[34]

Lanark is an expansive, quintessential statement of Gray's concern with entrapment of the individual by systems of control, illustrating in particular an exploration of ways to escape the enclosing cages of language and representation and the world-view they produce. Firstly, the novel challenges the literary production of social reality by embedding realist depiction within fantasy – the Thaw narrative within Lanark's dystopian version. Formally the text also disrupts realism with its foregrounded deploying of metafictional strategies, not only commenting on its own production in the 'Epilogue', but also including an 'Index of Plagiarisms'; this takes up space on the page marginal to the main narrative and lists precisely the instances of literary influence and copying throughout the novel, undermining the notion of originality that informs western literary production. Finally, Gray's typographical experiments, such as the 'Index', strategically deploy typeface to blast the linearity of the text on the page, creating sometimes anarchic profusions of form that disrupt and deform the typical reading experience.

Gray's second published novel, *1982, Janine* (1984) is even more illustrative of these themes and formal strategies as narrator Jock McLeish is a troubled individual who works as a designer of security systems and who meditates on Scotland's and his own state of entrapment: 'Scotland has been fucked and I am one of the fuckers who fucked her.'[35] Gray controversially employs explicit imagery – Jock's pornography-inspired fantasies involve the entrapment of a character named Janine – to pursue a 'theory of political sexuality [which] argues that our erotic fantasies parallel our political and economic behaviour, or are even versions of each other'.[36] Significantly Jock has a typographically vivid suicidal breakdown in the explosion of typeface that is 'The Ministry of Voices' section, recovering to recount in realist *bildungsroman* style his own journey to bitter and repressed adulthood. The question often asked of Gray's postmodern techniques is whether they create a critique of or provide more elaborate forms of entrapment, that 'ultimately cooperate with that process of "entrapment" itself [providing] not means of *escape*, but comfortable terms of surrender'.[37] It probably does both: 'makes possible and negates the values [of the economic system] at one and the same time.'[38]

We find a different approach to this postmodern condition in the work of James Kelman, whose style, though seemingly opposite to Gray's typographical dexterity, is equally radical in challenging textual hierarchies. Kelman's novels of this devolutionary period focus solely on the minute details of daily life for their single central male characters. In *The Busconductor Hines* (1984), *A Chancer* (1985), *A Disaffection* (1989), and the controversial Booker Prize winner *How Late It Was, How Late* (1994), iterations of a working-class Glaswegian consciousness are presented in a form that, in contrast to Gray's textual spectacle, appear more standard and uniform on the page and read like first-person narratives. Kelman's innovation, however, is no less radical in both the subject and form of his fiction. Prioritising the psychic interiority of his characters, Kelman achieves a 'fiction of psychological immersion' that 'aims to realise *subjectivity* (original emphasis)'[39] for the marginalised constituency he believes to be misrepresented in literature:

> Whenever I did find somebody from my background in English Literature there they were confined to the margins, kept in their place, stuck in the dialogue. You only ever saw them or heard them. You never got into their mind. You did find them in the narrative but from without, seldom from within.[40]

In this period of deindustrialisation, however, Kelman's task of working-class representation is a complex one, 'driven by the inequalities of late capitalism, the disruption of traditional working-class solidarities, and an attendant loss of meaning from the world, its events and institutions'.[41] This is 'a working-class without a possible salvation through the political or economic transformation of history'.[42] In such a context, traditional paradigms of heroic escape from class constraints or the prevalent model of the Scottish 'hard man' are not helpful as social critique. In contrast, Kelman's men are anxious and uncertain, experience failure and demonstrate a profound existential dilemma: 'how to assert selfhood in the face of the dehumanising pressure of social conditions'.[43] Though echoing Gray's concern with individual entrapment, Kelman's work is more Kafkaesque, depicting an alienating social regime and characterisation that is a 'mix of self-abnegation and self-assertion in a prose which disorientates the reader with baffling wayward spirals of defeated agency'.[44] Depicting the daily grind of a disaffected life necessitates profound literary innovation.

Though intent on 'realising subjectivity', Kelman's prose presents us with a compromised interiority which establishes the limits of individual agency and autonomy. Developed in the crucible of his short stories, this style blurs the boundaries and hierarchies of narration; the narrative voice blends with dialogue, sharing the vernacular with no speech markers, flowing between pronouns and between what can be thought of as speech, thought and narrative. Kelman is 'creating a linguistic unity between speech and narration'[45] as in the opening of *How Late* where the text travels between a reflective self-addressing second-person pronoun and a third-person perspective, ending with what could be direct interior monologue:

> Ye wake in a corner and stay there hoping yer body will disappear [...] Edging back into awareness, of where ye are: here, slumped in this corner, with these thoughts filling ye. And oh christ his back was sore; stiff, and the head pounding. He shivered and hunched up his shoulders, shut his eyes, rubbed into the corners with his fingertips; seeing all kinds of spots and lights. Where in the name of fuck ...

This is not simply a 'cunningly crafted artistic representation of speech';[46] as Craig argues, this 'liberation of the narrative voice from the constraints of written English is an act of linguistic solidarity'.[47] The vernacular voice is not enclosed, entrapped as monologue or dialogue, within a Standard English narration and the hierarchical value system it represents. However, this blurring of boundaries – between outside and inside perspectives, between 'he' and 'ye' or 'I', between objective description, self-reflective indirect discourse and direct expression – positions subjectivity on the border between the individual and their environment. The style raises the question of where exactly the self resides in this ongoing process of relational negotiation: inside or outside the individual or somewhere in between. In this constantly mobile focalisation individual autonomy is challenged and the self de-centred and dispersed. In particular, the masculine self, founded on autonomy, rational self-knowledge and self-control, and strong psychic and bodily boundaries, is undermined and relationality and vulnerability are foregrounded in a radical re-imagining of subjectivity.[48]

If women can be said to be outsiders to the preoccupations of these male-centred fictions, Janice Galloway resets this perspective in her fiction, appropriating Kelman's existential questions to interrogate 'how to be a woman under patriarchy'.[49] A feminine centre is key to Galloway's work; as she stated in 1999, her aim is 'to write as though having a female perspective is normal which is a damn sight harder than it sounds'.[50] To this end she employs both Gray's textual and typographical playfulness and Kelman's immersive but compromised interiority to address similar themes of alienation and entrapment in relation to female experience. Her innovative first novel, *The Trick Is to Keep Breathing* (1989), graphically presents one woman's breakdown amidst the particular estranging effects of popular culture. Joy Stone is struggling to grieve for her married lover whose accidental death has allowed him to be expropriated back into his family, leaving Joy no legitimate role or manner of mourning. Her crisis is represented by a fractured and fragmented narrative where Joy's first-person meditations on her circumstances are interrupted by italicised sections of the scene of Michael's death. Though this eruption of traumatic memory is a founding impulse of the text, Galloway's principal concern is the unstable self, its disintegration when unmoored from relation and society, but also its construction through the discourses of popular culture which pointedly disrupt the narrative in the form of magazine extracts, horoscopes, problem pages, recipes, references to self-help books. The playful typography emphasises these jarring intrusions with a variety of typefaces, inclusion of playscripts, lists and other graphic representations. More disturbingly there are sometimes missing page numbers, words floating in the margins, gaps and blank pages which express the incoherence and illegibility of Joy's melancholy self. These are postmodern experiments with form to challenge the autonomy of the subject; Galloway's writing is 'deconstructive [...] exposing and undermining the language, textual practices and discourses we live by'.[51] But *The Trick* is also 'reconstructive', ending on Joy's survival and reconfiguration of herself in the terms of 'a little light fiction [...] I read somewhere the trick is to keep breathing, make out it's not unnatural at all. They say it comes with practice.'[52] Such openness makes Galloway's fiction inspirational to 'the dominant trend in post-devolution Scottish literature [...] the displacement and not definitive fixing of identity'.[53]

A similar explosive creativity in the novel, putatively a 'Scottish renaissance of the 1990s',[54] continued with Irvine Welsh spearheading the ongoing resistance to mainstream conceptions of 'the literary', and developing the concern with identity and specifically with the all-consuming effects of popular and consumer culture explored by Galloway. Significantly relocating radical literary practice to an Edinburgh of the margins, Welsh's first novel *Trainspotting* (1993) was met by a critical reception which 'demurred or flatly refused to confer upon it the status of a novel',[55] such was its outlandish novelty. Yet neither did the text conform to any popular genre fiction, articulating a 'detachment not only from mainstream culture, but also from the cultural "fringe"'.[56] Its innovation was in 'reviving what have traditionally been Scottish literature's chief preoccupations: identity, class, language and fantasy' from a social location so marginal it failed to register in any literary mapping – 'an underclass previously without voice or visibility in Scottish literature'.[57] Welsh's 1990s novels create an intoxicating medium of delirious vernacular that mobilises surreal and violently absurd imagery; *Marabou Stork Nightmares* (1995) is narrated by football casual Roy Strang, comatose after a failed suicide attempt, and in *Filth* (1998) the narration of corrupt policeman Bruce Robertson is interrupted by a tapeworm in his gut. However, the influence of *Trainspotting* is far-reaching, due in part to its intermedial sensibility which transferred effortlessly to Danny Boyle's hugely successful 1996 film adaptation. It is, though, the novel's fragmented, hybrid form itself which expresses both complicity with and critique of its postmodern, neoliberal moment. Episodic and in some ways choral in nature,[58] the text vacillates between its main characters Renton, Sick Boy, Spud and Begbie, and between first-person and reflective third-person narration with Renton's italicised 'junk dilemmas' interspersed throughout. Identity is unmoored from moral, social, political or even somatic certainty, reflected in language ferociously vernacular, profane and scatological, as well as expertly manipulative of the affectations of linguistic and cultural discourses of a world in which, through de-industrialisation, whole communities have lost their meaning and their social referents. Welsh interrogates the rueful absurdity of a climate where the neoliberal individualism of the mainstream is mirrored by the nihilistic individualism of what it considers its amoral and indecent other, illustrating the violent competitiveness of survival common to both. But with searing irony, the self-annihilation associated with the heroin consumer culture is countered by the life force of the narration:

> it is a language in whose rhythm can be heard the sneer of punk and the rhythms of rave and hip-hop, in whose design can be seen the influence of visual culture and whose intense physicality provided an alternative to the increasing abstraction of modern literature and life.[59]

Welsh's innovations, like those of Gray before him, inspired writers of his generation, such as Laura Hird, Niall Griffiths and Alan Warner.

Morvern Callar (1995), Warner's first novel, is a beguiling female-centred response to Welsh's anarchic incontinence. On the one hand it explores a suggestive model of selfhood unbounded by the rave scene, the club and dance culture prominent since the late 1980s, where a pleasurable loss of self is facilitated by the sustained sensual and collective experience of ecstasy-fuelled partying. On the other hand, the narrator Morvern is a coolly distant recounter of her own experience, a closed surface we never get beyond despite the dramatic events: she enacts a grisly disposal of her boyfriend's self-murdered corpse and appropriates and publishes his novel which funds an elongated sojourn in Mediterranean rave culture. The remarkable narrating voice, where a localised speech is suggested by syntax and creative vocabulary rather than transliteration of the vernacular, manages to convey silence and inscrutability as well as keenly observed feminine experience. In contrast, *The Sopranos* (1998; later republished as *Our Ladies*) veers away from this puzzling detachment towards the chaotic noise of the chattering schoolgirls who are travelling to the capital for a choir competition. This is a loud and exuberant expression of presence, an explicitly female life force signalled in the novel's *Wuthering Heights* epigraph that notes 'a love for life here almost possible', countering Welsh's 'ah choose not tae choose life'.[60] Warner brings experimental narrative to bear on a new location, a thinly disguised Oban which gives proximity to the Highlands – not ignoring the rural environs but imbuing them with the brash, anarchic sensation of Warner's urban predecessors.

Until now I have prioritised those urban fictions so foregrounded in the hegemonic story of the devolutionary novel. However, to do so is to downplay the diversity of fiction in this era; there were, of course, other significant literary trends, equally as searching as well as more familiar and traditional, but as engaged in processing the contemporary context. This is intriguingly illustrated by a 'provocative Scottish coup'[61] that saw Kelman's 1994 Booker Prize-winning novel *How Late It Was, How Late* and George Mackay Brown's *Beside the Ocean of Time* together on that year's shortlist. Brown's elegiac and poetic text evoking the history and mythic Nordic past of the fictional Orkney island of Norday could not present a greater contrast to Kelman's urban angst. The ambivalence of 'island writers', addressing 'the island as a place of mythic renewal and as inherently unsustainable',[62] is also present in the work of Lewis-raised Iain Crichton Smith, for example, who in *The Dream* (1990) 'finally comes to terms with his divided island and city experience [...] offering release from rural disillusion'.[63] Brown's creation of a 're-ordered identity in a mythopoeic process' similarly presents a 'move from elegy to qualified hope',[64] in a diversity of literariness echoed by other writers of the period. A. L. Kennedy's first novel, *Looking for the Possible Dance* (1993), presents a finely tuned structure and characterisation to chart Margaret's journey from Glasgow to London and back, and from relational estrangement to possible reconciliation in an urban context struggling to maintain human connection. In her second novel, *So I Am Glad* (1995), Kennedy spikes her sceptical realism with a fantastical plot involving the putative reincarnation of seventeenth-century French Renaissance man Savinien Cyrano de Bergerac in contemporary Glasgow. This gothic disruption signals a confident challenging of genre boundaries and embrace of ontological instability also notable in texts such as Iain Banks's *The Wasp Factory* (1984) and *The Bridge* (1986), and Irvine Welsh's *Marabou Stork Nightmares* (1995). This preoccupation moves fiction writing in the direction of fulfilling Gardiner's demand for Scottish writers to 'inaugurate an entirely genre-free way of looking at literature, where a text's "literariness" inheres in the effects it has'.[65] Ironically, it is an explosion in 'genre fiction' in this period that reinforces this aspiration.

Crime fiction, in particular, began its spectacular rise to popularity in the 1980s, taking inspiration from McIlvanney's *Laidlaw* (1977) and its challenge to generic conventions – as a 'whydunnit' instead of a 'whodunnit'.[66] The eponymous Glasgow detective, appearing in two further novels, *The Papers of Tony Veitch* (1983) and *Strange Loyalties* (1991), is an ambivalent character whose difference from the criminals he is investigating is blurred; 'Laidlaw invites us to join him in a place where there is no them and us. There is only us.'⁶⁷ This captures a trend of Scottish writers 'adopting the genre as a means of exploring systemic rather than individual criminality'.⁶⁸ This model is developed by Ian Rankin in his Inspector Rebus series, where the moral clarity of the 'Edinburgh Laidlaw' is further complicated by his mental breakdown and PTSD. In the first novel, *Knots and Crosses* (1987) Rebus is positioned as policeman, victim and suspect in a narrative that foregrounds uncertainty and self-doubt, and the necessity of facing the past. In the 1990s, Denise Mina's *Garnethill* (1998) continues these themes from a feminine perspective, female vulnerability under oppressive patriarchal conditions arguably yielding greater sensitive insight into social breakdown; 'Mina's is a world in which those systems central to a healthy body politic – the law, medicine, social services – have broken down or been withdrawn, leaving the individual to negotiate a corrupt society as best they can.'⁶⁹ Central character Maureen O'Donnell is another unreliable agent who has suffered mental breakdown after a history of abuse, and also 'occupies the textual space of investigator, victim and criminal, blurring the traditional boundaries of crime fiction'.⁷⁰ Gill Plain argues that this 'ethical instability is typical of the devolutionary moment'; if the 'writing of a national consciousness is characteristic'⁷¹ of the period, these conflicted, anxious and uncertain narratives suggest a nation uneasy with its past and potential for recuperative action in the present. Other popular texts, such as Christopher Brookmyre's more satirical take on corruption in *Quite Ugly One Morning* (1996), with its 'boldly Manichean dynamic',⁷² or Alexander McCall Smith's more sedate, Botswana-set *No 1 Ladies Detective Agency* series (from 1998), closer to Agatha Christie than the American hardboiled model, do little to productively resolve this tension.

A 'wrestling with im/possible futures'⁷³ would seem naturally to be a preoccupation of science fiction, another phenomenally successful genre in Scottish writing since the 1980s with top-selling authors like Iain M. Banks and Ken MacLeod. Another politically exploratory genre, Caroline McCracken-Flesher suggests this derives from Scottish ambiguity and ambivalence:

> Scottish science fiction authors focus on the possibilities generated at the margins [...] this oddly imperial yet strangely subaltern literature, positioned both inside and outside the grand literary and critical narratives of the genre, thus operates as a form of criticism at once geographic and political, scientific and literary.⁷⁴

In Banks's 'Culture' novels, for instance, beginning with *Consider Phlebas* (1987), he propounds 'his vision of a future anarchist-socialist utopia', espousing a 'feminine mythology' which is 'a kind of "deterritorialisation", manifest in the loss of notions of "ownership" and a corresponding acceptance of a global or cosmological interconnectedness'.[75] Further, 'homogeneity in the Culture emerges from a vast constellation of difference, thereby creating opportunities for expanded notions of democracy'.[76] These optimistic readings, though not universally promoted – Gavin Miller accuses Banks of an 'implicit fear of subjectivity' in his 'computational view of life and mind'[77] – concur with Tim Baker's claim that by 'looking beyond both generic and national categorical models' Scottish science fiction 'embraces the novel as a form of unlimited possibility'.[78]

As the institution of the new Scottish parliament approached in 1999, that pushing of boundaries was tested in endeavours to address the 'constellation of difference' that comprised Scottish society which began gradually to increase the diversity of the novel's subjects. Luke Sutherland's *Jelly Roll* (1998) explores racism through the Highland tour of a jazz group with a new substitute saxophone player, Liam, who is black. It is noteworthy that the text, though preoccupied with the effects of Liam's presence, is narrated by fellow white band member Roddy, an ambivalent admirer of Liam who eventually admits betraying him to a horrific racist attack. Jackie Kay's *Trumpet* (1998) is also set in the world of jazz, the central figure of this narrative being successful trumpeter Joss Moody. Already dead at the start of the novel, Joss's life and the effects of his death, where his female embodiment is discovered and made public, are mediated by family, friends, the professional administrators of death, and a prospective sensationalist biographer. Interestingly these black Scottish characters are denied a direct 'voice', suggesting a reluctance to fix non-white identity and instead explore the damaging stereotypes through which non-white Scottish experience is mis/represented. Kay's engagement with queerness also marks a point of resistance to clear identity definition; Joss's transgendered self cannot be categorised or resolved as anything other than in process. Such complex representations maintain the 'displacement and not definitive fixing of identity' highlighted and valued by Wallace as Scotland enters a new democratic configuration in the realisation of devolution.

As we reach that significant moment in 1999, one novel stands out on that threshold as seeking atonement in its critique of the moral compromises of the past. Andrew O'Hagan's *Our Fathers* (1999), focused on the history of the postwar built environment of Glasgow, chronicles the relationship between three generations of one family – Hugh Bawn, who was council director of public housing for the city in the regeneration of the 1960s, his son Robert, an alcoholic drop-out, and his grandson Jamie, who has returned to the city to help demolish the compromised, failing high-rise blocks erected by Hugh. Anger and estrangement give way to understanding and uneasy reconciliation on Hugh's death;

> in suggesting what needs to be overcome and cleared away in Scotland may be not only the errors of the recent past, but also any excessive reaction against that past, *Our Fathers* exemplifies the kind of forward-looking and provisionally optimistic work that has been called paradigmatic of contemporary Scottish fiction.[79]

In sombre contrast to Gray's postmodernism, O'Hagan's 'poetic literary modernism'[80] is a circumspect culmination to an exhilarating period in the history of the Scottish novel, an era where the painful compromise of politics is assuaged by radical new fictional visions exploring complex selves and potential futures. Emerging from the uncertainty and doubt of 1979 the devolutionary Scottish novel lives by McIlvanney's dictum that 'hope begins in confronting the reality of ourselves'.

DOCUMENT 7

'Elitism and English Literature'[1]

From *When I was that age did art exist?* (revised, PM Press, forthcoming; Secker & Warburg, 2002)

James Kelman

I was a great reader as a boy and was born lucky. There was a library at the bottom of my street, inside the entrance to Elder Park, Glasgow. I started going along from the age of four with my big brother. There was no writer I enjoyed more than Enid Blyton and that lasted a couple of years. Later there was no genre I enjoyed more than school stories and that went on until probably I was about eleven or twelve years old. The books featured different schools and different pupils, males and females, but they all seemed related, and most were written by the same man, Frank Richards.

The schools he wrote about were upper-class establishments. It is a peculiar thing that children like myself could identify with the pupils in those schools. It was inconceivable that I ever would meet up with young people from my own background between these pages. I'm not talking about Scottish kids in general I'm talking about Scottish working-class kids in general because it was possible to meet a scholarship boy or one from a colonial background, whether from Scotland or India or someplace. I cannot remember any African or Chinese boys making an entrance but perhaps they did. These colonial natives were aristocrats back in their own country, even if they wore kilts, loincloths or turbans, or whatever, they were accepted as lower-rung aristocracy.

They were exotic creatures and never made it as heroes in their own right. The English language as spoken by these young colonials exhibited idiosyncratic mannerisms that were quite funny. At the same time they were always supportive and loyal to boys such as Harry Wharton and Tom Merry. Kids like myself would identify with the last pair and other upper-class English heroes, white Christians to the core. There was no chance of somebody like me identifying let alone making a hero of an

---

[1] This essay was written as a talk delivered to students.

exotic young colonial, even if he did happen to be Scottish. At twelve years of age who wants to be an oddball outsider with no sense of style and a funny way of talking.

At senior school I had no contact with literature but outside of school hours I was reading various things, including adventure stories by R. M. Ballantyne. Then a major court case happened. It was a full-blown scandal to do with a novel, all because of language and sex, it was *Lady Chatterley's Lover* by D. H. Lawrence. I was fourteen. I went out and bought the paperback. My mother discovered it and burned it, but not before I read a few pages and browsed a few more. Apart from the juicy stuff I remember I was struck by the weird use of language by the central male character, a salt-of-the-earth, working-class country-yokel sort of guy; he used to go about saying salt-of-the-earth things like 'If thar shits and thar pisses.' I had never heard anything like that in my life. It was amazing. So that was how these salt-of-the-earth working-class country yokels spoke in England! Well well well. Yet, oddly, the way the writer used language reminded me of the school stories by Frank Richards. I carried on with my own reading, mainly cowboy and private-eye novels written by American writers.

One English writer I read was John Buchan. He was actually Scottish, what some might call an assimilated member of British society. Probably that is what you would call him, British, an assimilated Scotsman. One definition of assimilation is somebody who denies their culture. But perhaps it is unfair to say that someone like John Buchan denied his culture. A shorthand definition of Britain is Greater England; somebody who is content to be labelled a 'Brit' is a Greater Englander. Buchan was an upper-middle-class guy who worked on behalf of the British Empire, and that was what he was paid for by the British State. He was very high up in Government and wrote novels in his spare time; *The Thirty-Nine Steps* is one many of you will know, at least as a movie. His books are good adventure yarns, especially for the politically naïve and readers of a reactionary bent; anyone at all with a soft spot for imperial splendour. There's an entire genre of that kind of stuff. Perhaps the creator of Sherlock Holmes is part of it.

Many academics and other literary critics argue that writers like Conan Doyle and Buchan should be treated with more respect. Writers of more recent generations, working in related genres and value systems, might include Ian Fleming, Frederick Forsyth and John Le Carré; others like John Grisham and Tom Clancy. I would not be bothered denying any of them was a good writer, at least not a bad writer, not unless I was pushed, but who cares. Nowadays there's a crowd of writers into that sort of right-wing secret-agent stuff, CIA, MI5 and SAS heroes, high-flying financier heroes, quirky politician heroes, stalwart soldier heroes, and so on.

In these genres 'white' and 'Christian' can be voiced utterances of approbation, e.g. 'His behaviour was exemplary, he was an absolute white man' or 'My horse has a wonderful temperament, he is a proper Christian.' Eventually the whole thing just done my nut. The heroes belonged to these incredible clubs that were extensions of boarding school, situated in secluded lanes around London's West End, all with log fires and great wee libraries, and these plush, leather-bound armchairs in which crotchety old bods with handlebar moustaches would nod off in a corner over the *Telegraph* obituary columns.

Certain villains might also be attached to such clubs, maybe by fraudulent means or through an administrative mess; these characters are always the 'masterminds' or 'evil brains' behind the villainy.

In such clubs there was always 'a man' to bring you a cigar and a large port or claret. It was always 'a man', never a servant. Not only did the 'man' call you 'sir' or 'lord', if not 'your Majesty', but he tucked you up in bed at night and then he came first thing in the morning and dressed you in appropriate clothes. As far as I know the monarchy still get that done for them, and not just the monarchy.

All the English heroes in that genre seem to have these 'men' in one guise or another throughout their lives, they get called various names, 'batman' for example. Maybe the young master has been a commanding officer in the armed forces and the guy now employed as his personal servant was formerly his 'batman' out in the Sudan or the Raj or the west coast of Ireland or islands of Scotland or someplace. Occasionally when a 'batman' exhibits obedience or devotion beyond the call of duty the young master will bring him home after the war to continue his personal 'batman' services. These 'servants', although they seldom get called that, can be from Africa or the Middle East, or the Near East or the Far East, they can even be indigenous Australasians. Any old outpost of Empire will do. Usually they exhibit quirky physical characteristics, or quirky behavioural patterns; these are both endearing and irritating. No matter where they come from the servants always exhibit peculiar speech mannerisms or patterns. If Scottish the 'man' will speak with what is called a 'heavy burr'. This is what the general run of lower-order Scottish people have in English literature, 'heavy burrs'. The writers may highlight this within the text. Colonial servants and underlings are integral to English literature and different literary conventions exist to deal with them. One such convention is the apparent attempt at phonetic transcription; I mean by that the spelling of words to give an impression of sound. I say 'apparent' because there is no authentic attempt going on.

These servants and underlings do not have to be from so-called countries either, many of these so-called 'people' can be from provincial locations much closer to Westminster and Buckingham Palace: they can be Cumbrians, Lancastrians or Yorkshiremen; they even may be born within hearing distance of Bow Bells; yes, a 'batman' can be Cockney, whatever, just as long as he is working-class, speaks funnily and assimilates to the values of the ruling class, at the same time offering an unquestioning obedience to its individual representatives.

Although I still had not finished with its fictionalisation, by the time I turned nineteen I no longer identified with youthful members of the English aristocracy and upper-middle classes. This is not because I was growing up. Very many adults continue identifying with the English upper classes and the values of that culture right throughout their life. British society has been premised on that. I don't think that it is any longer, at least not to anything like the same extent; there have been a few changes in the last hundred years.

There is no one reason why I gave up reading that fictionalised stuff, but I do remember one time in Manchester I was involved in some yarn with the usual uppercrust white Christian heroes. I was living in a lodging house and either I was unemployed or else working as a labourer in a Salford copper mill. It was a novel by John Buchan I was reading, one of an 'omnibus' collection. I just gave up halfway through, and that was that.

When I went to university I was twenty-nine years old and had published my first collection of stories nearly three years previously; and my second collection was due to appear in a few months' time. I had strong ideas about art: honesty, truth, integrity, justice, humanity; these were the marks of the artist. I use the term 'artist' here in its general sense; an artist can be a poet, a novelist, a sculptor, a dancer, a song-writer, a painter and so on. I felt uneasy when a writer I didn't think deserved to be called an artist was being described as 'good', and often 'major', by the academics. Even the fact that you were given such writers at university meant they were *assumed* to be 'good'. The lecturers and university authorities hold the power: they can say something is good without having to prove it. If you, as a student, want to deny that something is good then *you* are forced to prove 'it'.

And proving anything is never easy. Atheists in the company will know what I'm talking about: it is never the person who actually believes in 'god' who has to find the proof, only those who don't. Proving something doesn't exist is harder than proving something does exist. Some of the greatest philosophers of the past three thousand years have been defeated by that.

Anyway, at university I felt that if certain writers were going to be described as artists then something smelled about the very concept itself: art was just not as great as it is cracked up to be. So I wanted to distinguish between writers who were artists and writers who weren't artists; take for example the poet T. S. Eliot or the novelist Evelyn Waugh, both of whose elitism I rejected. Evelyn Waugh seemed to be so right-wing you'd be forgiven for calling him a Fascist. And how could you call a Fascist an artist? That struck me as by way of a contradiction in terms. Eventually I found it possible to say: here is a writer who okay might be 'good' but either s/he is a bad artist or s/he is not an artist at all, because surely someone who is a good artist cannot be someone who hates people of a different coloured skin, who hates people that speak a different language or whose racial origin differs from her/his own; surely a good artist will not be somebody who hates people of a different religion, people who come from a different cultural or economic background, who are not heterosexual, not homosexual, whatever.

But at that time I was not aware that so much of this business of the 'good' in literature, at least as it applies in education establishments, starts and ends with things like grammar and punctuation; if a schoolteacher or university lecturer calls a writer 'good' it might just mean the writer in question knows how to use colons, semicolons and paragraphs in a certain manner, or has a very large vocabulary, or uses a great variety of rhetorical devices, or exhibits a certain educational or cultural background, or shows a wide knowledge of foreign words and phrases. And all of that sort of stuff was not what good writing should have been about, as far as I could see, and certainly not what good art was about.

When I started to write stories I was twenty-two and naturally enough I thought to use my own background and experience. I wanted to write as one of my own people, I wanted to write and remain a member of my own community. That advice you get in the early days of writing, at any writers' workshop or writers' group, 'Write from your own experience!' Yes, that was what I set out to do, taking it for granted that was how writers began. I soon discovered that this was easier said than done. In fact, as far as I could see, looking around me, it never had been done. If it had, I could never find it. There was nothing I saw anywhere. Whenever

I did find somebody from my own sort of background in English literature, there they were confined to the margins, kept in their place, stuck in the dialogue. You only ever saw them or heard them. You never got into their mind. You did find them in the narrative but from the outside, never from the inside, always they were 'the other'. They never rang true, they were never like anybody you ever met in real life.

There were no literary models I could look to from my own culture. There was nothing whatsoever. I am not saying these models did not exist. But if they did then I could not find them; because of this dearth of home-grown literary models I had to look elsewhere. As I say, there was nothing at all in English Literature, but in English-language literature – well, I came upon a few American writers. I found folk whom I regarded as ordinary; here they were existing in stories, not as clichés, not as stereotypes. I was also discovering foreign language literature through translation; the Russians and others. I found literary models. I found ways into writing stories that I wanted to write; I could realise the freedom I had. I mean just the freedom other writers seemed to take for granted, the freedom to write from their own experience. Now I could create stories based on things I knew about; snooker halls and betting shops and pubs and DSS (DWP) offices; the broo, waiting in the queue at the Council Housing office; I could write stories about my friends and relations and neighbours and family and whatever I wanted. The whole world became available. Quite a heady experience.

It was after that came the other problems. Things were not as straightforward as I thought. It had not dawned on me that there might be very good reasons why these literary models did not exist in my own backyard; yes, censorship and suppression. I quickly bumped against it through the elementary matter of my chosen artform, language.

You cannot write a short story without language. That seems an odd statement. Yet received wisdom in this society has demanded it. Yes, they say, go and write a story, whatever story you want, but do not use whatever language is necessary. Go and write any story at all, providing of course you stay within the bounds, not the bounds of decency or propriety or anything tangible; because that is not the way it works. Nobody issues such instructions. It is all carried out by a series of nudges and winks and tacit agreements. What it amounts to is: go and write a story about a bunch of guys who stand talking in a pub all day but if you have them talking then do not have them talking the language they talk.

Pardon?

Write a story wherein people are talking, but not talking the language they talk.

Oh.

By implication those in authority ask the writer to censor and suppress her or his own work. They demand it. If you do not comply then your work is not produced. That is the way it is. That is the way it always has been. You land on the assembly line of compromise, the end result of which is dishonesty, deceit, falsity. Or else silence. Our mainstream media are full of silences. Why is it the better writers never work for the newspapers, for television, radio or the movies? Do you think it is because they prefer art forms like prose and poetry? Well sometimes that is true, but often it is just because every other medium is out of bounds given their first demands of a writer are compromise and dishonesty.

Back in 1987 I edited an anthology of poetry and prose by people attending a writers' group in the east end of Glasgow. Some of the work is of a kind not readily available on the shelves of libraries and bookshops. This is because it is attempting a realistic portrayal of the lives of ordinary people. Many folk are startled to discover such a thing can be classified as 'literature'. In our society we are not used to thinking of literature as a form of art that might concern the day-to-day existence of ordinary women and men, whether these ordinary women and men are the subjects of the poetry and stories, or the actual writers themselves. It is something we do not expect. And why should we? There is such a barrage of elitist nonsense spoken and written about literature that anything else would be surprising.

The propaganda of elitism operates in different ways but those are the ways of all forms of prejudice: it makes a wide range of statements and will not allow a challenge unless it be done on its own terms, and it continues to make such statements until eventually part of the foundation of the dogma comes to be accepted as a kind of 'truth': fat women have got hearts of gold, men with red hair lose their temper, Catholics are inferior to Protestants; people from Aberdeen are greedy, Jews are greedy, Pakistanis are greedy; people on the dole are lazy; whites are superior to blacks; folk who go to university are born clever; foreigners are evil; strangers are dangerous; asylum seekers are lazy, greedy, inferior, evil, dangerous liars, and anybody who lives in a council housing estate cannot possibly be interested in reading or writing poetry or prose.

A typical misconception when beginning as a writer, when you start creating literature, is that before you get down to the writing itself you have to rush away and do a course in English. You study for your 'O' grade and then you study for your 'H' grade and then the 'A' grade and then you start thinking maybe you should go to college or university and study for your 'Degree in English Literature' – because it seems somehow obvious that the more progress you make in the study of the subject the bigger the chance you'll have of becoming an actual writer, a creator of stories or poems. Absolute rubbish. This lies at the heart of the fallacy that when you are studying English literature within the higher education system you are at the same time studying the ways in which literature is created. Some people even believe that a person who qualifies to teach English is therefore qualified to teach 'creative writing'. They would be as well to believe the person was qualified to teach 'creative sculpting', 'creative musical composition', 'creative movie-making'.

Maybe it is time to stop using the phrase 'creative writing'. Maybe we should talk about 'literary art' or 'literature', about people creating literary art or people creating literature, instead of people 'doing creative writing'. Everybody uses language creatively, even teachers of English. If we are forced to use the phrase 'creative writing' let us insist on adopting a fuller phrase, let us call it 'creating creative writing'. But even that does not work properly, so just to avoid confusion we should stick with 'literary art' or 'literature'; literary artists create literature. Generally speaking, academics will prefer the phrase 'creative writing' in its current application because it allows literature to remain their property.

When a person writes a poem, play, short story or novel the person has become involved in the creation of literary art, the person is creating literature. The one way to write a poem, play, short story or novel is to sit down at the desk with your computer or your typewriter or with your pen and paper, and start writing. Literature is no different from other forms of art: when you want to create it and you have the tools and the materials then you just get to work, you begin. The writing comes first, not the theory. When people are involved in creating literature they are involved in a practice, they are engaged in an activity; in other words they have to be doing something as opposed to talking about doing something, or listening, reading, thinking about doing something. The vast majority of those who have studied literature at an advanced level, including English teachers, university lecturers and professors, have never created one piece of literary art in their entire lives. Of course a few have. But there again, so have a few doctors and lorry drivers; painters and construction workers; shop assistants and builders' labourers; people who are on the broo, people forced to be housebound while having to raise their families. Anyone who is able to read and write has the capacity to create a poem or story. And by practising and paying attention to the work they are doing it cannot help but improve. Everything else is secondary.

Of course it is difficult to make the start and it is difficult to continue having faith in what you do, in the face of what often seems to be straightforward hostility. Writers have to develop the habit of relying on themselves. It is as if there is a massive KEEP OUT sign hoisted above every area of literature. This is an effect of the hopeless elitism referred to earlier. But there are other reasons. The very idea of literary art as something alive and lurking within reach of ordinary women and men is not necessarily the sort of idea those who control the power in society will welcome with open arms. Maybe it is naïve to expect otherwise. Good literature is nothing when it is not being dangerous in some way or another and those in positions of power will always be suspicious of anything that might affect their security.

True literary art makes some folk uncomfortable. It can scare them. One method to cope with being scared is not to look, to turn away and then kid on whatever it is does not exist. Another method of coping is to get your tormentors to stop what it is they are doing. In some countries writers find their work is no longer being published or produced. Writers in other countries can get dumped into prison or banished into exile. Occasionally writers disappear suddenly and are never heard of again. In this country writers are suppressed and censored. It takes different forms. Censors can cut out words and lines from poems, stories, plays or films. They often ask the writers concerned to substitute other words and lines. Sometimes they just substitute words and lines they have invented by themselves. The censors may search through a writer's collection of stories and poems and take out ones that offend them; the censors will emphasise the ones that do not offend them. This is a method of silencing criticism because it makes it seem as if they are dealing fairly with the writers they have just finished censoring.

The folk in control of the power in society feel safest and most prefer it when writers agree to suppress and censor themselves. This happens throughout the media. The BBC is a fine example of it. So too are all other television companies and radio stations, plus almost the entire magazine and newspaper industry. Almost every writer working for the media, and wanting to continue working for the media, accepts that there are 'dangerous' things that are not to be written about and 'dangerous' language that is not to be used. Those who break these taboos and refuse to take the censoring will very soon discover that their work is no longer being used. Writers who persist in being 'dangerous' (i.e. honest to their art) will become notorious; they will be regarded as perverse, selfish, egocentric. They will be regarded as psychologically suspect, as though they are involved in some masochistic pursuit of failure. The logic is precise. If writers were truly interested not just in 'success' but in 'getting their message across' then they would jolly well stop being so bloody difficult and start suppressing and censoring themselves immediately, just like the rest of their third-rate colleagues.

While this is going on in the media at large, preparations for it are seen in the classroom. This is where folk are first made aware of what society expects in literary art. It is here they first discover how NOT to appreciate the potential of literature as a living art form, as a dynamic activity that might involve their friends, family and neighbours. The classroom is where we discover what is 'good' literature. Very soon 'good' literature and 'literature' become one and the same thing. Literature becomes the thing we are allowed to see in the classroom. The other stuff is the stuff we are not allowed to see.

I saw a letter to the *Independent* or *Guardian* recently in which someone wrote about the film *Billy Elliot* and said how it could be used as a text by schoolteachers if only the language was not so 'bad'. Why had those responsible not thought about such a thing in the first place. Did they not realise that by cleaning up their language their work would be of use to the classroom!

It is pointless being angry at the retired teacher who wrote the letter, if it was a retired teacher. The attitudes on display are simply those of the people in control of the education system, the media and society as a whole. If a writer wants to see his or her work made available in schools then it is high time repression and self-censorship began. When work is created by those who remain honest to their art then they are going to be proscribed, their stories, poetry and whatever will be banned from the classroom and the shelves of the school libraries.

If writers cannot sell their work to the media and cannot have their work sold across bookshop counters then sooner or later they must find other occupations. There was a collection of short stories entitled *Lean Tales* which has work by Agnes Owens, Alasdair Gray and myself. Agnes was also a novelist, published by Bloomsbury, the same as J. K. Rowling. But for most of her life she has never been able to give her best time to her literary work. Instead she had to find paying work in whatever capacity she could, and for long periods the only job she could get was as a servant, as a cleaner of the homes of middle-class people. In our society being a servant pays a wage whereas creating a literary art which attempts honesty in its portrayal of ordinary men and women pays almost nothing at all. Our schools and other institutions, including the media, encourage this actively.

Ninety-nine per cent of traditional English literature concerns people who never have to worry about money at all. We always seem to be watching or reading about emotional crises among folk who live in a world of great fortune both in matters of luck and money; stories and fantasies about rock stars and film stars, sporting millionaires and models; jet-setting members of the aristocracy and international financiers. Or else we are given straight genre fiction: detectives and murderers and cops and robbers; cowboys and indians and doctors and nurses; heroic spies and nasty Communists; science fiction, historical romance, diverse pornography; ghost stories, faery stories, vampire stories, horror tales of the supernatural, and so on.

The unifying feature of genre fiction is the way it denies reality. This is structural. In other words if reality had a part to play in genre fiction then it would stop being genre fiction. This is what distinguishes it from other forms of literature. But even in the romantic fantasies mentioned above we can catch a glimpse of something approaching reality, as when a dashing financier white Christian hero is about to rush off to catch a friend's private jet to Rio de Janeiro for lunch with a beautiful albeit 'dusky' South American princess, and he just remembers in the nick of time to give last-minute orders to his 'man' to phone the restaurant, not to reserve a table, just to check out the chef is the same as last time. But that kind of detail is rare. Usually the dashing young heroes do not even have to bother with things like visas and passports, the sort of petty details that trouble other travellers, let alone the kind of basic day-to-day worries that encroach on the lives of the rest of the population.

But should we expect anything else? Should we expect those in control of power in society to promote and encourage a literature that is explicitly concerned with the day-to-day existence of ordinary women and men? and by 'ordinary' here the context is run-of-the-mill day-to-day experience, as experienced by the overwhelming majority of the population. It would be quite pleasant to think this is the way things are. It would be nice to believe that ordinary women and men were being given every available opportunity to create a literature of poetry, prose, drama and song about homeless folk having to survive out in the streets or living off the edges of rubbish dumps; a literary art being created out of life on supplementary benefit, concerning itself with drug addiction, child prostitution, gluesniffing, alcoholism, kids of sixteen being forced on to the streets; stories, poetry and song about old people surviving the outrageous costs of medicine, heating and public transport; the latest round of humiliations being endured in the offices of the DSS or the Gas Board or the Housing Department or wherever the daily humiliation happens to be occurring this morning; police brutality, racial abuses, sectarian abuses, trade union corruption, political corruption, and everything else that comprises the reality of this country. Are we really surprised that these things dealt with properly, i.e. honestly and with artistic integrity, cannot be found in the literature promoted in schools and in the media generally? The fact is that we are consistently encouraged to accept that they have no place in English literature.

As I have mentioned before, I left school at the earliest opportunity, which in my day was fifteen years of age. I was an ordinary working-class boy making a dash for freedom at the very first opportunity the schools would allow. Like most working-class kids I was aware not only of the stigma of inferiority on my own forehead but also the one on the foreheads of my parents and neighbours. It is one of the more sophisticated features of the elitism in this country that prior to leaving school the majority of kids know not only what society thinks of them but what it thinks of their parents.

There was in Scotland a journal for English teachers entitled *Teaching English* and I remember a review of a novel just then published. The teacher responsible for the review seemed to like the novel yet he concluded the review by saying that:

> Its usefulness as a school text is unfortunately limited by the realistic inclusion in the dialogue of that element which [other writers have felt] necessary to suppress and, by references to frequent and prolonged bouts of drinking and occasional houghmagandie, the parents of your average 'S' grade candidate would certainly be moved to protest. But do read it for yourselves.

Let me tell you that 'houghmagandie' is a Scottish word for sex, not used very often, you will be amazed to hear, but it can still be heard, generally for purposes of irony. In that context it is not difficult to imagine a priest, church minister, Cabinet Minister, or even a Scottish Prime Minister using the same term. One thing it indicates is that the user of the term is at home in his culture; he is very comfortable in regard to booze, sex, drugs and rock and roll. Although he never gets too involved himself he certainly is not impressed by those who do, especially so-called writers who may want to create so-called literature around those areas for 'realistic' purposes. In his personal opinion writers who do create such work only do so for effect: such so-called 'realism' is a kind of adolescent exhibitionism.

It didn't occur to me for about five or six years after leaving school that literature was something I could be involved in. Then I discovered it was possible to write stories myself, I just had to go out and buy a couple of reliable ball-point pens and a good-sized notebook. I could even write stories about ordinary people if I wanted to. There wasn't anybody going to stop me by using physical force. After that I found out there were other people in this country also doing such things, and there were other people who had been doing such things for a couple of hundred years. It was just that nobody in any of the positions of power in society had got round to telling me.

Some of you may have noticed in the above extract from *Teaching English* how it is not just the kids being assessed, the actual parents have become 'S' grade; only 'S' grade parents have 'S' grade children. Here is the relevant part of the quote:

> by references to frequent and prolonged bouts of drinking and occasional houghmagandie, the parents of your average 'S' grade candidate would certainly be moved to protest. But do read it for yourselves.

Yes, see the execrable contempt! The English education authority has presupposed that 'the parents of your average 'S' grade candidate' will be less likely to recognise a work of 'realistic' literature than will the parents of your average 'O' grade candidate who in turn will be less likely than the parents of your average 'H' grade candidate who in turn will be less likely than the parents of your average 'A' grade candidate who will, of course, be much less likely than the parents of your average 'English-Degree-at-University' candidate. This kind of shameful nonsense is horrendous when laid out in cold print; it is how matters exist in our society. At best you end up with the patronising tones of the teacher-officer of English giving us to understand that it is fine for 'realistic' novels to be read by those who are properly qualified to do so, certainly not by 'S' grade adults. Of course there are those of us dumplings who do not even have an 'S' grade. Some of us dumplings do not even know what the hell an 'S' grade is, including myself and perhaps Agnes Owens, the woman who wrote the novel under review in *Teaching English*. It is one of the absurdities of this type of elitism that prior to when I went to university I was not qualified to read properly my own short stories and much of the earlier drafts of my first two novels.

Aye, on ye go.

CHAPTER TEN

The First Hundred Years of the Gaelic Novel

Moray Watson

It would not have been a realistic proposition to write a chapter on the Gaelic novel much before around 2000. In a general Scottish volume, this may strike many readers as surprising, when we consider the long and rich history of novel-writing that can be seen in the other two main languages we associate with the country. But we must always bear in mind that novel-writing is not a given in every community that has a literature, and that most languages of the world do not even enjoy any version of what we might properly describe as a literature. In *An Introduction to Gaelic Fiction* (2011), I discussed this situation at length, and noted that most of what we would think of as the body of Gaelic literature consisted of poetry until the early part of this century.[1] While poetry has remained important into the current century, there has been a marked change in the attention given to other forms, including both drama[2] and the novel, as well as a substantial increase in the production of these kinds of texts. In this chapter, I will explain the changes that have taken place that now make a discussion of the Gaelic novel viable, note some of the most salient features of the various surges in novel-writing activity, discuss the major figures whose work has set the standard for the form, and then finish by taking a look at the emergence of some new influences and areas of interest. Before beginning, it is worth noting that I am writing exclusively about novels written for adults. Since the 1960s, there have been short novels appearing that were aimed at children and teenagers. These books deserve their own critical attention, but they will not be discussed here as they have tended to be written for specific purposes and they are often directed towards educational goals. If this were a longer chapter, it would be worthwhile including them, and in any case they are overdue a thorough analysis in their own right. It is worth acknowledging that several of the recent books produced for adults have also been written at least partly with language education as a goal.

The present burgeoning in novel-writing and criticism is only the latest in a series of 'waves' in the development of the form. While it might be possible to point to some activity in the nineteenth century if we were trying to track down the first Gaelic novels, we can apply two criteria of convenience in our effort to date the emergence of the novel: namely, completion and appearance under their own cover. These criteria are by no means absolute, but they allow us to pinpoint a useful starting point for our survey: that is, a period between 1908 and 1923 when three novels and one novella appeared. Iain MacCormaic, a prolific writer of short stories, brought out his story *Gun D'Thug I Spéis Do 'n Àrmuinn* in 1908, described in its own publicity as 'a novelette'. This was followed four years later by the same author's *Dùn-Aluinn: no an t-Oighre 'na Dhìobarach*, representing the first 'full-sized' novel. The following year, MacCormaic's close contemporary and literary rival Aonghas MacDhonnchaidh published his *An t-Ogha Mór: no am Fear-Sgeòil air Uilinn*. This short flurry of activity was capped a decade later by Seumas MacLeòid's *Cailin Sgiathanach: no Faodalach na h-Abaid*. (Hereafter, the three novels will be referred to by their main titles only, for the sake of conciseness.) There then followed a hiatus of almost fifty years before sporadic production resumed during the 1970s, only to fade away again in the 1980s. A third period of productivity flared into life in the 1990s. This irregular and unpredictable activity relied on the efforts of certain energetic individuals, including MacCormaic, MacDhonnchaidh, their contemporary Ruaraidh Erskine of Mar, and, in the second half of the twentieth century, most crucially the editor, academic and publisher Derick Thomson. At the beginning of the current century, Thomson's retirement, and the consequent winding down of both his magazine *Gairm* and publishing house became the catalysts for a major effort to establish fiction writing on a steady and continuing footing. This took various forms, including fund-raising, awareness-raising, and the establishment of publishing contracts and literary prizes. The early 2000s thus marked the beginning of a period of novel-writing that has very quickly eclipsed everything that went before it, in terms of quantity and scope. As we embark on the third decade of this century, the stream of new novels continues unabated and, for the first time, we anticipate with some confidence the publication of more and more content with every year that passes. So, with this brief historical sketch in mind, let us consider some of the salient features of each of the waves of activity that I outlined here.

One of the things that most starkly characterises the early set of Gaelic novels is a strong sense of their being 'out of time'. The novella and all three novels of this initial (1908–1923) period give the impression of having been written deep in the nineteenth century, in terms of their concerns, their writing style, their deployment of literary devices and their plot and character development. While they are all set in the past, and could be said to be 'historical novels', it is unlikely that the anachronistic writing style is a deliberate feature used to authenticate their setting (contrast this with elements of Aonghas Pàdraig Caimbeul's *An Oidhche Mus Do Sheòl Sinn* of 2003, where the out-of-time style most certainly is a deliberate authenticating feature). Instead, these features suggest that the writers lacked either the interest or the confidence to produce work that showed an awareness of the full artistic context. This is in marked contrast to the poetry of the first half of the twentieth century, which gave us many important highlights and ultimately resulted in the very significant writing of Deòrsa Caimbeul Hay and Somhairle MacGill-Eain.[3] In *An Introduction to Gaelic Fiction* (2011), I have hinted that this might be part of the reason why the early efforts to create a body of extended fiction ultimately failed and left the floor to the poets.

The attentive reader might well have noticed that I used the term 'full-sized', including inverted commas, when referring to the first novel, MacCormaic's *Dùn-Aluinn*. This usage was based on two doubts: the first is that there is no established word count that we would all agree constitutes the minimum length for a novel, and the second is that all of the first three Gaelic novels are rather short. *Dùn-Aluinn* is only slightly more than fifty thousand words long, a size that has it hovering just scarcely beyond the range of a typical novella. Both *An t-Ogha Mór* and *Cailin Sgiathanach* are also on the shorter side. If we briefly lurch forward in time to the period between 1971 and 2002, we discover that this restricted length remained the norm in the world of Gaelic fiction until the most recent two decades. We have not identified the reasons for this tendency, although we could speculate that there were cost implications and other issues to do with business-related risks for authors, publishers and the readership. Another possibility here could be that writers lacked confidence or experience in the production of extended prose, that there was a lack of qualified editors, or that there were doubts about the audience's appetite for longer fiction in Gaelic.[4] It may well be that a combination of all these factors (and others) was at play. In any case, the three early novels are on the shorter side, despite plotlines that ramble and leave the reader with an impression of having trudged through a long and exhausting journey.

The 1970s saw a second stuttering attempt to bring the novel into the Gaelic milieu. Again, it might be more proper to refer to these books as novellas. In particular, Iain Mac a' Ghobhainn's *An t-Aonaran* (1976) and Tormod Caimbeul's *Deireadh an Fhoghair* (1979) more closely resemble the form of the novella, in their tight focus on small groups of characters, limited action, relatively restricted point-of-view and particularly low word count: for the most part, the volumes of the 1970s, and the one that appeared in 1989, are even briefer than the three novels of 1912–1923. At the same time, it is fair to say that *An t-Aonaran* and *Deireadh an Fhoghair*, and, to some extent, Cailein T. MacCoinnich's *A' Leth Eile* (1971) are in many ways considerably more substantial than any of those three earlier novels. Their deployment of technical devices and their emphasis on characterisation and character development distinguishes the 1970s novels from their predecessors. Even the relatively more lightweight *Gainmheach an Fhàsaich* (1971) by Màiri Nic Gill-Eain is more effective and convincing than the first wave of novels. Both *An t-Aonaran* and *Deireadh an Fhoghair* are thematically dense despite their brevity, and reward repeated re-reading. Both books have scarcely anything that could be called plot. In the case of *An t-Aonaran*, the plot centres on the thoughts, feelings and few actions of its solitary main character; as for *Deireadh an Fhoghair*, there are three main characters, whose interactions and dialogue form the bulk of the work. Atmospherically, these two novels have a good deal in common, but there are also many points of dissimilarity. The most striking of these is in the depiction of the characters' place in the community. In *An t-Aonaran*, the main character does not integrate into the community where he lives, whereas in *Deireadh an Fhoghair*, our three main characters effectively are the community, albeit that they are the remnant of a community that will die out imminently.

There is one other work that appeared during the 'revival' decade, although it has never been published under its own cover. That is Iain Mac a' Ghobhainn's experimental, surreal novel *Murchadh*, which was serialised in the magazine *Gairm* between 1979 and 1980. The serial format suits *Murchadh*, which is episodic in structure. In fact, the book very deliberately resists a plot or features of formal realism. Instead, it uses its fragmentary nature to explore ideas of nihilism, solipsism, and altered perceptions of reality, where the eponymous hero tries to reconcile his sense of significance with the evident lack of meaning in everything around him. The novel represents a descent into madness for its main character and yet that descent is offset by a tongue-in-cheek and even, at times, zany humour. It is tempting to see the influence of figures such as Eugène Ionesco or Samuel Beckett, and there are certainly elements that locate this novel in the context of the Absurd. *Murchadh*'s search for meaning is the only recurring central theme, and the reader is always aware that that search is doomed to futility. Readers of this chapter who are not familiar with Gaelic might nevertheless be familiar with the Murchadh character and some of his foibles, as he has also appeared in English as Murdo, the hero of *Thoughts of Murdo* (1993) and *Murdo: The Life and Works* (2001). Indeed, *Murchadh* has this fact in common with two of Iain Mac a' Ghobhainn's other novels, *An t-Aonaran* and *Am Miseanaraidh* (2005). Although not direct translations, English versions of both have appeared (as short stories!) under the author's anglophone name Iain Crichton Smith.

Mac a' Ghobhainn's final Gaelic novel was *Na Speuclairean Dubha* which came out in 1989. (I have described this as Mac a' Ghobhainn's final Gaelic novel, even though *Am Miseanaraidh* appeared later. This is because *Am Miseanaraidh* was evidently written in the 1970s and then either lost or abandoned. It was discovered after the author's death and brought out in 2005 as part of the Ùr-Sgeul initiative.) Unlike the other three, this one has no English version available. It is, however, similarly slight in size. Despite this, it is one of the most significant Gaelic novels and ranks alongside *An t-Aonaran* and *Deireadh an Fhoghair* in terms of merits. Readers familiar with some of Iain Crichton Smith's novels in English would find a lot to recognise in *Na Speuclairean Dubha*. In particular, it is reminiscent of books like *In the Middle of the Wood*, *An End to Autumn* and *My Last Duchess*. Like those other books, *Na Speuclairean Dubha* features a main character who struggles to express himself despite his obvious gifts with language. This theme returns regularly both in Mac a' Ghobhainn's work and also in a good deal of the other prose literature in the language and may metonymically represent a sense of frustration that such a richly expressive language as Gaelic has so few people who use it.

Chronologically, *Na Speuclairean Dubha* belongs more with the group of novels that appeared in the 1990s, but stylistically and thematically it feels more like the set that appeared in the 1970s. In that sense, it provides a bridge to what became an unexpectedly productive decade. No fewer than eight new novels were published during the 1990s. This was the period when writers began experimenting with genres (although *Gainmheach an Fhàsaich* was an earlier attempt to introduce the romantic drama genre into the language). This decade saw more overt political commentary, aimed both at government and also at corporations. Clear examples of this are *Clann Iseabail* (1993) by Màiri NicGumaraid, which has the British occupation of Northern Ireland as an important background, and *Cùmhantan* (1996) by Tormod MacGill-Eain, which takes a swipe at the business practices and greed of those involved in media industries in the early 1990s. Both *Cùmhnantan* and MacGill-Eain's other novel from this era, *Keino* (1998), introduce a good deal more humour into the mode than was evident in previous novels, despite their serious subject-matters and, at times, graphic use of verbal and physical violence. MacGill-Eain was to continue in the same vein with two further novels in 2005 and 2008, with the latter two relying even more heavily on humour.

We might consider the 1990s as the point where the Gaelic novel's audience began to diversify, and where writers began making an effort to appeal to a wider range of different types of readers. For instance, we have Calum MacMhaoilein's two short novels that are reminiscent of some of the books being produced for teenagers around the same time and which take Highland culture as their inspiration, combining elements of saga and vivid depiction of the community, while three years after the second of these, we have Dòmhnall Iain MacIomhair's attempt at a first Gaelic whodunnit, *Cò Rinn E?* (1996). (This is the first novel-length attempt at a whodunnit, though the genre was explored through the medium of the short story between the end of the nineteenth century and the early part of the twentieth.) Then again, Alasdair Caimbeul's *Am Fear Meadhanach* (1992) has a good deal in common with the highlights of the previous wave, up to and including *Na Speuclairean Dubha*. Caimbeul's novel is set in a recognisably Gaelic heartland community and employs idiomatic language and typical cultural elements to add authenticity to both narrative and dialogue. It is rather literary in character, as is Tormod Calum Dòmhnallach's formidable *An Sgàineadh* (1993), whose deliberately fragmentary structure recalls both Hogg's *Confessions* and Gray's *Lanark*.

As I noted in the introduction to this chapter, a seismic shift in the Gaelic publishing world took place when it lost one of its greatest assets to retirement. Derick Thomson finally stepped back from his publishing ventures and from editing the important literary magazine *Gairm* when the new century dawned. The significance of this cannot be overstated, as the magazine and the imprint of the same name had been enormously influential for half a century. As it turned out, what looked like a potential disaster for Gaelic publishing turned out to be a catalyst that has resulted in a huge boost for the industry. Various efforts have been put into replacing *Gairm* magazine, but our interest in the present chapter lies with what happened in terms of the production and distribution of novels. I have written elsewhere[5] about the establishment of the Ùr-Sgeul project and the opportunities it created for authors and publishers, but let us take a brief glance at some of the fruits borne not only directly but also indirectly by the efforts of the enterprising individuals who were behind Ùr-Sgeul.

I noted that we are seeing indirect benefits of Ùr-Sgeul, and these benefits continue to reveal themselves. Once that initiative normalised the idea of novel-writing within the Gaelic community and created ever-greater expectations among the audience and the publishers, other novel-writing activities increased substantially. As a result, we now have several publishers who are involved in producing extended prose fiction in Gaelic, and the range of writers involved has also increased considerably. The publisher who took on the Ùr-Sgeul contract was CLÀR, an Inverness-based imprint which has since continued producing important books for adults, including fiction. The follow-up initiative to Ùr-Sgeul, known as Aiteal, went to the Lewis-based publisher Acair. Similarly, since the conclusion of Aiteal, Acair has continued producing novels in addition to its pre-existing wide range of Gaelic and Gaelic-related books. Other publishers who have begun making substantial contributions include Luath Press and Sandstone Press, and we may hope that this diversification is a sign of increased vitality and potential sustainability.

It is reasonable to state that, despite attempts at the start and end of the twentieth century, it was only in the early 2000s that the Gaelic novel really established itself. Right from the start of this 'nouvelle vague' (I am using this term with tongue firmly in cheek, of course, but it fits with the metaphor I used earlier to describe the various 'waves' of Gaelic novel-writing), writers demonstrated a willingness to experiment with new forms, techniques, subject-matter and genres. Aonghas Pàdraig Caimbeul kicked things off with his *An Oidhche Mus Do Sheòl Sinn* (2003), a novel that attempted a grand, sweeping narrative on a scale never seen before in the language. And yet, scarcely a year later, he was back with *Là a' Dèanamh Sgèil Do Là* (2004), a much tighter story that combined science fiction elements with very contemporary concerns pertaining to both the language and its community. But Caimbeul was by no means the last to indulge in these modernising efforts. For a grand, sweeping narrative, for instance, we could look to the trilogy (2006, 2008, 2011) by Norma NicLeòid, a saga following a group of families across generations. For harder science fiction, we can look to *Air Cuan Dubh Drìlseach* (2013) by Tim Armstrong, which is set almost entirely in space. Among authors attempting something 'new' in the Gaelic novel, we have Màrtainn Mac an t-Saoir, who, by the time he brought out *An Latha as Fhaide* (2008), was already well established as a writer of fiction. In *An*

Latha as Fhaide, Mac an t-Saoir turns form on its head and subverts the idea of movement that we associate with a novel, making the action of the entire book take place in a single day. His novel becomes, in a way, a very long short story. Mac an t-Saoir's earlier *Gymnippers Diciadain* (2005) had also experimented with form, introducing short inter-chapters to contextualise the events of the story and to fill in more detail about the lives of the two main characters. Like *An Latha as Fhaide*, the novel maintained a strict control over formal elements, for instance in that the greater bulk of the story takes place in the same setting. If the first three novels could be described as historical fiction, Iain F. MacLeòid brought that back with his *Am Bounty* (2008), but then took things further by introducing the high fantasy genre to Gaelic in *An Sgoil Dhubh* (2014) after the end of the Ùr-Sgeul period. Then again, perhaps we could call Fionnlagh MacLeòid's prize-winning *Gormshuil an Rìgh* (2010) an earlier attempt at epic fantasy, although it is heavily grounded in a Gaelic mythopoeic world in contrast with Iain F. MacLeòid's more familiar blended world-building that is reminiscent of 'traditional' high fantasy. In that sense, though, we could argue that *Gormshuil an Rìgh* anticipates to some degree the current trends in embracing diversity in high fantasy world-building. At the same time, *An Sgoil Dhubh* incorporates elements that look as if they have been taken from a Gaelic folkloric context as well. What distinguishes *An Sgoil Dhubh* is its emphasis on plot and on the depiction of action sequences involving sword fighting and magical duels. Its author, Iain F. MacLeòid, also demonstrated his ability with the depiction of action sequences and gritty dialogue in some of the highlight moments in his 2005 book *Na Klondykers*.

As well as creating a platform for the emergence of new talent, the Ùr-Sgeul period also provided opportunities for established novelists such as Tormod and Alasdair Caimbeul. Tormod Caimbeul's *Deireadh an Fhoghair* had been one of the most important highlights of the revival period, so it was no surprise when his *Shrapnel* (2006) pushed the boundaries in terms of subject-matter, technical devices and characterisation. Petra Johana Poncarová suggests that 'there is probably no other Gaelic novel which would be as bold and new in terms of topic and setting and as assured and daring in terms of narrative structure, language, and the wide range of references'.[6] *Shrapnel* follows the lead of *Deireadh an Fhoghair* in having its plot take a back seat in favour of character interaction. Caimbeul's 2011 *An Druim Bho Thuath* continues this trend, giving the strong impression that Caimbeul's interest in the novel lay primarily in the realm of dramatic tension. He revels in throwing together characters whose reactions to each other and to their situation are reminiscent of drama. Indeed, Poncarová also notes, in relation to *An Druim Bho Thuath* (although it is also true of the other two novels), that there are dialogue exchanges that read 'like a short play'.[7] Tormod's brother Alasdair writes prose that is similarly influenced by the dramatic form, having been a successful playwright before taking up novel-writing with his *Am Fear Meadhanach*. In the case of Alasdair Caimbeul's 2011 novel *Cuid a' Chorra-Ghrithich*, Ronald Black's review even likens the experience of reading it to the experience of reading a play.[8] And, although Black suggests that he might not choose to sit down to read a play as such, the richness of language has meant that he, nevertheless, enjoyed the novel.

The Ùr-Sgeul initiative was a fixed-term project, with limited funding and specific end goals. Its success can be measured in the dramatically altered literary landscape that Ùr-Sgeul left behind. As well as books of short stories, one or two novellas and a translated novel, Ùr-Sgeul provided us with more than twenty original novels over a period of less than a decade. It is no surprise therefore that follow-on funding was provided to encourage the further development of prose fiction for adults. The publisher that took this forward was the long-established Acair, based in Stornoway. Fewer novels were produced during this follow-on 'Aiteal' phase, with the emphasis shifting slightly to incorporate a larger number of short story collections. Nevertheless, more advances were made. As well as the aforementioned *An Sgoil Dhubh* and another title by the same author, the Aiteal books include the historical novel *Còisir nan Gunna* (2013) by the gifted debutant Anndra A. Dunn. The other Aiteal novelists were already active during the Ùr-Sgeul phase, including Norma NicLeòid, author of the first trilogy and Catrìona Lexy Chaimbeul, who previously wrote the genre-expanding *Samhraidhean Dìomhair* (2009). A highlight of the Aiteal phase is Màrtainn Mac an t-Saoir's 2014 short novel *Cala Bendita 's a Bheannachdan*, which offers a stark contrast with his *An Latha as Fhaide* mentioned above. And yet, despite being very different in many ways, these two novels of Mac an t-Saoir's both develop the structural experimentalism we noted as also being true of his *Gymnippers Diciadain* (2005). In *Cala Bendita 's a Bheannachdan*, Mac an t-Saoir gives tantalising little clues and invites the reader to piece together the events of the plot. This, along with surprising shifts of point-of-view, and the use of various other languages (including an entire chapter in a dialect of English), combine to make the novel both challenging and fascinating. It is difficult to imagine a writer attempting anything like this had it not been for the Ùr-Sgeul period that preceded it and, in many ways, paved the way for the wide range of styles, genres, techniques and devices that have become regular features of the contemporary novel.

A notable feature of the earliest wave of Gaelic novels was that they were produced by a group of writers who were already well-known for writing in other modes. This was also true of the second and third waves of the 1970s to the 1990s. By the time we reached the Ùr-Sgeul and post-Ùr-Sgeul period, this was no longer necessarily the case: authors were first emerging onto the literary scene fully-formed as novelists. However, there are numerous exceptions to this statement, such as in the case of Maoilios Caimbeul, who was one of the leading poets in Gaelic, and a successful children's author, for many years before he began his novel-writing career. Caimbeul's *Teas* (2010), for instance, proves a more convincing introduction to the crime-based drama than what we received in *Cò Rinn E* fourteen years earlier. In *Teas*, Caimbeul writes a series of different and intriguing characters, demonstrating his typical gift for language. There are sections of the novel where he deploys the epistolary technique to good effect, moving on both the plot and the relationships between the characters and their sub-plots.

Finally, it is worth mentioning the fact that translated literature has been a relatively late arrival in Gaelic. That is not to say that there was never any translated work, but rather that the translation of novels has only very recently been taken up. We may find that surprising, in light of Even-Zohar's (1978) suggestion that translated texts have important parts to play in a literature like that of Gaelic.[9] There were short texts translated into Gaelic, primarily from English, but no novels until the past few years. Aonghas Pàdraig Caimbeul's recent (2021) translation of *Animal Farm* is a very welcome addition to the suite of literature available to Gaelic readers. With the increase in translation of graphic novels over the past few years, and with fiction like Ian Rankin's short stories now making their way into Gaelic, we may hope that Caimbeul's efforts will inspire further endeavours in this area. I am not entirely innocent in this regard myself, having translated *Alice's Adventures in Wonderland* into Gaelic a decade ago and now being in the process of proofing my translation of *The Hobbit*. Interestingly, there has always been plenty translation *out of* Gaelic, perhaps demonstrating a cultural self-confidence and a desire to be recognised more widely, and this has carried on into the current period of fiction-writing: notable examples of this being translations into French of Màrtainn Mac an t-Saoir's short stories and into Czech of the novel *Deireadh an Fhoghair*. Although these do not add to the set of texts available for us to read in Gaelic, they do help to remind us that there already exists a great deal of material that is well worth reading: so worthy of being read, indeed, that people want to make them available to readers of other languages.

It is remarkable how much things have changed in such a short period of time. When I began reading Gaelic fiction, there was some excitement because *An t-Aonaran* was available again after a brief hiatus. There were no other novels that could be bought unless you were lucky enough to stumble upon them in a second-hand bookshop. Only the most impressively stocked libraries had copies. Reading the three early novels was a chore, because they used outdated orthography (with some deliberate obscure usages as well), dialect-specific vocabulary that was not always readily available in dictionaries, and expressions that have since gone out of use in the everyday vernacular: notwithstanding the fact that they were, in varying degrees, weak attempts at writing, due to plodding plotlines, thin characterisation, unconvincing motivation and clunky dialogue. The upsurge of activity in the 1990s was welcome but limited in scope, quantity and, at times, quality. In the past two decades, the situation has undergone a complete sea-change. Illustrative of this, we may look to the online shop at the Gaelic Books Council. Where the fiction section might previously have been divided between short stories and novels (if we were being optimistic), now we see sections for 'Teenage/Young Adult', 'Adventure & Thriller', 'Audiobooks', 'Crime', 'Fantasy & Science Fiction', 'Fiction in Translation', 'Graphic Novels', 'Historical Fiction', as well as other sections for drama, short stories and periodical fiction. We now have a range of annual literary prizes, commission grants for authors, publishing grants, writer-in-residence schemes, literary mentoring schemes, and support for an MLitt in Publishing for Gaelic speakers. This is all indicative of a growing confidence in the novel (among other forms), as well as a sustained appetite for it. It would be reasonable to conclude this survey by stating that the Gaelic novel has finally come of age and that it truly now caters for a diverse audience with a broad range of interests.

CHAPTER ELEVEN

Scottish Detective Fiction

Matthew Wickman

It is doubtful that future literary historians will remember Irvine Welsh because of novels like *Crime* (2008). Even for Welsh, the novel seems to have been something of an afterthought – literally. It reprises the character Lennox who plays the sidekick in *Filth* (1998), Welsh's previous – filthy – crime story. And it recapitulates many a trope associated with the genre of detective fiction, particularly the popular Scottish brand of such fiction known as 'Tartan Noir'. In Welsh's iteration of the genre, a burned-out detective is on holiday in Florida when he stumbles across an international paedophilia ring, which he ultimately assists in vanquishing. The subject matter is at once serious and sentimental, and traces of that uneasy pairing reflect across a set of stereotypes for which the novel expresses both humorous disdain and emotional attachment. An alligator consumes a West Highland terrier named Braveheart; one character offers a drunken, barstool defence of Robert Burns while another, later, expresses sober appreciation for Burns's outsized influence; the tale Welsh spins inevitably spirals into a saga of conspiracy; and, perhaps most tellingly for the genre to which the novel belongs, it reflects on the connection between America and Scotland, the former 'more than a country of big cars and strange sports' and the latter more than a nation of 'Calvinistic gloom [Lennox's] tribe could wear like a plaid'.[1]

In its way, Tartan Noir has always been a genre of 'more than'. It is more than a copycat of an American original, more than a product of the moodiness of Scottish weather (an occasional claim for the resonance of hard-boiled fiction in and with Scotland) and more than a cash cow for an ever-expanding pantheon of successful novelists. As I have discussed elsewhere, Tartan Noir has also served as a medium of serious reflection onto the question of what it means to 'be' – what it means to be Scottish, to be modern, to be human.[2] Such reflection creeps into corners of Welsh's *Crime* (e.g. 'How well can we truly know others when we only see them through the lens of the self?'),[3] often taking the form of camp – of cheeky, lowbrow simulations of high philosophy. One of the most vivid manifestations of this sensibility in the novel is when Lennox's fiancée, Trudi, is channel surfing and comes across a kitschy, all-too-American television programme in which 'a grinning couple' shows its viewers how to exercise by using pets as weights. '"This is a tricky one, but remember, if your cat gets uncomfortable and leaves, you're going too fast"' – he 'slowly raises the animal with a leg extension' – '"Slooowww … that's the way, almost imperceptible. Luckily, Heidegger's a little tired right now"'.[4]

Heidegger: the nominal foil (in pet name absurdity) to Braveheart the terrier. But also a consummate, if understated, emblem of Tartan Noir. For Martin Heidegger is the great philosopher of Being, and questions of being pervade the genre. This is what may be most compelling about Welsh's novel. Where some critics read *Crime* as staking out new directions in Welsh's fiction, the novel's generic quality – its style of posing ontological questions in a manner evocative of Ian Rankin, Raymond Chandler, and other exponents of high-class pulp – tells a compelling story in its own right.[5] For genres bear histories, and the Tartan Noir brand of detective fiction, exploring modern being, possesses a revealing one. While I lack the space in this chapter to sketch a full history, I will set forth some key aspects of such a history and bring attention to indicative exhibits of the genre. This chapter makes a case for Tartan Noir as one branch of a much wider literary phenomenon, but a branch of particular interest given the degree to which these novels give expression to questions of modern life. My two-fold aim, then, will be, first, to trace the conceptual parameters of the hard-boiled genre and then, second, to illustrate a few key (but by no means exhaustive) examples of how Tartan Noir at once reflects and redirects aspects of the genre's legacy.

*

In part, and for all its worldly brio, hard-boiled fiction bears a strongly sentimental heritage. As Leonard Cassuto observes, 'stereotypically masculine hard-boiled crime fiction and stereotypically feminine, evangelical, and domestic sentimental fiction are two branches of the same tree'. At its core, then, and in keeping with this heritage, 'crime fiction is really about the pleasures and challenges of community,' such that '[i]nside every crime story is a sentimental narrative that's trying to come out'.[6] This slice of history is important, for it underscores the desire hard-boiled fiction retains for community amid peril. The campiness of the genre, the self-mimicry of its worldly cynicism superimposed over its sentimental core, thus represents a measure of self-consciousness with respect to this communal desire, an awareness of the labile quality of anything like *the collective spirit* in a modern era widely associated with various kinds of corruption: moral, corporate, political, ecological and more. This complexity – of genre; of the corrupt seepage of sentimentality – helps explain why in so many ways noir becomes popular as an American genre. And this, in turn, makes the trashy Floridian setting of Welsh's novel all the more apt. 'Tart Noir', Lee Horsley labels the Scottish slant on this brand of fiction.[7]

Albeit in roundabout fashion, this returns our attention for a moment to Heidegger, particularly in reflecting on Tartan Noir and on what seems distinctively Scottish about the genre. In his *Introduction to Metaphysics* (delivered as lectures in 1935, published in 1953), Heidegger famously remarked that Europe

> lies today in the great pincers between Russia on the one side and America on the other. Russia and America, seen metaphysically, are both the same: the same hopeless frenzy of unchained technology and of the rootless organization of the average man.[8]

Heidegger's philosophy – as he believed for a short spell in the mid-1930s, sustained by Nazi politics – was to be the great alternative, the medium of a fuller, less 'average' sense of community. Of interest here is less Heidegger's own interpretation of German philosophical destiny than his appeal to liminality. For, if Heidegger's Europe found itself in this liminal space, Scotland has been more liminal still, not only geographically but nationally and existentially, caught between America and Russia, Britain and independence, Brexit and the EU. And caught, too, between the earnestness of Heidegger's desideratum and the conventionality, even the kitschiness, of its enunciation.

I have explored this elsewhere, but it bears brief rehearsal here.[9] Beginning with William McIlvanney's *Laidlaw* (1977), published the year after Heidegger's death, Tartan Noir has long given expression to thoughts of an ontological and existential nature. In many cases, as in *Laidlaw*, the philosophical connections are obvious. Laidlaw, the protagonist of McIlvanney's novel, keeps 'Kierkegaard, Camus and Unamuno' in his desk and alludes to Heidegger in instructing his partner, Harkness: 'Your way of life is taught to you like a language. It's how you express yourself. But any language conceals as much as it reveals.'[10] The passage evokes a famous meditation of Heidegger's on the status of truth as 'unconcealment' in the 1936 essay 'The Origin of the Work of Art'. In other instances, the connections between Tartan Noir and Heideggerian ontology are less pronounced. That they are present at all says less about the philosophical reading habits of every last exponent of Tartan Noir (with some notable exceptions, McIlvanney and Ian Rankin perhaps foremost among them) than about the cognitive reflexes of Heidegger's thought, which reads uncannily like hard-boiled fiction. A 1946 lecture subsequently published as 'What Are Poets For?' evokes familiar hard-boiled motifs:

> The closer the world's night draws toward midnight, the more exclusively does the destitute prevail, in such a way that it withdraws its very nature and presence. Not only is the holy lost as the track toward the godhead; even the traces leading to that lost track are well-nigh obliterated. The more obscure the traces become less can a single mortal, reaching into the abyss, attend there to institutions and signs.[11]

For all its metaphysical pathos over modern 'destitut[ion]', the passage's references to corruption, ambiguous clues (the 'withdraw[n] [...] nature and presence') and heroic 'mortal[s] reaching into the abyss' evoke the quintessential hard-boiled scenario described by Raymond Chandler:

> down these mean streets a man must go who is not himself mean, who is neither tarnished nor afraid. The detective in this kind of story [...] is the hero, he is everything [...]. The story is his adventure in search of a hidden truth, and it would be no adventure if it did not happen to a man fit for adventure.[12]

Heidegger struck this note on several occasions. In 'What Is Metaphysics?' he mediates philosophy through the logic of conspiracy: 'every metaphysical question always encompasses the whole', one thing implicating everything else'.[13] He also returns to imagery of 'mystery' and the philosopher's role in solving it: 'What conserves letting-be in this relatedness to concealing? Nothing less than [...] the mystery; not a particular mystery regarding this or that, but rather the one mystery.'[14] '[T]hat which frees – the mystery – is concealed and always concealing itself.'[15] '[I]n being struck by what is actual, man may be debarred precisely from what concerns and touches him – touches him in the surely mysterious way of escaping him by its withdrawal.'[16] 'Whatever has to remain unspoken will be held in reserve in the unsaid. It will linger in what is concealed as something unshowable. It is mystery.'[17] A novel like *Laidlaw*, and Tartan Noir more generally, thus presents an interpretive circle, a structure Heidegger identifies with ontological inquiry: hard-boiled fiction employs philosophical motifs that in turn evoke the conventions of detective fiction. What we behold here is not a matter of influence but rather an uncanny convergence of thought, a pattern of perception. It bears an estranging effect on theory as much as Tartan Noir. The latter becomes a vehicle for serious inquiry even as theory flattens into the familiar, pulpy shape of the hard-boiled detective genre.

The strangeness of this conjuncture of (serious) philosophy and (campy) form may help us solve a riddle: detective novels are popular because they are fun, but that begs the question of why we find that kind of story (crime – suspense – solution) appealing in the first place. There is an element here of problem-solving through vicarious experience, or play, as detective stories externalise processes of inference that pervade our lives, such that the solution of whodunnits vicariously promises resolution to our own crises.[18] Other scholars, however, like Lee Horsley, argue that noir in particular introduces an important complication into this anthropological explanation by inscribing itself within a traumatic divide. For Horsley, mysteries not only serve an Aristotelian cathartic function – clarifying our situation by enacting and resolving its complexities – but also harrow us with images of experiences our stories cannot help us reconcile. To a degree, then, noir is about the failure of narrative.[19] That failure, though, serves as an index of desire: hard-boiled detective fiction, in which the protagonist becomes embroiled in the crime under investigation, portrays a profoundly interconnected world; it gives expression to a yearning for wholeness, and thus to something like epic. Hard-boiled detective fiction, we might say, is a perennially popular and durable but also unstable genre: Koichi Suwabe argues that detective fiction 'aims to restore the (already lost) paradise more straightforwardly than "serious" fiction'.[20]

Traces of this yearning instability cling to hard-boiled detectives, who embody preternatural powers of discernment while also openly exhibiting any number of moral flaws. To a degree, this was already true with early detectives like Arthur Conan Doyle's Sherlock Holmes, with his cocaine and morphine addictions.[21] Such flaws are then exaggerated in Tartan Noir, if not in the substances its characters ingest, then in the gusto with which they proclaim their fallen humanity. (One small example, taken from Ian Rankin's DI Rebus: '"I'm serious, John,"' Rebus's physician tells him. '"You smoke, you drink like a fish, and you don't exercise [...] [Y]our diet's gone to hell'". Rebus, unfazed and perpetually rebellious, answers with ironic disdain: '"So," he said, "see you in the pub later?"'[22]) This may help explain why there is a less defined sense of whodunnit in hard-boiled novels. As Jon Thompson remarks, crime in this genre – the stain of mortally flawed humanity – is less a strictly delimited act than an existential condition: 'Ultimately, there can be no solution to a crime' in hard-boiled fiction 'because crime is not extrinsic to the system but intrinsic, part of it'.[23] Everyone and everything is not only fallen, but embroiled, implicated. So it is, Ronald R. Thomas observes, that hard-boiled detectives do not really solve crimes as much as come to terms with pervasive corruption or else hold out tragically against it; detectives in this genre are 'not commissioned to identify or bring to justice a single culprit, but to investigate a proliferating state of corruption that can at best be stabilized, not corrected'.[24]

This helps account for the characteristic curmudgeonliness of the hard-boiled detective, explaining as well his or her cynicism, antinomian behaviour, and deep moral ambivalence. For the French theorist Gilles Deleuze, this also helps us understand the relationship between classical detective fiction and its noir descendant – and why and how the former, but not the latter, was 'philosophical': classical detective fiction depicts a world in which truth is still possible, motivating the search for the same.[25] By contrast, Ernst Bloch observes, the post-classical, hard-boiled turn in detective fiction divulges 'totality' triumphing over truth; it favours the experiential immediacy of Henri Bergson over the rationalism of John Stuart Mill.[26] All this lends hard-boiled detective fiction a deeply phenomenological quality: it underscores how and not just what we see. As Lee Horsley explains,

> The noir narrative is frequently focused through the mind of a single character who is bemused or disingenuous; it ironises his evasions and disguises; it calls into question his judgements; [and] it foregrounds the difficulties of interpreting a mendacious society.[27]

It thus seems fitting that McIlvanney's Laidlaw sounds like Heidegger, given the latter's emergence from the phenomenological tradition of Edmund Husserl that called philosophy into question. But it also seems apt that Heidegger should sound like Laidlaw, given that in the latter and his avatars one finds the kitschy, exaggerated features and cadence of the meta-philosophical turn Heidegger was instituting in modern thought.

Welsh's *Crime* – a Scottish novel set in America, channelling German philosophy – thus divulges more than it probably realises: Welsh's relatively pedestrian novel contains within itself key elements from the history of the genre. For detective fiction was nominally born in America, though its roots are more deeply Scottish and its branches bear German fruit. Edgar Allan Poe's 'Murders in the Rue Morgue' (1841), which sets itself in Paris, brings the inspector – C. Auguste Dupin – into the world. And Dupin arrives speaking the Scottish commonsense philosophy of Thomas Reid, specifically Reid's criticism of the sceptical metaphysics of David Hume: 'the mental features discoursed of as analytical are, in themselves, but little susceptible of analysis.'[28] For Glenn W. Most, such dialogue injects mystery into the investigation of crime – a mystery that pertains to the mind of the analyst as much as to the matter under examination: 'the mysteries that can be solved are not as mysterious as those posed by the power that solves them.'[29] How do we understand the world? In what does cognition consist? Commonsense philosophy, too easily dismissed as anti-intellectual (as 'common' sense), posed precisely these kinds of questions. As I discuss elsewhere, drawing on the work of Cairns Craig, the nineteenth-century Scottish philosopher Andrew Seth presented Reid's thought as the forgotten alternative to the tradition running from Descartes to Kant. Where the latter erroneously differentiated world from mind, causing thinkers to seek an illusory origin of mentality (in, say, the Cartesian *cogito*), Reid's philosophy situated thought instead within a complex system of relations. Such relations rooted themselves in our pasts and in the myriad impressions we receive in the present. Paul Gorner has revealed how this circumvention of idealism would pass from eighteenth-century Scotland into the German phenomenological tradition of Husserl and Heidegger.[30] To that extent, while Welsh's Lennox or McIlvanney's Laidlaw occasionally break into Heideggerian lingo, Heidegger's native philosophical language itself bears a Scottish accent.

Conan Doyle's Sherlock Holmes at once reflects and distorts these conceptual and generic origins. To a great extent, Doyle was responsive to the conventions Poe had employed, as he was to the public's growing taste for sensationalised tales of crime (fed in part, Jon Thompson observes, by growing attention to such stories in the mass media: 'Conan Doyle's detective fiction appealed not only to a wider readership [...] but also to an increased public interest in sensational crime'[31]). Also consistently with Poe, the Sherlock Holmes narratives were equally informed by other developments in intellectual culture. Ronald R. Thomas rehearses longstanding criticism associating Doyle's methods with Darwin's in biology as well as with the Scottish geologist Charles Lyell's.[32] The connecting thread between detective fiction, evolutionary biology, and geology consists in what we today call 'deep time', amounting for Darwin, Lyell, and Doyle to a penchant for excavating and revising history. To address the weight of history (even if only in the petty form of unsolved domestic mysteries), Doyle created a character in Holmes who is part forensic scientist, part artist, and part critic (e.g. of the failed methods of detection – of historical excavation – espoused by others). Thomas goes so far as to liken Holmes to a machine, proposing that photography, an invention hyper-attuned to detail, laid the cultural and conceptual groundwork for the Holmesian brand of detection. 'That might explain why popular images of Holmes almost always picture him gazing through the lens of a magnifying glass, presenting himself as a virtual camera-like instrument of supervision and inspection.'[33] An embodied technology, Holmes thus personifies instrumental reason. This is precisely the kind of idealised rationality, this (photographic) equivalence between man and machine, that hard-boiled detective fiction would expose (photographic pun intended). And, in so doing, and in a gesture of genealogical self-reflexivity, this later iteration of the genre reprises, its own philosophical origins in the Scottish, commonsensical critique of Cartesian, Kantian thought.

In actuality, then, 'common sense' was anything but. It insisted, rather, on the authority of experience even when the latter descended, as noir later would, into areas of the inexplicable. For Thomas Reid, this descent included a (surreal) scenario in which the mind, imagined as an autonomous eyeball dwelling in a universe shaped like a sphere, follows the trajectory of a line sketched on the surface of the sphere until that line rejoins itself, anticipating the kinds of thought experiments that would accompany non-Euclidean geometry a century later.[34] But the implications of common sense might also take the form of James Hogg's presentation of the supernatural as the common experience of the Scottish Borders, or Robert Louis Stevenson's harrowing tale of science gone wrong in *The Strange Case of Dr Jekyll and Mr Hyde*. Ian Rankin would credit Hogg and Stevenson as influences in his early Inspector Rebus novels: 'In my early books especially I was keen to point out parallels between my work and predecessors such as *Jekyll and Hyde* and [Hogg's] *Confessions of a Justified Sinner*.'[35] And while he partly dismisses these influences as the result of his own early aspirations to become a literature professor, he also remarks that 'Edinburgh really did seem a divided city', accommodating very different facets of human experience.[36] That diversity – high and low, upstanding and illicit, mannered and angst-ridden – informs all the Rebus novels. The series thus exemplifies Dennis Porter's observation that hard-boiled fiction 'was a reaction not against British sophistication but against British innocence'[37] – as much, in its way, as Welsh's gritty denunciation of Thatcherite social dynamics in *Trainspotting* (1993).

The image of mythic innocence had a strong hold in Britain, Charles Rzepka argues, which is why it took a long time for the hard-boiled genre to develop there.[38] For this reason, Scotland's turn to the form seems especially powerful if somewhat anachronistic. Tartan Noir obviously draws from the American hard-boiled tradition, but, as Poe's implication in Reid's philosophy indicates, that American tradition owes something to Scotland as well. Ronald R. Thomas reminds us that Allan Pinkerton, a Scot, set up a famous private detective agency in the US in the 1850s and helped pioneer the use of photographic equipment for forensic purposes.[39] Mark Twain would later satirise Pinkerton in the Simon Wheeler character in 'The Celebrated Jumping Frog of Calaveras County' (1865), although Frank A. Salamone also notes that it was Twain, along with Hemingway, who actually helped develop hard-boiled style.[40] Dashiell Hammett, one of early American exponents of the hard-boiled genre, began his career as a detective in the Pinkerton Detective Agency, making his character Sam Spade the product of a Scots-American union.

When Tartan Noir arrived in the 1970s with McIlvanney and then, a decade later, was reinforced with Rankin, the Scottish branch of the genre already shared with American precursors like Raymond Chandler the tendency to sow existential thoughts in a field usually associated with lowbrow writing.[41] To cite one example, early in McIlvanney's 1983 novel *The Papers of Tony Veitch*, Laidlaw visits the Royal Infirmary and the free-indirect-discursive narrator, channelling Laidlaw's thoughts, comments that 'The place was a confessional. You came here to admit to frailty, brittle bones, thin skin, frangible organs – the pathetic, haphazard machinery we make bear the weight of our pretensions.'[42] Or, citing one other, Russel D. McLean's Dundee detective J. McNee soliloquises this line from the seventeenth-century French philosopher and theologian Blaise Pascal: '*Our nature consists in movement. Absolute rest is death.*'[43] Stephen Knight connects this tendency toward philosophical reflection to the wider Scottish literary tradition, though he sees there a penchant for 'plodding realism' – a strange assertion if one surveys the broader sweep of Scottish fiction and its contribution to genres like fantasy and science fiction.[44] However, and perhaps justly, Knight joins the genre to the work of Lewis Grassic Gibbon, whom Margery Palmer McCulloch describes as a quasi-realist among the more experimental Scottish writers like Hugh MacDiarmid, importing the concerns of urban critique into the familiar preoccupation with style.[45] And Gibbon is potentially an indicative figure here because of his propensity for weaving far-reaching, metaphysical thoughts into the grain of his narratives:

> And then a queer thought came to her there in the drookèd fields, that nothing endured, nothing but the land she passed across, tossed and turned and perpetually changed below the hands of the crofter folk since the oldest of them had set the Standing Stones by the loch of Blawearie [...].[46]

Like Gibbon in *A Scots Quair*, Tartan Noir novelists ask searching questions about the meaning of national being. Rankin's book about his best-selling series, *Rebus's Scotland*, exhibits an ontologising tendency from its opening epigraph, taken from the opening lines of Hugh MacDiarmid's 1943 poem 'Scotland':

> It requires great love of it deeply to read
> The configuration of a land,
> Gradually grow conscious of fine shadings,
> Of great meanings in slight symbols.[47]

It is this tendency towards fine perception that explains why hard-boiled novels lean heavily towards description: they are novels as much about 'being' as 'doing,' as much about mood as action. In the Rebus novels, this attunement to the atmospherics of the place wed rumination and plot. Here, the dynamics of Heideggerian reflection on being – 'Dasein', 'being-there' – pass by way of a fascination with what is 'out there', evocatively calling the detective and his culture to heightened ontological self-consciousness. In perhaps Rankin's finest Rebus novel, *Black and Blue* (1997), Rebus is hunting the historical serial killer who went by the name of Bible John.

> [T]here were plenty of coppers who thought they knew who Bible John was, and knew him to be dead. But there were others more sceptical, and Rebus was among them. A DNA match probably wouldn't have been enough to change his mind. There was always the chance that Bible John was *out there* [my emphasis].[48]

Later, Gill Templar, Rebus's partner, troubled over his drinking – a common motif – remarks, in casual concern, 'There are people out there who're worried about you'.[49] These things 'out there' can thus be malevolent or benign; what this sense of (call it) intimate exteriority signifies is that things outside oneself shape how one sees and thinks about oneself and one's environment.

In effect, what is 'out there' in the Rebus novels shapes Rebus's sense, and our sense, of 'being'. 'Rebus knew there were those out there – always had been – who believed there to be no connection, other than pure circumstance, between the three killings' under investigation. But 'Rebus, no great champion of coincidence, still believed in a single, driven killer [...]. He'd felt that if Bible John walked into a crowded room, he would know him.'[50] Rebus is right – and wrong. There is, indeed, 'a single, driven killer': Bible John is alive and plotting in *Black and Blue*. However, Rebus eventually finds himself in the same room with Bible John, and even chats with him at a bar, but does not recognise him. The point is that the 'out there' – the murderer, friends, other forensic scientists, *mystery* – is less about what is factually than ontologically true: Rebus may not catch the killer, but he absorbs the atmosphere of corruption. This echoes Heidegger's reflections on anxiety in his 1929 essay 'What Is Metaphysics?' where he asserts that anxiety is 'different from fear' in that it attunes us to the state of existence as a whole. It is a sensitivity to what is 'out there,' inflecting and calibrating our sense of being. 'We "hover" in anxiety [...]. In the altogether unsettling experience of this hovering where there is nothing to hold onto, pure Da-sein is all that is still there.'[51]

For all these parallels between hard-boiled detective fiction and high philosophy, Rankin recognises that some readers – and critics – might be sceptical:

> I'm conscious of a question readers may well want answering: can crime fiction ever give a true and all-embracing account of a nation? The answer should be a resounding 'Yes!', but only if we include works by the likes of Dickens and Dostoevsky under the umbrella term of 'crime'.[52]

While Rankin eventually spurned the overtly literary references he encrypted into his early novels, he nevertheless set them against a backdrop of serious issues: corporate malfeasance, human trafficking, addiction, collective trauma, political intrigue, and more. 'Crime' in these novels is thus a source of reflection as much as a driver of plot.

*

'There's a thesis to be written on why so many of Britain's most notorious serial killers have had a Scottish connection', Rankin muses.[53] And, I would add, there may be a second thesis to write on the forms of ontological enquiry in Tartan Noir. And it is with a brief survey of this subject that I will conclude.

Reading across the ever-expanding catalogue of Tartan Noir, one begins to detect certain persistent, almost obligatory, even cheeky features of the genre. The second novel in Russel D. McLean's J. McNee series, *The Lost Sister* (2009), presents many of them: cynicism, paranoia, existentialism, guilt, alienation, anxiety, the uncanny, conspiracy and more. 'You walk around like you're carrying the weight of the world on your shoulders', one character tells McNee (p. 117).[54] Accordingly, McNee frequently waxes existential: 'I was an only child whose parents had died too young. Who had allowed himself to play the role that other people expected of him: distanced' (p. 228); 'I wasn't a copper any more. But I still carried their sins' (p. 208); '[M]y own paranoia was playing tricks on me' (p. 103); 'Here's the reality: she wasn't coming back. I was alone. In the end, that was the one inescapable truth of my life' (p. 34, paragraphs merged). Hard-boiled rhetoric resounds throughout: 'The business could eat your life. Best if you didn't have one to start with' (p. 8, paragraphs merged). 'The Association of British Investigators has a code of ethics for all members. I sometimes wonder if that's why more people don't join' (p. 167). Views of Scotland – more specifically, in this series, Dundee – are thus mediated through this medium: 'Bringing the experience inside was the only way to do it in Dundee. The local weather was hardly suited to the task' (p. 16). 'It was a phenomenon, how only when you lived in the place did you discover another side. As though Dundee was desperate to keep itself hidden from outsiders' (p. 232).

The atmospherics of place, particularly of Scottish places, inform even the more 'literary', less pulpy exhibits of the genre. *All the Colours of the Town* (2009), the debut novel from Liam McIlvanney, William's son, sets a fair amount of its plot in Belfast, but it reserves special commentary for Glasgow, from which its journalist – detecting, but not detective – protagonist derives. And like McNee's Dundee, McIlvanney's Glasgow is less a location of plot than a place of thought. The city, we are told,

> likes its gangsters [...]. Gangsters are a local speciality, like charismatic socialists and dour-faced football managers. People connect them to an

older Glasgow, a darker, truer city, before the stone-cleaning and the logos, Princes Square and the City of Culture.[55]

Accompanying such loco-specific reflection, and the serious issues it raises (like the vestige of the Troubles in Northern Ireland) is the protagonist's lyrical and occasionally hard-boiled voice. For example, Conway, the protagonist, tells us that, while standing at a toilet, he 'put a line through everything' in a string of instructions 'except "PLEASE FLUSH". Then [he] left without flushing' (p. 47). Or again: 'A week in Belfast. Seven days of cooked breakfasts and starched bedsheets and expense-account bar-bills on the strength of a worn snapshot and an old-fashioned hunch' (p. 103). The novel is hardly reducible to hard-boiled shtick, but the shtick fits its mood. Or, perhaps better said, the mood of self-searching, vaguely ontological enquiry already has something hard-boiled about it. 'I like the Walk', the Orange parade, Conway reflects. 'I know you're not supposed to. I know it's a throwback, a discharge of hate, a line of orange pus clogging the streets of central Scotland. But I like it anyway. I like the cheap music, the deliberate jauntiness' (p. 86). The Walk, for all its grim history (indeed, because of it), becomes an occasion for self-assertion – as is hard-boiled style itself.

Even novels that try self-consciously to refuse the conventions of hard-boiled fiction find themselves invoking them, sometimes parodically so. Stuart MacBride's Aberdeen-based Logan Macrae series debuts, with *Cold Granite* (2005), by taking up a theme familiar to Tartan Noir – a paedophile ring. It refuses, however, some of the smuttiness that inflects corners of the genre (most notoriously, perhaps, Irvine Welsh's *Filth*) as well as some of the atmospherics of noir, appealing more frequently to dreich weather than to the insidiousness of the urban climate. Even here, however, hard-boiled fiction makes an appearance in the novel, with one of its detectives, 'Desperate Doug' caught 'reading a book. With a guilty jump he stuffed the Ian Rankin under his seat'.[56] Karen Campbell is another author who deploys the detective genre while refusing some of its stereotypes. A one-time police officer, Campbell has a great feel for street and police jargon. And her writing, lyrical and edgy, evokes paratactic, high modernist style more than lowbrow, hard-boiled poetics:

> The stench of these blankets crept through the cell, and he found his breath catching in his throat, like the air was thickening and crawling away and he was moving down a narrow tunnel, then the tunnel was a throat, his throat, and it was swallowing him.[57]

Contrary to the traditional conventions of the hard-boiled genre, Campbell's female protagonists present occasions to reflect on the existential condition of women:

> For always, ever, one unalienable fact. Women are wombs. You might ignore that open sore at your centre, but it was there all the same. Monthly pain and lifetime wonders flitting in and out and round like a pesky fly. And, if you do succumb to that tug in your gut, then nothing is ever the same again.[58]

Even here, however, and true to Tartan Noir, ontological reflection abounds relative to the places of Scotland and Scottishness:

> Glasgow was not a pretty town, but it was a gallus. It sprawled and lolled, taking up more than its fair share of the west of Scotland, like a fat woman on the bus. Ringed with post-war schemes, built over stately homes and green fields, the city was a sink with a grey rim.[59]

> What difference did this circular pantomime they were performing in make anyway [...] the hundreds of jaded souls that looped round and round in grim, misshapen wheels? The match had finished – Scotland glorious once more in defeat.[60]

Traces of Tartan Noir even creep outside the detective genre altogether, inflecting the existentially reaching poetry – and poetic fiction – of, for example, John Burnside. In his poem 'Urban Myths', Burnside evokes 'The secret versions of ourselves, / truthful because they seem / remembered'. And what we remember are 'terrors we meant to avoid / tracking us through a long / acquaintance' before taking us on what seems a strange detour: 'blood on the kitchen floor, blood in the roof; / networks of bone and nerve in drifted leaves', as though we were witnesses – or perpetrators – of murder.[61] So it is in a later novel, *Glister* (2008), that Burnside spins a tale about a group of boys that go missing in a depressed Scottish town several years after the closure of a toxic chemical plant. The aura of corruption and misdeed is everywhere, though we never entirely solve the crime that seeps across the pages. Nor is that the aim of the novel. Instead, the plot acts as a whitewashing storefront for an ontological exploration of nature, evil, the narrative impulse toward meaning, and religion. And it pulses with the aura of mystery and clues. The Moth Man, a beatnik philosophical character of ill (but earnest, sentimental) intent – and named, it seems, after the Buffalo Bill character in the movie *The Silence of the Lambs* (a Tartan Noir favourite) – reflects with the young, first-person protagonist, 'Some people say there are no mysteries any more [...]. Do you think that's true, Leonard Wilson?' Wilson thinks – and thinks, and thinks. 'I shake my head. Here comes the God part. "*I* don't know," I say. "So *that's* the mystery," he says. Then he just sits there, smiling'.[62] Other Tartan Noir hallmarks also permeate the novel, from rumination on guilt and the presence of Jekyll-and-Hyde-style doubles to T. S. Eliotic echoes of a scorched earth present: 'this apparent wasteland', this blighted landscape in the shadow of the derelict chemical plant, 'is all the church we have'. (p. 66)

The few examples I have provided here fall far short of a survey of the field or even the range of writing – an undertaking that far exceeds the boundaries of this essay. (What, no mention of Val McDermid? What about Alexander McCall Smith or Louise Welsh? Or Lin Anderson, Peter May, Tony Black, Kate Atkinson, Christopher Brookmyre, Denise Mina, or so many others?) But what this essay provides, hopefully, is a perspective onto the breadth and diversity of Scottish detective fiction, particularly the hard-boiled brand of Tartan Noir. This diversity is explained not only by the popularity of the genre – an enticing incentive for its established and burgeoning exponents, to be sure – but also by the genre's form and history. Tartan Noir resonates with a range of modern affects and concerns. What is more, the prehistory of the genre (philosophically and in the emergence of modern detective agencies) bears a distinctively Scottish imprint. Most significantly, perhaps, it has become an important and accessible vehicle for reflection on what it means to be in present-day Scotland – or just about anywhere else.

CHAPTER TWELVE

Scottish Science Fiction and Fantasy

Anna McFarlane

David Pringle is one of several critics who have worried at the lack of a distinctive tradition of science fiction writing in Scotland,[1] especially given that Scotland was, from the late eighteenth century, one of the most industrialised countries in Europe and, by the 1840s, through the work of Lord Kelvin and James Clerk Maxwell, the country at the leading edge of the transformative development of 'energy physics'. Pringle suggests that apart from Leslie Mitchell's *Three Go Back* (1932) and *Gay Hunter* (1934), 'there are really no major Scottish science fiction novels prior to the commencement of the career of Iain M. Banks'[2] in the 1980s. In part, however, this may be the result of the way in which the genre of science fiction has come to be defined. It is often traced to the *voyages extraordinaires* of Jules Verne, published in the 1860s and 1870s (one of Verne's novels *Les Indes Noires/The Child of the Cavern* (1877) is set in a once exhausted Scottish coal-mine but which, as a result of the discovery of vast new strata of coal, becomes the site of an underground city powered by electricity) and the futurology of H. G. Wells's scientific romances such as *The Time Machine* (1895) and *The War of the Worlds* (1897), works whose emphasis on technological innovation laid the groundwork for the emergence of the techno-optimism of American science fiction's 'golden age' in the 1920s and 1930s.

This lineage was reinforced by the critical work of Darko Suvin, the first serious analyst of the genre in the 1960s, who insists that science fiction must be based on a *novum* (a technological innovation) which is consistent with what we already know or can reasonably hypothesise about the workings of the material universe. The *novum*, in other words, must have a natural rather than a supernatural explanation even if it is, as yet, an unrealised or unrealisable possibility. Suvin, for instance, denies that Robert Louis Stevenson's *Strange Case of Dr Jekyll and Mr Hyde*

(1886) can be considered as a work of science fiction because there is no explanation within the story of the nature of the chemical ingredient that brings about the bodily transformation of the central character. As Gavin Miller has explained, for Suvin *Jekyll and Hyde* cannot be *science fiction* since it offers no plausible causal explanation for events of the story.[3] However, as Colin Manlove has pointed out in relation to George MacDonald's *Phantastes* (1858), what is subtitled as 'A Faerie Romance for Men and Women' is actually structured by MacDonald's understanding of the as yet uncodified workings of electro-magnetism: the surface texture of the work may be that of fairy tale and magical transformation but those are set in motion by a deeper structure of scientific innovation – a view of the material world as fundamentally composed of energy that can be reshaped into alternative physical forms.[4] The world of modern science, Manlove suggests, is so extraordinarily different from the Newtonian world of earlier science that it cannot be effectively represented by the realist traditions of the novel from which science fiction, as presented by Suvin, has emerged. Caroline McCracken-Flesher has suggested that a specifically Scottish science fiction has different origins and different aims from the imperial trajectories of the colonisation of other planets so often taken to be central to popular 'sci-fi': 'the most interesting Scottish science fiction authors', she writes,

> do not dwell on the future against the past, or against the rest of galactic civilisation – the clichés of much mainstream genre writing. Rather, through a subtle blend of science and fantasy, they focus on the possibilities generated at the margins between and in the alternate spaces that slip beyond these too-easy oppositions.[5]

Taking a more open, less taxonomical view of genre, and considering science fiction and fantasy together as part of a familial group of literary genres that John Clute has described as 'fantastika' is therefore a more useful way to view Scottish speculative science and fantasy fictions.[6] In Scottish literature there is often a fusion of these related genres, and this approach is more likely to reveal the nature of the literature on its own terms, and in light of its specific original influences.

In Scotland, the roots of a tradition in science fiction and fantasy come not from the novel, but from poetry, and particularly the ballad form. The championing of the Borders Ballad by Sir Walter Scott, alongside Robert Burns's contribution in gathering and preserving the Scottish ballads of his childhood, created a Scottish literary culture that was self-consciously indebted to such tales of magic and wonder. Authors were inspired to carry on in that tradition, at times in an effort to preserve fairy tales and mythical creatures specific to Scotland and, at others, to contribute to international conversations about morality in an allegorical fashion. The Scottish contribution to fantasy in the form of the novel began in the nineteenth century with a series of authors who became celebrated internationally. Foremost amongst these is George MacDonald, a Christian minister and theologian who is known as the father of fantasy literature and was the inspiration for a number of the twentieth century's most important fantasy authors, particularly C. S. Lewis. Lewis wrote of reading MacDonald's *Phantastes* (1858) that, 'what it actually did to me was to convert, even to baptise [...] my imagination'.[7] MacDonald was known for his children's stories, particularly *The Princess and the Goblin* (1872), but also developed his fantasy style for adults. The title of *Phantastes: A Faerie Romance for Men and Women* lays out the author's intention to write a story that would draw on the traditions of folk and fairy tales, particularly the German tradition of the *Kunstmärchen*, while recognising the potential for fantasy literature to go beyond children's stories and to act as a way for adults to explore their own minds and ways of being in the world. MacDonald's contribution leads Colin Manlove to describe him as 'the founder of much modern fantasy'.[8] His inspirations are many and varied, but he clearly sees himself primarily as a writer in the Romantic tradition, and regularly draws on German and Romantic texts for epigraphs to each chapter of *Phantastes*. He was particularly inspired by Novalis (the pen name of Georg Philipp Friedrich Freiherr von Hardenberg), a line of influence that feeds into his work's concern with pastoral beauty, the individuation of man, and his relationship to his own subconscious mental processes.

Phantastes tells the story of Anodos, who inherits the keys to his deceased father's writing desk on the occasion of his twenty-first birthday. He finds within a tiny woman who announces that he will find the door to fairyland the following day. Sure enough, Anodos awakens to find the mundane furniture of his room transformed to a wooded fairyland, dotted with ancient statuary and peopled with wonderful creatures and mysterious women. The symbolism of the book, and the impression that the protagonist is in some sense exploring the landscape of his own subconscious, lends the book to Jungian readings. Take, for example, this scene where Anodos explores a palace:

> I was wandering through one lighted arcade and corridor after another. At length I arrived, through a door that closed behind me, in another vast hall of the palace. It was filled with a subdued crimson light; by which I saw that slender pillars of black, built close to walls of white marble, rose to a great height, and then, dividing into innumerable divergent arches, supported a roof, like the walls, of white marble, upon which the arches intersected intricately, forming a fretting of black upon the white, like the network of a skeleton-leaf. The floor was black. Between several pairs of the pillars upon every side, the place of the wall behind was occupied by a crimson curtain of thick silk, hanging in heavy and rich folds. Behind each of these curtains burned a powerful light, and these were the sources of the glow that filled the hall.[9]

The womb-like imagery of the crimson light and silk curtains, paired with the combination of classical architecture and organic imagery, evokes the symbolic structures of human nature and culture and, in the image of the corridor with several doors, explores how this natural-cultural positioning shapes decision-making and therefore the direction of a human life – particularly important for Anodos as he reaches his majority at the age of twenty-one and must now navigate his life as an adult, without the patriarchal deferral of power to his recently deceased father. MacDonald's complex visions, generally channelled into children's fiction over the course of his career, produced another major fantasy novel for adults. *Lilith* (1895) is a complex contribution, drawing on religious and archetypal imagery to take the reader into a mirror world where the eponymous Lilith, the first wife of Adam, fights a war against Adam and Eve. Colin Manlove has argued that both *Phantastes* and *Lilith* are deeply influenced by scientific developments in electromagnetism, which was being discovered piecemeal over the nineteenth century alongside MacDonald's career, highlighting the power of touch (as conduction) and earthing in MacDonald's fictions.[10] In Manlove's reading, the 'father of fantasy' is also offering an alternative model for exploring scientific development in fiction beyond the techno-optimism of science fiction as it is commonly categorised.

While MacDonald is associated with fantasy, Scotland is also involved in the development of science fiction. Mary Shelley famously spent some time in Tayside, staying with the Baxter family near Dundee as a young girl, and later said that the seeds for some of the picturesque scenes in *Frankenstein* (1816), considered by many to be the first science fiction novel, were sown during this time.¹¹ In the introduction to the 1831 edition of *Frankenstein*, Shelley wrote that,

> my habitual residence was on the blank and dreary northern shores of the Tay, near Dundee. Blank and dreary on retrospection I call them; they were not so to me then. They were the eyry of freedom, and the pleasant region where unheeded I could commune with the creatures of my fancy.¹²

Taking inspiration from the scenery around Tayside, placing Scotland as a key scene for the development of the genre of science fiction, Shelley had Dr Frankenstein follow his monster to the north of Scotland. R. L. Stevenson's *The Strange Case of Dr Jekyll and Mr Hyde* (1886) developed some of the themes begun in *Frankenstein* that would shape contemporary science fiction. The image of the scientist as a modern Prometheus, usurping power that was meant only for gods is crucial to the text, and Stevenson drew on the gothic cityscape of nineteenth-century Edinburgh, Auld Reekie, for his evocation of Victorian London. Like MacDonald's work, which grew from his belief in Christianity, Stevenson's *Jekyll and Hyde* was written with the aim of exploring a philosophical theme: that of the duality of human nature, a theme that has long been a concern of Scottish literature, most famously explored in James Hogg's *Confessions of a Justified Sinner* (1824), and later theorised by Gregory Smith as Caledonian antisyzygy.¹³

As argued by David Pringle, Scotland was also host to a more recognisable strain of science fiction in the form of the lost-world fiction. Thomas Connolly shows that lost-world fiction 'was an important subgenre for early SF, providing a key testing ground for ideas and motifs that would later become central to the genre'.¹⁴ Between 1912 and 1929 Sir Arthur Conan Doyle produced a series of novels and short stories featuring his character Professor Challenger, a Scottish professor of zoology best known for his appearance in *The Lost World* (1912). *The Lost World*, taking inspiration from Jules Verne, features an expedition to an area of South America that has been left undisturbed since prehistory, allowing its protagonist in effect to become a time traveller. In the interwar period, James Leslie Mitchell took inspiration from Conan Doyle in his two speculative novels *Three Go Back* (1932) and *Gay Hunter* (1934), both concerned with the themes of warfare and the threat of fascism. *Three Go Back* sees an odd throuple – a pacifist activist, an arms manufacturer, and an intrepid lady novelist – sent back in time to a land of sabre-toothed tigers and Neanderthals. While Mitchell clearly thought of these novels as pulpy distractions from his more serious work – in his dedication to *Three Go Back* he says, 'I wrote this novel as a holiday from more serious things'[15] – Mitchell uses the setting to consider the future of humankind, and to pitch the philosophies of the two (male) characters against each other, predominantly using Clair Stranlay, the novelist, as a focalising character. Justifications for war, peace, and human nature in general are brought to the fore through the prehistoric setting which takes an evolutionary-sociological approach to ask whether humankind has been shaped by the conditions of the species' emergence, and whether considering this can lead to a reappraisal of social organisation in the present. The pacificist argues, 'We know that man's a fighting animal by nature, that cruelty's his birthright; and we also know that what keeps us in the pit as animals are the armies and armaments'.[16] In *Three Go Back*, a trip to the past is a confrontation with man's animalistic and violent nature, and it brings with it a reckoning for how best to incorporate these tendencies into civilisation. Mitchell describes *Gay Hunter* as 'a companion book'[17] to *Three Go Back*. The protagonist is twenty-three-year-old Gay Hunter, an American archaeologist in England for a conference where she meets and helps an injured fascist, overcoming her revulsion for his politics. The two agree to attempt to access a premonition of the future using techniques detailed in J. W. Dunne's *An Experiment With Time* (1927). Dunne's book was a literary sensation and gave an account of techniques that would allow the practitioner to become aware of the premonitions that Dunne believed the dreaming mind could access. When Gay Hunter and the fascist try Dunne's suggestions, they do not just access premonitions, but find themselves transported to a future dystopia in a mirroring of *Three Go Back*'s visit to the past, a journey that once again engages with the ideological and evolutionary influences on human behaviour and on the formation of human societies.

Dystopia was the mode chosen by Neil Gunn to explore the fascism of the Second World War in *The Green Isle of the Great Deep* (1944). *The Green Isle* draws on Celtic mythology as the two protagonists, Young Art and Old Hector, find themselves transported through a pool to a dystopian, authoritarian world in which the citizens are controlled by manufactured food. Once again, the novel eludes easy distinctions between fantasy and science fiction. While the novel makes use of the mythology of the Highlands, its setting is distinctly science fictional and dystopian, leading a reviewer for *Foundation: The International Review of Science Fiction* to compare it to *Walden Two* (1948), B. F. Skinner's utopian exploration of behaviour modification.[18] Like Gunn, Naomi Mitchison used dystopia and fantastic themes in *We Have Been Warned* (1935) to show the possibilities of the growth of fascism. The novel is, in large part, autobiographical, telling the story of a young wife as her husband runs for office for the Labour party, and takes a trip to Soviet Russia, both experiences that Mitchison herself had had in the years leading up to the novel's publication. Fantastical elements enter into the text as the two sisters at the heart of the novel, Dione and Phoebe, find out more about their ancestor Green Jean the witch. At the novel's climax, Green Jean gives the sisters a dystopian vision of Britain under fascist control, offering the warning of the novel's title and giving a dystopian vision through fantastical means, much like Gunn's *Green Isle of the Great Deep*. Mitchison later turned to a more recognisable form of science fiction with *Memoirs of a Spacewoman* (1962). *Memoirs* was a significant contribution to feminist science fiction, and benefits from being read in the context of roughly contemporary North American authors Ursula K. Le Guin, Joanna Russ, and Marge Piercy. Mitchison's spacewoman works as a translator, communicating with aliens and contemplating the connections between different species. The novel has since been read as an early example of posthumanist sensibilities in feminist science fiction.[19] While the novel's main character explores alien planets and species, the onus is never on patriarchal colonisation, but on understanding these alien ecosystems and using them to reflect on the development of human behaviour as contingent, shaped by the material conditions of earthbound life. Mitchison returned to science fiction with *Solution Three* (1975) and *Not By Bread Alone* (1983), which discussed the politics of cloning and genetic modification in food production.

The blending of genres and forms has also impacted the reading of Alasdair Gray's *Lanark* (1981). The novel's unusual structure and its combination of realist and fantastic approaches has meant that it is more often read in terms of postmodernism than as a genre novel, or one that partakes in the motifs of fantasy proper.[20] It is split into four 'books'. The first is a realist, autobiographical account of a young boy, Thaw, growing up in Glasgow and attending the Glasgow School of Art. Drawing on Gray's own experiences with art school, asthma, and Glaswegian life, the novel famously makes a case for the importance of imagination in laying claim to a sense of place:

> 'Glasgow is a magnificent city,' said McAlpin. 'Why do we hardly ever notice that?' 'Because nobody imagines living here,' said Thaw [...] 'Think

of Florence, Paris, London, New York. Nobody visiting them for the first time is a stranger because he's already visited them in paintings, novels, history books and films. But if a city hasn't been used by an artist, not even the inhabitants live there imaginatively.'[21]

This claim for the importance of imaginary thinking is made in the realist section of the novel, and Gray goes on to embellish his realist Glasgow with fantasy elements that breathe life into the city, giving it a fantastical dimension that, paradoxically, renders it more real. *Lanark*'s engagement with fantasy and science fiction was to be the inspiration of much Scottish writing in the 1980s and 1990s, particularly evident in the work of Iain Banks, whose first novel, *The Wasp Factory* (1984), is a rewriting of the Frankenstein myth, its narrator Frank having been transformed from female to male by his father's chemical experiments. Banks's *The Bridge* (1986) imitates *Lanark* by envisaging a version of the Forth Bridge as being the Kafkaesque totality of modern civilisation, in which the novel's protagonist is apparently endlessly trapped. The science fiction elements of these novels were, however, expanded in the works written as Iain M. Banks, particularly the Culture series of space-opera novels set in a post-scarcity civilisation. In the Culture, labour is performed by advanced artificial intelligences (AIs), freeing up the human characters to a life of plenty characterised by posthuman transformations. Due to the potential for conflict and drama offered by societies beyond this utopian stability, much of the series is set on the outskirts of the Culture, the frontier territories where different interest groups fight for dominance, and joining the Culture might be seen as a matter of progressive development or the worst kind of colonisation. The unassimilated societies encountered by the Culture are often, as in *The Player of Games* (1988), versions of modern Western societies, characterised by economic dispossession and institutional violence.

That literary influence is not always from the earlier to the later is revealed, perhaps, in Alasdair Gray's *Poor Things* (1992), which rewrites *Frankenstein* in a fashion similar to *The Wasp Factory* and follows the Culture novels in its satirical presentation of modern colonialism and capitalism. In Mary Shelley's original narrative, Frankenstein's refusal to create a female mate for his monster leads to their mutual destruction, but in Gray's novel, the Frankenstein-figure, Godwin Baxter, is himself a scientific experiment in returning dead organs to life, a process which he repeats to bring a female suicide back to life by transplanting into her the brain of her own unborn foetus. The creature that then becomes Bella

Baxter, supposedly Godwin's niece, thus lives in two timescales: that of an adult body born into the repressive ethos of the Victorian age and that of the child's brain, which will experience a later era's overthrow of Victorian values. Bella's self-education, like that of Frankenstein's 'creature', reveals all the horrors of modern societies which depend on colonialist capitalism for the maintenance of 'civilisation'. The story, however, is a 'found' text by one Archibald McCandless, 'a Scottish Public Health Officer', which his wife Victoria insists is puerile fantasy, despite the fact that she is, herself, according to McCandless, the living continuation of Bella. This double narrative allows Gray to disrupt notions of historical progress by producing what the fake blurb of the book's dustjacket ironically describes as an 'up-to-date nineteenth-century novel'.

A writer who has perhaps come closest to taking on Banks's mantle of writing science fiction while being taken seriously by audiences of literary fiction is Michel Faber, born in Holland, raised in Australia, but settled in Scotland for the most prolific period of his writing career to date. Faber came to attention with his first novel, *Under the Skin* (2000), an eerie tale of an alien picking up hitchhikers on Scotland's A9 road and farming them for their meat. Faber did not stay with science fiction, and is also well known for his historical novel *The Crimson Petal and the White* (2002), but when *Under the Skin* was filmed by Jonathan Glazer in 2013 it cemented Faber's legacy as an important figure in science fiction, while committing an eerie vision of Scotland to film. Locations included Glasgow, Auchmithie Beach near Arbroath, and the forest around Lochgoilhead, all filmed as though through the extra-terrestrial perspective of Isserley (Scarlet Johansson) as she negotiates an alien (to her) landscape populated by inscrutable, and sometimes violent, men. Faber returned to science fiction with 2014's *The Book of Strange New Things*, a novel partly inspired by the terminal cancer of his wife, Eva, whom Faber has credited as an inspiration to and early reader of his work, advising him to a point bordering on collaboration. *The Book of Strange New Things* tells the story of a missionary to an alien planet whose people cannot heal – once they are hurt they cannot recover. The pain of illness that cannot be solved, and the intergalactic distance that separates the missionary from his wife, combine to give this novel its themes of lost love and isolation.

Faber's Scotland, and its adaptation by Glazer, situated the country as an alien landscape, but there was a counter representation of Scotland and its people through attempts to represent Scottish linguistic variation in print, thereby giving it a legitimacy that it was often seen to lack. The international success of Irvine Welsh's *Trainspotting* had shown in 1993 that the Scots language and Scottish slang could be welcomed by readers, and this position was developed in science fiction by Matthew Fitt's *But n Ben A-Go-Go* (2000). The novel primarily uses vocabulary from lowland Scots and is set in 2090, a juxtaposition that changes perceptions of the Scots language as a dying one belonging to the past by showing it as a lingua franca of the future in what John Corbett describes as 'an act of will that is both political and counterintuitive'.[22] Fitt describes the novel in terms of the juxtaposition of past and future as he places, 'words your granny liked tae use and your mither tellt ye no tae use in the unusual setting of a modern novel set in the future'.[23] The Scots language is associated with previous generations, with a past that young people are happy to set behind them, as well as a prohibition against Scots that is characteristic of Scottish society and schools. While the combination of the Scots language with science fiction is the key innovation of the novel, it is also notable for dealing with a number of important contemporary issues: the characters must deal with the consequences of a deadly pandemic (an HIV-like virus known as Senga), and much of Scotland is underwater due to the impact of climate change. The characters also interact on the VINE, a version of cyberspace. The setting allows Fitt to revel in the exuberance of Scots and its linguistic possibilities, combining old Scots words with neologisms that give him the scope to express the full gamut of his new and unusual future world. Fitt shows that Scots is well able to be used to describe a surveillance society with advanced technology:

> An as he skellied intae the white bleeze, a troop o droid surveillance puggies advanced in heelstergowdie formation alang the corridor roof, skited by owre his heid an wi a clatter o metallic cleuks, skittered awa eastwards doon the shadowy vennel.[24]

The contrast between the past and the future is also played out in the work of Andrew Crumey, a writer with a PhD in theoretical physics, who won the Saltire First Book Award and, later, the Scottish Arts Council Book Award. His writing uses scientific concepts such as quantum energy, parallel universes, and the uncertainty principle to stretch the limits of realism in his novels. His work has a metafictional dimension as characters struggle with their own fictionality, and there is an element of alternative history as parallel worlds are constructed and invade the narrative. Common figures appear from one novel to the next, making a good argument for treating Crumey's oeuvre as a megatext, or a multiverse. *Mobius Dick* (2004) takes a nuclear power station as the site of some mysterious experiments in quantum physics. The nuclear power plant, reminiscent of the real Dounreay nuclear site in the Highlands, represents a kind of retro-future; it evokes a vision that was futuristic in the 1950s but is now about to be decommissioned, making the plant a relic of a lost future. (The use of the nuclear plant as a site of culture that dominates the nature of the rural landscape is echoed in James Robertson's *And the Land Lay Still* (2010), representing that same clash between a rural, self-determined past and a technological future that never seems to arrive on time.) Crumey continues the metafictional nature of his work in *The Secret Knowledge* (2013) and *The Great Chain of Unbeing* (2018) which again engage with quantum physics and feature some of the same characters found in *Mobius Dick* and Crumey's other earlier novels.

In twenty-first-century Scottish science fiction the tendency towards genre-bending, with the distinction between science fiction and fantasy unclear, continues as authors consider the potential dangers of technological authoritarianism. For Ken MacLeod, this is most obvious in 2011's dystopia, *Intrusion*. The novel is set in London, and describes a UK run by authoritarian governments. The intrusion of the title might be the intrusion of the state into private decision making. The government are demanding that pregnant women take 'the fix', a pill that 'cures' all genetic disease in a foetus's genome, but the family at the core of the story – Hope, Hugh, and their son – are sceptical of the eugenic potential, and ultimately try to escape the state's systems of surveillance so that they can live freely. The other intrusion in the book is that of the past, or a fantasy world, into the present. Hugh and his son have the ability to look into another world, one that they can access on the Isle of Lewis, Hugh's childhood home. This door to another world gives them their means of escape from their straitjacketed surveillance society. Similar themes of eugenics and control arise in the work of Helen Sedgwick, a scientist-turned-author, whose *The Growing Season* (2016) shows an alternate 2016 in which ectogenesis (the gestation of the foetus outside of the womb) in a pouch has been in practice for two generations and uses the subject matter to explore gender roles in society, asking whether patriarchal domination would come to an end were reproduction to be unhitched from the female body. Again, Sedgwick primarily sets her novel in London but uses

Scotland as a remote foil to the main events of the plot, a setting for the inventor of the pouch, Freida, to escape to, living in solitude as she regrets her Frankensteinian involvement in a technology whose consequences she failed to predict. The novel deals with many of the same themes as MacLeod's work, with medical improvements acting as an excuse for the colonisation of the body by outside forces – in MacLeod's work it is the state, while Sedgwick frames the intrusion as a result of the increased power of corporations and I have argued elsewhere that the portrayal of the corporation in Sedgwick's text is emblematic of contemporary anxieties about the privatisation of the National Health Service.[25] While both novels are predominantly set in England, Scotland offers a remote place of quietude from which the protagonists can think, regroup, and even find an escape – not unlike the use of Scotland in Jackie Kay's *Trumpet* (1998), as a place far away from the mainstream press and the concerns of British society. In this sense, contemporary science fiction continues to see Scotland as a place outside of the future, one more in touch with the past and with oral or fairy tale traditions than with the critical futurology of science fiction.

Judging these texts' treatment of science fiction by the yardstick of a colonialist/globalist teleology of technological progress might risk accusing these representations of framing Scotland as backwards, or under-developed, stuck in a past that has little to offer the present, let alone a future characterised by techno-utopianism. Alternatively, Scotland in these texts can be read, as Miller has argued, as offering a feminist alternative to such patriarchal conceptions. As Miller puts it, 'a feminist, yet recognizably Scottish challenge to the masculine vision of a "phallic" unilinear progression based on the technological domination of nature.'[26] It is no coincidence that the technology in *Intrusion* or *The Growing Season* circulates around the reproductive female body, and the use of Scotland as a remote setting with access to the discourse of fantasy presents it as a healthy parallel to a British society marred by surveillance, control, and the occupation of ideological space by a tabloid mentality. Kirsty Logan's *The Gracekeepers* (2015) draws on a lyrical dystopianism to portray a post-climate change world, while Jenni Fagan's debut novel *The Panopticon* (2012) takes a similarly dystopian subject matter, but works it into the fabric of the Scottish countryside, using a first-person, vernacular narrator. The theme of witchcraft arises as a spectre haunting the young woman we first meet in the back of a police car on the way to the prison where she will be under complete surveillance. Anais thinks about what she knows about the fate of a woman who found herself outside the protection of patriarchy during the time of the witch hunts:

> If there wasnae a male authority figure tae say she was godly – then they thought she was weak for the devil. Bound tae be bad. Or even if her crops were doing well, better than her neighbours, or she wasnae scared tae answer back? Fucking witch. Prick it, poke it, peel its fingernails off and burn it in the square for the whole town to see.[27]

Anais's account weaves together the language of her teacher – in a phrase like 'male authority figure' – with her own dialect, rereading the story of the witches through her own experiences. For Anais, a witch was a woman who 'wasnae scared tae answer back', an ethos that she, as a juvenile delinquent, identifies with. The recurring theme of surveillance and the female body pits technological advances in the service of authoritarian, regressive systems. These themes appear more regularly in Scottish science fiction or fantasy as time goes by. Francine Toon's ethereal *Pine* (2020), winner of the 2020 McIlvanney Prize, captures a spirit of New Age practices that could be found in Scotland in the early 2000s while drawing on the legacy of witches and witchcraft to explore the past of the protagonist, whose mother went missing when she was a child. Part crime novel, part ghost story, the Highlands once again act as a space where generic distinctions are broken down.

More recently, Scotland has played host to a thriving fan community that has produced a number of celebrated writers. The Glasgow Science Fiction Writers' Circle is well established and, in 2016, produced a short story collection, *Thirty Years of Rain*, to celebrate the group's thirtieth anniversary. Notable writers who have been associated with the circle include the fantasy writer Hal Duncan, whose published works include the novels *Vellum* (2005) and *Ink* (2007), a two-part series set in the world of the Book of All Hours, a book made of angel skin and written in blood, in which all of the world's timelines are written. The novels are set in a world where time exists in three dimensions, like space, and is riven by an apocalyptic event known as the Evenfall. The series' fight between the powers of order and chaos is reflected in the writing with its plethora of references, the narrative often breaking off to find the characters in a different existence, in a different 'fold' in the vellum. The novels are densely written and highly descriptive, giving them a psychedelic flavour as they remix narrative with religion and mythology. Another significant alumna is Amal El-Mohtar, whose novella *This is How You Lose the Time*

War (2019), written with Max Gladstone, was recognised with a number of awards, including the British Science Fiction Association's award for shorter fiction, a Nebula award and a Hugo award. Like Duncan's work, *Time War* plays with the timeline, focusing on two protagonists on either side of a 'time war', a war that also appears to separate people ideologically, differentiating the posthuman Red, cyborgised beyond recognition with body modifications, from Blue, whose people are committed to a return to 'nature'. The novel is written in epistolary form as Red and Blue tease each other, encounter each other across time and space, and finally realise that the connection between them defies the complicated weave of the timeline itself. The Edinburgh-based magazine *Shoreline of Infinity* has also made a significant contribution to Scottish SF culture, running regular events and producing the collection *Scotland in Space: Creative Visions and Critical Reflections on Scotland's Space Futures* (2019).

Conclusion

The appearance of this twenty-first-century fantastic tradition, one that melds genres including fantasy and science fiction to produce something uniquely Scottish might be seen as a sign of growing cultural confidence. The momentum of the Scottish independence referendum campaign, and the reshaping of the cultural and political landscape it left in its wake, have given a new sense of Scotland as a place that might occupy a place in history, that might have a future, but at the same time can use its place outside of a wider British history to critique the patriarchal practice of viewing technological industrial progress as the teleology for reading the success of human life and culture. To return to Miller, contemporary Scottish science fiction writers recognise the 'dangers of nostalgia for a technological, capitalist, and masculinist future that has already failed'.[28] Considering Scottish science fiction, and particularly its development in the Scottish novel, through the more open generic criteria of the 'fantastika' umbrella recognises the nation as a zone of influence, taking in inspiration from outside, from several genres, and reacting to wider global discussions from a specific historical and geographical position.

CHAPTER THIRTEEN

Scottish Children's and Young Adult Fiction

Fiona McCulloch

George MacDonald regarded *The Princess and the Goblin* (1872), a modern fairy tale for children and 'the childlike', as 'the most complete thing I have done'.[1] Likewise, according to W. W. Robson, 'Most readers agree with Henry James that *Treasure Island* (1883) is perfect of its kind',[2] while the continuing popularity of J. M. Barrie's *Peter Pan* (1904 as a play; 1911 as the novel *Peter and Wendy*) in various theatrical and filmic adaptations attests to its unique role in modern culture. The upsurge in Scottish literary studies in the second half of the twentieth century that brought so many forgotten writers – particularly women writers – to renewed prominence has not, according to Sarah Dunnigan, had a similar impact on the perception of children's fiction: we still inhabit 'a Scottish critical and literary-historical landscape which has made little room for children's literature'.[3] If this is true, and this series' sister volume *The International Companion to Scottish Children's Literature* (2024)[4] offers ample perspectives on this, it produces multiple ironies.

First, the works of Scotland's most influential novelist, Sir Walter Scott, had, by the latter part of the nineteenth century, been reduced to recommended reading for school children. Paul Barnaby quotes Leslie Stephen's judgement that if *Ivanhoe* 'is no longer a work for men, but it still is, or ought to be, delightful reading for boys', so that we 'should not be ungrateful to Scott for wasting his splendid talents on what we can hardly call by a loftier name than most amusing nonsense'.[5] Scott's career could thus be read as symptomatic of a national literature in which childhood provided an escape both from the modern world and from adult responsibility, so that writing for children became a symptom of failed maturity. A second irony is that one of the most successful novels of the second half of the twentieth century, William Golding's *Lord of the Flies* (1954), is based on the children's tale which helped shape both *Treasure Island* and *Peter Pan*, R. M. Ballantyne's *The Coral Island* (1858). Golding's reversal of the optimistic values of Victorian Christianity nonetheless acknowledged the continuing power of Ballantyne's work. And, thirdly, some of the most significant and influential of modern Scottish novels drew directly on themes and techniques of earlier children's literature: Muriel Spark's *The Hothouse by the East River* (1973) is, for instance, a modern version of Barrie's Neverland, involving a new production of *Peter Pan* in New York, and Alasdair Gray's *Lanark* (1981), one of the most influential of Scottish novels, acknowledges its indebtedness to George MacDonald for several key episodes.[6]

Part of the problem in due appreciation being given to children's – and its more recent sibling, Young Adult (YA) – fiction is the assumption that literature for younger readers must be undemanding in terms of generic expectations and literary technique, since the intended readers will have neither a wide knowledge of previous literature nor the ability to question the text's presuppositions. Thus, as Jacqueline Rose has argued, even the most 'fabulous' of tales must assume the unproblematic relationship between language and what it refers to, so that 'realism and fantasy' both attempt 'to reduce to an absolute minimum our awareness of the language in which the story is written'.[7] This assumes, however, that the writer of fiction for children will be conscious only of his or her audience's reaction, and not of the much more complex relationship between the author, the narrator and the audience's expectations. The case of Ballantyne's *The Coral Island* is instructive, for the author had never seen a coral island, or, indeed, a palm tree or a coconut, and his novel is a construction out of his reading of other books, some of which are pillaged to the point of plagiarism. This textual *bricolage* is matched by the ironic presentation of the imperial values which it is generally assumed the book exists to promote: a pirate by the name of 'Bloody Bill' is allowed to articulate how useful religion is to the advancement of trade (and plunder):

> the only place among the southern islands where a ship can put in and get what she wants in comfort is where the Gospel has been sent to [...]. For my part, I don't know and I don't care what the Gospel does to them, but I know that when any o' the islands chance to get it, trade goes all smooth and easy.[8]

Whatever Ballantyne's intent – and after several years of working in Canada for the Hudson's Bay Company he became a committed Christian – the novel cannot prevent its various rhetorical strategies from undermining one another. The narrator, who is a more mature version of one

248 FIONA MCCULLOCH

of the shipwrecked boys, is therefore himself a character in the story whose views cannot be directly attributed to the author. Indeed, the retrospective reconstruction of the events on the island casts in doubt both their verity and validity.

As in the case of Barrie's *Peter Pan*, the performance of imperialism as *play* reveals the extent to which the ideology of imperialism distorts the economic realities by which it is driven, realities which break through unexpectedly into the generic structure of romance. Thus, when Barrie has Mrs Darling clearing up her children's minds as they go off to sleep, she discovers the apparently straightforward mental map of the island:

> for the Neverland is always more or less an island, with astonishing splashes of colour here and there, and coral reefs and rakish-looking craft in the offing, and savages and lonely lairs [...]. It would be an easy map if that were all; but there is also first day at school, religion, fathers, the round pond, needlework, murders, hangings, verbs that take the dative [...] and either these are part of the island or they are another map showing through, and it is all rather confusing, especially as nothing will stand still.[9]

The 'doubling' of the world which the Neverland maps points directly to the structure of Barrie's story, in which the realities of imperialism – the violent expropriation of the land of native peoples, the legally justified 'piracy' of seizing the ships of imperial competitors, the endless threat of individual and social violence – breaks through to implicate its readers in a very different environment from that of the benign spread of Christian civilisation:

> Let us now kill a pirate, to show Hook's method, Skylights will do. As they pass, Skylights lurches clumsily against him, ruffling his lace collar; the hook shoots forth, there is a tearing sound and one screech, and then the body is kicked aside, and the pirates pass on. He has not even taken the cigar from his mouth.[10]

Just as Ballantyne's narrator is an adult recalling a (supposed) childhood adventure which can never be fully incorporated into the adult's Christian-imperial ideology, so Barrie's playful Neverland suddenly opens up to reveal the real nature of the imperialism that keeps the Darling household safe in civilised London. As W. W. Robson notes, the juxtaposition of adult interpretations with childhood experiences produces the doubled narrative of not only Stevenson's classic text of children's literature, *Treasure Island* (1883), but of his later *The Strange Case of Dr Jekyll and Mr Hyde* (1886): 'I saw that of the two natures that contended in the field of my consciousness, if I could rightly be said to be either, it was only because I was radically both.'[11] The juxtaposition of the child's experiences with the adult's recollection of them produces a sophisticated interplay which not only prefigures more recent theoretical accounts of the impossibility of interpretive closure but which will become a major element in the formal experiments of later Scottish writers. Children's literature, one might say, provided the model in the 1970s and 1980s for a society shuffling off a religious and imperial identity and seeking alternative ways of understanding both its past and its possible future. 'In the relative infancy of a devolved Scotland', I have suggested elsewhere, 'it seems timely to demonstrate that children's fiction, far from comprising a mere afterthought within Scotland's creative psyche, plays a fundamental role in the shaping of that collectively imagined space'.[12]

It does so, however, in a world that has been becoming more 'globalised', both in terms of economic interactions and population flows, while, at the same time, producing the retrenchment of notions of national singularity we see across Europe in various movements of resistance to migrants and migration that culminate in myths of the 'great replacement' of traditional European cultures by the populations of their former colonies. In the case of Scotland, such tensions long predate the modern era because of the country's huge loss of population to outward migration from the eighteenth to the twentieth centuries as well the very substantial inward migration from Ireland and from Eastern Europe in the second half of the nineteenth century and from such countries as Italy in the twentieth. Though the Church of Scotland may have sought to defend Scotland's 'ethnic purity' in the 1920s,[13] in order to maintain its religious purity, it was a 'purity' long since undermined by waves of migration, both inward and outward. The expectations in the late 1990s, as ethnic notions of nationalism were displaced by a new and inclusive 'civic nationalism', was that Scotland would become a new – and different – country.[14]

In the case of Scotland since the independence referendum of 2014, however, the nation has been riven between those seeking escape from and those determined to maintain the authority of Westminster's control in Scotland and what, to many Scottish nationalists, is English hegemonic control over the British state. If the recovery and redeployment of Scottish children's literature has been one of the literary markers of Scotland's journey towards semi-independence, it may be that what has come to be denominated as 'Young Adult' fiction corresponds to its current condition, one, like teenagers, struggling to come to terms with the adult world and potential adult responsibilities. Critics have tended to distinguish between YA (approximately ages thirteen to eighteen), NA (New Adult; approximately ages eighteen to thirty), and adult fiction, but such sharp delineations are problematic, since children have always read books intended for adults while, more recently, so-called crossover fiction has appealed to teenagers and adults (sometimes labelled kidults) alike. Equally, such terms differ geopolitically, culturally and historically so that benchmarks can only ever be approximate. According to Roberta Seelinger Trites, YA fiction interdependently emerged with postmodernism and its interrogation of the Althusserian and Foucauldian power dynamics of subjectivity.[15] Rather than adhere to Western society's linear childhood development towards Cartesian fixed selfhood, postmodernism and, by association YA fiction, tests the boundaries of subjectivity and reconfigures it as a multifaceted construction enmeshed within discursive positionings.

Given post-devolution's decentring of Westminster-driven power offset by 2014's failure to fulfil self-determination (where devolved potential is constrained by limited autonomy), YA fiction seems particularly appropriate as a context to ponder the nation's geopolitical interstitial impasse: adolescent desire for autonomy, one might say, complements the compulsion for the nation's maturation to reach a grown-up state of independence. The post-devolution momentum that culminated in the 2014 independence referendum ignited juvenile engagement in grassroots movements; recognising this, the Scottish Government allowed those sixteen and over to vote. By aligning themselves with matters of citizenship, Scotland's youth actively participated in the nation's trajectory to forge their future. They are also, as a result of further waves of inward migration, as well as changes in social policy such as the legalisation of gay marriage, and the effort to overcome the marginalisation of those side-lined by the politics of gender, sexuality, race, ethnicity or disability, necessarily engaged in the imagining and reimagining of a more heterogeneous society.

In this context, Michael Gardiner's Deleuzian and Guattarian view of 'minor literature' is useful in its assessment of post-devolution Scottish fiction's impact, where 'the minor is invariably more literary than the major'.[16] For Gardiner, Scotland's minority positioning ensures 'a literature of effect and becoming rather than one of static assumptions',[17] with its marginal status a key driver that impels it towards a dynamic heterogeneity rather than defensive fixity. Here Gardiner's analysis intersects with recent discussions of the 'new cosmopolitanism' that arises not from an elite that is at home everywhere but from transnational flows of population that have created a world where no one is any longer at home within a single identity. According to Bruce Robbins and Paulo Lemos Horta, 'cosmopolitanism can be defined as any one of many possible modes of life, thought and sensibility that are produced when commitments and loyalties are multiple and overlapping', with the result that cosmopolitanism 'has come to be seen as characteristic of substantial social collectivities, often non-elite collectivities that had cosmopolitanism thrust upon them by traumatic histories of dislocation and dispossession', what has been described as the 'cosmopolitanism of the poor'.[18] A similar account can be found in the work of Rosi Braidotti, who also utilises Deleuze and Guattari's concept of 'becoming' to define cosmopolitanism in terms of the experience of a philosophically nomadic citizen who rejects static territorialism in favour of 'multiple belongings'[19] to the world. A minor literature, we might suggest, serves as a viable political force insofar as it resists static assumptions and strives for a cosmopolitical outlook of fluid becoming.

Thus Anne Donovan's YA novel, *Being Emily* (2008) depicts contemporary Glasgow, with its gentrification as a city of style, business and affluence, negatively impacting upon its historical roots as '*The dear green place*' since '*There'll be nae green left and it's already far too dear tae live here*'.[20] This rebuke, uttered by the father of teenage narrator, Fiona, highlights Glasgow's diminishing environmental, community and cultural space in the wake of corporate development. As a means of resisting such deracination of 'hame', Donovan's text incurs alternative cosmopolitan connections between self/other, while emphasising art and literature's role in politically resisting neoliberal commodification, symbolised in the city's Festival of Light, bringing people together to experience its 'reborn'[21] splendour. Rather than multicultural rhetoric – berated as '*paying lip service to the real diversity of our culture and smoothing over the racism and suspicion that divides us*'[22] – Donovan projects a unified cosmopolitan citizenship, epitomised in the relationships forged by Fiona, particularly her union with Glaswegian Sikh, Jas, and the heteronormative disruption of nuclear family with her gay brother, Patrick, and her lesbian aunt, Janice.[23] Similarly, Julie Bertagna's *Exodus* (2002–2011) trilogy, an environmental dystopia, interrogates the impact of self-serving governance and responds to climate change's destructive consequences by geopolitically relocating the nation's populace further north in remote Greenland. The protagonist, Mara, resists the opportunistic governments' top-down disempowerment of citizens by leading her people elsewhere, towards a northern 'land of the people'.[24] Rather than remaining subjects of self-interested capitalist leadership, Bertagna's eco-community aligns with Braidotti's cosmofeminist concept of spatial fluidity's 'multiple belongings': Mara's composite cohort strive towards achieving a symbiotic relationship with nature in their relocation.[25] With its titular focus upon the journey trope, Bertagna's trilogy emphasises the importance of geopolitical relocation from a divisive centralised power structure in favour of solidarity and fellowship between citizens and their ecosystem.[26]

In Claire McFall's *Bombmaker* (2014), an alternative contemporary history represents an 'elsewhere' that assimilates much of Britain's post-devolution and post-Brexit anxiety by situating her dystopian text in a fragmented disunited Kingdom: Celts are deemed enemies of the English state and any found to transgress its borders are punished as illegal immigrants. In McFall's vision, global instability and economic collapse leads alliances to disintegrate: 'China and the USA were at each other's throats, with Europe caught in the crossfire [...] So we left the EU [...] It didn't work very well'.[27] *Bombmaker*'s overt political context both influences and is influenced by adolescent interest in national and world issues, and her prescient narrative depicts isolationism rather than cooperation, thereafter experienced in the real-world geopolitics of Trumpism, Brexit and Covid-19. In McFall's 2014 publication, after Britain exits the EU, 'the country was bankrupt, the people starving. The government in London made the decision to dissolve the United Kingdom [...] They cut off Scotland, Northern Ireland and Wales'.[28] Britishness unravels with economic decline, and anyone who attempts to surmount its border walls is facially branded with a 'Celtic knot'.[29] McFall's dystopia negatively depicts a struggling hinterland: 'there was little in the way of government in Scotland any more, and absolutely no welfare state. There were no jobs, no money, no food. No chances.'[30] England's outliers are given no capacity for economic, social, or cultural betterment in this bleak outlook. However, the notable villain of the piece is not Scotland's struggle for autonomy but, rather, a hegemonic Anglo state that partitions itself in isolation. Not only 'cut off', England dehumanises those outwith its citadel, amplifying historical and continuing alterity. Teenage heroine Lizzie refers to 'news reports running almost nightly on EBC', where her Scottish otherness is framed as 'dangerous, untrustworthy, devious. Certainly not someone you should welcome into your home.'[31] *Bombmaker*'s EBC, a thinly veiled version of the BBC (often accused of pro-Union bias)[32], has become England's propaganda tool. McFall's text – published the same year as the 2014 'Indyref' – apparently warns against Scottish independence, but also indicates an interrogation of how Britain's internal borders are perceived, policed and managed in an unequal Union of hegemonic ubiquitous control. In that vein, it would seem the novel urges a self-determination to countermand any dismantling of its devolved powers or future aspirations.[33]

Scotland's historical alterity is further considered in Donald Lightwood's children's novel, *The Long Revenge* (2002), which charts the impact of the Highland Clearances on the lives of brothers, Duncan and Angus Paterson, and their widowed mother, Morag, who relocate to Edinburgh. The textual historiography weaves fictional characters into a pivotal moment in Scottish history. Real-life figures also appear, including Sir Walter Scott and the grave robbers Burke and Hare. Often omitted from school history lessons, the Clearances are a historical palimpsest in Scotland's cultural psyche where, habitually, citizens have a vague comprehension of such an atrocity. *The Long Revenge*'s re-imagining invites young readers to offset historical amnesia, with events enclosed within a contemporary framework, importantly forging a link between past and present. Australian father and son tourists visit Perthshire's 'Craigmuir Heritage Centre', composed 'of the ruins of an old Highland township that had been destroyed in 1822' when 'folks were cleared out of their houses so the landlord could graze sheep'.[34] Paterson junior notices their family name on the clachan's list, sparking the historical narrative chronicling their ancestral flit to Edinburgh. Notably, at the novel's close, the father/son tourists are named: Duncan and Angus Paterson share their ancestors' names. For Lightwood, Scotland's historical events are not separated by a distant past, but resonate in contemporary society, just as Duncan/Angus Paterson dually inhabit past and present. Likewise, the Clearance's resultant diaspora generated Scottish enclaves across the globe: 'Our history teacher said loads of Scots came to settle in Australia.'[35] It is noticeable that it is Paterson junior rather than senior who wishes to linger at the heritage centre better to understand his own ancestral narrative, which connects the list of evicted families with his history lessons on Australia's Scottish immigrants. *The Long Revenge* seeks to educate Scotland's future citizens on their cultural past and its correlation to geopolitical events, including the nation's demographic exodus.

The main narrative charts the Paterson's (brothers Duncan and Angus, and their mother, Morag) eviction and resultant Edinburgh relocation.

Morag 'knew well enough the Duke had the right to do what he wanted with his land. Now he wanted to put sheep on it. The crofters were no longer wanted.'[36] Only receiving the eviction notice 'that morning',[37] the dispossessed clachan forms part of the Clearances' topographical reshaping of Highland culture: 'One sentence. That's all it took to destroy people's lives.'[38] Brothers Duncan and Angus watch their croft alight and people 'trying to get into the church, but the minister was [...] forbidding them entry'.[39] Choosing Church preservation over protecting his flock, the cleric's complicity fails his 'congregation [...] who brought you here in the first place!'.[40] Establishment figures prioritise property and profit, while clachans 'must go far away from this place where they value sheep more than they do people'.[41] Having endured the Highland's social cleansing, Morag observes its commodification as Walter Scott, during the notorious king's visit of 1822, endorses fashionable tartan: 'Bless the man for his foolish notions [...] Edinburgh's gentry wanting to dress themselves up like Highland lairds and ladies.'[42] While this newfound demand for tartan pays Edinburgh workers, including Morag, she articulates the trend towards performative mimicry of impoverished Highlanders – cast asunder during the Clearances – by affluent Scottish and English establishment figures.

The relationship between past and present Scotland is also implicit in Ross Sayers's YA novel *Sonny and Me* (2019). Narrated by Billy, it charts his life at Battlefield High in Bannockburn, symbolic site of the Scottish Wars of Independence, but questions what 'independence' means in the modern world. Neither Billy nor his best friend Sonny belongs to the 'in' crowd, but are outsiders because Sonny is gay. They live in an environment of entrenched homophobia, dramatised when '*"POOF" had been scrawled in big letters across the front ae Sonny's jotter* [...] *"POOF" [was] written across my jotter tae*'.[43] Though straight, Billy's surname is 'Daughter' and he is labelled gay by association, so that both boys are subjected to homophobic bullying. Rather than investigate, English teacher, Mr Naismith, simply instructs them to replace the jotters, but Billy challenges this: '*If it's no worth findin oot who did it, then it's no worth replacin them. I'm fine wi my poof jotter. In fact, why do we no write it on everybody's jotter?*'[44] Despite Scotland's advances on LGBT rights and gender equality, Sayers portrays a conservative reactionary attitude to alterity, indicative of entrenched cultural malaise. While '*Maist folk were tryin no tae laugh*'[45] at the defaced jotters, teachers ignore the pack persecution to which they are witness. Sayers portrays a reactionary school system's unwillingness to address and educate on matters of

LGBT marginalisation and bullying. Even the headteacher, Mrs Campbell (who, it transpires, has murdered her father-in-law for money), regards Sonny as 'a perverted idiot'.[46] When Billy mistakenly assumes 'Ye're the only gay guy in oor year. Howarth's the only bi yin', Sonny replies: 'Mate, dinnae tell me ye're that naïve. Howarth and me arenae the only two',[47] signalling the extensive number of pupils silenced by education's heteronormative matrix.

Sonny's revelation to Billy is one of the few moments of insight to his character throughout the novel, which is largely focalised from the narrator's perspective. The narrative distances the reader from Sonny's experiences, since they tend to be filtered through Billy. When Billy complains about the jotter incident, Sonny remains silent and complies with the teacher's instruction to replace the jotter: he '*got up quickly, probably relieved tae hide for even a few seconds in the supply cupboard*'.[48] However, Billy's protests result in their exclusion from class: '*Sonny's eyes were red, but he smiled at me as he followed me oot intae the corridor*'.[49] Rather than initiate resistance, Sonny follows Billy's lead, grateful for an ally. Billy also chides Howarth: 'dinnae tell folk tae man up [...] That doesnae help anybody. Ye better no be sayin that tae Sonny'.[50] Despite Howarth's bisexuality, Billy's defence of Sonny demonstrates greater knowledge of gender constructions. Denigrated as 'rentboys', Billy retaliates, 'We're gay. Gid yin', while 'Sonny's aready backed away and I dinnae blame him really. No fair tae ask him tae listen tae this'.[51] A gay perspective is again deferred to the straight narrative gaze, with Billy not 'really' blaming Sonny, suggesting partial resentment. When his friend is called a 'big queer', Billy is 'kick[ed] in the ribs'.[52] Defending him on multiple occasions, Billy is the protector for silent Sonny. Billy concedes, 'I'm sorry I dinnae ken how tae talk tae ye aboot ye bein gay'.[53] Billy's inability to allow Sonny to safely express himself in an intimate space further gags him. In a patriarchal culture, Billy contradictorily challenges gender constructions yet responds to homophobic threats with aggressive retorts, separating his heteronormative credentials from a bullied feminised other by conflating gender and sexuality in a reassertion of his own masculinity. His inability to communicate with Sonny is a lost opportunity to pluralise a masculine code of conduct to accommodate a broader spectrum of sexuality. Just as Billy acknowledges shutting down a dialogic space where Sonny's perspective is heard, heteronormativity's hegemonic narrative ultimately quashes counter-narratives.

A similar interplay between the hegemonic and the dialogic is evident in Martin Stewart's *The Sacrifice Box* (2018), which is focused on disability.

In this case it is the protagonist, Sep, who is deaf in one ear due to a childhood infection caused by pushing mud into his ear to muffle the sound of his mother's then-boyfriend, who habitually shouted at her. Stewart outlines the volatility of family life and its pressures on children, a prevalent theme in YA fiction as adolescents grapple to navigate unstable home lives and uncertain worlds. Further, despite his mother's cancer remission during the narrative, its impact haunts Sep. Increasingly isolated from friends, he retreats into schoolwork, hoping to escape his island home for the mainland boarding school and then university. His sense of remoteness is accentuated with rural island life's diminishment by the mainland city's beacon-like allure across the sea, appearing 'distant and solid – and everything the island was not',[54] a symbol of freedom and renewal. That desire is fuelled by his recollection of visiting relatives there before his mother's illness: its effervescence offers Sep a possible antidote to the small-town claustrophobia that is magnified by his mother's cancer.

Unsurprisingly, 'He wanted that life – the busy, vibrant anonymity, not the Hill Ford fishbowl', while the 'city's engineering college' turns into a burning desire, beating its mantra 'with a single impulse. *Leave the island*'.[55] Hill Ford sounds like hill-fort, conjuring a bastion of primitive seclusion, juxtaposed with the illuminated urban sprawl's promise of unfettered modernity and adventure. Although island and city remain unnamed, Stewart's paratext confirms the Island is Arran – 'the town of Hill Ford is a composite of Brodick and Lamlash'[56] – so that the mainland city must be Glasgow. Scotland's landscape plays a vital role in Stewart's text both as geographical locales and literary tropes. The insular glare of the island community is amplified by Sep's childhood responsibility of being his mother's carer, as well as being friendless. Despite his mother's remission and her burgeoning relationship with the school headmaster, Sep's constricted life is punctuated only with study and part-time work. Predominantly set in 1986, with an introductory chapter in 1982 and flashbacks to 1941, spatiotemporal distance increases his isolation from the present of Stewart's twenty-first-century readers more familiar with a globally interconnected world.

To offset remote 1980s Scottish island living, Stewart emphasises the vital role of friendships and community. Headmaster Tench relocates from the mainland to experience 'small town' existence and share 'each other's lives in a kind of ... family of families'.[57] Sep's headmaster regards island living as a 'shared happiness' that 'connect[s] to the very essence of the human animal, and all the spiritual nourishment community can bring'.[58] Tench symbiotically links 'the human animal' to the island's biosphere, harmoniously fusing human, landscape, and animal. Conversely, Sep's desire for city dwelling is fuelled by his growing detachment from home, experiencing 'the barrier between him and the rest of the class like a coil of wire',[59] as the chasm widens. Resultantly, his employer and only friend, Mario, warns 'Do not hate, Sep. The only thing there is in the world, at the end, is love.'[60] Bullied as a child in Greece because he 'liked the boys [...] Sexually',[61] Mario implies that destructive 'hate' is remedied by restorative 'love'.

Love's necessity is thematically pervasive: resentment harboured by Sep and his former friends at their lost camaraderie emits negativity into the atmosphere. Their 1982 friendship pact involved sacrificing a symbolic possession to the titular box discovered in the woods. In 1986 that pact unravels, unleashing disruptive forces upon their lives as well as their elders who used the box in 1941. While *The Sacrifice Box* has a realist setting and themes, like school and family life, it is replete with Scottish gothic influence: zombified animals, corpses and animated toys unleash murderous nightmarish events. The box's malevolence contaminates the landscape, which 'really stinks':[62] 'Even the forest knows it. Nothin' growin' except the mushrooms.'[63] Gamekeeper Roxburgh informs them, 'all that resentment's like storm clouds around your heads. Forgive each other, then you'll have a chance.'[64] Their divisions expose a festering detachment: 'you were meant to be my friends [...] I've spent the past four years alone',[65] which echoes humanity's abandonment of nature and community. Sep's former friend Mack opens the box to trigger a reunion which, inadvertently, releases darkness: 'Mrs Maguire had sacrificed a doll in childhood – and it had returned to kill her. They had unwittingly sacrificed painful, secret things – and the box was using them as weapons.'[66] Sep visits hospitalised Maguire [his teacher] to determine how to reverse the Pandora-like ills, and she advises, 'People are hurt [...] That's what happens when you break a promise [...] there aren't many things in life as fierce as the bond between children. Between friends, who love each other.'[67] Love is a 'fierce' force that must be nurtured not left to stagnate. Echoing her childhood friend, Roxburgh, she warns: 'Forgive. Love. Make new offerings [...] that show your love for one another'.[68] Genuine connection maintains fellowship; the next chapter flashbacks to 1941 when Maguire and Roxburgh's group of friends make offerings to the box; she says 'I made this for all of you [...] and for everyone who needs it, even the Germans – they've got children and mothers and fathers too. If we could just love each other, maybe everything would be all right.'[69] During a devastating epoch that includes the

Holocaust, Stewart amplifies love's significance as a curative yet scarce resource in a world at war.

Humanity's capacity for evil is only resolved by its potential for benevolent friendship, not only between individuals but, geopolitically, within and between nations. Rather than self/other, Stewart centralises a need for interdependence between individuals and nations. This reflects, perhaps, a fundamental strand of Scottish philosophical thought, with Ian D. Suttie and John Macmurray deeming it a vital element of social cohesion.[70] Stewart's novel prioritises cosmopolitan connectivity over division and conflict to an adolescent readership who will form the demographic of Scotland's future citizens. When Sep and his friends reconcile, he realises '*That's all there is, at the end, isn't it? [...] People, and what you've shared.*'[71] By sacrificing himself to save community and friends, he finally connects; defeating the 'box's poison', Sep 'absorbed the wonder of his world: the crackle of growing grass, the pull of the tide and the soft breath of people', and 'reached out his love towards'[72] his mother. Imminent demise triggers epiphanic interdependence between self, landscape, community and family. Ultimately, his friends save him and, despite embarking on the ferry for the mainland, he remains anchored to home: 'a sense of place that ran up from the soles of his feet.'[73] No longer resentfully fleeing his past, his exodus positively embraces a future securely rooted in his formative community.

Like Sep, sixteen-year-old Alex in Sylvia Hehir's *Sea Change* (2019) lives with his widowed mother on their croft, helping her cope with grief: making 'tea' and 'supplementing what his mum earned'[74] by creel fishing for the local hotel. Like Stewart's novel, *Sea Change* is influenced by Scottish gothic, particularly tartan noir. Alex discovers a cadaver on the beach, assuming the corpse is unsavoury newcomer, Chuck. It transpires though that the deceased is Ellie – his best friend, Daniel's twin sister – and Chuck is her murderer. Alex's father also meets an untimely death, and the repressed inability of mother and son to articulate their loss engenders trauma:

> It had been well over a year since his dad died but neither Alex nor his mum ever mentioned him [...] He shouldn't have been hand diving for scallops after that bout of flu [...] Alex had a vision of his body drifting spread-eagled over the silty seabed.[75]

Gothic scenes haunt his unconscious, accentuating teenage turbulence. Briefly recounting the plot, Daniel, adopted son of the local Minister, goes missing after going to the bus station to meet up with his newfound sister. Chuck befriends Alex to get to Daniel who, it is later disclosed, is Chuck's half-brother. Ellie's murder and Daniel's attempted murder are Chuck's sinister efforts to prevent his mother discovering his father's infidelity. Alex sets off to the old Manse where Daniel once lived, only to be knocked out and tied up by Chuck. Finally freeing himself, Alex prevents Chuck from drowning Daniel, and is subsequently assisted by Caitlin (Daniel's girlfriend) and school acquaintance, Angus, who arrive at the scene. Ultimately, Chuck is arrested and life resumes its familiar rhythm in the unnamed Highland town, with Alex arranging his customary visit to Daniel 'after tea',[76] though the latter is obviously altered by his ordeal and Alex has matured, now accepting his burgeoning feelings for Angus.

While Stewart's novel depicts a remote island locale, Hehir's *Sea Change* is rooted in a secluded Highland community. Like Sayers's novel it also depicts a gay character but Hehir casts the main character, Alex, in this role. Her decision to place her gay hero in a rural Highland setting provides a comparison with Sayers's more urban locale of Stirling, as both texts confront the difficulties facing marginalised adolescents at school. *Sea Change*'s Alex feels alienated at school, and even his lifelong friendship with Daniel experiences a rift early in the narrative, later remedied when Alex saves him from Chuck. While Sayers's straight hero Billy defends Sonny from homophobic bullying, inversely, in Hehir's novel, Alex saves Daniel's life. Further, Alex journeys towards an acceptance of his own alterity by the novel's close. By acknowledging his homosexuality, he simultaneously admits his feelings for Angus: 'Alex turned so that they were face to face. He took hold of Angus's other hand. Their kiss this time was long and hard and Alex wanted it never to stop.'[77] While Alex faces his internalised fear and comes out to Angus, it is unclear how far either of them will enjoy full authenticity in their hometown. When Alex asks if Angus's parents know their son is gay, he replies, 'Not that I'm aware. I don't think they would even consider it a possibility. My dad's a road worker, my granddad was a road worker.'[78] Angus conceals his true self and fits into patriarchy's familial masculine matrix by excelling at sports.

At the novel's close, 'A bunch of kids on bikes turned the corner. "Alex and Daniel up a tree. K.I.S.S.I.N.G," they chanted'.[79] In an earlier scene in the school changing room they are referred to as 'lover boys'.[80] Daniel's discomfort is clear both times: he 'shook off Alex's hand'[81] and 'looked uncomfortable at the homophobic rant but Alex glanced at Angus and almost smiled'.[82] Although Daniel has experience of othering as an adopted child, it is uncertain whether he will mature enough to support Alex should he confide in him about being gay. Daniel's unwillingness to interrogate heteronormativity indicates an internalisation of cultural homophobia, just as Billy cannot discuss Sonny's homosexuality with him. Daniel's failure to evolve in his response to homophobic bullying indicates a deep-seated cultural malaise generationally entrenched within this remote community and, externally, wider Scottish culture that Hehir's text encourages her adolescent reader to address.

More promising, though, is Alex's relationship with Angus, where they both signal a willingness to defend each other. Daniel confirms his lack of maturation when he says, 'Just because he [Angus] helped save my life doesn't mean I have to like him'.[83] Such disregard for Angus's altruism indicates Daniel may reject Alex's friendship if his homosexuality is disclosed, even though both boys rescued him from Chuck. Alex, on the other hand, appreciates Angus's support:

> Daniel's wasn't the only life that had been saved by Angus that night [...] last night Alex had had nightmares about Chuck's rotting dead body [...] He knew that could easily have been a consequence if Angus hadn't been there.[84]

Although Chuck is villainous, Angus's generosity of spirit also saves him from drowning. Crucially, while Daniel and Caitlin go to science classes, Alex heads 'to the Hospitality room'.[85] Interrogated by his Aunty Joan – 'Why you can't do some proper subjects at that school. Baking cakes and fiddling around with bits of wood'[86] – Alex's preferences mirror his refusal to fit heteronormative masculinity's matrix. A skilled cook, he attends Hospitality classes, which amplifies his emerging openness and warmth towards others, including himself: 'Hospitality room',[87] the novel's closing words, evokes a space for kinship, solidarity and cosmopolitanism that complements Angus and indicates their compatibility. Alex's passion for creating gastronomic delights equates cosmopolitanism's concept of breaking bread with others as a community experience. Importantly, 'The sharing of food has always been part of the human story' and signifies 'the power of a meal to forge relationships, bury anger, provoke laughter'.[88] Likewise, informing Aunty Joan that he is also 'doing Higher English'[89] evokes a cosmopolitan interest in understanding others, since literature engages with other worlds, cultures and individuals beyond hegemonic norms. English, often diminutively feminised as a non-vocational ethereal subject, ensures Alex's academic interests challenge patriarchal conventions. Of course, studying Higher English in Scotland problematises its relationship with a dominating hegemonic culture but, optimistically, texts like Hehir's might conceivably find their way onto the curriculum and enable such 'minor' literature to intervene and resist that hegemony.

Laura Guthrie's *Anna* (2020) also engages with otherness, its titular narrator a thirteen-year-old with Asperger's syndrome. The authorial note explains, Asperger's 'became Autistic Spectrum Disorder Level 1'[90] but, since Anna's diagnosis predates this, Guthrie retains the original diagnostic term. Further, after an unexplained spinal accident, Anna spends a considerable time in hospital and, upon her release, is negotiating her new life as a wheelchair user. Before being discharged from hospital, though, the consultant informs her about a potential medical trial 'to repair spinal cord injuries like yours'.[91] Whether she applies or is accepted is left unsaid, and Guthrie explains, 'I didn't want Anna's happiness to hinge on [...] being able to walk again', unlike 'the original *Pollyanna* [which] treats Anna's possibly-permanent paraplegia as a giant tragedy'.[92] In a reimagining of Eleanor Porter's 1913 narrative, Guthrie's paratext elucidates her novel's exploration of Anna's accident as a way to resist the historical othering of disabilities, which 'only become tragedies when non-disabled people turn them into things that block opportunities, or treat people with them as somehow pitiable, incomplete, marred or at worst, dispensable'.[93] In response to such dehumanising discursive positioning of disabled people, *Anna* centralises an adolescent's struggles to navigate through life with the additional challenges of a neurodevelopmental disorder and, later, physical disabilities.

Anna's empathetic resilience is integral to healing several other characters, including her hitherto estranged mother, who concedes, 'I'm not strong [...] Not like you.'[94] Anna later confirms, 'I am strong. I can be true to myself, and I can blaze my own trail'.[95] Rather than internalise negative disability narratives, she regards her journey through life as an opportunity to forge her 'own trail'. From her deceased father who taught her the Happy Game, Anna learns 'to find a happy aspect in everything, no matter how dire',[96] mirroring Polyanna's Glad Game. As well as her developmental journey, Anna also geographically travels from London to Livingston to live with her estranged mother, following her father's death from a fire in their flat. Anna returns to her birthplace as a new Scot, learning to adjust to an unfamiliar culture from her London home. Ever optimistic, she adapts, makes friends, and dismantles her mother's aloofness to reignite a close mother/daughter bond. Bereft of her father, she creates a new family unit, helping to reunite her mother and maternal grandfather, and gains friends in her new neighbourhood and her mother's local church. Her opinion of her father deteriorates when informed of her mother's lost custody battle. Simultaneously, while her father disliked religion, Anna's developing interest in it is ignited through attending services with her mother. While a balanced view of both parents is useful, Anna is influenced by parental narratives and religion's grand narrative. Newfound ties strengthen her to overcome challenges of grief, relocation, Asperger's, and spinal injury, signalling that, despite these struggles, Anna will continue to thrive in a supportive new Scottish home. But will being 'true to myself' afford her necessary maturation and the space to inscribe 'my own trail', or merely parrot overwritten narratives?

Ultimately, these texts disrupt the myopic notion that literature for children and adolescents is a diminutive form that must be, by necessity, less valid to the nation's culture than its adult counterpart. What emerges instead through these readings is an awareness of the heterogeneous nature of such an intricate field that contains a multiplicity of genres spread across a complex literary spectrum, including realism, fantasy, sci-fi, historical, and gothic, to name just a few. To encompass not just one genre, but such a vibrant fertile landscape, signals a breadth and depth of diverse layers that exponentially enrich Scotland's cultural heritage. For Roderick McGillis, 'Children's literature is not hermetically sealed from either other literature or from the field of cultural production generally',[97] and this can no less be the case in relation to Scottish children's and YA texts. While only scratching the surface of available material, nevertheless, I hope to have, as Dunnigan argues above, contributed to the critical conversation of making 'room for children's literature'. As our initiation into literary worlds, such works are vital shapers of our cultural and cortical development,[98] laying the foundation stones of intellectual stimulation, and sparking a malleable grey matter that often, in turn, produces grown-up authors vital to our culture industry. Boasting the likes of Ballantyne to J. K. Rowling's *Harry Potter* series, with its journey from middle-England to a Scottish fantasy setting, these works help to remap the route of Scotland's literary topography and broaden its impact nationally and internationally. Having considered the significance of Rowling's work elsewhere,[99] I have not included her here, but to discount the phenomenal literary, cultural, and economic contribution to Scottish culture of such a global success, would be absurd.

The texts discussed here demonstrate their thematic maturity in handling historical events and informing new generations about, for instance, the Clearances, adding voice to an often-suppressed national wound. Likewise, there is a willingness to deal head on with contemporary social disturbances, contributing to the debates around, for instance, Brexit and Scotland's position within an uneasy Union. Within such weighty themes, children's and YA fiction has depicted characters capable of empathetic cosmopolitan connections and resilience in the face of challenges bigger and older than themselves, including homophobia, misogyny and poverty. Always popular with readers, Scottish children's and YA texts are gradually being given due notice critically, not just within children's literature studies, but by being recognised as an integral component of a wider Scottish cultural vista. To those who would disparage their infantile irrelevance, I offer McGillis's argument that

> The possibilities for interpretation of this literature are as varied as they are for any literature [...] many books for the young are disarming in their ostensible simplicity. Theory has taught us that what appears simple does so because we have not looked closely enough at that simple thing.[100]

To dismiss Scottish children's and YA literature as superficial, inevitably reinforces a rudimentary reading that locks it in arrested development, doing a disservice to its richness and robbing a nation of its key relevance. However, to dig inquisitively with a depth of interest will undoubtedly uncover an array of fascinating discoveries and recover the neglected roots of its positionality and kinship within the critical continuity of Scotland's cultural genealogy.

CHAPTER FOURTEEN

Into the Twenty-First Century

Cairns Craig

Surviving the Second World War

In its linguistically playful presentation of what appears to be a comedy of modern manners, Ali Smith's *There but for the* (2011) uses the four words of its title as subtitles for the book's four sections, the subtitle becoming the implied first word of the section's opening sentence. Each section thus depends on a word which, in the title, fails to become a portion of a complete sentence, as though neither 'grace' nor 'God' are any longer relevant to an 'I' that has now nowhere to go, imaged in the 'man who, one night at a dinner party, went upstairs and locked himself in one of the bedrooms of the house',[1] and remained there for months, pedalling incessantly on an exercise bike going nowhere. It is as if the man – named Miles, as though born to travel – were a revival of the time-traveller in H. G. Wells's *The Time Machine* (1894), who pedals his way into the future while remaining physically on the same spot in what was once London, but the surreal cyclist of the modern age is in a house in Greenwich, where in 1884, the world's timezones were codified by the international acceptance of Greenwich mean time as the fixed point from which all other times are measured. Miles travels nowhere, however, as though time has stalled, but those he has left in the world of time become time-travellers: Anna Hardie to the time when she first met Miles on a European trip in the 1970s; Mark (with whom Miles went to the fateful dinner) to the death in the 1960s of his mother, an influential Jewish artist; and, through Anna and Mark's influence, the nine-year-old Brooke Bayoude, who has a Moleskine notebook inscribed by Anna as 'History', revisits in imagination the youth of Elizabeth I in that same Greenwich. More than halfway through the book, in the third part, subtitled 'For', the narrative is suddenly taken over by the consciousness of May Young: her name is ironic since she is actually very old, despite her husband's insistence at the altar on 7 June 1947 that 'You'll always be "young" now you've married me' [...] But she was no fool, she knew exactly how old she was'.² She also knows exactly how many years it is since her daughter, Jennifer, died suddenly at age sixteen in 1979, a memory reinforced by that fact that one of her daughter's friends, Miles Garth, visits Mrs Young every year on the anniversary of her death: 'him turning up at the door every year couldn't help but mean another year had passed that May's own girl hadn't had'.³ Thirty years later, Mrs Young is in a nursing home when Miles has incarcerated himself in that bedroom in Greenwich. Similarly incarcerated in a care home, May travels in time, traversing back from Jennifer's childhood to her own visits to the cinema to see Gracie Fields's movies, at one of which she first encounters Philip Young, in 'Air Force uniform, he's young. He's not bad-looking'.⁴ She recalls,

> The eyes of the men after the war. Like rabbits in headlights. We all were. All of them who never came back. All them going up into the air and then not coming down. A line through the name in the morning, Philip told me. And that was that. Well, we came through, Philip and me.⁵

She may have 'come through', but it is to the years of the war that her memories return and through the consciousness of old Mrs Young, the events of 2010 become rooted in the Second World War. Not being able to visit her as usual on the anniversary of her daughter's death, Miles arranges for someone to sit with her, who turns out to be a rebellious young woman who helps May escape the care home and join the crowds gathered in celebration at the scene of Miles's strange vigil, but she sees only the past, 'a great celebration. It was just like after the war.'⁶ The immediacy of a modern world that is apparently radically different from the past becomes an after-echo of the conclusion of the war, as though the war is still the 'there' that defines the 'the' of our present becoming.

Like Ali Smith, Scottish novelists born long after the end of the war return to it relentlessly in their twenty-first-century writing, as though their world is defined not by the 'question of Scotland' but the question of the Britain which won the war and lost an empire, and the consequences of those intertwined events. Andrew Greig's *That Summer* (2000), for instance, charts the relationship between a Hurricane fighter-pilot – Len – and a member of the Women's Auxiliary Air Force – Stella – who works as a radar operator during the Battle of Britain in 1940–41. Their every meeting is bordered by the awareness of having survived one more day, and by the knowledge that they may not survive the next: 'It is really not a good idea to get interested in this man', Stella tells herself, 'I read the papers. Even if the scores are true, his survival is not, I think, very likely.'[7] They are participants in a world whose trajectory is unknowable:

> None of these people know the outcome of anything – the War, the next week, who will survive and who won't, if the troopship barges amassing across the Channel will shortly be launched. They are the most up-to date people on the planet and still they don't know.[8]

The consequence is that what survives the war will be entirely unlike what preceded it:

> Sometimes it seems the whole country is on the move, I thought. Nothing will be the same again. The War isn't something fought by somebody else. It's ours now – the Home Guard, the air-raid wardens, the people running trains and working in armaments factories and farming the land.[9]

The war is not simply an 'interruption of normal life'.[10] For those who survive, it will redefine everything with the same finality as for those who do not. Thinking of a possible future in which she is married and will have children, Stella realises 'why our parents kept their war to themselves. It was too horrible yet precious, it had gone too deep.'[11] However much they will try to ignore it, the war has become fundamental to who they can be for as long as they survive.

Similarly, A. L. Kennedy's *Day* (2007) follows the career of its eponymous protagonist, Alfie Day, the rear gunner of a Lancaster bomber who, when he has nearly completed the thirty missions after which he will be stood down, finds himself 'so near, too near, and you're sure this should not be mentioned: the terrible idea that sometimes mouths inside your head *I might live*'.[12] His life, however, is now premised on the deaths of those unknown others on whom his crew has dropped their bombs, a guilt which is compounded when they carry out a new kind of fire-bombing that leaves Alfie's Irish comrade Molloy feeling that 'when we did what we did this week – that was the end of heaven'.[13] The effects of 'a whole new kind of fire'[14] are as searing to their consciousnesses as it is destructive of the enemy's cities:

> *But the twenty-seventh was the worst. It was our ruination. When they ordered us back two days later and we went.*
> *'Jesus, you can see it from here.'*

> '*Shut up.*'
> '*Still hot.*'
> '*Shut up.*'
> '*Still burning.*'
> '*Poor fucking bastards.*'
> We went back and we bombed them again.[15]

As though now cursed, their Lancaster is riddled by anti-aircraft defences and only Alfie survives, parachuting into German territory where he is made a prisoner of war. Alfie's survival is as accidental and unpredictable as the life of the girl whom he met in an air raid shelter during the London blitz. She expects to hear that her husband, Donald, captured by the Japanese, is dead, but later writes to the imprisoned Alfie to tell of Donald's survival: 'What were the chances that both of her men would come back.'[16] Whatever life they manage to construct after the war – 'It will be complicated'[17] – will always be defined by being survivors of the chances of war.

Equally haunted is Andrew O'Hagan's *Personality* (2003), despite the fact that its main narrative follows the career in postwar consumerist Britain of Maria Tambini, a child star who shoots to fame after her appearance on a television talent show. Tambini is from an Italian migrant family in Scotland, the daughter of a brief relationship between her mother, Lucia, and an American serviceman. Maria may be the offspring of the war's conclusion, but for the Tambinis, grandmother, mother and daughter, there is no escape from the early days of the war, because Maria's grandmother's life is mutilated by the death of her older daughter, Sophia, in 1940. Lucia had begun a relationship with an Italian singer – Enrico Colangelo – who was interned at the outbreak of hostilities. About to be transported to a camp in Canada, Enrico smuggles Lucia and her daughter on board the ship during embarkation; the ship is the *Arandora Star* which was torpedoed off the Irish coast on 2 July 1940. Lucia is haunted by the disappearance of her first daughter – 'I knew it then and I know it now as I'm telling that this day was the end of me.'[18] As a consequence, Maria is present in her family's life only as a reflection of absences – the absence of her father who has gone back to America, the absence of her aunt Sophia – and after she has become an international success, her grandmother confuses her with Sophia in their phone calls.[19] Maria's life as a television superstar is spectrally accompanied by the girl who did not survive. As she settles to sleep in an American hotel room, she glances at the window: 'The glass was clear, but just before the darkness of sleep, for the briefest second, she was sure she saw the face of a small girl. The girl looked in, tapped at the glass, and disappeared.'[20] As Maria's subsequent anorexia intensifies, it is as if this other girl not only accompanies her in her travels but is physically consuming her bodily existence. Her own life an outcome of Sophia's absence, Maria attempts, by her refusal to eat, to make herself both central to and, at the same time, absent from the world into which she has been projected:

> She walked up and down the strip. She saw her shadow moving along the pavement in front of her, and after an hour she began to feel happy again, passing food places and breathing in the smells of onions and hamburgers. She passed all the places again and again and felt gratified with her shadow on the ground. It was like levitating. She needed nothing. She would eat nothing. She walked down the street and it was as if the whole street and the whole of Las Vegas had been built for Maria Tambini.[21]

The accidents of her family's survival are transformed into a world apparently designed for the coming of Maria, a wonder of the televisual age and yet unable to escape the absence created by the war, a fact underlined by Michael Aigus, the boy from Rothesay who was her distant admirer before she became famous and who, when they meet again in London, becomes her lover. Michael is the editor of a braille magazine for the war-blinded. Part of his job is to help co-ordinate special events for BBC programmes such as *Songs of Praise*, through which he discovers that Maria is being considered as a more modern replacement for Vera Lynn – a renewed version of the cultural spirit of the war. As Lucia declares when she lights candles in the chapel for Sophia and for the 'man on the *Arandora Star*', 'You think things are past but they never are.'[22]

The same is true for the central characters of James Robertson's *And the Land Lay Still* (2010). Don Lennie and Jack Gordon are survivors of military campaigns in Europe and the Far East and their banal but secure postwar lives are insistently disrupted by the memory of their wartime experiences. In Don's case, it is his accidental survival after an American bombing raid which mistakenly targets the British company he is involved with – 'then he saw that some of the debris was pieces of the men he'd been talking to a few minutes earlier'[23] – while in Jack's case it is the memory of a fellow prisoner in Burma, MacLaren, who decided to walk to freedom in India. Jack's account of MacLaren's recapture becomes a memory that can wake Don like an intruder in his house:

The name of the intruder was MacLaren. The man who tried to walk two thousand miles to India. The prisoner who wanted freedom at any price. The starving wreck they brought back and finished off with a sword sweep in a jungle clearing. And Jack had made a paper company of him, ranks of MacLarens marching across a page.[24]

Unable to suppress the memory of MacLaren's fate, Jack walks out on his wife and child and becomes himself a ghost haunting the modern Scotland in which Don continues to live:

> he'd be at his work, and a man coming round the front of the lorry would be Jack for a second, and then not Jack, just his ghost [...] That was what it was like: Jack haunted Don not because he was dead – which he almost surely was – but because he might still be out there somewhere, alive.[25]

The war may be over but its shaping influence over modern Scotland does not end. As Mike Pendreich says to the audience at the opening of the exhibition titled 'The Angus Angle', a collection of his father's photographs that Mike has curated, and with which the novel ends,

> History is written by the survivors [...]. We don't know what the story is when we're in it, and even after we tell it we're not sure. Because the story doesn't end. As William Faulkner put it, 'The past is never dead. It's not even past'.[26]

The insistent presence of the past is dramatically realised when Don Lennie discovers that among the photographs on display is one of Jack Gordon, a tramp whom Angus had inveigled into a photograph with the Dounreay nuclear power station in the background – a future that never happened. But Jack's accidental encounter with the Pendreich family was proof that he had again survived, just as he survives once more in the time-transcending medium of Angus's art.

A characteristic feature of these novels is the juxtaposition of an apparently objective historical perspective with subjective interior monologue, as when Alfie Day kills his abusive father by tipping him into a canal and throwing bricks at him:

> He doesn't complain when the second brick hits. You have the range now.
> Then there are only noises.
> *Took him a while. I like that it took him a while.*[27]

Similarly, Len's and Stella's perspectives in *That Summer* are juxtaposed against the known chronology of the Battle of Britain, while in *Personality*, O'Hagan segments his narrative so that a variety of characters are allowed to take up the first-person narration. Lucia, for instance, lays out clothes from a suitcase meant for Sophia:

> I have never seen them before and yet they are more personal to me than anything in this house. I don't own them in any way, but I was meant to own them, they are relics of some life that failed.[28]

A life failed by war is equally the theme of Suhayl Saadi's *Joseph's Box* (2009) which, though its geography ranges from Glasgow to the Himalayas, nonetheless has at its core the dying Archie Enoch McPherson, who claims to his doctor that he had been a fighter pilot in the war, though in fact he was always part of the ground crew. In the third person, historical view, Archie dies of cancer but from his first-person perspective, as his body is cremated, he is finally completing his alternative life as a fighter pilot:

> the aircraft fall from the sky and like torn sheaves their pilots burn to nothing.
> Archie feels all of this, every lick of flame, every invertebrate twitch, every last sound of pain and decay. Finally, it is happening.[29]

An extravagant use of such juxtaposition of historical events with a self-addressing interior monologue makes up Part Three of Robertson's *And the Land Lay Still*, in which the political history of postwar Scotland rolls out of the consciousness of Peter Bond, who was originally named 'James', but after the success of Sean Connery in the Bond movies renamed himself as Peter. He nonetheless believes that he is a secret agent, working for the British state, and therefore has a mastery of Scotland's public and underground political history: what he recalls may be the unacknowledged truth of modern Scotland or simply the deluded fantasy of a human wreck. One of Peter's recollections is being accosted in a pub in Glasgow by his 'handler', Croick, who, when Peter is drunk, mimics the Eagles's 'Hotel California' on the jukebox, 'but he was singing, "Welcome to the Hotel Caledonia" [...] And I knew I was doomed.'[30] Controlled by a British state that has itself been co-opted by American military and cultural power, Peter Bond is the antithesis of the James Bond who allows Britain and Scotland to pretend still to play a leading role on the world stage in the aftermath of the war.

Living in the Aftermath

Andrew Crumey's *The Great Chain of Unbeing* (2018) begins with the testing of a British hydrogen bomb on Christmas Island in the late 1950s. The narrator's father was one of the military personnel present: 'My father said even with his back to the fireball, and with his eyes closed, he could see the bones of his own hands.'[31] The consequence, however, was that 'a high-energy photon from the blast […] severed a chemical bond inside his body' so that the narrator is born blind and his father dies from cancer.[32] The lives and deaths of father and son are defined by a thermonuclear explosion undertaken to prove that Britain is still a world power, but instead of adding to the nation's 'being', it signals a chain reaction of 'unbeing'. A similar reversal from 'being' to 'unbeing' is the theme of Alan Spence's *The Pure Land* (2006), which begins in the aftermath of the dropping of the atom bomb on Nagasaki on 9 August 1945. Tomisaburo, a citizen of Nagasaki, looks out on 'the terrible end of everything; annihilation, nothingness. One single blast had laid waste half the city.'[33] The destruction of Nagasaki is itself, however, an aftermath – the aftermath of the American and European incursion into the previously closed world of Japan, in which Tomisaburo's father, Thomas Blake Glover, the founder of Mitsubishi, had played a significant role. Glover, from Aberdeen, had not only inspired Japanese industrialisation by importing Western technologies but helped provide armaments to those sections of Japanese society which overthrew the old order and set the country on the path of imperial expansion: 'I was the greatest rebel', Glover tells an American journalist, 'Without me the new Japan would not exist.'[34] But in the end, despite his achievements, Glover has nothing but regrets to leave to his son, who, in a parallel to the plot of *Madam Butterfly*, was born to a courtesan and later 'adopted' by Glover and his wife. Glover's last words to his son as he presents him with a Samurai sword are 'I'm sorry',[35] a sorrow that acknowledges how both are now trapped in the consequences of events over which they never had control. In Nagasaki in 1945, Tomisaburo has neither a valued past nor a possible future. The Japanese society he and his father had helped to shape is destroyed by the very power it sought to emulate, leaving Tomisaburo to commit ritual suicide using his father's Samurai sword in a re-assertion of his Japanese identity – his pre-modern identity – and an undoing of the world his Scottish father had created. In contrast to the male characters, Tomisaburo's mother, Maki, journeys from courtesan – a plaything of Western power – to outcast mother of an illegitimate child and then to a Buddhist nun, renamed Ryonan, who sees each new stage in her identity as 'another incarnation, a dream'.[36] The aftermath of her relationship with Glover is a stripping away of her possible identities until she grasps the necessity of 'unbeing':

> The city sparkled beneath her. This place. This time. The Pure Land.
> One day it would all be dust again. Civilisations came and went, rose and fell. Tathagata breathed in, breathed out.
> Form is emptiness.[37]

In the end she discovers that 'she had gone beyond it all':[38] she is both a symbol of the dissolution of her national culture and also of humanity's capacity to transcend such destruction by accepting that unbeing rather than being is the reality of the universe.

To live in such an aftermath is to live in a world so traumatised by a past event that there is no escape from its consequences: characters become the ghosts of unrealised futures that have turned into dead ends from which there is no escape. It was such a world that James Kelman envisaged in his 2001 novel *Translated Accounts*, which presents us with a series of fragmentary reports and recollections from an unnamed country which has, after a revolution, become a totalitarian state. Because the accounts are so fragmentary and translated from non-English sources by unidentified intermediaries, the relationship between language and the world it refers to is as profoundly ruptured as the relationships between the various characters we are introduced to, characters who cannot, in a world of spies and traitors, ever commit themselves to a statement they cannot retract:

> I cannot listen to you. Dreams of homecomings, I cannot listen. You wish to go back but there is no such going back it is not possible does not exist, dream world. Live in this world which is a real world, where we now are in this decay, destroyed building, destroyed lives and dreams of life, deaths of children, killings of children, live in this world, this is why we now exist continue to exist spiting, spiting, this is why, not for dreams, lives as they once were […].[39]

The people of *Translated Accounts* live in a failed future: their world is endless – in the sense of having no purpose or aim – and endlessly destructive; its inhabitants cling to 'old moments, ghost moments, everywhere around us, no people, broken buildings, silences'.[40] In this world there are only absences: the absence of those who have been executed or 'disappeared' and the absence of a self that can no longer connect with its past, and the absence of any relationship between language and the world: language veers from any stable grammatical order as past, present and future become disconnected – 'I cannot say about a beginning, or beginnings, if there is to be the cause of all, I do not see this'[41] – so that the narrative dynamics of the novel are continually subverting its trajectory into the future. Kelman's subsequent novels, such as *You Have to Be Careful in the Land of the Free* (2004) or *Kieron Smith, Boy* (2008), may be less apocalyptic than *Translated Accounts* but they are no less determined by a past over which the characters have no control: Jeremiah Brown knows 'I was aye out of my time; half a fucking century too late. The same when I was a wee boy, I aye missed out because I was a late child';[42] and while Kieron may be told that he is one of a people remade – 'We are a new school in a new scheme and we are new people, we are all ourselves new from what went before so here are new chances and new life'[43] – he knows differently: 'But I knew I would not get a job later. I would never get one. That was just me, if it was Fate, I did not f*****g care.'[44]

In such novels plot is displaced by isolated incidents, almost a sequence of short stories, and this mode has become typical of recent Scottish novels. It is the style, for instance, of Alan Warner's *The Man Who Walks* (2003), which is a picaresque journey in search of a relative whose mind has been damaged by years of drug-taking, as well as of Jenni Fagan's *Panopticon* (2013), in which the protagonist, Anais, is trying to survive a childhood of children's homes and failed fostering, as well as of Douglas Stuart's *Shuggie Bain* (2020), in which the protagonist has to grow up coping with his mother's regular descent into and then partial recovery from alcoholism. In each chapter of such books the forward trajectory of the narrative is suspended by a focus on isolated incidents which turn out to be prologues to or the repetition of previous experiences. Thus, Ewan Morrison's *How to Survive Everything* (2021) takes as its theme the preparations by the father of the narrator to survive the aftermath of a pandemic which he expects to destroy civil society. So intense is his commitment that he cuts off the electrical supply to the house that he has prepared as a survival capsule to ensure his companions' continuing belief in his predictions. They live, effectively, in two distinct narrative worlds, the one in which the father's imaginings as recounted in his 'survival guide' become 'reality', and the occasionally perceived continuation of a normal world which shows no symptoms yet of the anticipated pandemic chaos. The characters are living through the catastrophic aftermath of an event which has not yet occurred, but discover that life in the aftermath, because energised by the preparation for survival, is better than the life they had known as 'consumers' in a sated, globalised culture:

> Suddenly, there is a reason to get fit. To get up early. To take night classes. To hoard. To plan. To build. Suddenly, every minute counts. Now that you have accepted the coming pandemic and your own death, you have a passionate, lucid reason to live.[45]

Unsurprisingly, perhaps, the increasing number of novelists from Scottish immigrant communities, for whom life is always lived in the aftermath of the events which led to their migrations, share such structures. Zaf, the Pakistani Glaswegian DJ in Suhayl Saadi's *Psychoraag* (2004), says of himself and his university education:

> He had studied the migration patterns of his own people – quite dispassionately, as though they had been geese. By degrees, he had learned to dissociate, *Cognito ergo sum*. That wis the best migration pattern of all. The one you couldn't stop even if you'd wanted to – the one that never ended. The one in your head.[46]

Zaf discovers that 'without realisin it, you became separated from the whole of your past and everything in it. One day, you turn round and there's nuthin behind you';[47] the 'nuthin', however, is also the nothing ahead of you. Zaf's story is told during the last broadcast of an all-night programme on a local Asian radio station which is closing down; Zaf's life is also closing down in terms of his efforts to build relationships that will create a future for himself as a Pakistani Glaswegian. The novel gets its creative dynamism from the interaction of multiple languages and cultures, but it as though the vitality of the novel consumes the vitality of the character and leaves him emptily exhausted, suspended between the aim of his father's migration and his own attempted accommodations with that choice. Like the old valve radio his father had brought from Pakistan, there is no wavelength that will communicate between the past and the future. This is also true of Najwa, the narrator-protagonist of Leila Aboulela's *Minaret* (2005), in which forced migration – Najwa's father is a member of a Sudanese government which is overthrown and the family flee to London – results both in a loss of social status (declining from one who was looked after by servants to being herself a servant) and the loss of the younger man with whom she has formed a relationship, whose wealthy family consider her an unsuitable partner. Najwa ends up dreaming that she is back in her parents' house in her native land but it is now in ruins:

> I need my parents' room. I need their bed; its clean sheets, the privilege. I climb dark steep stairs to their room [...] all the possessions that distinguish us in ruins. I am not surprised. It is a natural decay and I accept it.[48]

There is nowhere to go back to; the ruined past is also a lost future; the aftermath of catastrophe is endless.

What such novels dramatise is the disjunction between the narrative of a globalised modern history of continual progress and the individual's experience of an alienating and destructive environment. Ali Smith's *Hotel World* (2001), for example, opens with a ghost's memory of her death when she fell four floors down the chute of a dumb waiter in the hotel where she was working. The novel recounts the aftermath of the moment when Sara Wilby became a present absence, haunting those who knew her. Sara's younger sibling, Clare, in turn haunts the Global Hotel where Sara died, its name ironically underlining that we are all simply temporary residents who will soon be moved on: 'They're history'.[49] A city which appears to be 'historical' is simply 'somewhere for tourists to bring their traveller's cheques to in the summer. Actual history is gone.'[50] The history which has actually gone, however, is the history of a lost future. A homeless woman recalls from her schooling that the philanthropist Robert Owen had built a new town for his workers: 'New Lanark was the name of his mills, like his philanthropy made a new place in the world. The poor. What history worked to improve, to make things better for. But that was then. This is now.'[51] And in the 'now' the newspaper that the homeless woman wraps round her feet declares 'BRITAIN MASSIVELY MORE UNEQUAL THAN 20 YEARS AGO. ONE IN FIVE PEOPLE LIVES BELOW THE BREADLINE.'[52] Owen's possible future in which poverty is abolished is an absence that haunts the present like the suddenly dead Sara.

In 1989, Francis Fukuyama's *The End of History and the Last Man*, published in the aftermath of the collapse of communism, envisaged a world in which liberal democracies would turn out to be the end-point to which history, however hesitantly, had all along been moving. In the aftermath of the Second World War, Fukuyama suggested, history had reached a benign trajectory towards the resolution of the conflicts that had afflicted the earlier stages of modern society. Smith's novel suggests, however, that even those who live prosperously in that modern world have been reduced to ghostly consumers who cannot imagine any possible transformation of their lives:

> A Marks and Spencer carrier bag snagged by the wind on a fence can call the ghosts of a thousand middle-aged ladies back to linger by the jumpers and cardigans once more, wandering the isles [...] to smell the scent of the new, with the ghosts of their husbands waiting by the door, arms folded, bored, eternally impatient.[53]

The world of global consumerism is a world haunted and taunted by the absence of a significant future: the novel ends with the girl in the watch shop for whom S. Wilby 'fell' when she delivered her watch for repair, envisaging that some day she will phone all the Wilbys in the phone directory to find the girl who has never returned to collect her watch. But what 'will be' will not include Sara Wilby, deprived both of will and being. Although the girl in the watch shop does not yet know it, she is living in a world which cannot, like Sara Wilby's watch, be fixed.

A parallel loss of future afflicts Joe Coyle in Andrew Crumey's *Sputnik Caledonia* (2008). Joe's son, Robert, had, like Sara, died at age nineteen. According to his diagnosis Robert's death is caused by a brain tumour, but Joe believes the tumour has resulted from Robbie finding his way into a secret military establishment where he had acquired a strange glass ball that he kept under his pillow – a glass ball Joe believes to have been nuclear waste. Robbie's death is, for Joe (a trade unionist and socialist), collateral damage in the machinery of a war economy designed to prevent the overthrow of American capitalism, an outcome Joe had hoped would follow victory in the war. Instead, Joe and his wife live in the continual deferral of the possibility of socialism, because the United States controls politics in Britain: 'it was a plot. The CIA bought Wilson off and put in Callaghan, then he turned out to be a dud so they picked Maggie.'[54] Joe is stranded in the aftermath of his son's death, and the death of the socialist future he had once believed in. The novel, however, provides Robbie with an alternative life in a different history, one in which he can fulfil his childhood ambition 'to be teleported into space, not become a door-to-door salesman',[55] because in this alternative world a postwar 'Caledonia' is part of 'the British Democratic Republic',[56] which, since 1948, has had a 'special relationship' not with the USA but with the USSR. The secret facility Robbie had broken into becomes the geographical location of his training as a cosmonaut in a Russian-dominated Britain, fulfilling both his father's desire for a socialist economy and his own dreams of space travel inspired by the successes of the Russian space programme of the 1950s. This new world, however, is no less alienating than the one in which Robbie died, since the town where he is based is effectively a prison camp that one can only enter by having one's memory of the past erased. The dream of progressive history is no more than the continuation of the exploitation of the weak and vulnerable by those who have seized the levers of power. In this world, Robbie has lost all agency, since the mission for which he is being prepared is – as in the early Russian experiments of sending animals into space – one from which it is not intended he should return alive. Having died in the American-dominated capitalist world of the 1960s, Robbie apparently dies again in its Russian equivalent, but just as he seemed to have evaded death at nineteen, so he seems again to have evaded death twenty-five years later, when an older Robert Coyle returns – like a Time Lord in the *Doctor Who* television series which Robbie had watched as a child – to revisit modern Scotland, where he will unknowingly meet his father, who will die believing that Robbie's *Doctor Who*-like assistant is Robbie himself, returned as he was when a child. No matter how often he dies in parallel historical worlds, Robbie's narrative continues, not because this is what is possible in a novel (reviewers often compared *Sputnik Caledonia* to Alasdair Gray's *Lanark*) but because if the universe is infinite, as some theories of physics suggest, it contains somewhere, in some kink of time, another version of his life: the Red Star towards which Cosmonaut Robert Coyle is catapulted tells him, 'Your life is over, Robert – but not your story'.[57] The narrative may present the endless and purposeless march of modern history but it also gestures to a universe in which Robbie, like the cat in Schrödinger's famous thought experiment about quantum physics, is both alive and dead in ontologically equivalent but quite distinct worlds.

The Return of Myth

The Britain of these aftermathic novels is a past without a future, filled with the debris of futures that never came to fruition. Robbie's return in *Sputnik Caledonia* gestures to a possible resurrection beyond the controlling narrative of historical decline. This is the theme of James Robertson's *News of the Dead* (2021), which is told through various narrative forms, from diaries and histories to folktales and ancient epic. At its core is a version of 'surviving the Second World War', in the story of Maja, a child who manages to escape war-torn Europe to find refuge in Glen Conach, where she spends her life in safety, until, in 2020, she and it are under attack from Coronavirus. The novel contrasts Maja's experiences in modern Scotland with a historical account of the same glen in the earlier Europe of 1809, as presented in the journal of Charles Kirkliston Gibb, a self-confessed fraud who poses as a historian in order to gain access to – and prise a living from – wealthy families whose libraries contain works he claims require investigation. Gibb's journal allows the glen of 1809, in the midst of the Napoleonic wars, to be contrasted with the glen of Maja's traumatised aftermath to the Second World War, but both are set in opposition to the text that Gibb has come to investigate – a late medieval account in Latin of the life of an early Christian missionary named Conach, who has supposedly given his name to the glen. However, neither the Latin text nor its contents, some of which form digressive narratives within the novel, can be authenticated, since the text was written some five hundred years after the events it records, and there is no other evidence to substantiate the existence of Conach as, despite the local attribution to him of the term 'saint', he was never acknowledged by the Church. Gibb's translation and interpretation of the Conach text is challenged by Jessie, the daughter of the landowner whose family has kept the manuscript safe for several hundreds of years; their debate is recorded in Gibb's journal:

> ME (attempting to reassert my authority): 'Jessie, this is a document of antiquity. I am not writing a romance.'
> J: 'Oh, but whoever composed it was doing just that. You surely don't believe any of it is true?'
> ME: 'I believe it is genuine, which is not the same. I cannot invent things and add them simply to make it more interesting.'
> J: 'But writers of romance do that all the time.'
> ME: 'I am a historian, Jessie.'
> J: 'And historians do too, I am sure. They want their heroes to look as heroic as possible.'[58]

History is a genre which steals from romance, just as romance, as in the case of Robertson's novel, may steal from history. Jessie wants to displace the history that Gibb seeks to reformulate:

J: '[...] The stories the old people tell of Conach are more – engaging. But you are concerned with history, not idle tales that must become more absurd and impossible with every generation that tells them. Do you think history must always be duller than fiction?'
ME: 'I could not say. I do not read many works of fiction.'
J: 'Nor do I, if by that you mean novelles. There are very few of those on these shelves. I meant, rather, legends and romances. Your task must be to eliminate everything that cannot be proven to be true. My task is to imagine whatever men such as you eliminate.'[59]

Romance describes a different world from history, one which history must banish in order to protect its authenticity, but it is precisely romance which makes the stories of Conach sufficiently interesting to those who recount them to have passed them on from generation to generation for hundreds of years. There would be no Conach for history to investigate if it were not for the attractions of romance. Equally, the story of Maja is significant not because it is true but because her story recapitulates and gives continuing life to many such stories:

> I think of all the wars she could have come from, all the violence and suffering she could have witnessed and experienced and escaped, and it doesn't seem to matter much which war or which century or which continent.[60]

This child walks out of a terrible period of history into a place which is largely unrecorded, 'a strange, unknowable region' haunted by a past in which 'the hazier everything becomes, the more whatever facts there are become entangled with myth and legend'.[61] It is a realm that undermines the categories by which the modern world understands itself: 'when you return to the present, it may seem that fact and fiction were never that discrete from one another after all.'[62] By its juxtapositions of different historical epochs the novel undermines the chronology on which history is based, and discovers in myth and legend continuities unknown to the historical investigator.

But the stories of Conach, Gibb and Maja are framed by two very different and anti-historical narrative perspectives. The first is presented through the visionary experiences of young boy named Lachie who visits Maja when she is very old and who has seen a ghost that might be the after-echo of the young Maja when she first arrived in the Glen. Lachie's ghost defies the logic of time, intruding into a history to which it does not belong, as Maja has intruded into Glen Conach, but points towards a supernatural level of experience familiar to 'myth and legend' but inexplicable in history. The second is, quite literally, the story of the ground that makes up the glen and which

> is made, in its upper reaches at least, of rocks formed more than five hundred million years ago when Scotland was a scattered jigsaw puzzle of four pieces, and the Earth a shifting, cracking, groaning pot of energy subjected to relentless, immensely powerful stresses and strains.[63]

Historical time is the merest flicker on the face of geological time, on those depths in relation to which modern humanity must now judge its significance and, 'to adapt the famous words of the "father of modern geology", James Hutton – if there was any vestige of a beginning, there was surely no prospect of an end'.[64] As the origin of the discipline of geology, and as one of the oldest landmasses on earth, Scotland is emblematic of the ancient forces by which the earth has been shaped long before the advent of humanity and its belief in the progress of history.

The dissolution of history by 'legend and romance' is also both the tale and the technique of novels such as John Burnside's *A Summer of Drowning* (2012), in which the protagonist, Liv, comes – almost – to believe that the events she is witness to one summer in her teens are the return of the ancient myths and legends collected by her nearest neighbour, Kyrre Opdahl. Thus, Kyrre sees in the drownings, only days apart, of two brothers who had been at school with Liv, not a terrible accident, or the psychological impact on the second brother of the first's death, but the recurrence of the legendary figure of the *huldra*, which appears as a beautiful young woman come from the sea to seduce men to their deaths. Initially Liv dismisses this interpretation as impossible – 'Afterwards, Kyrre Opdahl would say [...] that it was because of her, because of the huldra; but that was ridiculous. There was no huldra'[65] – but when she actually witnesses the similar death of Martin Crosbie, a city dweller who is spending the summer in Kyrre's cottage, she is forced to acknowledge that there may be truths that modernity has forgotten:

> For if Kyrre's stories had one thing in common, it was this: no matter what form we give it, or how elaborately it is contrived, order is an illusion and, eventually, something will emerge from the background noise and the shadows and upset everything we are so determined to believe in. Or

that's how it is in stories – in real life, that something is always there, hidden in plain view, waiting to flower. A turn of phrase, a blemish, an unspoken wish – it doesn't take much to open the floodgates and let the chaos in.[66]

The return of myth is the return of a world before it was given order, whether by God or by humanity. Kyrre's own death, apparently at the hands of the huldra, is both proof of the destructive return of ancient myth but also a justification of the apparent reality of a world very different from that in which modernity believes. Liv refuses to accept Kyrre's stories because they tell a winter's tale of a dark world while she is spending an apparently endless northern summer with her mother, where there is only light.

Similar themes were taken up when Ali Smith decided to write a series of four novels, each thematically devoted to a season,[67] but also attempting to incorporate the immediate events of the time of their writing – from the Brexit outcome of the 2016 UK Referendum to the pandemic lockdowns of the 2020s. She committed herself to the juxtaposition of the immediacy of the 'historical' present with the 'sempiternal' not only of the return of the seasons but of the myths which, since Frazer's *The Golden Bough*, had been seen to be fundamental to traditional cultures. Such myths are called up in each novel's echoes of Shakespearian plays – *The Tempest* in *Autumn*,[68] *Cymbeline* in *Winter*,[69] *Macbeth* in *Spring*[70] and, ironically, *The Winter's Tale* in *Summer*[71] – since, as the theories of Northrop Frye suggest, Shakespeare's plays are, themselves, versions of the cycle of the seasons, with the comedies in particular dramatising nature's reassertion of vitality and creativity over the threat of infertility and death:

> We may call it the drama of the green world, its plot being assimilated to the ritual theme of the triumph of life and love over the waste land […] Thus the action of the comedy begins in a world represented as a normal world, moves into the green world, goes into a metamorphosis there in which the comic resolution is achieved, and returns to the normal world.[72]

As though in acknowledgement of this tradition, the final volume of the seasonal quartet, *Summer*, is focused on a family named Greenlaw, in which the mother is symbolically named 'Grace' and her son, Robert, regards himself as an outlaw to society but a benign one, like Robin Hood, following the 'green law' of his name. As in Frye's account, the characters of the novel undergo a metamorphosis as they rediscover the laws of the green world and their relationship to the transformative power of art.[73]

The central figure of a quartet of very dispersed characters is Daniel Gluck, a survivor of the Second World War and the son of a German migrant who fled to Britain from Germany during the rise of Nazism. The young Gluck had, however, spent his summers in Germany with his relatives and became known to his sister Hannah as her 'summer brother', as though his identity changes with the seasons; she, however, becomes the missing 'autumn sister' who haunts the aftermath of the war, having died working for the Resistance in France. After the war Gluck forges a career for himself as a songwriter, art providing compensation for loss with the success of song lyrics such as 'Summer Brother' in the 1960s: 'Summer brother autumn sister / Autumn's gone so summers don't exist.'[74] Art, however, cannot bring back the dead and Gluck's life is dominated by absence – not only the absence of Hannah but the absence of Pauline Boty, the 'Pop artist' whose work Gluck admires in the 1960s, who dies young and whose work largely disappears; but also the absence of one half of his Barbara Hepworth sculpture, purloined by a lover with whom he had a brief relationship. Living with the burden of migration, exile and loss, Gluck's life is transformed by his friendship with a child, Elisabeth, who is his next-door neighbour and who might be a substitute for his lost sister. Gluck's description of one of Boty's collages inspires Elisabeth to become an art historian and to research and bring back to public notice Boty's achievements. Elisabeth too, however, becomes an absence to Gluck when she goes to college and plans to marry, but her discovery of a remaindered book of Boty's works takes her back to visit Gluck again and to the realisation that just as Gluck had fallen in love with what he saw through Boty's eyes, as captured in her art, so she has always been in love with what she saw through Gluck's eyes, and becomes his constant visitor in a care home, and then, when the pandemic strikes, has him transferred to her own home in order to safeguard him. In a novel full of absent fathers, Gluck becomes to Elisabeth the father she has never known and she, like Perdita in *The Winter's Tale*, a daughter recovered.

In terms of mythic structure, Gluck, who is 104 years old in this novel, represents the declining world that has to be saved from extinction by the recovery of vitality from the 'green world': thus, comic romance must bring the Greenlaws to Gluck in an environment where everyone can undergo a metamorphic transformation. The accidental agent of this transformation is the 'outlaw' Robert Greenlaw who superglues an eggtimer to his sister, Sacha's, fingers so that she will cease to worry about the times they live in because she will always have 'time on your hands'.[75] Robert is obsessed by Einstein's conception of time and, in thus subverting mechanical time, Robert the outlaw accidentally opens the way to the 'Green world', since Sacha is helped to hospital by a couple the reader may have already met in *Winter*, Arthur and his girlfriend Charlotte, who are now temporarily back together after their breakup in the previous novel. Their accidental encounter with Sacha happens while they are travelling to Suffolk to fulfil one of the injunctions in Arthur's mother's will, which is to return to a Mr Gluck the sculpted stone which she took from him after a brief affair. As they pause in the Greenlaw home, however, enthused by the family's lifestyle, they offer to have Grace and her two children accompany them on their visit. Out of the banality of a visit to an old invalid comes a green world metamorphosis since, when they arrive at Elisabeth's home, Gluck sees in Robert the return of his sister Hannah, the transformation of the boy into a girl being, of course, one of the conventions of Shakespearean romance:

What Daniel sees then is his sister.
    Is it? Hannah?
    It's Hannah herself standing there looking in.
    It is.
    It's her.
    It's her young self.
    It's the copy of her young self.
    She opens the window's door and it's Hannah, God help him, there in the room, aged twelve, in the shape of a boy.
    Oh hello, Daniel says.
    Hi, Hannah says.
    Where've you been all this time? he says.
    The traffic was busier than they thought it'd be, Hannah says.
    But so very long, Daniel says. I thought time had quite undone us.
    On the contrary, time and space are what lace us all up together, Hannah says. What makes us part of the larger picture. Universally speaking. The problem is, we tend to think we're separate. But it's a delusion.
    Ah, Daniel says.
    Of course I'm quoting Einstein, Hannah says.[76]

The time that dominates the wasted land of modernity, the time of destruction and loss symbolised by the return of plague in the form of Covid-19, is revealed to be but the gateway to a world reborn, a rebirth symbolised in Grace's recovered memory of the summer in which she played the statue of the mother that comes back to life in *The Winter's Tale*, and by the reunion of the two pieces of Barbara Hepworth's sculpture entitled 'The mother and child maquette'. That reunion reveals to the readers (but not to the characters) that the woman who had purloined the stone statue was Arthur's mother, who, by returning the stolen piece, allows the lost father and his son to be re-united through the magic of Art, the name by which Arthur has been known to us in both novels. And Art will find completion in his love for his father's lost 'daughter', Elisabeth, all made possible by art's ability to bring back to life that which was turned to stone. An aftermath of desolation becomes an aftermath of transformation, art and nature colluding in a cycle of renewal that binds up the wounds of history and the depredations of time.

Endnotes

Introduction

1. J. H. Millar, *A Literary History of Scotland* (T. Fisher Unwin, 1903), p. vii.
2. Ibid., p. 5.
3. For the text of the report, see education-uk.org/documents/newbolt/newbolt1921.html.
4. Raymond Williams, *The Country and the City* (Chatto & Windus, 1973), p. 2.
5. Ibid.
6. Ian Watt, *The Rise of the Novel: Studies in Defoe, Richardson and Fielding* (1957; Penguin, 1963), p. 35.
7. Ibid., p. 31.
8. Ibid., p. 301.
9. Ibid., p. 312.
10. Ibid., p. 310.
11. J. B. Priestley, *The English Novel* (Thomas Nelson, 1927), p. 35.
12. See 'Document 2'.
13. Ian Duncan (ed.), Sir Walter Scott, *Ivanhoe* (Oxford University Press, 1996), p. vii.
14. Sarah Green, *Scotch Novel Reading; or, Modern quackery, by a Cockney* [S. Green], vol. 1 (Newman & Co, 1824), p. 47.
15. John Sutherland, *The Life of Walter Scott: A Critical Biography* (Blackwell, 1995), p. 120.
16. Lewis Grassic Gibbon and Hugh MacDiarmid, *Scottish Scene: or the Intelligent Man's Guide to Albyn* (Hutchinson, 1934), p. 168.
17. Francis Russell Hart, *The Scottish Novel: A Critical Survey* (John Murray, 1978), p. 30.
18. Ibid., p. 2.
19. Edwin Muir, *Scott and Scotland: The Predicament of the Scottish Writer with an Introduction by Allan Massie* (Polygon, 1982), p. v.

20 Jonathan Bate, 'General Editor's Preface', in Randall Stevenson, *The Oxford English Literary History: Vol. 12: 1960–2000: The Last of England?* (Oxford University Press, 2004), pp. iii–x (p. ix).
21 Northrop Frye, *The Secular Scripture: A Study of the Structure of Romance* (Harvard University Press, 1976), pp. 4–6.
22 Katie Trumpener, *Bardic Nationalism: The Romantic Novel and the British Empire* (Princeton University Press, 1997), p. 141.
23 Georg Lukacs, *The Historical Novel*, trans. Hannah and Stanley Mitchell (1962; Peregrine, 1969), pp. 58–59.
24 Sydney Owenson, Lady Morgan, *The Wild Irish Girl*, ed. Kathryn Kirkpatrick (Oxford World's Classics, 1999), p. 174.
25 Ibid., pp. 174–75.
26 John Carey (ed.), James Hogg, *The Private Memoirs and Confessions of a Justified Sinner* (Oxford World's Classics, 1969), p. 254.
27 Trumpener, *Bardic Nationalism*, p. 132.
28 Tom Nairn, *The Break-Up of Britain: Crisis and Neo-Nationalism* (1977; Verso, 1981), p. 119.
29 Walter Scott, '14 March 1826', *Journals of Sir Walter Scott*, ed. W. E. K. Anderson (Oxford University Press, 1972).
30 Tom Nairn, *The Break-up of Britain*, p. 155.
31 Peter Guthrie Tait and Balfour Stewart, *The Unseen Universe* (Macmillan, 1875), p. 159.
32 Jenni Calder (ed.), Margaret Oliphant, *The Beleaguered City and Other Tales of the Seen and the Unseen* (Canongate, 2000), p. 55.
33 Jenni Calder (ed.), Robert Louis Stevenson, *The Strange Case of Dr Jekyll and Mr Hyde and Other Stories* (Penguin Books, 1979), p. 48.
34 Ibid.
35 J. M. Barrie, *Peter Pan or The Boy Who Would Not Grow Up* (Samuel French, 1928).
36 Masson, *Recent British Philosophy* (Macmillan, 1865), p. 150.
37 David Masson, *Essays Biographical and Critical, Chiefly on English Poets* (Macmillan, 1856), p. 473.
38 Glenda Norquay (ed.), *R. L. Stevenson on Fiction: An Anthology of Literary and Critical Essays* (Edinburgh University Press, 1999), pp. 81–91 (p. 85); see Document 4.
39 See P. M. Harman, *The Natural Philosophy of James Clerk Maxwell* (Cambridge University Press, 1998).
40 G. B. Tennyson (ed.), Thomas Carlyle, *A Carlyle Reader: Selections from the Writings of Thomas Carlyle* (1969; Cambridge University Press, 1984), pp. 34, 35.

41 Thomas Carlyle, *Critical and Miscellaneous Essays*, 5 vols (Charles Scribner, 1904), IV, p. 128.
42 See, for instance, 'On Heroes and Hero-Worship', in which Dante and Shakespeare are designated as two poets of world significance; 'Italy produced the one world-voice; we English had the honour of producing the other', G. B. Tennyson (ed.), *Carlyle Reader*, p. 395.
43 See Arthur Herman, *The Scottish Enlightenment* (Fourth Estate, 2001); and my own account of 'When Was the Scottish Enlightenment?', Ch. 2 of *Intending Scotland: Explorations in Scottish Culture since the Enlightenment* (Edinburgh University Press, 2009).
44 See Garry Wills, *Inventing America: Jefferson's Declaration of Independence* (Doubleday, 1978).
45 A. J. P. Taylor, *English History 1914–1945*, vol. 15 of the *Oxford History of England* (Oxford University Press, 1965), p. v. See, for instance, Krishan Kumar, *The Making of English National Identity* (Cambridge University Press, 2003), pp. 3–17.
46 Joseph H. Jackson, *Writing Black Scotland: Race, Nation and the Devolution of Black Britain* (Edinburgh University Press, 2021), p. 28.
47 See Gerard Carruthers and Colin Kidd (eds), *Literature and Union: Scottish Texts, British Contexts* (Oxford University Press, 2018).
48 Ali Smith, *There but for the* (2011; Penguin, 2012), p. 30.
49 Andrew Greig, *Rose Nicolson* (Riverrun, 2021).

1. Smollett and the Novel in Scotland

1 Tobias Smollett, *The Adventures of Roderick Random*, ed. Paul-Gabriel Boucé (Oxford University Press, 2008), p. 1.
2 Robert Crawford, *Devolving English Literature* (Clarendon Press, 1992), p. 60.
3 [Frances Coventry], *An Essay on the New Species of Writing founded by Mr. Fielding* (W. Owen, 1751).
4 For an overview of the author's diverse achievements see Ian Campbell Ross, 'Tobias Smollett', in Susan Manning et al. (eds), *The Edinburgh History of Scottish Literature: Enlightenment, Britain and Empire (1707–1918)* (Edinburgh University Press, 2007), pp. 163–68.
5 *The Adventures of Ferdinand Count Fathom*, ed. Jerry C. Beasley (University of Georgia Press, 1988), p. 4. The quotation continues to discuss the role of a 'principal personage' or hero.
6 On the debate over Smollett's adherence to picaresque models see 'Picaresque and Quixotic Fiction' in Aileen Douglas, 'Tobias Smollett', *Oxford Bibliographies Online*, doi:10.1093/obo/9780199846719-0093

7 David Daiches, 'Smollett Reconsidered', in Alan Bold (ed.), *Smollett: Author of the First Distinction* (Vision and Barnes and Noble, 1982), pp. 13–46 (p. 46).
8 Rivka Swenson, *Essential Scots and the Idea of Unionism in Anglo-Scottish Literature, 1603–1832* (Bucknell University Press, 2015), p. 74. Swenson sees Smollett's novels as responding to 'Scottish emigration history' (p. 75); see also Leith Davis, *Acts of Union: Scotland and the Literary Negotiation of the British Nation, 1707–1830* (Stanford University Press, 1998), p. 68.
9 For a detailed comparison of the works, careers, and canonical status of Smollett and Fielding see Linda Bree, 'Fielding and Smollett: Rival Novelists', in *Tobias Smollett, Scotland's First Novelist*, ed. O. M. Brack, Jr (University of Delaware Press, 2007), pp. 142–67.
10 See Crawford, *Devolving English*, pp. 57–58, and Davis, *Acts of Union*, p. 70.
11 David Hume, *A Treatise of Human Nature*, ed. L. A. Selby-Bigge and P. H. Nidditch (1739–40; Clarendon Press, 1985), p. 318.
12 See Davis, *Acts of Union*, p. 69.
13 Swenson, *Essential Scots*, p. 81.
14 *The Letters of Tobias Smollett*, ed. Lewis M. Knapp (Clarendon Press, 1970), p. 8.
15 *Letters*, p. 112.
16 Jerry C. Beasley, *Tobias Smollett, Novelist* (University of Georgia Press, 1998), p. 9.
17 *The Expedition of Humphry Clinker*, ed. Lewis M. Knapp and rev. Paul-Gabriel Boucé (1771; Oxford University Press, 2009), p. 217.
18 Louis L. Martz, *The Later Career of Tobias Smollett* (Archon Books, 1967), pp. 137–80.
19 For a reading of *Humphry Clinker* as Smollett's attempt to 'annul' charges against the Scots see Eric Rothstein, 'Scotophilia and *Humphry Clinker*: The Politics of Beggary, Bugs, and Buttocks', *University of Toronto Quarterly*, 52.1 (Fall 1982), pp. 63–78 (quotation, p. 63), doi:10.3138/utq.52.1.63
20 Tara Goshal Wallace, '"About savages and the awfulness of America": Colonial Corruptions in *Humphry Clinker*', *Eighteenth-Century Fiction*, 18.2 (Winter 2005–06), pp. 229–50, doi:10.1353/ecf.2006.0033
21 Crawford, p. 56.
22 Ibid., p. 75.

23 Evan Gottlieb, '"Fools of Prejudice": Sympathy and National Identity in the Scottish Enlightenment and *Humphry Clinker*', *Eighteenth-Century Fiction*, 18.1 (Fall 2005), p. 82, doi:10.1353/ecf.2006.0007
24 Janet Sorensen, *The Grammar of Empire in Eighteenth-Century British Writing* (Cambridge University Press, 2000), p. 137.
25 Walter Scott, 'Memoir of the Life of the Author', in *The Novels of Tobias Smollett, M.D.*, Ballantyne's Novelist's Library, vol. 2 (London, 1821), p. xxx–xxxi.

2. The Philosophical Foundations of the Scottish Novel

1 David Hume, *A Treatise of Human Nature*, ed. L. A. Selby-Bigge (1888; Clarendon Press, 1967), p. 415.
2 John Locke, *An Essay Concerning Human Understanding*, ed. Peter H. Nidditch (1689; Clarendon Press, 1975), p. 395.
3 Ibid.
4 Hume, *Treatise*, p. 93.
5 Dugald Stewart, *Elements of the Philosophy of the Human Mind* (1792; sixth edn, 1818), p. 20.
6 Adam Smith, 'The History of Astronomy' in *III: Essays on Philosophical Subjects*, The Glasgow Edition of the Works and Correspondence of Adam Smith, ed. W. P. D. Wightman and J. C. Bryce (1795; Liberty Fund, 1982), p. 105.
7 Hume, *Treatise*, pp. 268–69.
8 Ibid., p. 207.
9 Ibid., p. 269.
10 Ibid., p. 318.
11 Ibid., p. 319.
12 Adam Smith, *The Theory of Moral Sentiments*, ed. D. D. Raphael and A. L. Macfie (1759; Liberty Fund, 1984), p. 23.
13 Smith, *Theory of Moral Sentiments*, p. 10.
14 Henry MacKenzie, *The Man of Feeling*, ed. Brian Vickers (1771; Oxford World's Classics, 2001), p. 78.
15 John Mullan, *Sentiment and Sociability: The Language of Feeling in the Eighteenth Century* (Oxford University Press, 1990), p. 201.
16 Mackenzie, *Man of Feeling*, p. 26.
17 Ibid., pp. 96–97.
18 Christian Isobel Johnstone, *Clan-Albin: A National Tale*, ed. Andrew Monnickendam (1815; Association for Scottish Literary Studies, 2003), p. 269.

19 Mary Brunton, *Discipline* (1814; Pandora Press, 1986) p. 163.
20 Ibid., p. 56.
21 MacKenzie, *The Man of Feeling*, p. 25.
22 Brunton, *Discipline*, p. 286.
23 Ibid., p. 294.
24 Ibid., p. 296.
25 See, for instance, Ian Duncan, *Scott's Shadow: The Novel in Romantic Edinburgh* (Princeton University Press, 2007), pp. 124–25.
26 David Hume, *The History of Great Britain* (London, 1754), Ch. LVIII, pp. 28–29.
27 Tobias Smollett, *The Expedition of Humphry Clinker*, ed. Angus Ross (1771; Penguin, 1967), p. 376.
28 Ibid., p. 189; cf. p. 380.
29 Ibid., p. 269.
30 Ibid., p. 283.
31 Susan Ferrier, *Marriage*, ed. Herbert Foltinek (1818; Oxford University Press, 1971), p. 254.
32 Ibid.
33 Ibid., p. 327.
34 Ibid., p. 346.
35 Ibid.
36 Ibid., p. 468.
37 Ibid., p. 451.
38 Jane Porter, *Thaddeus of Warsaw: A Novel*, ed. Thomas McLean and Ruth Knezevich (1803; Edinburgh University Press, 2019), p. 146.
39 Ibid., p. 291.
40 Ibid., p. 333.
41 Brunton, *Discipline*, p. 349.
42 Jane Porter, *The Scottish Chiefs*, ed. Fiona Price (1810; Broadview Editions, 2007), p. 45.
43 Ibid., p. 46.
44 Ibid.
45 Ibid., p. 564.
46 Walter Scott, *Waverley*, ed. Andrew Hook (1814; Penguin, 1972), p. 56.
47 Ibid., p. 226.
48 Ibid., p. 295.
49 Ibid., p. 294.
50 Ibid., p. 333.
51 Walter Scott, *Redgauntlet*, ed. W. M. Parker (1824; J. M. Dent & Sons, 1958), p. 381.

52 James Hogg, *The Private Memoirs and Confessions of a Justified Sinner*, ed. John Carey (1824; Oxford University Press, 1970), pp. 191–92.
53 Ronald E. Beanblossom and Keith Lehrer (eds), *Thomas Reid's Inquiry and Essays* (Hackett, 1983), p. 86.
54 Ibid., p. 118.
55 Elizabeth Hamilton, *The Cottagers of Glenburnie and Other Educational Writing*, ed. Pam Perkins (Association for Scottish Literary Studies, 2010), pp. 122.
56 Ibid.
57 Ibid., p. 129.
58 Mary Brunton, *Self-Control*, ed. Anthony Mandal (1811; Pickering & Chatto, 2014), p. 13.
59 Ibid., p. 343.
60 Ibid., p. 352.
61 Porter, *Scottish Chiefs*, p. 681.
62 Johnstone, *Clan-Albin*, p. 526.
63 Ibid., p. 527.
64 Ibid., p. 475–76.
65 Thomas Carlyle, *Sartor Resartus*, ed. Kerry McSweeney and Peter Sabor (1833; Oxford University Press, 1987), p. 200.
66 George MacDonald, *David Elginbrod* (1863; Hurst and Blackett, 1871), p. 402.

3. Walter Scott, the Reader, and the Times After Time

1 E. M. Forster, *Aspects of the Novel* (1927; Penguin, 1976), p. 44.
2 Ibid., p. 40.
3 Ibid., pp. 41–42.
4 Sophie Laniel-Musitelli and Céline Sabiron, *Romanticism and Time: Literary Temporalities* (Open Book, 2021), p. ix.
5 Thomas Carlyle, '[review] *Memoirs of the Life of Sir Walter Scott, Baronet*', *London and Westminster Review*, 6 (1838), pp. 293–345; J. G. Lockhart, *Memoirs of the Life of Sir Walter Scott, Bart.*, 7 vols (Cadell, 1837–1838). Hereafter, *Life*.
6 Carlyle, p. 295.
7 Ibid., p. 297.
8 Ibid., p. 336.
9 Ibid., p. 301.
10 Ibid., p. 318.
11 Ibid., p. 334.
12 Ibid., p. 336.

13 Edwin Muir, *Scott and Scotland: The Predicament of the Scottish Writer* (Routledge, 1936), p. 11.
14 Ibid., pp. 11–12.
15 John Buchan, *Sir Walter Scott* (1932; Cassell, 1987), pp. 119, 334.
16 Georg Lukács, *The Historical Novel* (1937; Beacon, 1963), pp. 53, 32.
17 Cairns Craig, *Out of History* (Polygon, 1996), p. 41.
18 Ibid., p. 39.
19 Ibid., p. 45.
20 Ibid., 224.
21 See H. Philip Bolton, *Scott Dramatized* (Mansell, 1992); Katherine Haldane Grenier, *Tourism and Identity in Scotland, 1770–1914* (Ashgate, 2005), pp. 80–84.
22 Ann Rigney, *The Afterlives of Walter Scott: Memory on the Move* (Oxford University Press, 2012).
23 See Barnaby and Hubbard, 'The International Reception and Literary Impact of Scottish Literature, 1707–1918', in Susan Manning (ed.), *Edinburgh History of Scottish Literature*, vol. 2 (Edinburgh University Press, 2007), pp. 37–38; Robert Crawford, 'Walter Scott and European Union', *Studies in Romanticism* 40.1 (2001), pp. 137–52. .
24 Carlyle, p. 245.
25 Muir, *Scott and Scotland*, p. 12.
26 Walter Scott, *Minstrelsy of the Scottish Border*, 2 vols (James Ballantyne, 1802), pp. 244–95.
27 Ibid., 254.
28 Walter Scott, 'Fragment of a Romance which was to have been entitled, THOMAS THE RHYMER', *Waverley* (Cadell, 1829), pp. xli–liv; *Bride of Lammermoor* (1819; Edinburgh University Press, 1996), p. 139; *Castle Dangerous* (1831, d. 1832; Edinburgh University Press, 2006), pp. 38–40, 153–59.
29 Walter Scott, *Waverley*, ed. P. D. Garside (1814; Edinburgh University Press, 2007), pp. 3–6.
30 Ibid., p. 3.
31 Ibid., pp. 3–4.
32 Ibid., p. 4.
33 Jane Millgate, *Walter Scott: The Making of the Novelist* (University of Toronto Press, 1984), pp. 35–36.
34 Walter Scott, *Letters of Sir Walter Scott*, 12 vols (Constable, 1933–37), IV, p. 293.
35 J. G. Lockhart, *Life*, IV, pp. 177–78.

36 Walter Scott, *The Tale of Old Mortality*, ed. Douglas Mack (1816; Edinburgh University Press, 1993), p. 352.
37 Walter Scott, *The Antiquary* (1816; Edinburgh University Press, 1995), p. [3]. The 'Tales of My Landlord' ultimately included *The Black Dwarf* (1816), *The Tale of Old Mortality* (1816), *The Heart of Mid-Lothian* (1818), *The Bride of Lammermoor* (1819), *A Legend of the Wars of Montrose* (1819), *Count Robert of Paris* (1831) and *Castle Dangerous* (1831).
38 Millgate, *Walter Scott*, p. vii.
39 Ibid., p. viii.
40 Ibid., p. vii.
41 Craig, *Out of History*, p. 221.
42 Angus Calder, 'Introduction', *Old Mortality* (Penguin, 1974), p. 9.
43 See A. N. Wilson (ed.), *Ivanhoe* (Penguin, 1984), pp. 521–33.
44 Scott, *Waverley*, pp. 362–63.
45 Walter Scott, *The Monastery*, ed. Penny Fielding (1820; Edinburgh University Press, 2000), pp. 23–30.
46 Jerome McGann, *Walter Scott's Romantic Postmodernity*, in Leith Davis et al. (eds), *Scotland and the Borders of Romanticism* (Cambridge University Press, 2004), pp. 113–29 (p. 114).
47 Scott, *The Monastery*, pp. 22–23.
48 Ibid., pp. 360–61.
49 Ibid., p. 29.
50 Walter Scott, *Castle Dangerous*, ed. J. H. Alexander (1831; Edinburgh University Press, 2006), pp. 194–208.
51 Ibid., p. 195.
52 Laniel-Musitelli and Sabiron, p. xii.
53 Hutton delivered versions of his theory to the Royal Society of Edinburgh through 1785, and it was printed in the society's *Transactions*, 1.2, for 1788 as 'Theory of the Earth; or an Investigation of the Laws observable in the Composition, Dissolution, and Restoration of Land upon the Globe' (pp. 209–304). Scott had a family connection with Boulton (*Letters*, I: pp. 183–84) and was on friendly terms with Watt (*Life*, V: p. 81n); in 1824, Scott led with Francis Jeffrey to establish a memorial to the engineer (*Letters*, VIII: p. 326).
54 Ina Ferris, 'Temporality and Historical Fiction Reading in Scott', in Caroline McCracken-Flesher and Matthew Wickman (eds), *Walter Scott at 250: Looking Forward* (Edinburgh University Press, 2021), pp. 11–27 (p. 22).

55 Laniel-Musitelli and Sabiron, p. xii.
56 Ibid., p. xvi.
57 Ibid.
58 See Caroline McCracken-Flesher, *Possible Scotlands: Walter Scott and the Story of Tomorrow* (Oxford University Press, 2005), pp. 36–38.
59 Scott, *Waverley*, p. 35, p. 44.
60 Ibid., p. 189.
61 Ibid., pp. 197–98.
62 Ibid. p. 236.
63 Ibid., pp. 257–59, and p. 198.
64 Scott, *Old Mortality*, p. 34.
65 Scott, *Waverley*, p. 174.
66 Ibid., pp. 256–57.
67 Scott, *Old Mortality*, p. 198.
68 Ibid. p. 337, p. 341.
69 Robert Mayer, *Walter Scott and Fame* (Oxford University Press, 2017), pp. 18, 25.
70 Mikhail Bakhtin, *Dialogic Imagination: Four Essays*, ed. Michael Holquist (University of Texas Press, 1981), p. 253.
71 [Walter Scott and William Erskine], Review of *Tales of My Landlord*, *Quarterly Review*, 16 (1816–1817), pp. 430–80; see p. 431.
72 Scott, *The Monastery*, p. 3.
73 Walter Scott, *The Fortunes of Nigel*, ed. Frank Jordan (1822; Edinburgh University Press, 2004), p. 8.
74 Ibid., p. 9.
75 Ibid., p. 12.
76 Ibid., p. 15.
77 Walter Scott, *The Journal of Walter Scott*, ed. W. E. K. Anderson (Canongate, 1998), p. 73.
78 Ibid., p. 592.
79 Deidre Lynch and Evelyne Ender, 'Time for Reading', *PMLA*, 133.5 (2018), pp. 1073–82 (p. 1079), doi:10.1632/pmla.2018.133.5.1073
80 William E. Connolly, *A World of Becoming* (Duke University Press, 2011), p. 9.
81 For Hogg, see Penny Fielding, '"I bide my time": History and the Future Anterior in *The Bride of Lammermoor*', in McCracken-Flesher and Wickman (eds), pp. 28–45.
82 Scott, *Journal*, p. 63.

4. The Scottish Novel in the Wake of Walter Scott, 1815–1830

1 Henry Cockburn, *Memorials of His Time* (Adam and Charles Black, 1856), p. 282.
2 See, for instance, Arthur Herman, *The Scottish Enlightenment: The Scots' Invention of the Modern World* (Fourth Estate, 2002).
3 For detailed and nuanced accounts of the importance of serialisation of the novel during the eighteenth century, see Nicholas Seager, 'The Novel's Afterlife in the Newspaper, 1712–1750', in *The Afterlives of Eighteenth-Century Fiction*, ed. by Daniel Cook and Nicholas Seager (Cambridge University Press, 2015), pp. 111–32; and Gillian Hughes, 'Fiction in the Magazines', in *The Oxford History of the Novel in English: Volume 2: English and British Fiction 1750–1820*, ed. by Peter Garside and Karen O'Brien (Oxford University Press, 2015), pp. 461–77.
4 See Richard Sher, *The Enlightenment and the Book: Scottish Authors and their Publishers in Eighteenth Century Britain, Ireland and America* (University of Chicago Press, 2006).
5 Ian Duncan, *Scott's Shadow: The Novel in Romantic Edinburgh* (Princeton University Press, 2007), p. 20.
6 For a definitive yet dizzying account of how Scott encounters near financial ruin, see Edgar Johnson's chapter 'Cold Roads to Cold News (1825–1826)', vol. 2 of *Sir Walter Scott: The Great Unknown* (Macmillan, 1970), pp. 955–71.
7 Georg Lukács, *The Historical Novel*, trans. Hannah Mitchell and Stanley Mitchell (1937; University of Nebraska Press, 1983). To clarify, Lukács does not overtly announce Scott as the 'father' of the historical novel so much as he employs a kind of antiphrasis by asserting, 'What is lacking in the so-called historical novel before Sir Walter Scott is precisely the specifically historical, that is, derivation of the individuality of characters from the historical peculiarity of their age' (p. 19). Although a plethora of editions of Scott's twenty-eight novels exists, the Edinburgh Edition of the Waverley Novels – under the direction of David Hewitt as Series Editor – is now the definitive scholarly collection.
8 Ian Duncan, 'Scotland and the Novel', in *The Cambridge Companion to Fiction in the Romantic Period*, ed. by Richard Maxwell and Katie Trumpener (Cambridge University Press, 2008) pp. 251–64 (p. 252).
9 See Clifford Siskin's chapter 'Periodicals, Authorship, and the Romantic Rise of the Novel' (pp. 155–71), in *The Work of Writing: Literature and*

Social Change in Britain, 1700–1830, ed. by Clifford Siskin (The Johns Hopkins University Press, 1999), p. 168.

10 For a detailed account of Hogg's life as a shepherd and the emergence of his literary genius despite such odds, see 'Chapter 3: The Ettrick Shepherd', in Valentina Bold, *James Hogg: A Bard of Nature's Making* (Peter Lang, 2007), pp. 63–84.

11 D. M. Moir, *Sketches of the Poetical Literature of the Past Half-Century* (William Blackwood, 1851), pp. 101–02.

12 See, for example, *The Edinburgh Companion to James Hogg*, ed. by Gerard Carruthers and Colin Kidd (Edinburgh University Press, 2012).

13 James Hogg, *The Brownie of Bodsbeck*, ed. by Douglas S. Mack (1818; Scottish Academic Press, 1976), p. 29. Mack's is currently the only reliable edition; however, The Stirling/South Carolina Research Edition of the *Collected Works of James Hogg* (published by Edinburgh University Press) is due to release a new scholarly edition edited by Valentina Bold. Mack relies chiefly on Hogg's 1817 manuscript and elucidates where and how the 1818 first edition and subsequent 1837 republication vary substantively; for example, in the manuscript Hogg describes the brownie as 'wicked and benevolent', whereas the 1818 and 1837 editions describe it as 'wicked and malevolent'; see Mack's 'Note on the Text', pp. xx–xxvii.

14 Kirsten Stirling, *Bella Caledonia: Woman, Nation, Text* (Rodopi, 2008), p. 103.

15 G. Gregory Smith, *Scottish Literature: Character and Influence* (Macmillan and Company, 1919), p. 19.

16 Smith, p. 4.

17 Matthew Wickman, 'Tartan Noir, or, Hard-Boiled Heidegger', *Scottish Literary Review*, 5.1 (Spring/Summer 2013), pp. 87–109 (p. 98).

18 Hogg, *The Brownie of Bodsbeck*, p. 164.

19 Mack, *The Brownie of Bodsbeck*, p. xxii. Mack explains that there are 'deletions [in pencil on the manuscript] that seem to be intended to tone down Hogg's original text' and clarifies that such changes became a 'feature of the text of the first edition [and] is reinforced by another group of passages which were not deleted or altered in the printed text of 1818. These changes were presumably made at the proof stage, but it should be stressed that there is no clear evidence that Hogg read the proofs of the first edition. He was away from Edinburgh [at his Altrive Lake farm] when *The Brownie* was being printed' (pp. xxi–xxii).

20 Sharon Ragaz: '"Gelding" the Priest in *The Brownie of Bodsbeck*: A New Letter', *Studies in Hogg and his World*, 13 (2002), pp. 95–103 (p. 98). Ragaz cites a letter from printer James Ballantyne to William Blackwood on 3 March 1818 in which Ballantyne asks, 'Do you chance to be aware, that one of the incidents in the Brownie of Bodsbeck is the emasculation, the gelding of a priest by the said Brownie? In case you are not aware of this most irregular aberration, I take the liberty to point it out' (p. 98); however, in 'James Hogg's *The Brownie of Bodsbeck*: An Unconventional National Tale' (*Studies in Scottish Literature*, 42.1 [2016], pp. 49–67), Barbara Leonardi argues that Hogg's description of Clerk's castration 'presents the priest's punishment as morally right, as his desire to possess Katharine's body could violate the purity of what Hogg has established as the signifier of the vulnerable groups of the Scottish nation' (p. 58).

21 Coterie authorship was neither a new nor isolated literary phenomenon in early nineteenth-century Scotland. For example, in *Poetry and Politics in the Cockney School: Keats, Shelley, Hunt and their Circle* (Cambridge University Press, 1998), Jeffrey N. Cox reconstructs how what were typically hailed as the 'Keats Circle' or 'Shelley Circle' were actually incubators for literary imagination and collaborative creation; and in *Writing Women's Literary History* (The Johns Hopkins University Press, 1993), Margaret J. M. Ezell elucidates how seventeenth- and eighteenth-century authors like Aphra Behn, Margaret Cavendish, and Lady Mary Wortley Montagu worked within literary circles that both affirmed and complicated their writings.

22 Marshall Walker, *Scottish Literature since 1707* (Routledge, 1996), p. 152.

23 Samuel Baker, 'The Gothic, Supernatural and Religious', in *The International Companion to Nineteenth-Century Scottish Literature*, ed. by Sheila M. Kidd, Caroline McCracken-Flesher, and Kenneth McNeil (Scottish Literature International, 2022) pp. 50–57 (p. 51).

24 For a more thorough explanation of these tenets, see Peter Garside's 'Introduction', in James Hogg, *The Private Memoirs and Confessions of a Justified Sinner*, ed. by Peter Garside (Edinburgh University Press, 2002), pp. xi–xcix (pp. xxviii–xxx).

25 Ibid., p. lxxxv, n. 38.

26 James Hogg, *Memoirs of the Author's Life, and Familiar Anecdotes of Sir Walter Scott*, ed. by Douglas S. Mack (Scottish Academic Press, 1972), p. 55; Mack's edition contains the third and final revision of Hogg's *Memoirs* that was published in his 1832 *Altrive Tales*.

27 Douglas S. Mack, in James Hogg's *Memoirs*, p. 55, n. 8.
28 Hogg, *Confessions*, p. 3.
29 Duncan, 'Scotland and the Novel', p. 253.
30 John Galt, *The Autobiography of John Galt*, 2 vols (Cochrane & M'Crone, 1833), II, p. 219.
31 John Galt, *The Ayrshire Legatees; Or, The Pringle Family* (William Blackwood, 1821), p. 3.
32 Ibid., p. 3.
33 Galt's Southwest of Scotland readers in particular would also have recognised Galt's local knowledge with the arrival '[o]n the fourteenth day after the departure of the family from the manse, [of] the Rev. Mr Charles Snodgrass, who was appointed to officiate during the absence of the doctor' (Ibid., p. 20). Dr Pringle's interim clerical replacement, the Rev. Snodgrass, functions as a signifier of the novel's grounding in time and place by drawing upon the surname of a family which resided along the Garnock River 'between Irvine and Kilwinnng' long before the publication of the *Legatees* in 1821; the Snodgrass name affirms the novel's verisimilitude in Ayrshire geography and in the memories of its rural inhabitants. For maps showing the Snodgrass Family farm along the Garnock River, see Captain Andrew Armstrong and Son, *A New Map of Ayr Shire Comprehending Kyle, Cunningham & Carrick: the scale one inch to a mile*, ['Publish'd according to Act of Parliament, January 10th 1775'], (Stephen Pyle, Sculptor, Angel Court, Snow Hill, London; Norfolk, England, 1775), NLS Shelfmark, EMS.s.515; and John Thomson, *Northern Part of Ayrshire. Southern Part* (J. Thomson & Co., 1828), NLS Shelfmark, EMS.s.712(9). Relying upon *The Exchequer Rolls of Scotland* (1264–1600), George F. Black begins describing Snodgrass as 'An Ayrshire surname derived from the twenty shilling lands of old extent of Snodgers or Snodgrasse in the parish of Irvine and bailliary of Cunningham. Adam Snorgyrs appears as bailie of Are in 1372 (ER., II, p. 486)', in *The Surnames of Scotland: Their Origin, Meaning, and History* (New York Public Library, 1946), p. 735.
34 Franco Moretti, *Graphs, Maps, Trees: Abstract Models for a Literary History* (Verso, 2005), pp. 35–36.
35 Colin Kidd, 'Satire, Hypocrisy, and the Ayrshire–Renfrewshire Enlightenment', in *The International Companion to John Galt*, ed. by Gerard Carruthers and Colin Kidd (Scottish Literature International, 2017), pp. 15–33 (p. 16).
36 Moretti, p. 46–47.

37 For Galt's colonising efforts in Canada, which includes an early map of Guelph, see Gilbert A. Stelter, 'John Galt: The Writer as Town Booster and Builder', in *John Galt: Reappraisals*, ed. by Elizabeth Waterson (University of Guelph, 1985), pp. 17–43; and 'John Galt's "Whole Art of Colonization": Sound, Voice, Space', chapter 2 in Josephine McDonagh, *Literature in a Time of Migration: British Fiction and the Movement of People, 1815–1876* (Oxford University Press, 2021), pp. 70–111.
38 Daniel Maclise, 'Object: The Author of a "Life of Byron"' (Lithograph on chine collé; 18.5 x 14.0 cm), 1830; British Museum No.: 1859.0625.94.
39 Galt, *Autobiography*, II, pp. 227–28.
40 Katie Trumpener, *Bardic Nationalism: The Romantic Novel and the British Empire* (Princeton University Press, 1997), pp. 151–52.
41 Padma Rangarajan, 'Debating Insurrection in Galt's *Ringan Gilhaize*', *Studies in Scottish Literature*, 46.1 (2020), pp. 7–13 (p. 13).
42 Trumpener, p. 273. For the religious controversy surrounding Scott's *Old Morality*, Hogg's *Confessions*, and Galt's *Ringan Gilhaize*, see Douglas S. Mack, '"The rage of fanaticism in former days": James Hogg's *Confessions of a Justified Sinner* and the Controversy over *Old Mortality*', in *Nineteenth-Century Scottish Fiction: Critical Essays*, ed. by Ian Campbell (Carcanet New Press, 1979), pp. 37–50.
43 See Francis Jeffrey, 'Secondary Scottish Novels', *Edinburgh Review*, 39 (October 1823), pp. 158–79.
44 Ibid., pp. 161–62.
45 'History of Blackwood's Magazine', in *Noctes Ambrosianæ*, ed. by R. Shelton Mackenzie, 5 vols (Redfield, 1854), I, p. xiv.
46 J. H. Alexander clarifies in the introduction to his *Tavern Sages: Selections from the Noctes Ambrosianæ* (Association for Scottish Literary Studies, 1992) that 'Most of [the *Noctes*] are set in the actual tavern run by the Yorkshireman William Ambrose at 1 Gabriel's Road, and from No. 29 (November 1826) in his superior establishment, Ambrose's North British Hotel, Tavern, and Coffee-House at 15 Picardy Place' (p. vii).
47 Trevor Royle, 'Noctes Ambrosianae', in *Companion to Scottish Literature* (Gale, 1983), p. 228.
48 Margaret Oliphant, *Annals of a Publishing House: William Blackwood and His Sons, Their Magazine and Friends*, 2 vols (William Blackwood, 1897), I, p. 114.
49 John Wilson and John Gibson Lockhart, 'Noctes Ambrosianæ', *Blackwood's Edinburgh Magazine* (April 1822), pp. 155–74 (p. 169).

50 Quoted in Andrew Noble, 'John Wilson (Christopher North) and the Tory Hegemony', in *The History of Scottish Literature: Volume 3, Nineteenth Century*, ed. by Douglas Gifford (Aberdeen University Press, 1989), pp. 125–51, (p. 147).
51 Ibid., p. 148.
52 Francis Russell Hart, *The Scottish Novel: From Smollett to Spark* (Harvard University Press, 1978), pp. 72, 79.
53 [Walter Scott, unsigned review], 'Remarks on Frankenstein, or the Modern Prometheus; A Novel', *Blackwood's Edinburgh Magazine*, 2 (March 1818), pp. 613–20. Scott's authorial assumption includes sexist language such as, 'Even in the description of his marvels, however, the author who manages this stile [*sic*] of composition with address, gives them an indirect importance with the reader, when he is able to describe with nature [...]' (p. 613). For the details and controversies surrounding how and to what degree Percy Bysshe Shelley had a heavy hand in editing *Frankenstein*, see *The Frankenstein Notebooks: A Facsimile Edition of Mary Shelley's Manuscript Novel, 1816-1817*, ed. by Charles E. Robinson, 2 vols (Garland Publishing, 1996).
54 John A. Doyle, *Memoir and Correspondence of Susan Ferrier, 1782–1854* (John Murray, 1898), pp. 145–46.
55 [Susan Ferrier], *Destiny; Or, The Chief's Daughter*, 3 vols (Robert Cadell, 1831), p. vii.
56 See 'Fig. 2 Authorship of New Novels, 1800–1829: Gender Breakdown', in *The English Novel 1770–1829: A Bibliographical Survey of Prose Fiction Published in the British Isles: Volume II: 1800–1829*, ed. by Peter Garside, Rainer Schöwerling, Christopher Skelton-Foord, and Karin Wünsche, 2 vols (Oxford University Press, 2000), II, p. 74. Also see *British Fiction 1800–1829: A Database of Production, Circulation and Reception*, founded by Garside and housed at Cardiff University: www.british-fiction.cf.ac.uk.
57 Garside and others, *The English Novel 1770–1829*, II, p. 76.
58 Trumpener, p. 146.
59 For a first-hand account of this Royal Visit, see [Robert Mudie], *A Historical Account of His Majesty's Visit to Scotland* (Oliver & Boyd, 1822); this anonymous and highly popular account went through two editions in 1822; for a detailed historical account, see John Prebble, *The King's Jaunt: George IV in Scotland, August 1822: 'One and Twenty Daft Days'* (Collins, 1988).
60 For example, see Susan Ferrier, *Marriage: A Novel*, ed. by Dorothy McMillan (Association for Scottish Literary Studies, 2020); Cassandra

Phillips, 'A Scholarly Edition of Susan Ferrier's *The Inheritance*', unpublished Ph.D. Thesis, University of Saskatchewan, 2006; and *The Inheritance*, ed. by Ronnie Young (Kennedy & Boyd, 2009).

5. The Victorian Novel of Spiritual Crisis and the Disruption of Scottish Literary History

1. Christopher Harvie, 'Industry, Religion and the State of Scotland', in Douglas Gifford (ed.), *The History of Scottish Literature, Vol. 3: The Nineteenth Century* (Aberdeen University Press, 1988), p. 24; Paul H. Scott, 'The Last Purely Scotch Age' in Douglas Gifford, ibid., p. 13.
2. Douglas Gifford, 'Preparing for the Renaissance: Revaluing Nineteenth-Century Scottish Literature', in Gerard Carruthers, David Goldie, and Alastair Renfrew (eds), *Scotland and the 19th-Century World* (Rodopi, 2012), pp. 21–36 (p. 23).
3. Scott, 'The Last Purely Scotch Age', p. 19.
4. Callum G. Brown, *Religion and Society in Scotland since 1707*, p. 185.
5. Valerie Wallace and Colin Kidd, 'Between Nationhood and Nonconformity: The Scottish Whig-Presbyterian Novel and the Denominational Press', in Gerard Carruthers and Colin Kidd (eds), *Literature and Union: Scottish Texts, British Contexts* (Oxford University Press, 2018), pp. 193–220 (pp. 194, 193).
6. Ibid., p. 209.
7. Ibid.
8. Margaret Oliphant, *Passages in the Life of Mrs. Margaret Maitland of Sunnyside. Written by Herself* (Henry Colburn, 1849), p. 337.
9. Ibid., pp. 4–5.
10. Ibid., p. 1.
11. Ibid., pp. 338, 349.
12. Ibid., p. 44.
13. Ibid., p. 240.
14. *The Autobiography and Letters of Mrs. M. O. W. Oliphant*, ed. Mrs Harry Coghill (Wm Blackwood & Sons, 1899), p. 17. Although Oliphant's family was living in Liverpool in 1843, they nonetheless 'went out' with the Free Church, in which her elder brother Willie was for a short while a minister.
15. On domestic womanhood in Kailyard fiction, see Samantha Walton, 'Scottish Modernism, Kailyard Fiction, and the Woman at Home', in Kate MacDonald et al. (eds), *Transitions in Middlebrow Writing* (Macmillan, 2015), pp. 141–59 (pp. 142–44).
16. Margaret Oliphant, *A Son of the Soil* (1866; Macmillan, 1894), p. 363.

17 Ibid., p. 49.
18 Ibid., pp. 87, 369.
19 The Secessionists separated from the Church of Scotland in 1733 and then subdivided into those who agreed or refused to take the burgess oath, which signified approval of the established Church. The Antiburgher Secession Church thus opposed the Moderate Kirk and regarded itself – as many Presbyterian sects did – as the true heir to the Covenanters. See David S. Robb, *George MacDonald* (Scottish Academic Press, 1988), p. 6.
20 George MacDonald, *Robert Falconer* (1868; D. Lothrop, 1870), p. 176.
21 Ibid., p. 87.
22 Ibid., p. 392.
23 Ibid., p. 76.
24 Annie S. Swan, *Maitland of Laurieston* (Oliphant, Anderson and Ferrier, 1891), p. 31.
25 Ibid., p. 272.
26 Ibid., p. 67.
27 Ibid., p. 67.
28 Ibid., pp. 60, 10.
29 Ibid., p. 121.
30 Ibid., p. 212.
31 Ibid., p. 436.
32 Ibid., p. 368.
33 Ibid., p. 246.
34 See William Raeper, *George MacDonald* (Lion Publishing, 1987), pp. 201–08; and David Holbrook, *A Study of George MacDonald and the Image of Woman* (Edwin Mellin, 2000).
35 Oliphant, *Son of the Soil*, p. 247.
36 Ibid., p. 314.
37 Ibid., p. 248.
38 See, for instance, Robert and Vinetta Colby, 'Mrs. Oliphant's Scotland: The Romance of Reality', in Ian Campbell (ed.), *Nineteenth-Century Scottish Fiction* (Barnes & Noble, 1979), pp. 89–104; and Merryn Williams, 'Margaret Oliphant', in Douglas Gifford and Dorothy McMillan (eds), *A History of Scottish Women's Writing* (Edinburgh University Press, 1997), pp. 276–77.
39 Ibid., p. 237.
40 Ibid., p. 373.
41 Ibid., p. 371.
42 MacDonald, *Robert Falconer*, pp. 84, 392.

43 Ibid., p. 54.
44 Robert Lee Wolff, *The Golden Key* (Yale University Press, 1961), p. 236.
45 MacDonald, *Robert Falconer*, p. 84.
46 Ibid., pp. 120, 185.
47 Ibid., pp. 142–43.
48 Ibid., p. 250.
49 Ibid., p. 359.
50 Robb, *George MacDonald*, p. 30.
51 MacDonald, *Robert Falconer*, p. 131.
52 On the complicated gendering of God in this novel, see Philip Hicock, 'God and Gender in *Robert Falconer*: Deifying the Feminine', in Christopher MacLachlan, John Patrick Padziora, and Ginger Stelle (eds), *Rethinking George MacDonald: Contexts and Contemporaries* (Scottish Literature International, 2013), pp. 105–20.
53 Annie S. Swan, *My Life: An Autobiography* (Ivor Nicholson & Watson, 1934), p. 286.
54 Swan, *Maitland*, p. 440.
55 Ibid., pp. 280, 441.
56 See Margaret Oliphant, *The Autobiography of Margaret Oliphant*, ed. Elisabeth Jay (Broadview Press, 2002), pp. 36–46.
57 See for instance Merryn Williams, 'Margaret Oliphant', in Douglas Gifford and Dorothy McMillan (eds), *A History of Scottish Women's Writing* (Edinburgh University Press, 1997), p. 281; Linda Peterson, 'The Female *Bildungsroman*: Tradition and Subversion in Oliphant's Fiction', in D. J. Trela (ed.), *Margaret Oliphant: Critical Essays on a Gentle Subversive* (Susquehanna University Press, 1995), p. 82; and Elsie Michie, *The Vulgar Question of Money: Heiresses, Materialism, and the Novel of Manners from Jane Austen to Henry James* (Johns Hopkins University Press, 2013), p. 147.
58 Oliphant, *Son of the Soil*, p. 293.
59 Ibid., p. 428.
60 Ibid., pp. 428–29.
61 Ibid., p. 428.
62 MacDonald, p. 365. Teufelsdröckh discovers that 'to know thyself' is to 'know what thou canst work at', and urges, 'Whatsoever thy hand findeth to do, do it with thy whole might'. See Thomas Carlyle, *Sartor Resartus*, ed. Kerry McSweeney and Peter Sabor (Oxford University Press World's Classics, 1987), pp. 126, 149.
63 Robb, *George MacDonald*, p. 31.

64 MacDonald, *Robert Falconer*, p. 517.
65 For an account of the differences between the serialised and triple-decker versions of *Robert Falconer*, see Peter Butter, 'The strengths and weaknesses of *Robert Falconer*', *North Wind: A Journal of George MacDonald Studies*, 14 (1995), pp. 57–64 (p. 62).
66 MacDonald, *Robert Falconer*, p. 515.
67 Ibid., p. 521.

6. From the Nineteenth to the Twentieth Century

1 E.g. Cairns Craig, *Out of History* (Polygon, 1996); Andrew Nash, *Kailyard and Scottish Literature* (Rodopi, 2007); Michael Shaw, *The Fin-De-Siècle Scottish Revival: Romance, Decadence and Celtic Identity* (Edinburgh University Press, 2019)
2 John Buchan, *The Watcher by the Threshold: Shorter Scottish Fiction* (Canongate, 1997), pp. 260, 272.
3 Ibid., p. 288.
4 Andrew Lang, 'Realism and Romance', *Contemporary Review*, 52 (November 1887), pp. 683–93 (p. 690).
5 William Black, *White Heather* (1885; Sampson Low, 1893), pp. 258, 382.
6 Robert Buchanan, *A Child of Nature* (1881; Chatto & Windus, 1896), pp. 16, 105.
7 George MacDonald, *What's Mine's Mine* (1886; George Routledge, 1887), p. 336.
8 Fiona Macleod, *Pharais and The Mountain Lovers* (Heinemann, 1912), pp. 63–64.
9 Ibid., p. 380.
10 Fiona Macleod, *The Sin-Eater and other Tales* (Patrick Geddes, 1895), p. 9.
11 Fiona Macleod, *The Washer by the Ford and other Legendary Moralities* (Patrick Geddes, 1896), p. 6.
12 Neil Munro, *The Lost Pibroch and other Sheiling Stories* (William Blackwood, 1896), p. 58.
13 Ibid., pp. 5–6.
14 Alison Lumsden, 'Stevenson, Scott and Scottish History', in Penny Fielding (ed.), *The Edinburgh Companion to Robert Louis Stevenson* (Edinburgh University Press, 2009), pp. 70–85 (p. 73).
15 Ibid.
16 Robert Louis Stevenson, *Memories and Portraits* (Chatto & Windus, 1887), p. 251.

17 Robert Louis Stevenson, *Kidnapped*, ed. Ian Duncan (1886; Oxford World's Classics, 2014), pp. 110–11.
18 Stevenson, *Memories and Portraits*, p. 251.
19 Stevenson, *Kidnapped*, pp. 108, 177, 184.
20 Stevenson, *Memories and Portraits*, p. 283.
21 Robert Louis Stevenson, *The Master of Ballantrae* ed. Adrian Poole (1889; Penguin, 1996), pp. 157, 219.
22 S. R. Crockett, *The Raiders* (T. Fisher Unwin, 1894), pp. 11–12.
23 S. R. Crockett, *The Grey Man* (T. Fisher Unwin, 1896), p. 344.
24 Ibid., p. 272.
25 John Buchan, *The Thirty-Nine Steps*, ed. John Keegan (1915; Penguin, 2004), p. 27.
26 John Buchan, *John Burnet of Barns* (1898; Nelson, 1922), p. 216.
27 Violet Jacob, *Flemington*, ed. Carol Anderson (1911; Association for Scottish Literary Studies, 1994), Author's Note.
28 Ibid., pp. 60, 203, 110, 126–27.
29 Neil Munro, *The New Road* (William Blackwood, 1914), pp. 14–15.
30 Ibid., pp. 177, 120, 17, 290–91.
31 Sarah Tytler, *Logie Town* (1887; Ward & Downey, 1890), p. 1.
32 Ibid., pp. 171, 165.
33 'The Old Saloon', *Blackwood's Magazine* (August 1889), pp. 254–75 (p. 266).
34 Margaret Oliphant, *Kirsteen*, 3 vols (Macmillan, 1890), III, pp. 286, 291.
35 Ibid., I: p. 46, III: pp. 28, 50–51.
36 Elsie B. Michie, 'History After Waterloo: Margaret Oliphant Reads Walter Scott', *ELH*, 80 (2013), pp. 897–916 (p. 913), doi:10.1353/elh.2013.0034
37 Jane and Mary Findlater, *Crossriggs* (1908; Virago, 1996), p. 3.
38 Ibid., p. 162.
39 Ibid., pp. 214, 81–82, 90–91, 69, 359, 379.
40 Ibid., p. 8.
41 Sarah Tytler, *St Mungo's City*, 3 vols (Chatto & Windus, 1885), I, p. 249.
42 Ibid., III, pp. 271–22.
43 William Sime, *King Capital*, 2 vols (William Blackwood, 1883), I, p. 73.
44 Ibid., I: p. 15, II: p. 102, I: p. 154, II: pp. 64–65, II: p. 309.
45 John Maclaren Cobban, *The King of Andaman* (Methuen, 1895), p. 10.
46 Ibid., pp. 12, 1, 43, 37.
47 George Douglas Brown, *The House with the Green Shutters*, ed. Dorothy Porter (1901; Penguin, 1985), pp. 44, 93, 99.

48 J. MacDougall Hay, *Gillespie* (Constable, 1914), p. 30.
49 Ibid., pp. 14, 358–59, 607.
50 S. R. Crockett, *Cleg Kelly: Arab of the City* (Smith, Elder 1896), p. 1.
51 Patrick MacGill, *The Rat-Pit* (Herbert Jenkins, 1915), p. 227.
52 Frederick Niven, *Justice of the Peace* (1914; Nelson, 1917), p. 407.
53 J. M. Barrie, *Tommy and Grizel* (Cassell, 1900), p. 185.
54 See Andrew Nash, 'Barrie, Sentimentality, and Modern Literature', in Valentina Bold and Andrew Nash (eds), *Gateway to the Modern: Resituating J. M. Barrie* (Scottish Literature International, 2014), pp. 103–20.

7. The Scottish Novel in the Interwar Years

1. J. M. Reid, *Modern Scottish Literature*, Saltire Pamphlets 5 (Oliver and Boyd, 1945), p. 18.
2. Richard Overy, *The Morbid Age: Britain Between the Wars* (Allen Lane, 2009).
3. Reid, *Modern Scottish Literature*, p. 16.
4. Hugh MacDiarmid, 'New Scottish Fiction (II): Others', *Contemporary Scottish Studies*, ed. Alan Riach (Carcanet, 1995), p. 348.
5. Lewis Grassic Gibbon, 'Literary Lights', Lewis Grassic Gibbon and Hugh MacDiarmid, *Scottish Scene or the Intelligent Man's Guide to Albyn* (1934; Cedric Chivers, 1974), pp. 195–96.
6. Reid, *Modern Scottish Literature*, 18; William Power, *My Scotland* (The Porpoise Press, 1934), p. 300.
7. Alistair McCleery, 'The Porpoise Press 1922–26', *Scottish Literary Journal*, 12.2 (1985), pp. 53–68.
8. Lewis Grassic Gibbon, 'Literary Lights', *Scottish Scene*, p. 198.
9. Ibid., p. 199.
10. Ibid., p. 200.
11. Ibid., pp. 200–01.
12. Ibid., p. 201.
13. Ibid., p. 205.
14. Moray Watson, *An Introduction to Gaelic Fiction* (Edinburgh University Press, 2011), p. 58–59. See also Ch. 10 of this volume.
15. 'Literary Lights', p. 207.
16. Hanne Tange, 'Language, Class and Social Power in *A Scots Quair*', in Scott Lyall (ed.), *The International Companion to Lewis Grassic Gibbon* (Scottish Literature International, 2015), pp. 22–32 (pp. 30–31).
17. James Barke, *Land of the Leal* (Canongate, 1987), p. ix.

18 Keir Elder, 'James Barke: Politics, Cinema and Writing Scottish Urban Modernity', unpublished PhD Thesis, University of Dundee (2013).
19 Mary Seenan, *Nancy Brysson Morrison: A Literary Life* (Kennedy and Boyd, 2013), p. 135; Samantha Walton, *The Living World: Nan Shepherd and Environmental Thought* (Bloomsbury, 2020), pp. 23ff.
20 Glenda Norquay, 'Finding a Place: The Voice of Lorna Moon', *Études Écossaises*, 9 (2004), pp. 91–103. Moon's works include: short stories, *Doorways in Drumorty* (1926); novel, *Dark Star* (1929), in Glenda Norquay (ed.), *The Collected Works of Lorna Moon* (Black and White Publishing, 2002).
21 Carla Sassi, 'Prismatic Modernities: Towards a Recontextualization of Scottish Modernism', in Emma Dymock and Margery Palmer McCulloch (eds), *Scottish and International Modernisms* (Association for Scottish Literary Studies, 2011), pp. 184–197 (p. 192).
22 Fionn MacColla, 'Foreword', *The Albannach* (1932; Souvenir Press, 1971), p. 1.
23 Ian Macpherson, *Shepherd's Calendar* (Cape, 1931), p. 11.
24 Neil M. Gunn, *Highland River* (1937; Arrow, 1960), p. 78.
25 Cairns Craig, *The Modern Scottish Novel: Narrative and the National Imagination* (Edinburgh University Press, 1999), p. 150.
26 O. Douglas, *Penny Plain* (1920; Hodder & Stoughton, 1942), p. 156.
27 Joyce's daughter in *Hunger March* or Kitty in Rebecca West, *The Return of the Soldier* (1918).
28 Douglas, *Penny Plain*, p. 80.
29 Angus MacDonald 'Modern Scots Novelists', in H. J. C. Grierson (ed.), *Edinburgh Essays on Scots Literature* (1933; Books for Libraries Press, 1968), pp. 149–73 (p. 165).
30 Eric Linklater, *White Maa's Saga* (1929; Cape, 1934), p. 203.
31 Dot Allan, *Hunger March* (1934); Moira Burgess (ed.), *Makeshift and Hunger March* (Association for Scottish Literary Studies, 2010), p. 322.
32 Ibid., p. 333.
33 Macpherson, *Shepherd's Calendar*, p. 21.
34 Lewis Grassic Gibbon, *Sunset Song, A Scots Quair* (1932–34; Pan, 1987), p. 235.
35 Nan Shepherd, *The Weatherhouse, A Grampian Quartet* (1930; Canongate, 1996), p. 167.
36 Willa Muir, *Mrs Ritchie, Imagined Selves* (1933; Canongate, 1996), pp. 252–54.

37 Edwin Muir's *Scottish Journey* (1935) participates in this genre; George Orwell, *Coming Up for Air* (1939) is a perfect example.
38 Walton, *The Living World*.
39 Agnes Stewart, 'Some Scottish Novelists', *Northern Review*, 1.1 (May 1924), pp. 35–41 (p. 36).
40 Douglas Gifford, *Scottish Literature* (Edinburgh University Press, 2002), p. 717.
41 Power, *My Scotland*, p. 298.
42 Allan, *Hunger March*, p. 207.
43 Ibid., p. 275; p. 280.
44 James Barke, *Major Operation* (Collins, 1936), p. 16.
45 A. McArthur and H. Kingsley Long, *No Mean City* (1935; Chivers Press, 1989), p. 1.
46 George Blake, *The Shipbuilders* (Faber and Faber, 1935), p. 173.
47 Ibid., p. 230.
48 Katie Gramich, 'Caught in the Triple Net? Welsh, Scottish and Irish Women Writers', in Maroula Joannou (ed.), *The History of British Women's Writing (1900–1945)* (Palgrave, 2012), p. 228.
49 Alison Light, *Forever England: Femininity, Literature and Conservatism Between the Wars* (Routledge, 1991).
50 Blake, *The Shipbuilders*, p. 361.
51 Barke, *Major Operation*, p. 395.
52 Neil M. Gunn, *Wild Geese Overhead* (1939; Whittles Publishing, 2002), p. 22.
53 MacColla, *The Albannach*, p. vii.
54 Ibid., p. 10.
55 Ibid., p. 34.
56 Ibid., p. 237.
57 Macpherson, *Shepherd's Calendar*, p. 26.
58 Ibid., p. 265.
59 Hugh MacDiarmid, 'Neil M. Gunn', *Contemporary Scottish Studies*, p. 313.
60 Kurt Wittig, *The Scottish Tradition in Literature* (Oliver & Boyd, 1958), p. 338.
61 H. Gustav Klaus, 'James Barke: a Great-hearted Writer, a Hater of Oppression, a True Scot', in Andy Croft (ed.), *A Weapon in the Struggle: The Cultural History of the Communist Party in Britain* (Pluto Press, 1998), pp. 7–27 (p. 8).
62 *Wild Geese Overhead*, p. 216.

63 James Barke, 'Lewis Grassic Gibbon', *Left Review*, 2.5 (1936), pp. 220–25 (p. 220).
64 Christopher Whyte, 'Fishy Masculinities: Neil Gunn's *The Silver Darlings*', in Christopher Whyte (ed.), *Gendering the Nation* (Edinburgh University Press, 1995), p. 66.
65 Ken Keir, 'Modernist Myths and Mothers: Jung and "Mythic Parallelism" in Neil Gunn's *The Silver Darlings*', *Modern Humanities Research Association*, 5 (2011), pp. 1–2, doi:10.59860/wph.a1684db
66 Louisa Gairn, *Ecology and Modern Scottish Literature* (Edinburgh University Press, 2008); Andrew J. Sneddon, '"We will beat the landlords and the scenic sentimentalists": Neil M. Gunn and Landscape Discourse in the "Hydro" Debates', *International Journal of Scottish Literature*, 5 (2009).
67 J. Rubén Valdés Miyares, 'On the Trail of the Highland Clearances: The Clearances Metanarrative in Scottish Historical Fiction', *English Studies*, 98.6 (2017), pp. 585–97, doi:10.1080/0013838x.2017.1322384
68 Nan Shepherd, *The Quarry Wood*, *A Grampian Quartet* (Canongate, 1996), p. 4. The novel was rejected by thirteen publishers before being accepted by Constable.
69 Ibid., p. 210.
70 Elizabeth Kyle, 'Modern Women Authors', *Scots Observer*, 25 June 1931, p. 4; Margery Palmer McCulloch *Modernism and Nationalism: Literature and Society in Scotland 1918–1939* (Association for Scottish Literary Studies, 2004), pp. 203–08.
71 Emily Pickard, 'Re-Evaluating Willa Muir's "Mrs Muttoe and the Top Storey" in Light of COVID-19 Labour Disparities', *Scottish Literary Review*, 14.1 (Spring/Summer 2022), pp. 191–206.
72 See Scott Lyall (ed.), *The International Companion to Lewis Grassic Gibbon* (Scottish Literature International, 2015).
73 Morag Shiach, 'Lewis Grassic Gibbon and Modernism', in Lyall (ed.), ibid., pp. 9–21.
74 Carla Sassi, 'The Shifting Identities of Mitchell and Gibbon', in Lyall (ed.), ibid., pp. 33–46 (p. 33).
75 See Timothy C. Baker, 'Ian Macpherson's Writing of the Disaster', *IRSS*, 33 (2008), doi:10.21083/irss.v33i0.486
76 See Juliet Shields, *Scottish Women's Writing in the Long Nineteenth-Century* (Cambridge University Press, 2021).
77 Overy, p. 178.

78 Timothy C. Baker, 'Introduction', *Wild Harbour* (British Library, 2019), p. 9.
79 See Simon W. Hall, *The History of Orkney Literature* (John Donald, 2010).
80 Elizabeth Maslen, 'Naomi Mitchison's Historical Fiction', in Maroula Joannou (ed.), *Women Writers of the 1930s* (Edinburgh University Press, 1999), pp. 138–50 (p. 141).
81 Kate Macdonald and Nathan Waddell (eds), *John Buchan and the Idea of Modernity* (Pickering & Chatto, 2013).
82 David Goldie, 'Twin Loyalties: John Buchan's England', in Kate Macdonald (ed.), *Reassessing John Buchan* (Routledge, 2009), pp. 29–40 (p. 37).
83 John Miller, '"The Soul's Queer Corners": John Buchan and Psychoanalysis', in *John Buchan and the Idea of Modernity*, pp. 125–40.
84 Samantha Walton, 'The Scottish Landscape in the Crime Novels of Josephine Tey', in Kirsten Sandrock and Frauke Reitemeier (eds), *Crimelights: Scottish crime fiction then and now* (Wissenschaftelicher Verlag, 2014), p. 17.
85 Shields, *Scottish Women's Writing in the Long Nineteenth-Century*, p. 122.
86 Julia Ditter, '"Ghosts of the Future": Elegiac Temporalities and Planetary Futures in Nancy Brysson Morrison's *The Gowk Storm*', *Scottish Literary Review* 14.1 (Spring/Summer 2022), pp. 171–90.
87 Charlotte Lauder, 'Claire Spencer: A Lost Scottish Modernist', *Lost Modernists*, 1.1 (2021): lostmodernists.com/claire-spencer-a-lost-scottish-modernist/

8. From the Second World War to the 1970s

1 See Moira Burgess, 'Arcades – The 1940s and the 1950s', Ian Brown and Alan Riach (eds), *The Edinburgh Companion to Twentieth-Century Scottish Literature* (Edinburgh University Press, 2009), pp. 103–11 (p. 103).
2 Douglas Gifford, 'Modern Scottish Fiction', *Studies in Scottish Literature*, 13.1 (1978). Available at scholarcommons.sc.edu/ssl/vol13/iss1/20.
3 Liam McIlvanney (ed.), *Growing Up in the West* (Canongate Classics), p. vii.
4 J. F. Hendry, *Fernie Brae*, in McIlvanney (ed.), ibid., p. 260.
5 Ibid., p. 174.
6 Ibid., p. 252.
7 Ibid., p. 262.

8 Ibid., p. 293.
9 Ibid., p. 311.
10 See Gordon Jarvie's introduction to George Friel, *A Glasgow Trilogy* (Canongate Classics, 1999), p. ix.
11 Archie Hind, *The Dear Green Place* (Polygon, 1984), p. 65.
12 Ibid., p. 27.
13 William McIlvanney, *Remedy is None* (1966; W. & R. Chambers, 1992), p. 225.
14 William McIlvanney, *A Gift from Nessus* (Eyre & Spottiswood, 1968), p. 222.
15 William McIlvanney, 'Growing up in the West', in Karl Miller (ed.), *Memoirs of a Modern Scotland* (Faber: 1970), pp. 168–178 (p. 171).
16 William McIlvanney, *Surviving the Shipwreck* (Mainstream, 1991), p. 223.
17 Keith Dixon, 'Writing on the Borderline: The Works of William McIlvanney', *Studies in Scottish Literature*, 24.1 (1989). Available at scholarcommons.sc.edu/ssl/vol24/iss1/13 [Accessed 1 April 2023].
18 William McIlvanney, *Docherty* (George, Allen & Unwin, 1975), p. 277.
19 William McIlvanney, *Laidlaw* (Hodder and Stoughton,1977), p. 9.
20 Glenda Norquay, 'Four Novelists of the 1950s and 1960s', in Cairns Craig (ed.), *The History of Scottish Literature, Volume 4: Twentieth Century* (Aberdeen University Press, 1987), pp. 259–276 (p. 265).
21 Alan Sharp, *A Green Tree in Gedde* (1965; Richard Drew, 1985), p. 93.
22 Ibid., p. 94.
23 See Andrew Murray Scott, *Alexander Trocchi: The Making of the Monster* (Polygon, 1991).
24 See, for example, Adam Guy, *The Nouveau Roman and Writing in Britain after Modernism* (Oxford University Press, 2020).
25 Alexander Trocchi, *Cain's Book* (1963; John Calder, 1992), p. 45.
26 Ibid., p. 60.
27 Edwin Morgan, *The Midnight Letterbox: Selected Correspondence, 1950–2010*, ed. James McGonigal and John Coyle (Carcanet, 2015), p. 487.
28 Alan Bold, *Modern Scottish Literature* (Longman, 1983), p. 214.
29 Iain Crichton Smith, *Consider the Lilies* (1968; Canongate, 1987), p. 1.
30 Ibid., p. viii.
31 Douglas Gifford 'Scottish Fiction since 1945', in Norman Wilson (ed.), *Scottish Writing and Writers* (The Ramsay Head Press, 1977), pp. 11–29 (p. 15).
32 Ibid, p. 18.

33 Gavin Wallace and Douglas Gifford, 'The Range and Achievement of Robin Jenkins: An Introductory Overview', in Linden Bicket and Douglas Gifford (eds), *The Fiction of Robin Jenkins: Some Kind of Grace*, pp. 1–21 (p. 1).
34 Alastair R. Thomson, 'Faith and Love: An Examination of Some of the Themes in the Work of Robin Jenkins', *New Saltire*, 3 (Spring 1962), pp. 57–64 (p. 58).
35 Robin Jenkins, *Dust on the Paw* (1961; Richard Drew, 1986), p. 21.
36 Ibid., p. 256.
37 Penelope Jardine (ed.), *The Golden Fleece: Essays* (Carcanet, 2014), p. 30.
38 Ibid.
39 Martin McQuillan (ed.), *Theorising Muriel Spark: gender, race, deconstruction* (Macmillan, 2002), p. 158.
40 Alain Robbe-Grillet, 'The Writer's Only Commitment is to Literature', in Andrew Hook (ed.), *The Novel Today: Edinburgh International Festival 1962: Programme and Notes, International Writers' Conference* (Kennedy and Boyd, 2012), pp. 43–44.
41 Spark qtd in McQuillan, p. 216.
42 Ian Rankin, 'Surface and Structure: Reading Muriel Spark's "The Driver's Seat"', *The Journal of Narrative Technique*, 15.2 (1985), pp. 146–55.
43 Christopher Sinclair-Stevenson, 'Obituary: Elspeth Davie', *The Independent*, 15 November 1995: www.independent.co.uk/voices/obituary-elspeth-davie-1582056.html.
44 See Marina Spunta, 'A Universe of One's Own? Elspeth Davie and the Narrative of the "Gap"', *Chapman* 81, (1995), pp. 18–25.
45 John Sturrock, *The French New Novel* (Oxford University Press, 1969), p. 8.
46 See Eleanor Bell, 'Experiment and Nation in the 1960s', in Glenda Norquay (ed.), *The Edinburgh Companion to Scottish Women's Writing* (Edinburgh University Press, 2011), pp. 122–129 (p. 127).
47 Gill Benton, *Naomi Mitchison* (Pandora Press, 1990), p. 144.
48 Jenni Calder, *The Nine Lives of Naomi Mitchison* (Virago, 1997), p. 270.
49 Edwin Morgan, 'The Young Writer in Scotland', in Andrew Hook (ed.), *The Novel Today*, pp. 35–38 (p. 37).

9. The Scottish Novel 1979–1999

1 Cairns Craig, *The Modern Scottish Novel: Narrative and the National Imagination* (Edinburgh University Press, 1999), p. 36.
2 T. M. Devine, *The Scottish Nation 1700–2000* (Penguin, 2000), p. 588.

3   Duncan Petrie, *Contemporary Scottish Fictions: Film, Television and the Novel* (Edinburgh University Press, 2004), p. 2.
4   Ibid.
5   William McIlvanney, 'After: March 1979 – The Cowardly Lion', in *Surviving the Shipwreck* (Mainstream Publishing, 1991), p. 25. Similarly, Turnbull's cartoon in the *Glasgow Herald* depicted 'the Scottish lion admitting "I'm feart"' (Devine, *The Scottish Nation*, p. 589).
6   Neal Ascherson, *Stone Voices: The Search for Scotland* (Granta, 2002), p. 108.
7   Eleanor Bell, *Questioning Scotland: Literature, Nationalism, Postmodernism* (Palgrave Macmillan, 2004), p. 100.
8   Douglas Gifford, 'Breaking Boundaries: From Modern to Contemporary in Scottish Fiction', in Ian Brown et al, *Edinburgh History of Scottish Literature: Modern Transformations: New Identities (from 1918)* (Edinburgh University Press, 2007), pp. 237–52 (p. 237).
9   Robert Crawford, *Scotland's Books* (Penguin, 2007), p. 661.
10 Murray Pittock, *The Road to Independence?* (Reaktion, 2008), p. 114.
11 Liam McIlvanney, 'The Politics of Narrative in the Post-War Scottish Novel', in Zachary Leader (ed.), *On Modern British Fiction* (Oxford University Press, 2002), pp. 181–208 (p. 186).
12 Randall Stevenson, 'A Postmodern Scotland?', in Gerard Carruthers, David Goldie and Alastair Renfrew (eds), *Beyond Scotland: New Contexts for Twentieth-century Scottish Literature* (Rodopi, 2004), pp. 209–28 (p. 224).
13 Cairns Craig, *Intending Scotland: Explorations in Scottish Culture Since the Enlightenment* (Edinburgh University Press, 2009), p. 8.
14 See Gerard Carruthers, 'Scottish Literature: Second Renaissance', in Laura Marcus and Peter Nicholls (eds), *Cambridge History of Twentieth-Century English Literature* (Cambridge University Press, 2005), pp. 668–84.
15 Berthold Schoene, 'Going Cosmopolitan: Reconstituting "Scottishness" in Post-devolution Criticism', in Berthold Schoene (ed.), *Edinburgh Companion to Contemporary Scottish Literature* (Edinburgh University Press, 2007), pp. 7–16 (p. 7).
16 Matthew Wickman, 'The Emergence of Scottish Studies', in Gerard Carruthers and Liam McIlvanney (eds), *Cambridge Companion to Scottish Literature* (Cambridge University Press, 2012), pp. 248–60 (p. 256).
17 Scott Hames, 'Introduction: Don't Feel Bought, You're Buying', in Hames (ed.), *Unstated: Writers on Scottish Independence* (Word Power, 2012), pp. 1–18 (p. 7).

18 Ibid.
19 Scott Hames, *The Literary Politics of Scottish Devolution: Voice, Class, Nation* (Edinburgh University Press, 2020), p. 24.
20 Cairns Craig, 'Introduction', in Craig (ed.), *The History of Scottish Literature, Vol. 4: The Twentieth Century* (Aberdeen University Press, 1988), pp. 1–9 (p. 7).
21 Wickman, p. 249.
22 McIlvanney, *Surviving the Shipwreck*, p. 155.
23 Stevenson, 'A Postmodern Scotland?', p. 215.
24 McIlvanney, *Surviving the Shipwreck*, p. 162.
25 Ian A. Bell, 'Imagine Living There: Form and Ideology in Contemporary Scottish Fiction', in Suzanne Hageman (ed.), *Studies in Scottish Fiction: 1945 to the Present* (Peter Lang, 1996), pp. 217–33 (p. 226).
26 Michael Gardiner, *From Trocchi to Trainspotting: Scottish Critical Theory since 1960* (Edinburgh University Press, 2006), pp. 2, 3.
27 Gavin Wallace, 'Voices in Empty Houses: The Novel of Damaged Identity', in Gavin Wallace and Randall Stevenson (eds), *The Scottish Novel Since the Seventies* (Edinburgh University Press, 1993), pp. 217–31 (p. 220).
28 Schoene, 'Going Cosmopolitan', pp. 7, 9.
29 Ibid., p. 9.
30 Wallace, p. 217.
31 Gardiner, p. 10.
32 Stevenson, 'A Postmodern Scotland?', p. 220.
33 Cairns Craig, 'Going Down to Hell is Easy: *Lanark*, Realism and the Limits of the Imagination', in Robert Crawford and Thom Nairn (eds), *The Arts of Alasdair Gray* (Edinburgh University Press, 1991), pp. 90–107 (p. 92).
34 Alasdair Gray, *Lanark: A Life in Four Books* (Picador, 1994), p. 484.
35 Alasdair Gray, *1982, Janine* (Canongate, 2003), p. 126.
36 Douglas Gifford, 'Private Confessions and Public Satire in the Fiction of Alasdair Gray', in *Chapman* 50–51, 10.1–2 (1987), pp. 101–16 (p. 115).
37 Alison Lumsden, 'Innovation and Reaction in the Fiction of Alasdair Gray', in Wallace and Stevenson (eds), *The Scottish Novel Since the Seventies*, pp. 115–26 (pp. 124, 125).
38 Craig, 'Going Down to Hell is Easy', p. 107.
39 Hames, *The Literary Politics of Scottish Devolution*, p. 289.
40 James Kelman, 'The Importance of Glasgow in my Work', in *Some Recent Attacks* (AK Press, 1992), p. 82.

41 Aaron Kelly, 'James Kelman and the Deterritorialisation of Power', in Schoene (ed.), *Edinburgh Companion to Contemporary Scottish Literature*, pp. 175–83 (p. 178).
42 Cairns Craig, 'Resisting Arrest: James Kelman', in *The Scottish Novel Since the Seventies*, pp. 99–114 (p. 101).
43 Carole Jones, *Disappearing Men: Gender Disorientation in Scottish Fiction 1979–1999* (Rodopi, 2009), p. 33.
44 Ibid., p. 31.
45 Craig, 'Resisting Arrest', p. 103.
46 Crawford, *Scotland's Books*, p. 666.
47 Craig, 'Resisting Arrest', p. 103.
48 See Carole Jones, 'James Kelman's Melancholic Politics', *Scottish Literary Review*, 7.1 (2015), pp. 89–112.
49 Jones, *Disappearing Men*, p. 64.
50 Cristie (*recte* Christie) L. March, 'Interview with Janice Galloway', *Edinburgh Review*, 101 (1999), pp. 85–98 (p. 85).
51 Glenda Norquay, 'Janice Galloway's Novels: Fraudulent Mooching', in Aileen Christianson and Alison Lumsden (eds), *Contemporary Scottish Women Writers* (Edinburgh University Press, 2000), pp. 131–43 (p. 131).
52 Janice Galloway, *The Trick Is to Keep Breathing* (Minerva, 1991), p. 235.
53 Gavin Wallace, 'Voyages of Intent: Literature and Cultural Politics in Post-devolution Scotland', in Schoene (ed.), *Edinburgh Companion to Contemporary Scottish Literature*, pp. 17–28 (p. 26).
54 Robert A. Morace, *Irvine Welsh* (Palgrave Macmillan, 2007), p. 24.
55 Aaron Kelly, *Irvine Welsh* (Manchester University Press, 2005), p. 14.
56 Berthold Schoene (ed.), 'Introduction', *Edinburgh Companion to Irvine Welsh* (Edinburgh University Press, 2010), pp. 1–8 (p. 3).
57 Ibid., p. 2.
58 See Craig, *The Modern Scottish Novel*, p. 97: 'a community's self-narration in dialect'.
59 Morace, p. 26.
60 Irvine Welsh, *Trainspotting* (Minerva, 1994), p. 188.
61 Carole Jones, 'Post-Meta-Modern-Realism', in *The Review of Contemporary Fiction*, 32.3 (2012), pp. 79–86 (p. 79).
62 Timothy C. Baker, 'The Lonely Island: Exile and Community in Recent Island Writing', in Scott Lyall (ed.), *Community in Modern Scottish Literature* (Brill Rodopi, 2016), pp. 25–42 (p. 27).

63 Douglas Gifford, 'Breaking Boundaries', p. 244.
64 Ibid., p. 245.
65 Gardiner, *From Trocchi to Trainspotting*, p. 4.
66 McIlvanney, *Surviving the Shipwreck*, p. 155.
67 Ibid., p. 162.
68 Gill Plain, 'Concepts of Corruption: Crime Fiction and the Scottish "State"', in Schoene (ed.), *Edinburgh Companion to Contemporary Scottish Literature*, pp. 132–40 (p. 132).
69 Ibid., p. 133.
70 Ibid., p. 134.
71 Ibid.
72 Thomas Christie, *Notional Identities: Ideology, Genre and National Identity in Popular Scottish Fiction since the Seventies* (Cambridge Scholars, 2013), p. 158.
73 Caroline McCracken-Flesher (ed.), 'Introduction', in *Scotland as Science Fiction* (Bucknell University Press, 2012), p. 2.
74 Ibid.
75 Gavin Miller, 'Iain (M.) Banks: Utopia, Nationalism and the Posthuman', in Schoene (ed.), *Edinburgh Companion to Contemporary Scottish Literature*, pp. 203–09 (pp. 203, 207.)
76 John Garrison, 'Speculative Nationality: "Stands Scotland Where It Did?" in the Culture of Iain M. Banks', in McCracken-Flesher (ed.), *Scotland as Science Fiction*, p. 57.
77 Miller, p. 209.
78 Tim Baker, 'Writing Scotland's Future: Speculative Fiction and the National Imagination', *Studies in Scottish Literature*, 42.2 (2016), pp. 248–66 (p. 266).
79 Peter Clandfield and Christian Lloyd, 'Redevelopment Fiction: Architecture, Town-planning and "Unhomeliness"', in Schoene (ed.), *Edinburgh Companion to Contemporary Scottish Literature*, pp. 124–31 (p. 129).
80 Ibid., p. 128.

10. The First Hundred Years of the Gaelic Novel

1 See Moray Watson, *An Introduction to Gaelic Fiction* (Edinburgh University Press, 2011), pp. 1–11; W. Gillies, 'On the Study of Gaelic Literature' in Michel Byrne, Thomas Owen Clancy and Sheila Kidd (eds), *Litreachas & Eachdraidh: Rannsachadh na Gàidhlig 2: Glaschu 2002 / Literature & History: Papers from the Second Conference of Scottish Gaelic Studies: Glasgow 2002* (Roinn nan Cànanan Ceilteach,

2006), pp. 1–32; Derick Thomson, 'Scottish Gaelic Literary History and Criticism in the Twentieth Century', *Aiste: Rannsachadh air Litreachas Gàidhlig: Studies in Gaelic Literature*, 1 (2007), pp. 1–21.
2 Michelle Macleod, *A Century of Gaelic Drama* (Association for Scottish Literary Studies, 2021).
3 See Ronald Black's useful introductory essay in his anthology *An Tuil* (Polygon, 1999).
4 To understand the situation, consider both of Donald John MacLeod's articles titled 'Gaelic Prose' – *Transactions of the Gaelic Society of Inverness*, vol. XLIX (1974–1976), pp. 198–230; Cairns Craig (ed.), *The History of Scottish Literature, Volume 4: Twentieth Century* (Aberdeen University Press, 1987), pp. 331–35, for more information that might fill in the necessary context.
5 Moray Watson, *An Introduction to Gaelic Fiction* (Edinburgh University Press, 2011).
6 Petra Johana Poncarová, 'The Gaelic Cosmopolite', *Litteraria Pragensia*, 27 (2017), pp. 36–48 (p. 39).
7 Petra Johana Poncarová, '*An Druim Bho Thuath*: Tormod Caimbeul's Last Vista of Gaelic Scotland', *Litteraria Pragensia* 28 (2018), pp. 70–81 (p. 80).
8 R. MacIlleDhuibh (Ronald Black), 'O Choinneach Mòr gu Eilean Nog – an turas annasach aig Alasdair Caimbeul', *The Scotsman*, 1 October 2011.
9 Itamar Even-Zohar, 'The Position of Translated Literature within the Literary Polysystem', in James S. Holmes, J. Lambert, and R. van den Broeck (eds), *Literature and Translation: New Perspectives in Literary Studies* (Acco, 1978) pp. 117–27.

11. Scottish Detective Fiction

1 Irvine Welsh, *Crime* (Jonathan Cape, 2008), p. 332.
2 See Matthew Wickman, 'Tartan Noir, or, Hard-Boiled Heidegger', *Scottish Literary Review*, 5.1 (2013), pp. 87–109.
3 Welsh, *Crime*, p. 338.
4 Ibid., p. 173.
5 On the connection of Welsh's *Crime* to the detective novels of Raymond Chandler and Ian Rankin, see Linden Peach, *Masquerade, Crime and Fiction: Criminal Deceptions* (Palgrave, 2006), p. 19. On the departure of *Crime* from Welsh's previous work, see Berthold Schoene, 'Introduction', in Berthold Schoene (ed.), *The Edinburgh Companion to Irvine Welsh* (Edinburgh University Press, 2010), p. 8, and Matt

McGuire, 'Welsh's Novels', *The Edinburgh Companion to Irvine Welsh*, p. 29.
6   Leonard Cassuto, *Hard-Boiled Sentimentality: The Secret History of American Crime Stories* (Columbia University Press, 2009), pp. 2, 3, 7.
7   Lee Horsley, *The Noir Thriller* (Palgrave, 2001), p. 265.
8   Martin Heidegger, *Introduction to Metaphysics*, trans. Gregory Fried and Richard Polt (Yale Nota Bene, 2000), p. 40.
9   See Wickman, 'Tartan Noir, or, Hard-Boiled Heidegger', pp. 88–90.
10 William McIlvanney, *Laidlaw* (Harcourt, Brace, and Company, 1977), p. 9, p. 72.
11 Heidegger, 'What Are Poets For?', *Poetry, Language, Thought*, trans. Albert Hofstadter (Perennial, 1971), p. 92.
12 Raymond Chandler, 'The Simple Art of Murder', *Later Novels and Other Writings* (Library of America, 1995), pp. 991–92.
13 Heidegger, 'What Is Metaphysics?', *Basic Writings*, p. 94.
14 Heidegger, 'On the Essence of Truth', *Basic Writings*, p. 130.
15 Heidegger, 'The Question Concerning Technology', *Basic Writings*, p. 330.
16 Heidegger, 'What Calls for Thinking?', *Basic Writings*, p. 374.
17 Heidegger, 'The Way to Language', *Basic Writings*, p. 409.
18 See Michael Cohen, *Murder Most Fair: The Appeal of Mystery Fiction* (Marleigh Dickinson University Press, 2000), p. 110.
19 Horsley, *The Noir Thriller*, p. 16.
20 Koichi Suwabe, 'The Case of the Femme Fatale: A Poetics of Hard-boiled Detective Fiction', *The Journal of the American Literature Society of Japan*, 2 (2003), pp. 55–72 (p. 61). Cf. Patricia Merivale, 'Gumshoe Gothics: Poe's "Man of the Crowd"', in Merivale and Susan Elizabeth Sweeney (eds), *Detecting Texts: The Metaphysical Detective Story from Poe to Postmodernism* (University of Pennsylvania Press, 1999), pp. 101–16 (p. 101).
21 See, for example, Arthur Conan Doyle, *The Sign of Four*, in *Sherlock Holmes: The Complete Stories* (Wordsworth Editions, 1989), pp. 97–98.
22 Ian Rankin, *Let It Bleed* (St Martin's, 1996), p. 12.
23 Jon Thompson, *Fiction, Crime, and Empire: Clues to Modernity and Postmodernism* (University of Illinois Press, 1993), p. 146.
24 Ronald R. Thomas, *Detective Fiction and the Rise of Forensic Science* (Cambridge University Press, 1999), p. 91.
25 See Gilles Deleuze, 'The Philosophy of Crime Novels', trans. Michael Taormina, in David Lapoujade (ed.), Deleuze, *Desert Islands and Other Texts, 1953–1974* (Semiotext(e), 2004), p. 81, p. 82.

26 Ernst Bloch, 'A Philosophical View of the Detective Novel', trans. Roswitha Mueller and Stephen Thaman, *Discourse*, 2 (Summer 1980), pp. 32–52 (p. 40).
27 Horsley, *The Noir Thriller*, p. 9.
28 Edgar Allan Poe, *The Complete Tales and Poems* (Vintage, 1975), p. 141. Compare with Reid's argument concerning the inaccessibility of the mind's origins in the Introduction to *An Inquiry into the Human Mind, on the Principles of Common Sense* (1764).
29 Glenn W. Most, 'The Hippocratic Smile: John le Carré and the Traditions of the Detective Novel', in Most and William W. Stowe (eds), *The Poetics of Murder: Detective Fiction and Literary Theory* (Harcourt Brace Jovanovich, 1983), pp. 341–65 (p. 344).
30 See Paul Gorner, 'Reid, Husserl and Phenomenology', *British Journal for the History of Philosophy*, 9 (2001), pp. 545–55. For a broader discussion of the nineteenth-century Scottish revision of idealist philosophy, see Cairns Craig, *Associationism and the Literary Imagination: From the Phantasmal Chaos* (Edinburgh University Press, 2007), pp. 41–83.
31 Thompson, *Fiction, Crime, and Empire*, p. 63.
32 Thomas, *Detective Fiction and the Rise of Forensic Science*, p. 237.
33 Ibid., p. 119.
34 I discuss Reid's thought experiment more extensively in *Literature after Euclid: The Geometric Imagination in the Long Scottish Enlightenment* (University of Pennsylvania Press, 2016), pp. 45–46.
35 Ian Rankin, *Rebus's Scotland: A Personal Journey* (Orion, 2005), pp. 85–86.
36 Ibid.
37 Dennis Porter, *The Pursuit of Crime: Art and Ideology in Detective Fiction* (Yale University Press, 1981), p. 162.
38 See Charles J. Rzepka, *Detective Fiction* (Polity, 2005), p. 227. Lewis Moore briefly rehearses the 'surprising development' of the hard-boiled genre in Britain in *Cracking the Hard-Boiled Detective: A Critical History from the 1920s to the Present* (McFarland, 2006), p. 272.
39 See Thomas, *Detective Fiction and the Rise of Forensic Science*, p. 115.
40 See Frank A. Salamone, '*Black Mask* and the Origins of the Hard-Boiled Detective: An Anthropologist's View', *Dime Novel Round-Up*, 67.3 (1998), pp. 75–94 (p. 90). On Twain's satirising of Pinkerton, see Thomas, *Detective Fiction and the Rise of Forensic Science*, p. 244.
41 Sean McCann discusses how Raymond Chandler 'praised the language of the pulps. As a kind of 'vernacular' expression, pulp language

seemed to him less a form of mystification than a repository of neglected popular virtues.' *Gumshoe America: Hard-Boiled Crime Fiction and the Rise and Fall of New Deal Liberalism* (Duke University Press, 2000), p. 147.

42 William McIlvanney, *The Papers of Tony Veitch* (Harcourt Brace and Company, 1983), p. 18.
43 Russell D. McLean, *The Lost Sister* (Five Leaves Publications, 2009), p. 33.
44 See Stephen Knight, *Crime Fiction since 1800: Detection, Death, Diversity* (Palgrave Macmillan, 2010), pp. 160–61.
45 See Margery Palmer McCulloch, *Scottish Modernism and Its Contexts, 1918–1959: Literature, National Identity and Cultural Exchange* (Edinburgh University Press, 2009), pp. 131–53.
46 Lewis Grassic Gibbon, *Sunset Song* (1932; Penguin, 2007), p. 126.
47 Hugh MacDiarmid, 'Scotland', in Michael Grieve and W. R. Aitken (eds), *The Complete Poems of Hugh MacDiarmid*, 2 vols (Penguin, 1985), I: p. 652, ll. 1–4.
48 Ian Rankin, *Black and Blue* (Orion, 1998), p. 71.
49 Ibid., p. 144.
50 Ibid., p. 78.
51 Heidegger, 'What Is Metaphysics?', pp. 100–01.
52 Rankin, *Rebus's Scotland*, p. 128.
53 Ibid., p. 117.
54 Russel D. McLean, *The Lost Sister* (Five Leaves, 2009).
55 Liam McIlvanney, *All the Colours of the Town* (Faber and Faber, 2009), pp. 32–33.
56 Stuart MacBride, *Cold Granite* (HarperCollins, 2005), p. 447.
57 Karen Campbell, *After the Fire* (Hodder, 2009), p. 10.
58 Karen Campbell, *The Twilight Time* (Hodder, 2008), p. 294.
59 Ibid., p. 15.
60 Ibid., p. 335.
61 John Burnside, 'Urban Myths', in Donny O'Rourke (ed.), *Dream State: The New Scottish Poets* (Polygon, 1994), p. 8.
62 John Burnside, *Glister* (Vintage, 2008), pp. 121, 122.

12. Scottish Science Fiction and Fantasy

1 David Pringle, 'Introduction: Scotlands Old and New', in Neil Williamson and Andrew J. Wilson (eds), *Nova Scotia: New Scottish Speculative Fiction* (Crescent, 2005), p. x.
2 Ibid., p. xii.

3 Gavin Miller, 'Scottish Science Fiction: Writing Scottish Literature Back into History', *Études Écossaises*, 12 (2009), pp. 121–133 (p. 122), doi:10.4000/etudesecossaises.197
4 See Colin Manlove, *Scotland's Forgotten Treasure: The Visionary Romances of George MacDonald* (Aberdeen University Press, 2016), ch. 4, and 'The Elecromagnetic World of George MacDonald's Visionary Romances', *Journal of Scottish Thought*, 12 (2020), pp. 144–58, doi:10.57132/jst.10
5 Caroline McCracken-Flesher, 'Introduction', in Caroline McCracken-Flesher (ed.), *Scotland as Science Fiction* (Bucknell University Press, 2012) pp. 1–14 (p. 2).
6 John Clute, 'Fantastika: Or, the Sacred Grove', *Fantastika Journal*, 1.1, (2017), pp. 13–20.
7 C.S. Lewis, *George MacDonald: An Anthology* (Harper Collins, 2015), p. xxxiv.
8 Colin Manlove, *Scottish Fantasy Literature: A Critical Survey* (Tuckwell Press, 1994), p. v.
9 George MacDonald, *Phantastes: A Faerie Romance for Men and Women* (Smith, Elder & Co., 1858), p. 185.
10 Colin Manlove, 'The Elecromagnetic World of George MacDonald's Visionary Romances', pp. 144–58.
11 Brian Aldiss, *Billion Year Spree: The True History of Science Fiction* (Weidenfeld and Nicolson, 1973).
12 Mary Shelley, *Frankenstein* (Gallery 13, 2020), p. xxx.
13 George Gregory Smith, *Scottish Literature: Character and Influence* (Macmillan and Co., 1919). See also 'The Caledonian Antisyzygy of George Gregory Smith' in Gerard Carruthers, *Scottish Literature* (Edinburgh University Press, 2009), pp. 11–13.
14 Thomas Connolly, *After Human: A Critical History of the Human in Science Fiction from Shelley to Le Guin* (Liverpool University Press, 2021), p. 37.
15 James Leslie Mitchell, *Three Go Back* (Jarrolds Publishers, 1932), p. 9.
16 Ibid, p. 91.
17 James Leslie Mitchell, *Gay Hunter* (William Heinemann, 1934), p. vii.
18 George Hay, '*The Green Isle of the Great Deep* by Neil Gunn (Review)', *Foundation: The International Review of Science Fiction* (March 1977), p. 65.
19 Gavin Miller, 'Animals, empathy, and care in Naomi Mitchison's *Memoirs of a Spacewoman*', *Science Fiction Studies*, 35.2 (2008), pp. 251–65.

20 For example, see Claire Allen, 'Beyond Postmodernism in Alasdair Gray's *Lanark*', in Nicola Allen, David Simmons (eds), *Reassessing the Twentieth-Century Canon* (Palgrave Macmillan, 2014).
21 Alasdair Gray, *Lanark: A Life in Four Books* (Canongate, 1981), p. 243.
22 John Corbett, 'Past and Future Language: Matthew Fitt and Iain M. Banks', in Caroline McCracken-Flesher (ed.), *Scotland as Science Fiction* (Bucknell University Press, 2012), pp. 117–132 (p. 119).
23 Matthew Fitt, *But n Ben A-Go-Go* (Luath Press, 2000), p. 12.
24 Ibid, p. 5.
25 Anna McFarlane, 'Ectogenesis on the NHS: Reproduction and Privatisation in 21st Century British Science Fiction', in Sümeyra Buran and Sherryl Vint (eds), *Technologies of Feminist Speculative Fiction: Gender, Artificial Life, Reproduction* (Palgrave Macmillan, 2022), pp. 21–44.
26 Gavin Miller, 'Animals, empathy, and care in Naomi Mitchison's *Memoirs of a Spacewoman*', p. 127.
27 Jenni Fagan, *The Panopticon* (Windmill Books, 2013), p. 6.
28 Gavin Miller, 'Scottish Science Fiction: Writing Scottish Literature Back into History', p. 125.

13. Scottish Children's and Young Adult Fiction

1 Quoted in Robert Lee Wolff, *The Golden Key: A Study of the Fiction of George MacDonald* (Yale University Press, 1961), p. 168.
2 W. W. Robson, *The Definition of Literature and Other Essays* (Cambridge University Press, 1982), p. 95.
3 Sarah Dunnigan 'Introduction', in Sarah Dunnigan and Shu-Fang Lai (eds), *The Land of Story-Books: Scottish Children's Literature in the Long Nineteenth Century* (Scottish Literature International, 2019), p. x.
4 Maureen A. Farrell and Robert A. Davis (eds), *The International Companion to Scottish Children's Literature* (Scottish Literature International, 2024)
5 See Paul Barnaby, 'The Young Person's Sir Walter: Scott and the Nineteenth-Century Child Reader', in Dunnigan and Shu-Fang Lai, *The Land of Story-Books*, pp. 20–41.
6 Alasdair Gray, *Lanark* (Canongate, 1981), p. 493.
7 Jacqueline Rose, *The Case of Peter Pan: or the Impossibility of Children's Fiction* (Macmillan, 1994), p. 65.
8 R. M. Ballantyne, *The Coral Island* (Nelson, 1897), p. 212.
9 J. M. Barrie, *Peter Pan* (1911; Penguin, 1967), p. 19.

10 Ibid., p. 74.
11 Robson, *The Definition of Literature*, pp. 95–96.
12 Fiona McCulloch, 'A Key to the Future: Hybridity in Contemporary Children's Fiction', in Berthold Schoene (ed.), *The Edinburgh Companion to Contemporary Scottish Literature* (Edinburgh University Press, 2007), p. 141.
13 The 'Church and Nation Committee' of the Church of Scotland, under the convenorship of Dr John White, issued a report entitled '*The Menace of the Irish Race to our Scottish Nationality*', which initiated over a decade of anti-Catholic propaganda which culminated in mob violence.
14 See, for instance, the number of books that included 'New Scotland' in their title, for instance Alison Park, *New, New Politics* (2001); John Curtice, David McCrone, Alison Park and Lindsay Paterson (eds), *New Scotland, New Society* (2002); the re-establishment of the Scottish Parliament also initiated projects involving significant revisions of the Scottish past, such as Roger Mason et al. (eds), *The New Edinburgh History of Scotland* (2008–) and Ian Brown et al. (eds), *The Edinburgh History of Scottish Literature* (2007).
15 Roberta Seelinger Trites, *Disturbing the Universe: Power and Repression in Adolescent Literature* (University of Iowa Press, 2000), p. 19.
16 Michael Gardiner, 'Literature, Theory, Politics: Devolution as Iteration', in Berthold Schoene (ed.), *The Edinburgh Companion to Contemporary Scottish Literature*, p. 48.
17 Ibid.
18 Bruce Robbins and Paulo Lemos Horta, 'Introduction', in Robbins and Horta (eds), *Cosmopolitanisms* (New York University Press, 2017), p. 3; 'cosmopolitanism of the poor' they attribute to Silviano Santiago.
19 Rosi Braidotti, *Transpositions: On Nomadic Ethics* (Polity Press, 2006), p. 35.
20 Anne Donovan, *Being Emily* (2008; Canongate, 2009), p. 161.
21 Ibid., p. 204.
22 Ibid., p. 23.
23 For further discussion, see McCulloch, '"It Was Hame": Cosmopolitan Belonging in Anne Donovan's *Being Emily*', in *C21 Literature: Journal of 21st-Century Writings*, 5.2 (March 2017), pp. 1–23, doi:10.16995/c21.22
24 Julie Bertagna, *Exodus* (2002; Pan MacMillan, 2003), p. 178.
25 For further discussion, see McCulloch, '"A New Home in the World": Nomadic Writing and World Citizenship in Julie Bertagna's *Exodus*

Trilogy', in Fiona McCulloch, *Contemporary British Children's Fiction and Cosmopolitanism* (Routledge, 2017), pp. 150–74. For fuller consideration of cosmofeminism, see Carol A. Breckenridge, Sheldon Pollock, Homi K. Bhabha, and Dipesh Chakrabarty, *Cosmopolitanism* (Duke University Press, 2002).

26 See also Sarah Dunnigan, 'A "Spell of Stories": Scottish Children's Fantasy', in Farrel and Davis (eds), pp. 78–98.
27 Claire McFall, *Bombmaker* (Templar, 2014), p. 23.
28 Ibid.
29 Ibid., p. 24.
30 Ibid., pp. 26–27.
31 Ibid., p. 207.
32 See, for instance, 'BBC's Scottish independence coverage accused of pro-union bias', *Guardian*, 2 June 2014.
33 This novel is further discussed in Fiona McCulloch, 'Adolescent Citizenship in Cathy MacPhail's *Mosi's War* and Claire McFall's *Bombmaker*', in Farrell and Davis (eds), pp. 149–65.
34 Donald Lightwood, *The Long Revenge* (Scottish Children's Press, 2002), p. 5, p. 6.
35 Ibid., p. 125.
36 Ibid., p. 22.
37 Ibid., p. 22.
38 Ibid., pp. 22 and 23.
39 Ibid., p. 31.
40 Ibid., p. 32.
41 Ibid., p. 33.
42 Ibid., p. 40.
43 Ross Sayers, *Sonny and Me* (Cranachan Publishing, 2019), p. 25.
44 Ibid., p. 26.
45 Ibid., p. 25.
46 Ibid., p. 325.
47 Ibid., p. 334.
48 Ibid., p. 26.
49 Ibid., p. 27.
50 Ibid., p. 49.
51 Ibid., p. 64.
52 Ibid., p. 82.
53 Ibid., p. 320.
54 Martin Stewart, *The Sacrifice Box* (Penguin, 2018), p. 21.
55 Ibid.

56 Ibid., p. 390.
57 Ibid., p. 35.
58 Ibid., p. 35.
59 Ibid., p. 39.
60 Ibid., p. 58.
61 Ibid., pp. 58–59.
62 Ibid., p. 234.
63 Ibid., p. 245.
64 Ibid., p. 248.
65 Ibid., p. 257.
66 Ibid., p. 262.
67 Ibid., p. 269.
68 Ibid., p. 273.
69 Ibid., p. 276.
70 Cairns Craig, *Intending Scotland: Explorations in Scottish Culture Since the Enlightenment* (Edinburgh University Press, 2009).
71 Stewart, p. 381.
72 Ibid.
73 Ibid., p. 385.
74 Sylvia Hehir, *Sea Change* (Stone Cold Fox Press, 2019), p. 36.
75 Ibid.
76 Ibid., p. 307.
77 Ibid., p. 299.
78 Ibid., p. 298.
79 Ibid., p. 306.
80 Ibid., p. 60.
81 Ibid.
82 Ibid., p. 306.
83 Ibid., p. 307.
84 Ibid.
85 Ibid.
86 Ibid., p. 202.
87 Ibid., p. 307.
88 'The Joy of Food': www.nationalgeographic.com/foodfeatures/joy-of-food.
89 Ibid., p. 202.
90 Laura Guthrie, *Anna* (Cranachan Publishing, 2020), p. 350.
91 Ibid., p. 318.
92 Ibid., p. 351.
93 Ibid., p. 351.

94 Ibid., p. 239.
95 Ibid., p. 251.
96 Ibid., p. 6.
97 Roderick McGillis, 'Criticism Is the Theory of Literature': 'Theory Is the Criticism of Literature', in David Rudd (ed.), *The Routledge Companion to Children's Literature* (Routledge, 2010), p. 14.
98 For further discussion of the link between YA fiction and cortical development, see Fiona McCulloch, '"My World Has Become Smaller": Cortically Remapping Postfeminist Confinement in Louise O'Neill's *Asking For It*', in Anne Marie Hagen, *Mediation and Children's Reading: Relationships, Intervention, and Organization from the Eighteenth Century to the Present* (Lehigh University Press, 2022), pp. 199–224.
99 Fiona McCulloch, *Contemporary British Children's Fiction and Cosmopolitanism* (Routledge, 2017).
100 McGillis, p. 14.

14. Into the Twenty-First Century

1 Ali Smith, *There but for the* (2011; Penguin, 2012), p. 3.
2 Ibid., p. 201.
3 Ibid., p. 235.
4 Ibid., p. 231.
5 Ibid., pp. 246–47.
6 Ibid., p. 261.
7 Andrew Greig, *That Summer* (Faber and Faber, 2000), p. 30.
8 Ibid., p. 23.
9 Ibid., p. 113.
10 Ibid.
11 Ibid., p. 232.
12 A. L. Kennedy, *Day* (2007; Penguin, 2008), p. 234.
13 Ibid., p. 236.
14 Ibid., pp. 236–37.
15 Ibid., p. 237.
16 Ibid., p. 276.
17 Ibid., p. 279.
18 Andrew O'Hagan, *Personality* (Faber and Faber, 2003), p. 202.
19 Ibid., p. 185.
20 Ibid., p. 186.
21 Ibid., p. 177.
22 Ibid., p. 63.
23 James Robertson, *And the Land Lay Still* (2010; Penguin, 2011), p. 224.

24 Ibid., p. 198.
25 Ibid., p. 212.
26 Ibid., p. 645.
27 Kennedy, *Day*, pp. 197–98.
28 O'Hagan, *Personality*, pp. 186–87.
29 Saadi, *Joseph's Box*, p. 429.
30 Ibid., p. 337.
31 Andrew Crumey, *The Great Chain of Unbeing* (Dedalus Books, 2018), pp. 7–8.
32 Ibid., p. 15.
33 Alan Spence, *The Pure Land* (2006; Canongate, 2007), p. 1.
34 Ibid., p. 336.
35 Ibid., p. 355.
36 Ibid., p. 370
37 Ibid., p. 390.
38 Ibid.
39 James Kelman, *Translated Accounts* (2001; Polygon, 2009), p. 242.
40 Ibid., p. 238.
41 Ibid., p. 297.
42 James Kelman, *You Have to Be Careful in the Land of the Free* (Hamish Hamilton, 2004), p. 175.
43 James Kelman, *Kieron Smith, Boy* (Hamish Hamilton, 2008), pp. 198–99.
44 Ibid., p. 348.
45 Ewan Morrison, *How to Survive Everything* (Contraband, 2021), p. 359.
46 Suhayl Saadi, *Psychoraag* (Black and White, 2004), pp. 115–16.
47 Ibid.
48 Leila Aboulela, *Minaret* (Bloomsbury, 2005), p. 256.
49 Ali Smith, *Hotel World* (2001; Penguin, 2002), p. 47.
50 Ibid., p. 45.
51 Ibid., p. 44.
52 Ibid., p. 45.
53 Ibid., p. 226.
54 Andrew Crumey, *Sputnik Caledonia* (2008; Dedalus, 2015), pp. 407–08.
55 Ibid., p. 91.
56 Ibid., p. 125.
57 Crumey, p. 389.
58 James Robertson, *News of the Dead* (Penguin Books, 2021), pp. 229–30.
59 Ibid., pp. 79–80.

60 Ibid., p. 296.
61 Ibid., p. 5.
62 Ibid.
63 Ibid., p. 6.
64 Ibid.
65 John Burnside, *A Summer of Drowning* (Vintage, 2012), p. 4.
66 Ibid., p. 77.
67 Ali Smith, *Autumn* (Hamish Hamilton, 2016); *Winter* (Hamish Hamilton, 2017); *Spring* (Hamish Hamilton, 2019); *Summer* (Hamish Hamilton, 2020).
68 Smith, *Autumn*, p. 17.
69 Smith, *Winter*, pp. 197 ff.
70 Smith, *Spring*, p. 327.
71 Smith, *Summer*, p. 3.
72 Northrop Frye, *Anatomy of Criticism: Four Essays* (Princeton University Press, 1957), p. 182.
73 See, for instance, p. 48, p. 62, p. 71; 'On the archetypal level proper, where poetry is an artifact of human civilization, nature is the container of man. On the anagogic [i.e. spiritual] level, man is the container of nature, and his cities and gardens are no longer little hollowings on the surface of the earth, but the forms of a human universe', p. 145. Smith acknowledges the influence of Gillian Beer's 'immortal Winter's Tale tale', and Beer acknowledges the influence of Frye in Chapter 2 of her book on *The Romance* (Routledge, 1970).
74 Smith, *Autumn*, p. 235.
75 Ibid., p. 45.
76 Ibid., p. 195.

Further Reading

James Acheson and Sarah Ross (eds), *The Contemporary British Novel since 1980* (Palgrave Macmillan, 2005).
Neal Ascherson, *Stone Voices: The Search for Scotland* (Granta, 2002).
Timothy C. Baker, *Contemporary Scottish Gothic: Mourning, Authenticity, and Tradition* (Palgrave Macmillan, 2014).
Mikhail Bakhtin, 'Dialogic Imagination: Four Essays', in Michael Holquist (ed.) (University of Texas Press, 1981).
Jerry C. Beasley, *Tobias Smollett, Novelist* (University of Georgia Press, 1998).
Eleanor Bell, *Questioning Scotland: Literature, Nationalism, Postmodernism* (Palgrave Macmillan, 2004).
Stephen Bernstein, *Alasdair Gray* (Bucknell University Press, 1999).
Linden Bicket and Douglas Gifford (eds), *The Fiction of Robin Jenkins: Some Kind of Grace* (Brill | Rodopi, 2017).
Alan Bold (ed.), *Smollett: Author of the First Distinction* (Vision and Barnes and Noble, 1982).
Alan Bold, *Modern Scottish Literature* (Longman, 1983).
Valentina Bold, *James Hogg: A Bard of Nature's Making* (Peter Lang, 2007).
Valentina Bold and Andrew Nash (eds), *Gateway to the Modern: Resituating J.M. Barrie* (Scottish Literature International, 2014).
H. Philip Bolton, *Scott Dramatized* (Mansell, 1992).
Peter Boxall and Brian Cheyette (eds), *The Oxford History of the Novel in English: Vol. 7: British and Irish Fiction since 1940* (Oxford University Press, 2016).
O. M. Brack, Jr, (ed.), *Tobias Smollett, Scotland's First Novelist* (University of Delaware Press, 2007).
Callum G. Brown, *Religion and Society in Scotland since 1707* (Edinburgh University Press, 1997).

Ian Brown (ed.), *The Edinburgh History of Scottish Literature, Vol. 3 – Modern Transformations: New Identities (from 1918)* (Edinburgh University Press, 2007).

Ian Brown and Alan Riach (eds), *The Edinburgh Companion to Twentieth-Century Scottish Literature* (Edinburgh University Press, 2009).

John Buchan, *Sir Walter Scott* (1932; Cassell, 1987).

John Burns, *A Celebration of the Light: Zen in the Novels of Neil Gunn* (Canongate, 1988).

Michel Byrne, Thomas Owen Clancy and Sheila Kidd (eds), *Litreachas & Eachdraidh: Rannsachadh na Gàidhlig 2: Glaschu 2002 / Literature & History: Papers from the Second Conference of Scottish Gaelic Studies: Glasgow 2002* (Roinn nan Cànanan Ceilteach, 2006).

Ian Campbell (ed.), *Nineteenth-Century Scottish Fiction: Critical Essays* (Carcanet New Press, 1979).

Gerard Carruthers, David Goldie and Alastair Renfrew (eds), *Beyond Scotland: New Contexts for Twentieth-century Scottish Literature* (Rodopi, 2004).

Gerard Carruthers, *Scottish Literature* (Edinburgh University Press, 2009).

Gerard Carruthers, David Goldie, and Alastair Renfrew (eds), *Scotland and the 19th-century World* (Rodopi, 2012).

Gerard Carruthers and Liam McIlvanney (eds), *Cambridge Companion to Scottish Literature* (Cambridge University Press, 2012).

Gerard Carruthers and Colin Kidd (eds.), *The International Companion to John Galt* (Scottish Literature International, 2017).

Gerard Carruthers and Colin Kidd (eds), *Literature & Union: Scottish Texts, British Contexts* (Oxford University Press, 2018).

Aileen Christianson and Alison Lumsden (eds), *Contemporary Scottish Women Writers* (Edinburgh University Press, 2000).

Thomas Christie, *Notional Identities: Ideology, Genre and National Identity in Popular Scottish Fiction since the Seventies* (Cambridge Scholars, 2013).

Daniel Cook and Nicholas Seager (eds), *The Afterlives of Eighteenth-Century Fiction* (Cambridge University Press, 2015).

Cairns Craig (ed.), *The History of Scottish Literature, Vol. 4: The Twentieth Century* (Aberdeen University Press, 1988).

Cairns Craig, *Out of History* (Polygon, 1996).

Cairns Craig, *The Modern Scottish Novel: Narrative and the National Imagination* (Edinburgh University Press, 1999).

Cairns Craig, *Associationism and the Literary Imagination: From the Phantasmal Chaos* (Edinburgh University Press, 2007).

Cairns Craig, *Intending Scotland: Explorations in Scottish Culture Since the Enlightenment* (Edinburgh University Press, 2009).
Cairns Craig, *The Wealth of the Nation: Scotland, Culture and Independence* (Edinburgh University Press, 2018).
Cairns Craig, *Muriel Spark, Existentialism and the Art of Death* (Edinburgh University Press, 2019).
Robert Crawford and Thom Nairn (eds), *The Arts of Alasdair Gray* (Edinburgh University Press, 1991).
Robert Crawford, *Devolving English Literature* (Clarendon Press, 1992).
Leith Davis, *Acts of Union: Scotland and the Literary Negotiation of the British Nation, 1707-1830* (Stanford University Press, 1998).
Leith Davis et al. (eds), *Scotland and the Borders of Romanticism* (Cambridge University Press, 2004).
Leith Davis and Janet Sorenson (eds), *The International Companion to Scottish Literature of the Long Eighteenth Century* (Scottish Literature International, 2021)
T. M. Devine, *The Scottish Nation 1700-2000* (Penguin, 2000).
Ian Duncan, *Modern Romance: The Gothic, Scott, Dickens* (Cambridge University Press, 1992).
Ian Duncan, *Scott's Shadow: The Novel in Romantic Edinburgh* (Princeton University Press, 2007).
Ian Duncan and Douglas S. Mack (eds): *The Edinburgh Companion to James Hogg* (Edinburgh University Press, 2012).
Sarah Dunnigan and Shu-Fang Lai (eds), *The Land of Story-Books: Scottish Children's Literature in the Long Nineteenth Century* (Scottish Literature International, 2019).
Emma Dymock and Margery Palmer McCulloch (eds), *Scottish & International Modernisms* (Association for Scottish Literary Studies, 2011).
Maureen A. Farrell and Robert A. Davis (eds), *The International Companion to Scottish Children's Literature* (Scottish Literature International, 2024).
Penny Fielding (ed.), *The Edinburgh Companion to Robert Louis Stevenson* (Edinburgh University Press, 2009).
Penny Fielding, *Writing and Orality: Nationality, Culture and Nineteenth-Century Scottish Fiction* (Clarendon Press, 1996).
Penny Fielding, *Scotland and the Fictions of Geography: North Britain, 1760-1830* (Cambridge University Press, 2008).
E. M. Forster, *Aspects of the Novel* (1927; Penguin, 1976).
Northrop Frye, *Anatomy of Criticism: Four Essays* (Princeton University Press, 1957).

Northrop Frye, *The Secular Scripture: A Study of the Structure of Romance* (Harvard University Press, 1976).
Louisa Gairn, *Ecology and Modern Scottish Literature* (Edinburgh University Press, 2008).
Michael Gardiner, *From Trocchi to Trainspotting: Scottish Critical Theory since 1960* (Edinburgh University Press, 2006).
Michael Gardiner and Willy Maley (eds), *The Edinburgh Companion to Muriel Spark* (Edinburgh University Press, 2010).
Peter Garside, Rainer Schöwerling, Christopher Skelton-Foord, and Karin Wünsche (eds), *The English Novel 1770–1829: A Bibliographical Survey of Prose Fiction Published in the British Isles*, 2 vols (Oxford University Press, 2000).
Peter Garside and Karen O'Brien (eds), *The Oxford History of the Novel in English: Volume 2: English and British Fiction 1750–1820* (Oxford University Press, 2015).
Lewis Grassic Gibbon and Hugh MacDiarmid, *Scottish Scene or the Intelligent Man's Guide to Albyn* (1934; Cedric Chivers, 1974).
Douglas Gifford (ed.), *The History of Scottish Literature, vol. 3: The Nineteenth Century* (Aberdeen University Press, 1988).
Douglas Gifford and Dorothy McMillan (eds), *A History of Scottish Women's Writing* (Edinburgh University Press, 1997).
Douglas Gifford, *Neil M. Gunn and Lewis Grassic Gibbon* (Oliver & Boyd, 1983)
Douglas Gifford, *Scottish Literature* (Edinburgh University Press, 2002).
Adam Guy, *The Nouveau Roman and Writing in Britain after Modernism* (Oxford University Press, 2020).
Suzanne Hageman (ed.), *Studies in Scottish Fiction: 1945 to the Present* (Peter Lang, 1996).
Katherine Haldane Grenier, *Tourism and Identity in Scotland, 1770–1914* (Ashgate, 2005).
Scott Hames (ed.), *The Edinburgh Companion to James Kelman* (Edinburgh University Press, 2010).
Scott Hames (ed.), *Unstated: Writers on Scottish Independence* (Word Power, 2012).
Scott Hames, *The Literary Politics of Scottish Devolution: Voice, Class, Nation* (Edinburgh University Press, 2020).
Francis Russell Hart, *The Scottish Novel: A Critical Survey* (John Murray, 1978).
Arthur Herman, *The Scottish Enlightenment: The Scots' Invention of the Modern World* (Fourth Estate, 2002).

David Holbrook, *A Study of George MacDonald and the Image of Woman* (Edwin Mellin, 2000).
Joseph H. Jackson, *Writing Black Scotland: Race, Nation and the Devolution of Black Britain* (Edinburgh University Press, 2021).
Maroula Joannou (ed.), *The History of British Women's Writing (1900–1945)* (Palgrave, 2012).
Carole Jones, *Disappearing Men: Gender Disorientation in Scottish Fiction 1979-1999* (Rodopi, 2009).
Aaron Kelly, *Irvine Welsh* (Manchester University Press, 2005).
Sheila M. Kidd, Caroline McCracken-Flesher and Kenneth McNeil (eds), *The International Companion to Nineteenth-Century Scottish Literature* (Scottish Literature International, 2022).
Gustav H. Klaus, *James Kelman* (British Council, 2004).
Stephen Knight, *Crime Fiction since 1800: Detection, Death, Diversity* (Palgrave Macmillan, 2010).
Simon Kövesi, *James Kelman* (Manchester University Press, 2013).
Krishan Kumar, *The Making of English National Identity* (Cambridge University Press, 2003).
Sophie Laniel-Musitelli and Céline Sabiron, *Romanticism and Time: Literary Temporalities* (Open Book, 2021).
Zachary Leader (ed.), *On Modern British Fiction* (Oxford University Press, 2002).
Alison Light, *Forever England: Femininity, Literature and Conservatism Between the Wars* (Routledge, 1991).
Georg Lukács, *The Historical Novel*, trans. Hannah and Stanley Mitchell (1937; Peregrine, 1969).
Alison Lumsden, *Walter Scott and the Limits of Language* (Edinburgh University Press, 2008).
Scott Lyall (ed.), *Community in Modern Scottish Literature* (Brill Rodopi, 2016).
Scott Lyall (ed.), *The International Companion to Lewis Grassic Gibbon* (Scottish Literature International, 2015).
Caroline McCracken-Flesher, *Possible Scotlands: Walter Scott and the Story of Tomorrow* (Oxford University Press, 2005).
Caroline McCracken-Flesher (ed.), *Scotland as Science Fiction* (Bucknell University Press, 2012).
Caroline McCracken-Flesher and Matthew Wickman (eds), *Walter Scott at 250: Looking Forward* (Edinburgh University Press, 2021).
Kate MacDonald et al. (eds), *Transitions in Middlebrow Writing* (Macmillan, 2015).

Fiona McCulloch, *Contemporary British Children's Literature and Cosmopolitanism* (Routledge, 2016)

Margery Palmer McCulloch, *Modernism and Nationalism: Literature and Society in Scotland 1918–1939* (Association for Scottish Literary Studies, 2004).

Margery Palmer McCulloch, *Scottish Modernism and Its Contexts, 1918–1959: Literature, National Identity and Cultural Exchange* (Edinburgh University Press, 2009).

Josephine McDonagh, *Literature in a Time of Migration: British Fiction and the Movement of People, 1815–1876* (Oxford University Press, 2021).

Anna McFarlane, *Cyberpunk Culture and Psychology: Seeing through the Mirrorshades* (Routledge, 2021).

Christopher MacLachlan, John Patrick Padziora, and Ginger Stelle (eds), *Rethinking George MacDonald: Contexts and Contemporaries* (Scottish Literature International, 2013).

Martin McQuillan (ed.), *Theorizing Murial Spark: gender, race, deconstruction* (Macmillan, 2002).

William K. Malcolm, *Lewis Grassic Gibbon: A Revolutionary Writer* (Capercaille Books, 2016).

Colin Manlove, *Scottish Fantasy Literature: A Critical Survey* (Tuckwell Press, 1994).

Colin Manlove, *Scotland's Forgotten Treasure: The Visionary Romances of George MacDonald* (Aberdeen University Press, 2016).

Susan Manning (ed.), *The Edinburgh History of Scottish Literature: Vol. 2 – Enlightenment, Britain and Empire (1707-1918)* (Edinburgh University Press, 2007).

Louis L. Martz, *The Later Career of Tobias Smollett* (Archon Books, 1967).

Richard Maxwell and Katie Trumpener (eds), *The Cambridge Companion to Fiction in the Romantic Period* (Cambridge University Press, 2008).

Robert Mayer, *Walter Scott and Fame* (Oxford University Press, 2017).

Elsie Michie, *The Vulgar Question of Money: Heiresses, Materialism, and the Novel of Manners from Jane Austen to Henry James* (Johns Hopkins University Press, 2013).

Gavin Miller, *Alasdair Gray: The Fiction of Communion* (Rodopi, 2005)

Jane Millgate, *Walter Scott: The Making of the Novelist* (University of Toronto Press, 1984).

Robert A. Morace, *Irvine Welsh* (Palgrave Macmillan, 2007).

Edwin Muir, *Scott and Scotland: The Predicament of the Scottish Writer*, with an Introduction by Allan Massie (1936; Polygon, 1982).

John Mullan, *Sentiment and Sociability: The Language of Feeling in the Eighteenth Century* (Oxford University Press, 1990).
Tom Nairn, *The Break-Up of Britain: Crisis and Neo-Nationalism* (1977; Verso, 1981).
Andrew Nash, *Kailyard and Scottish Literature* (Rodopi, 2007).
Glenda Norquay (ed.), *R. L. Stevenson on Fiction: An Anthology of Literary and Critical Essays* (Edinburgh University Press, 1999).
Glenda Norquay (ed.), *The Edinburgh Companion to Scottish Women's Writing* (Edinburgh University Press, 2011).
Duncan Petrie, *Contemporary Scottish Fictions: Film, Television and the Novel* (Edinburgh University Press, 2004).
Murray Pittock, *The Road to Independence?* (Reaktion, 2008).
Murry Pittock, *Scottish and Irish Romanticism* (Oxford University Press, 2008)
Dennis Porter, *The Pursuit of Crime: Art and Ideology in Detective Fiction* (Yale University Press, 1981).
J. B. Priestley, *The English Novel* (Thomas Nelson, 1927).
Horst Prilinger, *Family and the Scottish Working-class Novel, 1984-1994* (Peter Lang, 2000).
William Raeper, *George MacDonald* (Lion Publishing, 1987).
Ann Rigney, *The Afterlives of Walter Scott: Memory on the Move* (Oxford University Press, 2012).
Fiona Robertson (ed.), *The Edinburgh Companion to Walter Scott* (Edinburgh University Press, 2012).
Jacqueline Rose, *The Case of Peter Pan: or the Impossibility of Children's Fiction* (Macmillan, 1994).
Charles J. Rzepka, *Detective Fiction* (Polity, 2005).
Berthold Schoene (ed.), *Edinburgh Companion to Contemporary Scottish Literature* (Edinburgh University Press, 2007).
Berthold Schoene (ed.), *Edinburgh Companion to Irvine Welsh* (Edinburgh University Press, 2010).
Andrew Murray Scott, *Alexander Trocchi: The Making of the Monster* (Polygon, 1991).
Mary Seenan, *Nancy Brysson Morrison: A Literary Life* (Kennedy and Boyd, 2013).
Michael Shaw, *The Fin-De-Siècle Scottish Revival: Romance, Decadence and Celtic Identity* (Edinburgh University Press, 2019).
Richard Sher, *The Enlightenment and the Book: Scottish Authors and their Publishers in Eighteenth Century Britain, Ireland and America* (University of Chicago Press, 2006).

Juliet Shields, *Scottish Women's Writing in the Long Nineteenth Century: The Romance of Everyday Life* (Cambridge University Press, 2021).

Juliet Shields, *Sentimental Literature and Anglo-Scottish Identity* (Cambridge University Press, 2010).

Clifford Siskin (ed.), *The Work of Writing: Literature and Social Change in Britain, 1700–1830* (The Johns Hopkins University Press, 1999).

George Gregory Smith, *Scottish Literature: Character and Influence* (Macmillan and Co., 1919).

Janet Sorensen, *The Grammar of Empire in Eighteenth-Century British Writing* (Cambridge University Press, 2000).

Randall Stevenson, *The Oxford English Literature History*, Vol. 12, 1960-2000, *The Last of England?* (Oxford University Press, 2004).

Kirsten Stirling, *Bella Caledonia: Woman, Nation, Text* (Rodopi, 2008).

John Sutherland, *The Life of Walter Scott: A Critical Biography* (Blackwell, 1995).

Rivka Swenson, *Essential Scots and the Idea of Unionism in Anglo-Scottish Literature, 1603-1832* (Bucknell University Press, 2015).

Derick Thomson, 'Scottish Gaelic Literary History and Criticism in the Twentieth Century', *Aiste: Rannsachadh air Litreachas Gàidhlig: Studies in Gaelic Literature Volume 1* (2007), pp. 1–21.

Jon Thompson, *Fiction, Crime, and Empire: Clues to Modernity and Postmodernism* (University of Illinois Press, 1993).

D. J. Trela (ed.), *Margaret Oliphant: Critical Essays on a Gentle Subversive* (Susquehanna University Press, 1995).

Katie Trumpener, *Bardic Nationalism: The Romantic Novel and the British Empire* (Princeton University Press, 1997).

Marshall Walker, *Scottish Literature since 1707* (Routledge, 1996).

Gavin Wallace and Randall Stevenson (eds), *The Scottish Novel Since the Seventies* (Edinburgh University Press, 1993).

Samantha Walton, *The Living World: Nan Shepherd and Environmental Thought* (Bloomsbury, 2020).

Elizabeth Waterson (ed.), *John Galt: Reappraisals* (University of Guelph, 1985).

Moray Watson, *An Introduction to Gaelic Fiction* (Edinburgh University Press, 2011).

Ian Watt, *The Rise of the Novel: Studies in Defoe, Richardson and Fielding* (1957; Penguin, 1963).

Christopher Whyte (ed.), *Gendering the Nation* (Edinburgh University Press, 1995).

Matthew Wickman, *Literature After Euclid: The Geometric Imagination in the Long Scottish Enlightenment* (University of Pennsylvania Press, 2016).

Raymond Williams, *The Country and the City* (Chatto & Windus, 1973).

Neil Williamson and Andrew J. Wilson (eds), *Nova Scotia: New Scottish Speculative Fiction* (Crescent, 2005).

Norman Wilson (ed.), *Scottish Writing and Writers* (The Ramsay Head Press, 1977).

Kurt Wittig, *The Scottish Tradition in Literature* (Oliver & Boyd, 1958).

Robert Lee Wolff, *The Golden Key: A Study of the Fiction of George MacDonald* (Yale University Press, 1961).

Notes on Contributors

Eleanor Bell is Senior Lecturer in Scottish Literature at Strathclyde University. Author of *Questioning Scotland: Literature, Nationalism, Postmodernism* (2004) and co-editor of *Scotland in Theory: Reflections on Culture and Literature* (2004), as well as two co-edited books on the Scottish 1960s, her monograph *Scottish Literary Magazine Culture from 1950 to 2000: Beatniks in the Kailyard* is forthcoming from Edinburgh University Press.

Cairns Craig is Professor Emeritus, Irish and Scottish Studies, Aberdeen University. General Editor of the four-volume *History of Scottish Literature* (Aberdeen UP, 1987–88), his many books on Scottish topics include *Out of History* (1996) and *The Wealth of the Nation* (2018). Founding *The Journal of Irish and Scottish Studies* and *The Journal of Scottish Thought* and editing both (2008–22), he published most recently *Muriel Spark, Existentialism and the Art of Death* (2019) and introductions to the first two volumes of *The Collected Works of Kenneth White* (2021).

Aileen Douglas is Professor of Eighteenth-Century Studies at Trinity College Dublin, teaching in the School of English. Her extensive work on eighteenth-century fiction in English includes *Uneasy Sensations: Smollett and the Body* (1995) as well as *Work in Hand: Script, Print and Writing, 1660–1840* (2017). She co-edited *The Vicar of Wakefield* (2024) in the Cambridge Edition of the Collected Works of Oliver Goldsmith.

Carole Jones is Honorary Fellow in the Department of English and Scottish literature at Edinburgh University, where she was Senior Lecturer from 2008, teaching contemporary Scottish fiction, queer fiction, and representation of gender and sexuality. Published widely on contemporary

Scottish and Scottish authors, including Nan Shepherd, Muriel Spark, James Kelman, Jenni Fagan and Shola von Reinhold, her *Disappearing Men: Gender Disorientation in Scottish Fiction 1979–1999* (2009) was published by Rodopi.

Caroline McCracken-Flesher is Professor of English at the University of Wyoming. Author of *Possible Scotlands: Walter Scott and the Story of Tomorrow* (2005) and *The Doctor Dissected: A Cultural Autopsy of the Burke and Hare Murders* (2012), she edited *Culture, Nation, and the New Scottish Parliament* (2007), *Scotland as Science Fiction* (2012) and *The International Companion to Nineteenth-Century Scottish Literature* (2022).

Fiona McCulloch, an independent scholar, was Lynn Wood Neag Distinguished Visiting Professor of British Literature (University of Connecticut, 2015). Her books include *The Fictional Role of Childhood in Victorian and Early Twentieth-Century Children's Literature* (2004), *Cosmopolitanism in Contemporary British Fiction* (2012), and *Contemporary British Children's Fiction and Cosmopolitanism* (2017); her articles and chapters include '"Connected to time": Ali Smith's Anachronistic Scottish Cosmopolitanism' (2022).

Anna McFarlane is James Murray Beattie Lecturer in Fantasy Literature at Glasgow University, coming there from Leeds University where she led the Medical Humanities Research Group. Visiting Collaborator on the Wellcome Trust-funded Future of Human Reproduction project at Lancaster University, she co-edited *The Routledge Companion to Cyberpunk Culture* (2020), *Fifty Key Figures in Cyberpunk Culture* (2022), and *The Edinburgh Companion to Science Fiction and the Medical Humanities* (2024) and wrote *Cyberpunk Culture and Psychology: Seeing Through the Mirrorshades* (2021).

Andrew Nash is Reader in Book History and Deputy Director of the Institute of English Studies, University of London, directing there the London Rare Books School. Author of *Kailyard and Scottish Literature* (2007) and co-editor (with Valentina Bold) of *Gateway to the Modern: Resituating J. M. Barrie* (2014) and volume 7 of *The Cambridge History of the Book in Britain* (2019), he has published extensively on Scottish and Victorian literature and the history of the book since 1800. Another co-edited volume, *Books, Readers and Libraries in Fiction*, is scheduled for 2025.

Glenda Norquay is Emeritus Professor of Scottish Literature at Liverpool John Moores University. Editor of *The Edinburgh Companion to Scottish Women's Writing* (2012), her books include *Robert Lous Stevenson and Theories of Reading* (2007) and *Robert Louis Stevenson, Literary Networks and Transatlantic Publishing in the 1890s* (2020). Currently working on geographies of identity in Scottish fiction, her Critical Lives volume on Stevenson is forthcoming.

Juliet Shields is Professor of English and Kahn Chair in the Humanities at Southern Methodist University. She works on the intersections between nationality, gender and race in eighteenth- and nineteenth-century British and American literature. She is the author of *Nation and Migration: The Making of British Atlantic Literature, 1765–1835* (2016), *Mary Prince, Slavery, and Print Culture in the Anglophone Atlantic World* (2021) and *Scottish Women's Writing in the Long Nineteenth Century* (2021). She also edited Christian Isobel Johnstone's *Clan-Albin: A National Tale* (1815) for the Chawton House Library of Women's Novels (2022).

Charles Snodgrass is Assistant Professor of English at Grambling State University. His articles and chapters on Walter Scott, John Galt, James Hogg, Susan Ferrier, and print culture in early nineteenth-century Scotland have appeared in *Scottish Literary Journal*, *Studies in Hogg and His World*, *Studies in Romanticism*, and *Nineteenth-Century Contexts*. Contributing Editor to *Selected Criticism, 1820–25* of Pickering & Chatto's six-volume *Blackwood's Magazine, 1817–25*, he co-edited (1997–2007) *Romantic Circles Reviews* book review feature.

Moray Watson is Professor of Gaelic and Translation at Aberdeen University. Director of Ionad Eòghainn MhicLachlainn: the National Centre for Gaelic Translation, his publications include *The Edinburgh Companion to the Gaelic Language* (2010), *An Introduction to Gaelic Fiction* (2011) and textbooks and pedagogical materials for Gaelic He edited Iain Crichton Smith's Gaelic poetry (2013) and short stories (2023) – both Donald Meek Prize nominations, the former winning. His translations from various languages into English and Gaelic include *Alice's Adventures in Wonderland* (2012), *The Hobbit* (2024) and *The Time Machine* (2024).

Matthew Wickman is Professor of English at Brigham Young University. Author of *The Ruins of Experience: Scotland's 'Romantick' Highlands and the Birth of the Modern Witness* (2007), *Literature After Euclid: The Geometric Imagination in the Long Scottish Enlightenment* (2016), and many articles on Scottish literary and intellectual history, he most recently co-edited, with Caroline McCracken-Flesher, *Walter Scott at 250: Looking Forward* (2021).

Index

Aboulela, Leila, 274–75
   Minaret, 274–75
Acair, 212, 214
Aiteal, 212, 214
Alexander, J. H., 299
   The Tavern Sages: Selections from the 'Noctes Ambrosianæ', 299
Alexander, William, 96
   Johnny Gibb of Gushetneuk, 96
Aldiss, Brian, 321
   Billion Year Spree: The True History of Science Fiction, 321
Alison, Archibald, 6
Allan, Dot, 139, 140, 141, 142
   Hunger March, 139
Anderson, Lin, 23
Aristotle, 7, 221
Argosy, 99
Armstrong, Tim, 212
   Air Cuan Dubh Drìlseach, 212
Arnold, Matthew, 115
   'On the Study of Celtic Literature', 115
Ascherson, Neal, 179, 313
   Stone Voices: The Search for Scotland, 313
'Association of Ideas', 34, 36

Association for Scottish Literary Studies, 17
Atkinson, Kate, 231
Austen, Jane, 3, 4, 51, 92
   Mansfield Park, 92
   Pride and Prejudice, 92

Bacon, Francis, 106
   'Of Marriage and the Single Life', 105
Baillie, Joanna, 10
   The Family Legend, 10
Baker, Samuel, 84, 297
   'The Gothic, Supernatural and Religion', 297
Baker, Timothy C. (Tim), 190, 309
   'Ian Macpherson's Writing of the Disaster', 309
   'Introduction', Ian Macpherson, *Wild Harbour* (2019), 310
   'Lonely Island: Exile and Community in Recent Island Writing', 315
   'Writing Scotland's Future: Speculative Fiction and the National Imagination', 316

Bakhtin, Mikhail, 71, 294
  Dialogic Imagination: Four Essays, 294
Ballantyne, R. M., 193, 246–48, 262
  The Coral Island, 246–48
Balzac, Honoré de, 4, 78
Banks, Iain (M.), 188, 189, 232, 239
  The Bridge, 188, 239
  Consider Phlebas, 190
  'Culture' series, 190, 239
  The Player of Games, 239
  The Wasp Factory, 188, 239
Bannatyne, James, 80
Barke, James, 135, 136, 140, 145
  The Land of the Leal, 136
  Major Operation, 139, 141, 142, 143
Barnaby, Paul, 246, 292
Barrie, J. M., 14, 15, 95, 112, 124, 246, 248
  Auld Licht Idylls, 124
  The Little White Bird, 127
  Peter Pan, 14, 246, 248
  Peter and Wendy, 246
  Sentimental Tommy, 127
  Tommy and Grizel, 127
  A Window in Thrums, 121
Beasley, Jerry C., 288
  Tobias Smollett, Novelist, 288
Beckett, Samuel, 160, 209
Beer, Gillian, 328
  Romance, 328
Bell, Eleanor, 179, 312, 313
  'Experiment and Nation in the 1960s', 31
  Questioning Scotland: Literature, Nationalism, Postmodernism, 313
Bell, Ian A., 181, 314
  'Imagine Living There: Form and Ideology in Contemporary Scottish Fiction', 314
Bell, J. J., 128
Benjamin, Walter, 5
Benton, Gill, 171, 312
  Naomi Mitchison, 312
Bergson, Henri, 222
Bertagna, Julie, 251
  Exodus, 251
Besant, Walter, 108, 109
  All Sorts and Conditions of Men, 108
Black, Ronald, (R. MacIlleDhuibh), 214, 317
  An Tuil, 317
Black, Tony, 231
Black, William, 113–14
  White Heather, 114
Blackwood's Edinburgh Magazine, 81, 90, 96, 105
  'Chaldee Manuscript', 90
  Noctes Ambrosianæ, 90
Blackmore, R. D., 118
  Lorna Doone, 118
Blackwood, William, 89
Blake, George, 136, 139, 140, 156
  The Shipbuilders, 139, 141, 142, 143
Blair, Hugh, 1
Bloch, Ernst, 222
  'A Philosophical View of the Detective Novel', 319
Bold, Alan, 165, 288, 311
  Modern Scottish Literature, 311
  Smollett: Author of the First Distinction, 288

Bold, Valentina, 296
   James Hogg: A Bard of Nature's Making, 296
Bolton, H. Philip, 292
   Scott Dramatized, 292
Boswell, James, 1, 8, 109
   The Life of Johnson, 109
Brack, O. M. Jr, 288
   Tobias Smollett, Scotland's First Novelist, 288
Bree, Linda, 288
   'Fielding and Smollett: Rival Novelists', 288
Bridie, James, 155
   Jonah and the Whale, 155
   Tobias and the Angel, 155
Brookmyre, Christopher, 189, 231
   Quite Ugly One Morning, 189
Broster, D. K., 61
Brown, Callum I., 95
Brown, George Douglas, 87, 125, 154
   The House with the Green Shutters, 87, 125, 154
Brown, George Mackay, 166, 188
   Beside the Ocean of Time, 188
   A Calendar of Love, 166
   Greenvoe, 166
   Loaves and Fishes, 166
   Magnus, 166
   A Time to Keep, 166
   The Year of the Whale, 166
Brown, John (Covenanter), 83, 86
Brunton, Mary, 38–39, 43–44, 47, 93
   Discipline, 38–39, 43–44, 93
   Self-Control, 47–48
Buchan, John, 61, 62, 113, 128, 135, 150–51, 156, 193

'Afternoon', 118
Castle Gay, 150
'Fountainblue', 113
Huntingtower, 139, 150
John Burnett of Barns, 118
John Macnab, 150
Midwinter, 151
The Northern Muse, 157
The Power-House, 113
Sir Walter Scott, 62
The Thirty-Nine Steps, 61, 118
'The Watcher by the Threshold', 113
Witch Wood, 151
Buchanan, Robert, 114
   A Child of Nature, 114
Burgess, Moira, 310
   'Arcades – The 1940s and the 1950s', 310
Burns, Robert, 5, 11, 129, 233
Burnside, John, 230–31, 280–81
   Glister, 230–31
   A Summer of Drowning, 280–81
   'Urban Myths', 320
Bute, John Stuart, Third Earl of Bute, 28

Cadel, Robert, 92
Caimbeul, Alasdair, 211
   Am Fear Meadhanach, 211
   Cuid a' Chorra-Ghritich, 214
Caimbeul, Aonghas Pàdraig, 208, 212
   An Oidhche Mus Do Sheòl Sinn, 208, 212
   Là a' Dèanamh Sgèil Do Là, 212
Caimbeul, Maoilios, 215
   Teas, 215

Caimbeul, Tormod, 165, 208, 213–14
   Deireadh an Fhoghair, 165–66, 208, 213
   An Druim Bho Thuath, 213–14
   Shrapnel, 213
Calder, Angus, 66
Calder, Jenni, 171, 312
   The Nine Lives of Naomi Mitchison, 312
Calder & Boyars, 160
Calvin, John (Cauvain, Jean), 11
Calvinism, 132
Campbell, Karen, 229–30
   After the Fire, 320
   The Twilight Time, 320
Campbell, Roy, 155
Camus, 162, 219
Canongate Classics, 16
Carlyle, Alexander, 26
Carlyle, Thomas, 1, 9, 15, 16, 49, 61, 63, 64, 105, 110
   'Chartism', 15
   Sartor Resartus, 15, 49, 105
   'Signs of the Times', 15, 16
Carré, John Le, 193
Carruthers, Gerard, 313
   'Scottish Literature: Second Renaissance', 313
Carruthers, John, 140
Carswell, Catherine, 140, 149
   The Camomile, 149
   The Life of Robert Burns, 157
   Open the Door!, 149
   The Savage Pilgrimage, 157
Cartesian, 223, 224, 250
Cassuto, Leonard, 218, 317
   Hard-Boiled Sentimentality: The Secret History of American Crime Stories, 318
Cato, 78
Cervantes, Miguel de, 3, 22
   Don Quixote, 3, 22
Chaimbeul, Catriona Lexy, 214
   Samhraidhean Dìomhair, 214
Chandler, Raymond, 218, 220, 225
   'The Simple Art of Murder', *Later Novels and Other Writings*, 318
Chateaubriand, François-René, 109
Chaucer, Geoffrey, 109
Christie, Thomas, 316
   Notional Identities: Ideology, Genre and National Identity in Popular Scottish Fiction since the Seventies, 316
CLÀR, 212
Clancy, Tom, 193
Clandfield, Peter and Christian Lloyd, 316
   'Redevelopment Fiction: Architecture, Town-planning and "Unhomeliness"', 316
Claverhouse, James Graham of, 83, 88
Clute, John, 233
   'Fantastika: Or, the Sacred Grove', 321
Cobban, John Maclaren, 124–25
   The King of Andaman, 124–25
Cockburn, Henry, 79, 94
Cockburn, John, 140
Cohen, Michael, 318
   Murder Most Fair: The Appeal of Mystery Fiction, 318
Connolly, Thomas, 236

After Human: A Critical History of the Human in Science Fiction from Shelley to Le Guin, 321
Conrad, Joseph, 155
Constable, Archibald, 89
Corbett, John, 240
Coventry, Frances, 287
  An Essay on the New Species of Writing founded by Mr. Fielding, 287
Craig, Cairns, 62, 66, 93, 137, 179, 180, 182, 184, 223, 307, 312, 313
  'Going Down to Hell is Easy: *Lanark*, Realism and the Limits of the Imagination', 314
  Intending Scotland: Explorations in Scottish Culture since the Enlightenment, 313
  The Modern Scottish Novel: Narrative and the National Imagination, 307, 312
  Out of History, 62
  'Resisting Arrest: James Kelman', 315
Crawford, Robert, 1, 63, 179, 287, 288, 292,
  Devolving English Literature, 287
  Scotland's Books, 313
  The Scottish Invention of English Literature, 1
Crockett, S. R., 95, 117–18
  Cleg Kelly, 126
  The Grey Man, 117–18
  The Raiders, 117
Cronin, A. J., 154, 158
  Hatter's Castle, 154
  Grand Canary, 158
  Three Loves, 158

Crumey, Andrew, 241–42, 271, 276–77
  The Great Chain of Unbeing, 242, 271
  Mobius Dick, 242
  The Secret Knowledge, 242
  Sputnik Caledonia, 276–77

Daiches, David, 22, 287
Dante (Alighieri), 50
Darwin, Charles, 11, 223–24
Davie, Elspeth, 170–71
  Creating a Scene, 170–71
Davis, Leith, 288
  Acts of Union: Scotland and the Literary Negotiation of the British Nation, 1707–1830, 288
  Scotland and the Borders of Romanticism, 293
De Quincey, Thomas, 90
Defoe, Daniel, 3
Deleuze, Gilles, and Guattari, Félix, 222, 250, 251
  'Philosophy of Crime Novels', 318
Derrida, Jacques, 82
Descartes, René, 223, 224
Devine, T. M., 312
  The Scottish Nation 1700–2000, 312
Disruption [of Church of Scotland], 95, 97, 107
Dixon, Keith, 162, 311
  'Writing on the Borderline: The Works of William McIlvanney', 311
Dòmhnallach, Tormod Calum, 211
  An Sgàineadh, 21
Don Juan, 109

Donovan, Anne, 251
  Being Emily, 251
Douglas, Norman, 155
Douglas, O. (Anna Buchan), 137–38, 151
  Penny Plain, 138, 139
Doyle, Arthur Conan, 118, 128, 193, 221, 223, 224, 236
  The Lost World, 236
Dryden, John, 5
Dunbar, William, 5
Duncan, Hal, 244
  Ink, 244
  Vellum, 244
Duncan, Ian, 4, 7, 79–80, 85, 290
  Modern Romance and Transformations of the Novel, 7
  'Scotland and the Novel', 295
  Scott's Shadow: The Novel in Romantic Edinburgh, 7, 290
Dunn, Anndra A., 214
  Còisir nan Gunna, 214
Dunne, J. W., 237
  An Experiment with Time, 237
Dunnigan, Sarah, 246
  International Companion to Scottish Children's Literature, 246
Duras, Marguerite, 171

Edgeworth, Maria, 10, 51, 92
Edinburgh, 30, 31, 129, 224
Einstein, Albert, 283
Einzig, Paul, 155
Encyclopedia Britannica, 11
Elder, Keir, 306
  'James Barke: Politics, Cinema and Writing Scottish Urban Modernity', 307

El-Mohtar, Amal, 244
  This is How You Lose the Time War, 244–45
Eliot, T. S., 23
Ender, Eveline, 73
Engels, Friedrich, 16
  The Condition of the Working Classes in England, 16
English Literature, 2
Erskine of Mar, Rhuraidh, 207
Ettrick Shepherd, *see* Hogg, James
Evans, Mary Ann (George Eliot), 10
Even-Zohar, Itamar, 215
  Papers in Historical Poetics, 215
  'Position of Translated Literature within the Literary Polysystem', 317

Faber, Michel, 240
  The Book of Strange New Things, 240
  Under the Skin, 240
Fagan, Jenni, 243–44, 273
  The Panopticon, 243–44, 273
Ferguson Adam, 9
  Essay on the History of Civil Society, 9
Ferguson, William, 12
Fergusson, Robert, 5
Ferrier, James, 90
Ferrier, Susan Edmondstone, 51, 89, 91–93, 94
  Destiny, 92
  Inheritance, 91
  Marriage, 41–42, 91
Ferris, Ina, 68–69
Fielding, Henry, 3, 5, 23, 33
  History of Tom Jones, 3, 4, 23, 109
  Joseph Andrews, 23
Fielding, Penny, 294

Findlater, Jane and Mary, 121–22
  Crossriggs, 121–22
  The Green Graves of Balgowrie, 122
Fitt, Matthew, 240
  But n Ben A-Go-Go, 240
Fleming, Ian, 193
Formal realism, 3–4
Forster, E. M., 60, 66, 73
  Aspects of the Novel, 60
Forsyth, Frederick, 193
Fowler, William, 19
Frankau, Gilbert, 158
Frankenstein, 91, 235–36, 239–40, 300, 321
Fraser's Magazine, 87, 96
Frazer, J. G., 11, 113, 158, 281
  The Golden Bough, 11, 281
French Revolution, 74
Freud, Sigmund, 155
Friel, George, 160
  The Bank of Time, 160
  The Boy Who Wanted Peace, 160
  Grace and Miss Partridge, 160
  Mr Alfred M.A., 160
Froude, Anthony, 99
  The Nemesis of Faith, 99
Frye, Northrop, 7, 281, 328
  Anatomy of Criticism, 328
Fukuyama, Francis, 275–76
  The End of History and the Last Man, 275–76

Gabaldon, Diana, 61
  Outlander, 61
Gaelic Books Council, 216
Gairm, 207, 211
Gairn, Louisa, 309
  Ecology and Modern Scottish Literature, 309

Gaitens, Edward, 159
  Dance of the Apprentices, 159
Galloway, Janice, 17, 180, 185
  The Trick is to Keep Breathing, 17, 185
Galt, John, 9, 80, 85, 87, 95, 97
  Annals of the Parish, 86, 87–88, 97
  Autobiography, 87
  The Ayrshire Legatees, 85, 86
  The Earthquake, 85
  The Gathering of the West, 85
  Glenfell, 85
  Majolo, 85
  Ringan Gilhaize; Or the Covenanters, 88–89
  The Steam-Boat, 85
  The Wandering Jew, 85
Gardiner, Michael, 188, 250–51, 314
  From Trocchi to Trainspotting: Scottish Critical Theory since 1960, 250–51, 314
Garrison, John, 316
  'Speculative Nationality: "Stands Scotland Where It Did?" in the Culture of Iain M. Banks', 316
Garside, Peter [P. D.], 92, 292
Geikie, Alexander, 11
  The Scenery of Scotland, 11
George IV, 93
Gerard, Alexander, 6
Gibbon, Charles, 122
  A Princess of Jutedom, 122
Gibbon, Edward, 109
Gibbon, Lewis Grassic (*see also* Mitchell, James Leslie), 5, 135, 136, 139, 141, 145, 148–49, 153–59, 226

Gibbon, Lewis Grassic (*cont.*)
   Cloud Howe, 148
   Gay Hunter, 149
   Grey Granite, 148
   A Scots Quair, 136, 226
   Stained Radiance, 149
   Sunset Song, 139, 148, 162
   The Thirteenth Disciple, 149
Gifford, Douglas, 95, 159, 166, 179, 314
   'Modern Scottish Fiction', 310, 311
   'Private Confessions and Public Satire in the Fiction of Alasdair Gray', 314
   'Range and Achievement of Robin Jenkins', 312
Gilfillan, George, 109
Ginsberg, Allen, 172
Glasgow, 30
Goethe, Johann Wolfgang von, 74, 77
   Egmont, 74
Goldie, David, 310
   'Twin Loyalties: John Buchan's England', 310
Golding, William, 246
   The Lord of the Flies, 246
Goldsmith, Oliver, 87
   The Vicar of Wakefield, 87
Good Words, 96
Gorner, Paul, 223
   'Reid, Husserl and Phenomenology', 318
Gottleib, Evan, 32, 289
Graham, R. B. Cunninghame, 155
Gramich, Katie, 308
   'Caught in the Triple Net? Welsh, Scottish and Irish Women Writers', 308

Gray, Alasdair, 17, 85, 123, 180, 181–83, 185, 191, 201, 211, 238–39, 246, 277
   1982 Janine, 182–83
   Lanark, 17, 85, 123, 181–82, 238–39, 247, 277
   Poor Things, 239–40
Green, Sarah, 4, 10
   Scotch Novel Reading or Modern Quackery, 4, 10
Greig, Andrew, 19, 265–66, 270
   Rose Nicolson, 19
   That Summer, 265–66, 270
Grenier, Katherine Haldane, 292
   Tourism and Identity in Scotland 1770–1914, 292
Grierson, H. J. C., 307
   Edinburgh Essays on Scots Literature, 307
Grieve, Christopher Murray (*see also* MacDiarmid, Hugh), 135
   Annals of the Fives Senses, 135
   Northern Numbers, 135
Griffiths, Niall, 187
Grisham, John, 193
Gunn, Neil M., 136, 137, 145–46, 156–57, 237–38
   Butcher's Broom, 146
   The Green Isle of the Great Deep, 237–38
   The Grey Coast, 145
   Highland River, 137, 138
   The Lost Glen, 145, 156
   Morning Tide, 145
   Sun Circle, 146, 156
   Wild Geese Overhead, 141, 144, 145
Guthrie, Laura, 261–62
   Anna, 261–62
Guy, Adam, 311

The Nouveau Roman and Writing in Britain after Modernism, 311

Haggard, H. Rider, 11, 157
Hall, Simon W., 310
   The History of Orkney Literature, 310
Hames, Scott, 180, 313
   'Introduction', *Unstated: Writers on Scottish Independence*, 313
   The Literary Politics of Scottish Devolution, 314
Hamilton, Elizabeth, 46
   The Cottagers of Glenburnie, 46–47
   Memoirs of Modern Philosophers, 46
Hamilton, W. H., 156
Hammett, Dashiell, 225
Hardy, Robina F., 126
   Jock Halliday: A Grassmarket Hero, 126
Hart, Francis Russell, 5, 6, 91, 285, 300
   The Scottish Novel: A Critical Survey, 5, 6, 285, 300
Harvie, Christopher, 95
Hay, Deòrsa Caimbeul, 208
Hay, John MacDougall, 125–26
   Gillespie, 125–26
Hegel, Georg Wilhelm Friedrich, 76–77
Hehir, Sylvia, 258–61
   Sea Change, 258–61
Heidegger, Martin, 82, 218, 218, 219, 220–21, 222, 223, 226
   Being and Time, 82
   Introduction to Metaphysics, 219, 318

   'On the Essence of Truth', *Basic Writings*, 318
   Poetry, Language, Thought, 318
   'Question Concerning Technology', *Basic Writings*, 318
   'Way to Language', *Basic Writings*, 318
   'What Are Poets For?', *Basic Writings*, 220, 318
   'What Calls for Thinking', *Basic Writings*, 318
   'What Is Metaphysics', *Basic Writings*, 220–21, 318
Hemingway, Ernest, 225
Hendry, J. F., 159–60
   Fernie Brae: A Scottish Childhood, 159
Henryson, Robert, 5, 129
Hepworth, Barbara, 282, 284
Herman, Arthur, 295
   The Scottish Enlightenment: The Scots' Invention of the Modern World, 295
Hind, Archie, 161
   The Dear Green Place, 161
Hird, Laura, 187
Hitler, Adolf, 175
Hogarth, William, 108
Hogg, James, 5, 9, 18, 80, 81, 83, 84, 85, 90, 95, 211, 224
   The Brownie of Bodsbeck and Other Tales, 82, 83, 84, 85
   Memoir of the Author's Life, 84
   The Mountain Bard, 81
   The Private Memoirs and Confessions of a Justified Sinner, 9, 18, 45, 82, 83, 84, 86, 211
   The Queen's Wake, 81

Hogg, James (*cont.*)
   The Three Perils of Man, 83, 86
   The Three Perils of Woman, 83
   Tales of the Wars of Montrose, 85
Holmes, Sherlock, 221, 223, 224
Homer, 53, 108
   Odyssey, 109
Hook, Andrew, 312
   The Novel Today: Edinburgh International Festival 1962: Programme and Notes, International Writers' Conference, 312
Horsley, Lee, 219, 221, 317
   The Noir Thriller, 317
Hubbard, Tom, 292
Hughes, Gillian, 295
   'Fiction in the Magazines', 295
Hume, David, 11, 17, 24, 30, 32, 34, 39, 46, 48–49, 288
   'bundle theory of the self', 36
   History of England, 39–40
   on sympathy, 36
   A Treatise of Human Nature, 34–35
Hunt, Leigh, 90
Husserl, Edmund, 222, 223
Hutton, James, 11, 68
   Theory of the Earth, 11, 68

Industrial Revolution, 133
Ionesco, Eugène, 160, 209

Jacob, Violet, 118–19, 146
   Flemington, 118–19
Jacobitism, 4, 81
Jackson, Joseph F., 18
   Writing Black Scotland: Race, Nation and the Devolution of Black Britain, 18

James IV, 132
James, Henry, 15, 67, 108, 110, 246
Jardine, Penelope, 312
   (ed.) Muriel Spark, *The Golden Fleece: Essays*, 312
Jarvis, Gordon, 311
   (ed.), George Friel, *A Glasgow Trilogy*, 311
Jeffrey, Francis, 89
Jenkins, Robin, 166–67, 172
   The Changeling, 166, 167
   The Cone Gatherers, 166, 167
   Dust on the Paw, 167
   Guests of War, 166
   Happy for the Child, 166
   Love Is a Fervent Fire, 166
   The Missionaries, 166
   The Thistle and the Grail, 166, 167
   A Very Scotch Affair, 167
Johnson, Samuel, 8
Johnstone, Christian Isobel, 37, 48, 93, 289
   Clan-Albin, 37–38, 48, 93, 289
Jones, Carole, 315
   Disappearing Men: Gender Disorientation in Scottish Fiction 1979–1999, 315
   'James Kelman's Melancholic Politics', 315
   'Post-Meta-Modern-Realism', 315
Joyce, James, 73, 154, 160

Kames, Lord (Henry Home), 6
Kant, Immanuel, 223, 224
Kay, Jackie, 190, 243
   Trumpet, 190, 243
Keir, Ken, 309
   'Modernist Myths and

Mothers: Jung and "Mythic Parallelism" in Neil Gunn's *The Silver Darlings*', 309
Kelly, Aaron, 315
　Irvine Welsh, 315
　'James Kelman and the Deterritorialisation of Power', 315
Kelman, James, 17, 162, 180, 183–85, 188, 192–205, 272–73, 314
　The Bus Conductor Hines, 17
　A Chancer, 183
　A Disaffection, 183
　How Late It Was, How Late, 183, 184
　'Importance of Glasgow in my Work', 314
　Kieron Smith, Boy, 273
　Lean Tales, 201
　Translated Accounts, 272–73
　You Have to Be Careful in the Land of the Free, 273
Keats, John, 90
Kennaway, James, 163
　The Bells of Shoreditch, 163
　The Cost of Living like This, 163
　Household Ghosts, 163
　The Mindbenders, 163
　Some Gorgeous Accident, 163
　Tunes of Glory, 163
Kennedy, A. L., 188, 266–67, 269
　Day, 266–67, 269
　Looking for the Possible Dance, 188
　So I Am Glad, 188
Kesson, Jessie, 146, 165
　Another Time, Another Place, 165
　Glitter of Mica, 165
　The White Bird Passes, 165
　Where the Apple Ripens, 165
Kidd, Colin, 86, 95–96
　'Satire, Hypocrisy, and the Ayrshire-Renfrewshire Enlightenment', 298
Kierkegaard, Søren, 162, 219
Klaus, H. Gustav, 308
　'James Barke: A Great-hearted Writer, a Hater of Oppression, a True Scot', 308
Knight, Stephen, 225–26
　Crime Fiction since 1800: Detection, Death, Diversity, 320
Kyle, Elizabeth, 309
　'Modern Women Authors', 309

Lamb, Charles, 60, 73
Lang, Andrew, 112, 113
Laniel-Musitelli, Sophie, 61, 68
Lauder, Charlotte, 310
　'Claire Spencer: A Lost Scottish Modernist', 310
Lauder, Thomas Dick, 93
　Elizabeth de Bruce, 93
　The Wolf of Badenoch, 93
Lawrence, D. H., 193
　Lady Chatterley's Lover, 193
Leavis, F. R., 2
　The Great Tradition, 2
Leigh, Dennis, 239
Leonardi, Barbara, 297
　'James Hogg's *Brownie of Bodsbeck*: An Unconventional National Tale', 297
Lewis, C. S., 234

Light, Alison, 143, 308
  For England: Femininity, Literature and Conservatism Between the Wars, 308
Lightwood, Donald, 253–54
  The Long Revenge, 253–54
Linklater, Eric, 139, 141, 149, 150, 154, 158, 166
  Juan in America, 150
  Magnus Merriman, 139, 150
  A Man over Forty, 166
  The Men of Ness, 50, 158
  The Merry Muse, 166
  Poet's Pub, 166
  A Terrible Freedom, 166
  White-Maa's Saga, 139, 150
Loch Lomond, 31
Lockhart, John Gibson, 61, 80, 84, 89, 90
  Adam Blair, 89
  Memoirs of the Life of Sir Walter Scott, Baronet, 61
  Reginald Dalton, 89
  Valerius, 89
Logan, Kirstie, 243
  The Gracekeepers, 243
Lumsden, Alison, 314
  'Innovation and Reaction in the Fiction of Alasdair Gray' 314
Lyell, Charles, 11, 224
  Principles of Geology, 11
Lynch, Deidre, 73
Luath Press, 212
Lucan, 78
Lukács, Georg, 4, 8, 74–78, 80
  The Historical Novel, 4, 8, 80

Mac an t-Saoir, Màrtainn, 212
  An Latha as Fhaide, 212
  Cala Bendita 's a Bheannachdan, 214
  Gymnippers Diciadain, 213
MacArthur, Alexander and H. Kingsley Long, 141
  No Mean City, 141
Macaulay, Thomas Babbington, 110
Mac a' Ghobhainn, Iain, *see* Smith, Iain Crichton
MacCoinnich, Cailein T., 209
  A' Leth Eile, 209
MacColla, Fionn (Thomas MacDonald), 136, 137, 140, 144, 307
  Albannach, 137, 144, 307
MacCormac, Iain, 207, 208
  Gun D'Thug I Spéis Do 'n Àrmuinn, 207
  Dùn-Aluinn: no an t-Oighre 'na Dhìobarach, 207, 208
MacDhonnchaidh, Aonghas, 207
  An t-Ogha Mór: no am Fear-Sgeòil air Uilinn, 207
MacDiarmid, Hugh (*see also* Grieve, Christopher Murray), 135, 137, 145, 226
  'Neil M. Gunn', 308
  'Scotland', 226
MacDonald, Angus, 138,
  'Modern Scots Novelists', 307
MacDonald, George, 17, 49, 98, 99, 100, 103–04, 106–07, 113, 114, 233, 234–35, 246, 247, 291
  David Elginbrod, 49
  Lilith, 113
  Phantastes, 113, 233, 234–35
  The Princess and the Goblin, 246
  Robert Falconer, 49, 98, 99, 100, 103–04, 106–07
  What's Mine's Mine, 114

MacDonald, Kate and Nathan
    Waddell, 310
  John Buchan and the Idea of
    Modernity, 310
  Reassessing John Buchan, 310
MacGill, Patrick, 126
  Children of the Dead End, 126
  The Rat-Pit, 126
MacGill-Eain, Somhairle (*see also*
    MacLean, Sorley), 208
MacGill-Eain, Tormod, 210–11
  Cùmhantan, 210–11
  Keino, 211
MacIomhair, Dòmhnall Iain, 211
  Cò Rinn E?, 211, 215
Mack, Douglas, 83, 84, 296
MacKenzie, Compton, 155
MacKenzie, Henry, 9, 37, 38, 87
  The Man of Feeling, 9, 37, 87
MacLean, Sorley, 208
Maclaren, Ian, 96
Macleod, Fiona (William Sharp),
    114–15
  Mountain Lovers, 115
  Pharais, 114–15
  The Washer of the Ford, 115
MacLeod, Ken, 189, 242
  Intrusion, 242
MacLeod, Seamus (James
    MacLeod), 136, 208
  Caitlin Sgiathanach: no
    Faodalach na h-Abaid
    (*'Skye Girl: or Foundling of*
    the Abbey', 136, 207, 208
MacLeòid, Iain F., 213
  Am Bounty, 213
  Na Klondykers, 213
  An Sgoil Dhubbh, 213
Maclise, Daniel, 87, 299
Macmillan's Magazine, 14, 99, 105

MacMhaoilein, Calum, 211
Macmurray, John, 258
Macpherson, Ian, 137, 139, 140,
    144, 149
  Land of our Fathers, 150
  Pride in the Valley, 150
  Shepherd's Calendar, 137, 141,
    144
  Wild Harbour, 150
Macpherson, James, 6, 8
  Fragments of Ancient Poetry,
    6, 8
Maginn, William, 90
Manlove, Colin, 233, 235
  Scotland's Forgotten Treasure:
    The Visionary Romances of
    George MacDonald, 321
  Scottish Fantasy Literature: A
    Critical Survey, 321
Mannin, Ethel 158
Manning, Susan, 287
  The Edinburgh History of
    Scottish Literature:
    Enlightenment, Britain and
    Empire (1707–1918), 287,
    292
March, Christie L, 315
  'Interview with Janice
    Galloway', 315
Martz, Louis L., 27, 288
  The Later Career of Tobias
    Smollett, 288
Maslen, Elizabeth, 150
Massie, Allan, 6
Masson, David, 14–15, 99
  Recent British Philosophy, 14
Maxwell, Gavin, 87
  Ring of Bright Water, 87
Maxwell, James Clerk, 11, 12, 15, 232
May, Peter, 231

Mayer, Robert, 71, 293
    Walter Scott and Fame, 294
McBride, Stuart, 229
    Cold Granite, 229
McCann, Sean, 319
    Gumshoe America: Hard-Boiled Crime Fiction and the Rise and Fall of New Deal Liberalism, 319
McCleery, Alistair, 306
    'The Porpoise Press 1922-26', 306
McCracken-Flesher, 189, 293, 294, 233
    'Introduction', *Scotland as Science Fiction*, 233, 316
    Possible Scotlands: Walter Scott and the Story of Tomorrow, 293
    Walter Scott at 250: Looking Forward, 294
McCulloch, Fiona, 249, 323
    'A Key to the Future: Hybridity in Contemporary Children's Fiction', 323
McCulloch, Margery Palmer, 309, 226
    Modernism and Nationalism: Literature and Society in Scotland 1918-1939, 309
McDermid, Val, 23
McFall, Claire, 252-53
    Bombmaker, 252-53
McFarlane, Anna, 322
    'Ectogenesis on the NHS: Reproduction and Privatisation in 21st Century British Science Fiction', 322

McGann, Jerome, 67
McGillis, Roderick, 262, 263
McGrath, John, 165
    The Cheviot, the Stag and the Black, Black Oil, 165
McGuire, Matt, 318
    'Welsh's Novels', 318
McIlvanney, Liam, 159, 179, 220, 228-29, 310, 313
    All the Colours of the Town, 228-29
    Growing Up in the West, 310
    'Politics of Narrative in the Post-War Scottish Novel', 313
McIlvanney, William, 82, 161-62, 179, 181, 188-89, 191, 219, 222, 225, 313
    'Cowardly Lion', 179
    Docherty, 162
    A Gift from Nessus, 161
    Laidlaw, 82, 162, 188, 219, 221
    The Papers of Tony Veitch, 188, 225
    Remedy is None, 161
    Strange Loyalties, 188
    Surviving the Shipwreck, 313
McLean, Russell D., 225, 228
    The Lost Sister, 228
McQuillan, Martin, 169, 312
    Theorising Muriel Spark: gender, race, deconstruction, 312
Michie, Elsie B., 121
Michelet, Jules, 110
Mill, John Stuart, 222
Millar, John Hepburn, 1
    A Literary History of Scotland, 1
Miller, Gavin, 190, 232, 243, 316, 321

'Iain (M.) Banks: Utopia, Nationalism and the Posthuman', 316
'Scottish Science Fiction: Writing Scottish Literature Back into History', 321
'Animals, empathy, and care in Naomi Mitchison's *Memoirs of a Spacewoman*', 321
Miller, Henry, 160
Miller, Hugh, 11
   The Old Red Sandstone, 11
Miller, John, 310
   '"The Soul's Queer Corners": John Buchan and Psychoanalysis', 310
Millgate, Jane, 66
Milton, John, 109
   Paradise Lost, 109
mimesis, 7
Mina, Denise, 189, 231
   Garnethill, 18
Mitchell, James Leslie (*see also* Gibbon, Lewis Grassic), 232, 236–37
   Gay Hunter, 236–37
   Three Go Back, 236, 237
Mitchison, Naomi, 135–36, 156, 171, 238
   Black Sparta, 156
   The Blood of the Martyrs, 150
   The Bull Calves, 171
   The Conquered, 156, 171
   The Corn King and the Spring Queen, 150, 171
   Memoirs of a Spacewoman, 171, 238
   Not by Bread Alone, 171, 238
   Solution Three, 171, 238
   We Have Been Warned, 50, 238
   What the Human Race is Up To, 172
Modern Scot, 154–55
Moir, David Macbeth, 81, 93
   The Life of Mansie Wauch, 93
Montrose, Marquis of, 157
Monty Python, 73
Moon, Lorna (Nora Helen Wilson Low), 136, 146
   Dark Star, 146
Morace, Robert A., 315
   Irvine Welsh, 315
Moretti, Franco, 86–87
Morgan, Edwin, 164–65, 172, 311
   Midnight Letterbox: Selected Correspondence 1950–2010, 31
   'The Young Writer in Scotland', 312
Morrison, Ewan, 273–74
   How to Survive Everything, 273–74
Morrison, Nancy Brysson, 136, 151–52
   The Gowk Storm, 152
Most, Glenn W., 223
   'The Hippocratic Smile: John le Carré and the Traditions of the Detective Novel', 319
Mullan, John, 37
Muir, Edwin, 5–6, 62, 63, 64, 155, 308
   Scott and Scotland, 5–6, 62
   Scottish Journey, 308
Muir, Willa, 17, 136, 147–48, 149, 156
   Imagined Corners, 17, 148
   Mrs Muttoe and the Top Storey, 148
   Mrs Ritchie, 139, 148

Munro, Neil, 115–16, 119, 128
    'Castle Dark', 115
    John Splendid, 116
    The New Road, 119
    *The Lost Pibroch and other
        Sheiling Stories*, 115
    Para Handy, 128
Murray, Charles, 156
Murray, Isobel, 165
Murry, Middleton, 157
Mussolini, Benito, 175

Newbolt report (1924), 2
NicGill-Eain, Màiri, 209
    Gainmheach an Fhàsaich, 209
NicGumaraid, Màiri, 210
    Clann Iseabail, 210
NicLeòid, Norma, 212
Niven, Frederick, 127
    Justice of the Peace, 127
Noble, Andrew, 91, 300
    'John Wison (Christopher
        North) and the Tory
        Hegemony'
Noctes Ambrosianæ, 81
Norquay, Glenda, 307, 163, 311, 315
    *Collected Works of Lorna
        Moon*, 307
    'Four Novelists of the 1950s
        and 1960s', 311
    'Janice Galloway's Novels', 315
North, Christopher, *see* Wilson,
    John
Novalis (Georg Philipp Friedrich
    Freiherr von Hardenberg),
    234

O'Hagan, Andrew, 190, 267–68
    Our Fathers, 190–91
    Personality, 267–68

Oliphant, Margaret (Mrs), 10, 13,
    50–59, 96, 99, 101, 102, 104,
    113, 120–21
    Kirsteen, 120–21
    Miss Marjoribanks, 105
    *Passages in the Life of Mrs
        Margaret Maitland*, 87,
        96–98, 101
    A Son of the Soil, 98, 99–100,
        102–03, 104
    Tales of the Seen and Unseen, 113
Orwell, George, 308
    Coming Up for Air, 308
Overy, Richard, 134
    *The Morbid Age: Britain
        Between the Wars*, 306
Owens, Agnes, 201, 205
Owenson, Sydney (Lady
    Morgan), 8
    The Wild Irish Girl, 8

Pascal, Blaise, 225
Peach, Linden, *Masquerade,
    Crime and Fiction: Criminal
    Deceptions*, 317
People's Friend, 96
Petrie, Duncan, 313
    *Contemporary Scottish
        Fictions: Film, Television
        and the Novel*, 313
Phidias, 108
Philpotts, Eden, 156
Pilgrim's Progress, 109
Pinkerton, Allan, 225
Pittock, Murray, 179
    Road to Independence?, 313
Plain, Gill, 189, 314
    'Concepts of Corruption:
        Crime Fiction and the
        Scottish "State"', 316

Playfair, John, 11
    Illustrations of the Huttonian Theory of the Earth, 11
Poe, Edgar Allan, 223
    Complete Tales and Poems, 319
Poncarová, Petra Johana, 213–14
    'An Druim Bho Thuath: Tormod Caimbeul's Last Vista of Gaelic Scotland', 317
    'The Gaelic Cosmopolite', 317
Porpoise Press, 135
Porter, Dennis, 225
    The Pursuit of Crime: Art and Ideology in Detective Fiction, 319
Porter, Eleanor H., 261
    Pollyanna, 261
Porter, Jane, 10, 42, 44, 48
    Thaddeus of Warsaw, 10, 42–43
    The Highland Chiefs, 10, 44, 48
Power, William, 135, 140
    My Scotland, 306
Priestley, J. B., 4
    The English Novel, 4
Pringle, David, 232, 236
    'Introduction: Scotlands Old and New', 320
Proust, Marcel, 155
Pushkin, Alexander Sergeyevich, 76

Quarterly Review, 71

Rae, Hugh C. (also published as Robert Crawford, R. B. Houston, James Albany), 162
    A Few Small Bones, 162
    The Marksman, 162
    Night Pillow, 162
    The Saturday Epic, 162–63
    The Shooting Gallery, 163
    Skinner, 162
Ragaz, Sharon, 83, 297
    '"Gelding" the Priest in *The Brownie of Bodsbeck*: A New Letter', 297
Ramsay, Allan, 29, 129
    The Ever Green, 29
Ramsay, Andrew Michael, 20
    A New Cyropaedia; or the Travels of Cyrus, 20
Rangarajan, Padma, 88
    'Debating Insurrection in Galt's Ringan Gilhaize', 299
Rankin, Ian, 85, 189, 215, 218, 220, 221, 224, 225, 226–28, 312
    Black and Blue, 226–27
    Knots and Crosses, 189
    Let it Bleed, 318
    Resurrection Men, 85
    Rebus's Scotland, 226, 319
    'Surface and Structure: Reading Muriel Spark's *The Driver's Seat*, 312
Reade, Charles, 109
Reid, J. M., 134–35
    Modern Scottish Literature, 306
Reid, Thomas, 11, 17, 46, 48, 223, 224
    An Inquiry into the Human Mind on the Principles of Common Sense, 46
Richards, Frank, 192, 193
Richardson, Samuel, 3, 51, 55
    Pamela, 51
    Sir Charles Grandison, 55

Rigney, Ann, 292
  The Afterlives of Walter Scott: Memory on the Move, 292
Robb, David S., 104, 106
Robbe-Grillet, Alain, 169, 171, 172, 312
  'The Writer's Only Commitment is to Literature', 312
Robbins, Bruce and Paulo Lemos Horta, 251
  (eds) *Cosmopolitanisms*, 323
Robertson, James, 241, 268–69, 270, 277–80
  And the Land Lay Still, 241, 268–69, 270
  News of the Dead, 277–80
Robertson, William, 30
Robinson, Crabb, 91
Robson, W. W., 246, 248–49
Rose, Jacqueline, 247
Ross, Ian Campbell, 287
Rothstein, Eric, 88
Rowling, J. K., 201, 262
  Harry Potter series, 262
Royal Society of Edinburgh, 68
Royle, Trevor, 90
Rubens, Peter Paul, 33
Rzepka, Charles, 225
  Detective Fiction, 319

Saadi, Suhayl, 274
  Psychoraag, 274
Sabiron, Céline, 61, 68
Sage, Alain René Le, 22
  The Adventures of Gil Blas of Santillane, 22
Salamone, Frank A., 225
  '*Black Mask* and the Origins of the Hard-Boiled Detective', 319
Salini, [Carlo], 108–09
Sampson, George, 2
  English for the English, 2
Sandrock, Kirsten and Frauke Reitemeier, 310
  Crimelights: Scottish crime fiction then and now, 310
Sarraute, Nathalie, 171
Sassi, Carla, 136, 149, 309
  'The Shifting Identities of Mitchell and Gibbon', 309
Sayers, Ross, 254–55, 258
  Sonny and Me, 254–55
The Scarlet Letter (Nathaniel Hawthorne), 109
Schoene, Berthold, 313
  The Edinburgh Companion to Irvine Welsh, 317
  'Going Cosmopolitan: Reconstituting "Scottishness" in Post-devolution Criticism', 313
Scott, Andrew Murray, 311
  Alexander Trocchi: The Making of the Monster, 311
Scott, Paul H., 95
Scott, Sir Walter, 3, 4, 5, 6, 7, 9, 10, 11, 19, 33, 44, 50–59, 56, 60–73, 74–78, 92, 95, 129–33, 157, 289, 233, 246, 254
  The Antiquary, 56, 65, 69
  The Bride of Lammermoor, 63, 292
  Castle Dangerous, 63, 292
  The Chronicles of the Canongate, 72
  The Fortunes of Nigel, 67, 72
  Guy Mannering, 57, 65, 66, 82
  The Heart of Mid-lothian, 51, 57–59, 65, 75–76

Ivanhoe, 4, 5, 11, 66, 86, 93, 246
Journal, 72
The Lady of the Lake, 51, 60, 80, 100, 109
The Lay of the Last Minstrel, 80
Letters, 292
Marmion, 80
Minstrelsy of the Scottish Border, 5, 63
The Monastery, 67, 72
Old Mortality, 65, 66, 67, 70–71, 84, 88–89
Redgauntlet, 45, 66, 81, 86
Rob Roy, 66, 81
Tales of my Landlord, 9, 65, 68
The Abbott, 67
'Thomas the Rhymer', 63, 64
Waverley, 4, 44–51, 54, 63, 64, 65, 66, 69–70, 79, 80, 81, 86, 87, 88, 292
Scott, Walter (of Braxenholme and Buccleuch), 19
Scottish Arts Council, 17
Scottish Assembly, 178
Scottish Literary Renaissance, 134
Scottish Literature, 130
Scottish Parliament, 178
Seager, Nicholas, 295
  'The Novel's Afterlife in the Newspaper, 1712–1750', 295
Sedgwick, Helen, 242–43
  The Growing Season, 242–43
Seenan, Mary, 307
  Nancy Brysson Morrison: A Literary Life, 307
Seth, Andrew (Pringle-Pattison), 223
Shakespeare, William, 5, 7, 15, 53, 55, 281
  As You Like It, 53

  Cymbeline, 281
  Macbeth, 281
  The Tempest, 55, 281
  A Winter's Tale, 59, 281
Sharp, Alan, 163–64
  A Green Tree in Gedde, 163–64
Sharp, William, *see* Macleod, Fiona
Shelley, Mary, 235–36, 239
  Frankenstein, 235–36, 239–40
Shelley, Percy Bysshe, 90
Shepherd, Nan, 17, 136, 147, 150
  A Pass in the Grampians, 147
  The Quarry Wood, 17, 147
  The Weatherhouse, 139, 147
Shiach, Morag, 149
Shields, Juliet, 151
  Scottish Women's Writing in the Long Nineteenth-Century, 309
Shoreline of Infinity, 244–45
  Scotland in Space: Creative Vision and Critical Reflection on Scotland's Space, 245
Sime, William, 123–24
  King Capital, 123–24
Sinclair-Stevenson, Christopher, 312
  'Obituary: Elspeth Davie', 312
Siskin, Clifford, 80
  'Periodicals, Authorship, and the Romantic Rise of the Novel', 295
Skinner, B. F., 237
  Walden Two, 237
Smiles, Samuel, 126
  Self-Help, 126
Smith, Adam, 1, 6, 17, 30, 32, 35, 49
  'Astronomy', 35
  The Theory of Moral Sentiments, 36
  The Wealth of Nations, 6

Smith, Alexander McCall, 189
　The No. 1 Ladies Detective Agency, 189
Smith, Ali, 18, 73, 264–65, 275–76, 281–84
　Autumn, 281
　Hotel World, 73, 275–76
　Spring, 281
　Summer, 281–84
　There but for the, 18, 264–65
　Winter, 281
Smith, G. Gregory, 82, 296
　Scottish Literature: Character and Influence, 82, 296
Smith, Iain Crichton (Iain Mac a' Ghobhainn), 87, 165, 172, 188
　An t-Aonaran, 165, 209
　Consider the Lilies, 87
　The Dream, 188
　An End to Autumn, 210
　In the Middle of the Wood, 210
　Murchadh, 209
　Murdo: The Life and Works, 210
　My Last Duchess, 210
　Na Speuclairean Dubha, 210
　Thoughts of Murdo, 210
Smith, William Robertson, 11, 12
Smith, Zadie, 18
　White Teeth, 18
Smollett, Tobias, 20–33
　The Adventures of Peregrine Pickle, 21
　The Adventures of Ferdinand Count Fathom, 21, 22
　The Adventures of Sir Launcelot Greaves, 21, 22
　The Adventures of Roderick Random, 20, 21, 22, 23–27, 33

A Complete History of England, 20, 40
　The Critical Review, 20
　The Expedition of Humphry Clinker, 21, 27–32, 33, 40–41, 43
　The Letters of Tobias Smollett, 288
　The Present State of Nations, 27
　Travels through France and Italy, 27
Sorenson, Janet, 32, 289
Spark, Muriel, 6, 85, 168–70, 173–77, 247
　The Bachelors, 168
　The Ballad of Peckham Rye, 85
　The Comforters, 168
　'Desegregation of Art', 173–77
　The Driver's Seat, 169–170
　The Hothouse by the East River, 247
　Memento Mori, 168
　The Prime of Miss Jean Brodie, 168–69
　Robinson, 168
Spence, Alan, 271–72
　The Pure Land, 271–72
Spenser, Edmund, 7
　The Faerie Queene, 7, 109
Spunta, Marina, 312
　'A Universe of One's Own? Elspeth Davie and the Narrative of the "Gap"', 312
Sterne, Laurence, 63
Stetler, Gilbert A., 299
　'John Galt: The Writer as Town Booster and Builder', 299
　'John Galt's "Whole Art of Colonization": Sound, Voice, Space', 299

Stephen, Leslie, 246
Stevenson, Randall, 179, 313
   'A Postmodern Scotland?', 313
Stevenson, Robert Louis, 6, 13, 15,
   108–11, 112, 116–17, 224, 232,
   236, 249
   'A Gossip on Romance', 116
   'A Humble Remonstrance', 15,
     108–11
   Kidnapped, 61, 116
   'Markheim', 112
   The Master of Ballantrae,
     116–17, 118
   'The Merry Men', 112
   'The Pavilion on the Links', 112
   Strange Case of Dr Jekyll and
     Mr Hyde, 13, 85, 224, 232,
     236, 249
   'Thrawn Janet', 112
   Treasure Island, 112, 249
Stewart, Agnes, 140
Stewart, Balfour, 12
   The Unseen Universe or
     Physical Speculations on a
     Future State, 12, 13
Stewart, Dugald, 35
   Elements of the Philosophy of
     the Human Mind, 35
Stewart, Martin, 255–58, 259
   The Sacrifice Box, 255–58
Stirling, Kirsten, 82
   Bella Caledonia: Women,
     Nation, Text, 296
Strahan, Alexander, 99
Strathesk, John, 96
   Blinkbonny, or Bell o' the
     Manse, 96
Strindberg, August, 155
Stuart, Douglas, 273
   Shuggie Bain, 272

Sturrock, John, 171, 312
   The French New Novel, 312
Sunday Magazine, 99
Sutherland, Luke, 190
   Jelly Roll, 190
Suttie, Ian D., 258
Suvin, Darko, 232–33
Suwabe, Koichi, 221, 318
   'The Case of the Femme
     Fatale: A Poetics of
     Hard-Boiled Fiction', 318
Swan, Annie S., 98, 99, 100, 104, 120
   Aldersyde: A Border Story of
     Seventy Years Ago, 120
   Maitland of Lauriston, 98, 99,
     100–02, 104–05
   Mary Garth, 124
Swenson, Rivka, 288
   Essential Scots and the Idea of
     Unionism in Anglo-Scottish
     Literature, 1603–1832, 288
Sym, Robert ('Timothy Tickler'),
   90–91
Stuart, Charles Edward ('Bonne
   Prince Charlie'), 102

Tacitus, 110
Tagore, Rabindranath, 153
Tait, Peter Guthrie, 12
   The Unseen Universe or
     Physical Speculations on a
     Future State, 12, 13
Tange, Hanne, 306
   'Language, Class and Social
     Power in *A Scots Quair*',
     306
Tartan Noir, 217, 221
Taylor, A. J. P., 17
   English History 1914–1945, 18
Tennyson, Alfred, 156

Tey, Josephine (Elizabeth Mackintosh; also writing as Gordon Daviot and F. Craigie Howe), 151
Thatcher, Margaret, 178
Thomas, Ronald R., 222, 223, 225, 318
  Detective Fiction and the Rise of Forensic Science, 318
Thompson, E. P., 16
  The Making of the English Working Classes, 16
Thompson, Jon, 222, 223, 318
  Fiction, Crime and Empire: Clues to Modernity and Postmodernity, 318
Thomson, Alastair R., 312
  'Faith and Love: An Examination of Some of the Themes in the Work of Robin Jenkins', 312
Thomson, Derick, 207, 211
  Gairm, 211
  'Scottish Gaelic Literary History and Criticism in the Twentieth Century', 317
Thomson, James, 1
Thomson, William (Lord Kelvin), 11, 12, 232
Ticonderoga, battle of, 29
Tolstoy, Leo, 4, 78
Trocchi, Alexander, 164
  Cain's Book, 164
Toon, Francine, 244
  Pine, 244
Trite, Roberta Seelinger, 250
Trumpener, Katie, 7, 9, 88
  Bardic Nationalism: The Romantic Novel and the British Empire, 7–8

Twain, Mark (Samuel Clemens), 158, 225
  'The Celebrated Jumping Frog of Calaveras County', 225
  A Tramp Abroad, 158
Tytler, Sarah (Henrietta Keddie), 120, 122–23
  Logie Town, 120, 123
  St Mungo's City, 122–23

Unamuno, Miguel de, 162, 219
Union [of Scotland and England, 1707], 1, 29, 32
Urquhart, Thomas, 20
  The Jewel, 20
Ùr-Sgeul, 211–12, 213, 214–15

Verne, Jules, 232
  Les Indes Noires/The Child of the Cavern, 232

Walker, Marshall, 8, 297
Wallace, Gavin, 166, 181, 190, 312, 314, 315
  'The Range and Achievement of Robin Jenkins', 312
  'Voices in Empty Houses: The Novel of Damaged Identity', 314
  'Voyages of Intent: Literature and Cultural Politics in Post-Devolution Scotland', 315
Wallace, Tara Goshal, 288
Wallace, Valerie, 95–96
Walton, Samantha, 140
  'The Scottish Landscape in the Crime Novels of Josephine Tey', 310
War of Jenkins Ear, 20

Ward, Mary Augusta, 99
　Robert Elsmere, 99
Warner, Alan, 187, 273
　The Man Who Walks, 273
　Morvern Callar, 187
　The Sopranos (Our Ladies), 187
Watson, Moray, 136, 206, 208, 306
　An Introduction to Gaelic Fiction, 206, 208, 306
Watson, Roderick, 16
Watt, Ian, 3, 6
　The Rise of the Novel, 3
Watt, James, 67–68
Webb, Cornelius, 90
Wells, H. G., 232
　The Time Machine, 232
　The War of the Worlds, 232
Welsh, Irvine, 162, 181, 186–87, 188, 217, 218, 219, 223, 224, 229
　Crime, 217, 223
　Filth, 186, 217, 229
　Marabou Stork Nightmares, 186, 188
　Trainspotting, 186, 224, 241
Welsh, Louise, 231
West, Rebecca, 152
　Judge, 152
　Return of the Soldier, 307
White, John, 323
　'The Menace of the Irish Race to our Scottish Nationality', 323

Whyte, Christopher, 309
　'Fishy Masculinities: Neil Gunn's *The Silver Darlings*', 309
Wickman, Matthew, 82–83, 180, 293, 313
　The Emergence of Scottish Studies, 313
　'Tartan Noir, or, Hard-Boiled Heidegger', 296, 317
　Walter Scott at 250: Looking Forward, 293
Williams, Gordon, 159
　From Scenes like These, 159
Williams, Raymond, 2
　The Country and the City, 2
Wilson, A. N., 66
Wilson, John ['Christopher North'], 80, 84, 89, 90, 91
　Lights and Shadows, 89
　The Trials of Margaret Lyndsay, 89, 91
Wittig, Kurt, 145
Wolff, Robert Lee, 103
Woolf, Virginia, 154
Wordsworth, William, 53, 91, 108

Yeats, W. B., 132

Zanoni (by Edward Bulwer-Lytton), 109

www.ingramcontent.com/pod-product-compliance
Lightning Source LLC
Chambersburg PA
CBHW052048230426
43671CB00011B/1837